D1760329

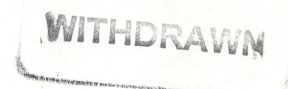

HISTORY AS RE-ENACTMENT

R. G. Collingwood's Idea of History

WILLIAM H. DRAY

OXFORD
UNIVERSITY PRESS

OXFORD

UNIVERSITY PRESS

Great Clarendon Street, Oxford OX2 6DP

Oxford University Press is a department of the University of Oxford.
It furthers the University's objective of excellence in research, scholarship,
and education by publishing worldwide in

Oxford New York

Athens Auckland Bangkok Bogotá Buenos Aires Calcutta
Cape Town Chennai Dar es Salaam Delhi Florence Hong Kong Istanbul
Karachi Kuala Lumpur Madrid Melbourne Mexico City Mumbai
Nairobi Paris São Paulo Singapore Taipei Tokyo Toronto Warsaw

with associated companies in Berlin Ibadan

Oxford is a registered trade mark of Oxford University Press
in the UK and in certain other countries

Published in the United States
by Oxford University Press Inc., New York

First published 1995
First issued in paperback 1999

British Library Cataloguing in Publication Data

Data available

Library of Congress Cataloging in Publication Data
Dray, William H.
History as re-enactment: R. G. Collingwood's idea of history/
William H. Dray.
Includes bibliographical references
1. Collingwood, R. G. (Robin George), 1889–1943—Contributions in
philosophy of history. 2. History—Philosophy. I. Title.
D.16.8.D688 1995 901—dc20 95-30553
ISBN 0-19-824293-X
ISBN 0-19-823881-9 (Pbk.)

Typeset in Palatino

Printed in Great Britain
on acid-free paper by
Biddles Ltd
Guildford and King's Lynn

To my family,
Doris, Chris, Liz,
with love

ACKNOWLEDGMENTS

I T will be clear to readers of this book how much I owe to scholars whose work is cited in the notes, and especially to pioneers in the study of Collingwood's philosophy of history like W. H. Walsh, Alan Donagan, and Louis Mink. My greatest single debt, however, is to W. J. van der Dussen, who was once my student, but who, in matters Collingwoodian, has long been my master, as well as a wonderfully helpful colleague and friend. I am grateful to him and to other good friends and Collingwood scholars, Michael Krausz, Rex Martin, David Boucher, Leon Pompa, Lionel Rubinoff, for critical comments on portions of the text. I can only wish that I had been able to respond to them better.

A predecessor of the present text, written largely in ignorance of the manuscripts which were deposited by Mrs Kathleen Collingwood in the Bodleian Library in 1978, was completed during a research leave in 1978–9 and then put aside. I should never have gotten back to the project without the encouragement of Michael Krausz, and I should never have persevered with it without the patience and helpfulness of Angela Blackburn, Frances Morphy, Tim Barton, and Peter Momtchiloff at the Oxford University Press. It is a pleasure to acknowledge help also from the University of Ottawa in the form of research grants which enabled me to study the manuscripts at the Bodleian during the summers of 1990 and 1993; and to thank my wife, Doris, for her support in a multitude of ways, as well as for understanding of an altogether higher order than the kind talked about so much in this book.

Permissions have been granted me to draw upon the following previously published work: Chapter 1 of my *Perspectives on History*, by Routledge and Kegan Paul; 'R. G. Collingwood and the Acquaintance Theory of Knowledge', by the *Revue internationale de philosophie*; 'R. G. Collingwood on Reflective Thought', by the *Journal of Philosophy*; 'Collingwood's Historical Individualism', by the *Canadian Journal of Philosophy*; and 'R. G. Collingwood on the A Priori of History', by *Clio*. My sincere thanks to all of them, and also to Mrs Teresa Smith, Collingwood's daughter, for kindly allowing me to quote at various points from the manuscripts.

W.H.D.

PREFACE TO THE PAPERBACK EDITION

SINCE the original edition of this book was written, the known corpus of Collingwood's writings on philosophy of history has been widened by the discovery of the long-lost portion of the original manuscript of 'The Principles of History', his projected final work on the subject. This welcome additional resource introduces some new themes, like the relationship between philosophy of history and aesthetic theory, and develops further a number of older ones, like the place of rationality and emotion in historical thinking. There seems to be nothing in it, however, that calls for any significant change in the arguments of the present book. This is a contention that readers can now test for themselves, since the whole of 'The Principles of History', together with other previously unpublished manuscripts of Collingwood's, has recently been published by Oxford University Press.[1] The companion manuscripts include most of those to which occasional reference is made in the present work.

It does need to be acknowledged, however, that an assumption occasionally made in the original edition, namely, that the 'lost' manuscript must have followed closely the 'Scheme for a book' which Collingwood sketched for it, and which has been known since 1978, has been falsified by the event. And among the ways in which its actual text diverges from what was planned is its making no mention of the idea of re-enactment. Possible explanations of this surprising omission are considered in the Editors' Introduction to the newly published volume. Suffice it to say here that, although the term 're-enactment' is not used, many passages of the new manuscript are easily read as expressing this idea in other language, and that what is said there on other topics, far from being incompatible with it, simply enlarges the context for what is maintained in this book about the nature and central role of re-enactment in Collingwood's theory of history.

It might be added that, although no substantial changes have been made in the original text, the opportunity has been taken to correct a few errors of spelling and punctuation, and, in two instances, to rephrase more clearly what was originally said.

October 1998

[1] *The Principles of History and other Writings in Philosophy of History*, ed. W. H. Dray and W. J. van der Dussen (Oxford, 1999).

CONTENTS

ABBREVIATIONS

After the first citation, the following works will be referred to both in the text and in the footnotes using the abbreviations indicated.

Philosophical Books by Collingwood

A	*An Autobiography* (1939)
EM	*An Essay on Metaphysics* (1940, rev. 1995)
EPH	*Essays in the Philosophy of History* (1965)
EPM	*An Essay on Philosophical Method* (1933)
IH	*The Idea of History* (1946, rev. 1993)
IN	*The Idea of Nature* (1945)
NL	*The New Leviathan* (1942, rev. 1992)
PA	*The Principles of Art* (1938)
RP	*Religion and Philosophy* (1916)
SM	*Speculum Mentis* (1924)

Published Essays by Collingwood

With the exception of SPAT, these essays are all reprinted in William Debbins (ed.), *Essays in the Philosophy of History by R. G. Collingwood* (hereafter abbreviated as *EPH*). The page numbers will be from this volume.

CPH	'Croce's Philosophy of History' (1921)
HSD	'Are History and Science Different Kinds of Knowledge?' (1922)
LHK	'The Limits of Historical Knowledge' (1928)
NAPH	'The Nature and Aims of a Philosophy of History' (1925)
PH	'The Philosophy of History' (1930)
PP	'A Philosophy of Progress' (1929)
SHC	'Oswald Spengler and the Theory of Historical Cycles' (1927)
SPAT	'Some Perplexities about Time: With an Attempted Solution' (1925–6)
THC	'The Theory of Historical Cycles' (1927)

Unpublished Manuscripts by Collingwood

CHBI	'Can Historians be Impartial?' (1936)
HUP	'History as the Understanding of the Present' (1934)

L29   'Lectures on the Philosophy of History' (1929)
L31   'The Origin and Growth of the Idea of a Philosophy of History' (1931)
L32   'The Philosophy of History' (1932)
NHH   'Notes on the History of Historiography and Philosophy of History' (1936)
NHV   'Notes on Historiography Written on a Voyage to the East Indies' (1938–9)
NTM   'Notes towards a Metaphysic' (1933–4)
RAH   'Reality as History' (1935)
RNI   'Inaugural. Rough Notes' (1935)

Manuscripts included in the Revised Edition of The Idea of History

To make it easy to identify these sources, the abbreviations L26, L27, and L28 will be used, but the page numbers will be from *The Idea of History*, rev. edn.

L26   'Lectures on the Philosophy of History' (1926)
L27   'The Idea of a Philosophy of Something and, in Particular, a Philosophy of History' (1927)
L28   'Outlines of a Philosophy of History' (1928)

Historical Books by Collingwood

RB   *Roman Britain* (1932 rev. edn.)
RBES   *Roman Britain and the English Settlements* (1936)

Books by Others

BPH   Haskell Fain, *Between Philosophy and History*
HE   Rex Martin, *Historical Explanation: Re-enactment and Practical Inference*
HS   W. J. van der Dussen, *History as a Science: The Philosophy of R. G. Collingwood*
HST   Gordon Leff, *History and Social Theory*
HU   L. O. Mink, *Historical Understanding*
IPH   W. H. Walsh, *Introduction to Philosophy of History*
KEH   R. F. Atkinson, *Knowledge and Explanation in History*
LPC   Alan Donagan, *The Later Philosophy of R. G. Collingwood*
MHD   L. O. Mink, *Mind, History, and Dialectic*
PHP   Nathan Rotenstreich, *Philosophy, History and Politics*
PHU   W. B. Gallie, *Philosophy and the Historical Understanding*
WIH   E. H. Carr, *What is History?*

1

HISTORY AND PHILOSOPHY

§ 1. *Collingwood's Status and Reception*

If the philosophy of history is now in a flourishing state in
English-speaking countries and in countries where English is
read, this is due in no small measure to the stimulus provided by
the writings of R. G. Collingwood. Much of the best work that has
been done in this field since the posthumous publication in 1946
of his well-known book *The Idea of History* has been a conscious
attempt to develop or to emend views which he expressed; and
much of the rest has owed a good deal of its interest to its connection with those views. The extent to which Collingwood pion-
eered the subject in British philosophy is suggested by his own
efforts in *The Idea of History* to name his British predecessors. His
search for more remote ones yielded only passing remarks by
rather unlikely figures: Bacon's assimilation of historical knowledge to memory; Locke's insistence upon a 'plain historical
method' in the study of human nature; Hume's occasional observations on what is acceptable and unacceptable in historical inference (*IH* 58, 206, 73–5). When he turned to more recent writers, he
could find little more than a single essay by F. H. Bradley, which
he regarded as quite a minor advance upon Hume, and some
highly speculative and, in his view, fundamentally misguided
theorizing by 'philosophical' historians like J. B. Bury and Arnold
Toynbee (*IH* 134 ff., 147 ff., 159 ff.).

Only in his contemporary, Michael Oakeshott, whose *Experience and its Modes*, published in 1933, he characterized as 'the
high-water mark of English thought upon history', did he admit
to finding a true peer (*IH* 159). Yet it is hard to regard the single
chapter devoted to historical thinking in that book as offering
more than an aperitif, set against Collingwood's own voluminous
writings on the subject over a period of more than twenty years.
Even when ostensibly devoted to other areas of philosophical

concern, this body of work, which includes several substantial monographs and many shorter pieces, gives impressive evidence of the seriousness with which Collingwood took his own doctrine that, just as the chief business of ancient, medieval, and early modern philosophy was to deal with the coming of age of mathematics, theology, and natural science, respectively, so the chief business of philosophy in our own day must be to come to terms with the more recent emergence of history as a well-defined branch of knowledge. To some of his critics, Collingwood's preoccupation with history has seemed to amount almost to an obsession. This is so especially with regard to his apparent contention in one of his later works, *An Essay on Metaphysics*, that philosophy itself dissolves, in the end, into a form of the history of ideas, a history of the most fundamental presuppositions which have been held at various places and times in the past—a doctrine, however, which is not easily squared with the clear distinction maintained throughout *The Idea of History* and some other writings between history and the philosophy of it.

In *An Autobiography*, another late work, Collingwood complained bitterly of the neglect of his ideas by the English philosophical establishment of his day. He saw himself, not without reason, as a lone thinker working against odds in a professional environment which displayed, not just indifference, but positive hostility to any claim that history might raise distinctive philosophical problems (*A* 53, 116).[1] Of course, what are now seen as his major writings on the subject did not appear until after his death—or, in the case of the *Autobiography*, just before it. But stages in the development of his thought were expounded in a provocative series of essays published in the 1920s and 1930s.[2] And his inaugural lecture as Waynflete Professor at Oxford, 'The Historical Imagination', and a lecture which he delivered to the British Academy, 'Human Nature and Human History', the latter an excellent general statement of what may be taken as his mature position, were available from 1935 and 1936, respectively.

---

[1] See also van der Dussen, *HS* 203.

[2] Most of these have been reprinted in William Debbins (ed.), *Essays in the Philosophy of History by R. G. Collingwood* (Austin, Tex., 1965) (cited hereafter as *EPH*). Individual essays will be referred to using the abbreviations listed above, with page numbers from *EPH*.

Collingwood also lectured several times on philosophy of history as part of his regular duties at Oxford in years following 1926, and his lectures were apparently popular. The dearth of critical discussion of his views thus does, in retrospect, appear rather strange. But the charge of neglect could scarcely be sustained today. For, especially since the appearance in 1962 of Alan Donagan's path-breaking monograph, *The Later Philosophy of R. G. Collingwood*, there has been a veritable spate of exegetical and critical writings on various aspects of his thought. A residue of the original cool reception nevertheless lingers on in the curious fact that most of this work has originated not in Great Britain, but in North America, Scandinavia, and other parts of Western Europe. A notable exception is the sympathetic consideration given to some of Collingwood's claims about history by W. H. Walsh in his influential *Introduction to Philosophy of History*, and in some other writings.[3]

Yet a good deal of the growing literature on Collingwood has focused less on his philosophy of history than on two other, closely related philosophical concerns. The first is the nature not of history, but of philosophy, as it emerges from Collingwood's long campaign to bring about what he called a *rapprochement* between philosophy and history, and which, as was noted, has sometimes seemed to entail the historicization of philosophy itself. The second is the essentially scholarly question of whether the doctrines set forth in Collingwood's various philosophical writings, these ranging in subject-matter from philosophy of religion, art, politics, science, and history to philosophy of philosophy itself, can be considered parts or aspects of a single system of ideas—the critic's primary task then being to find the 'key' to it—or whether they must be seen as, at most, successive, and perhaps ultimately incompatible, attempts at elaborating such a system. In consequence, what Collingwood had to say about history in particular has sometimes been obscured by a concern with larger questions.

This is particularly true of Lionel Rubinoff's dazzling monograph, *Collingwood and the Reform of Metaphysics*,[4] which develops

---

[3] (London, 1951). Walsh's excellent review article of 1947, 'R. G. Collingwood's Philosophy of History', *Philosophy*, 22 (1947), 153–60, is one of the earliest critical commentaries on his position.

[4] (Toronto, 1970) (cited hereafter as *Reform of Metaphysics*).

a quasi-Hegelian interpretation of the Collingwoodian corpus;
but it is true also of Louis Mink's more prosaic *Mind, History and
Dialectic*, despite the valuable critical review it offers of recurring
and often misconceived objections which have been urged against
central doctrines of *The Idea of History*. In fact, until the appearance
of W. J. van der Dussen's *History as a Science* in 1981, there existed
no systematic, book-length study devoted primarily to the exposition, interpretation, and criticism of Collingwood's account of
history as a form of knowledge and inquiry. Donagan's monograph contains an incisive and surprisingly comprehensive examination of it, but in just two chapters of a book the chief aim of
which was to set forth Collingwood's mature philosophy as a
whole. More recent books like Leon Goldstein's *Historical Knowing*, or Rex Martin's *Historical Explanation: Re-enactment and Practical Inference*, or Heikki Saari's *Re-enactment: A Study in R. G.
Collingwood's Philosophy of History*,[5] which display little interest
in Collingwood's philosophical system as a whole, are no more
concerned with his philosophy of history as a whole. They are,
rather, studies of selected issues which specific doctrines of
Collingwood's are seen as raising, such as the way human actions
are to be understood by historians or the way historical scepticism
is to be avoided—albeit in a Collingwoodian spirit and using
Collingwoodian dicta as points of departure. Much the same may
be said of the best-known articles on aspects of Collingwood's
philosophy of history by such authors as David Boucher,
L. B. Cebik, Lorraine Code, Gordon Couse, Patrick Gardiner,
Michael Krausz, Margit Nielsen, Nathan Rotenstreich, D. S. Taylor,
or Stephen Toulmin, to name only a few.

By contrast, van der Dussen's book is encyclopedic in scope, as
well as being a work of indefatigable and meticulous scholarship.
It has, in consequence, become recognized as an indispensable
reference for anyone now wishing to contribute to the interpretation of Collingwood's ideas on history. It charts the development
of Collingwood's thought in a number of dimensions through a
bewildering array of writings, both published and unpublished,
calling attention in illuminating ways to connections between his
philosophical ideas and his historical practice, and relating his
better-known ideas to further interests he pursued and issues he

---

[5] (Åbo, Finland, 1984). Saari's book cited hereafter as *Re-enactment*.

dealt with which were previously unsuspected: for example, his concern with folklore as a distinctive source of historical evidence, or his views on the relation of history to the social sciences, a matter on which *The Idea of History* is strangely silent. Van der Dussen's exhaustive documentation of the critical literature on Collingwood's writings, and his lively and informed commentary on it, will also guide discussion for some time to come. But although he is indisputably the best authority on what Collingwood wrote about history and cognate matters, and although, besides careful exposition, he offers valuable critical observations on many points of dispute, his book is more a propaedeutic to an eventual comprehensive analysis of Collingwood's philosophy of history than that analysis itself. As C. B. McCullagh has put it, what it offers is 'a complete resource book for scholars investigating R. G. Collingwood's philosophy of history'.[6] Van der Dussen has cleared the way for a new stage of Collingwoodian studies and has indicated directions in which such studies can now most fruitfully proceed. What follows, while dissenting occasionally from particular conclusions which he draws, is enormously in his debt.

§ 2. *The Aims of this Book*

I must nevertheless make it clear from the outset that the present study attempts no more than a further step, although, I hope, a significant one, towards the systematic critical examination of Collingwood's whole philosophy of history that van der Dussen's work has rendered so much more feasible. Its central focus, like that of the books by Martin and Saari, is on Collingwood's well-known contention that history is, or should be, a re-enactment of past experience or a re-thinking of past thought. This idea has been much discussed; but I do not think that its role in Collingwood's philosophy of history, or even its nature, has yet been made as clear as it needs to be. I shall take issue with what seem to me certain misconceptions associated with it, as well as responding to criticisms where this seems warranted. But I shall also try to explore more fully than has yet been done the relation

---

[6] Review of *HS*, in *Australasian Journal of Philosophy*, 61 (1983), 221.

which the notion of re-enactment bears to some of Collingwood's other leading ideas, in some cases ideas to which he did not himself explicitly relate it. To this extent, if no more, I shall be aiming at further elucidation of Collingwood's philosophy of history as a whole.

Good reasons could doubtless be given for selecting some other doctrine of Collingwood's as the point of entrée into his thought about history: for example, his alleged relativism, or his account of argument from evidence, or his theory of presuppositions, or his concept of a specifically historical imagination—ideas which are also prominent in it, and which have also been objects of considerable attention. There are, furthermore, students of Collingwood, like Cebik, who would deny that the idea of re-enactment has great importance for philosophy of history, my own choice of focus being to that extent unfortunate.[7] Even van der Dussen, although himself taking the idea seriously enough, observes that it has been overemphasized in the literature on Collingwood.[8] I can only endeavour to show, in what follows, that its importance is difficult to exaggerate. It is an idea, at any rate, upon which Collingwood himself laid great stress in *The Idea of History* and in other writings;[9] it has frequently been thought to throw light on other Collingwoodian claims, such as that historical reconstruction is a work of the imagination, or that historical understanding yields self-knowledge; and it is, arguably, the idea for which Collingwood is best known as a philosopher of history. Saari's reference to it as 'the *Leitmotif*' of Collingwood's later philosophy of history therefore seems to me apt.[10] I think, furthermore, that it is an idea which is both fundamentally sound and of considerable interest in itself for philosophy of history, at least in its general thrust, if not always in Collingwood's detailed formulations of it. At the same time, it is one which has often been represented by critics in ways which obscure its true force and significance.

---

[7] L. B. Cebik, 'Collingwood: Action, Re-enactment, and Evidence', *Philosophical Forum*, 2 (1970), 68–9 (cited hereafter as 'Collingwood').

[8] 'Collingwood's Unpublished Manuscripts', *History and Theory*, 18 (1979), 301.

[9] Epilegomena 1 and 4 are largely about it; the historical part of *IH* culminates in its emergence; it has a prominent place in *A*; it was hailed as an important discovery in L28; and it was to have been the main theme of a large section of 'The Principles of History'.

[10] Saari, *Re-enactment*, 23.

The plan of the present study is as follows. In Chapter 2, I shall look at some things which Collingwood had to say about what he saw as paradigmatic cases of re-enactment: cases in which the past actions of particular individuals are understood in terms of what the person concerned thought about his situation. I shall first analyse and explicate what I take to be Collingwood's chief claims in such cases, sometimes rephrasing them in language which he does not himself use but which will be more familiar to many readers. I shall then, in Chapter 3, besides noting some ways in which he appears not to have hewed consistently to his own analysis, either in theory or in practice, formulate and try to deal with some difficulties which have been raised by critics who find his position, even when dealing with what appear to be the most favourable cases, incoherent, or irrelevant, or at any rate incomplete in important ways. With a view to further explicating Collingwood's own position, I shall also contrast the analysis which I take him to be offering with some other accounts commonly given of the way the same sort of subject-matter might be understood. This will involve, among other things, some discussion of the nature of action, thought, event, uniqueness, laws, necessity, and so on.

In Chapters 4 and 5, I shall go on to consider the objection, often heard, that, even if Collingwood's account is acceptable for certain especially favourable cases, it will not stretch to fit many, and perhaps most, of the things that historians ordinarily seek to understand. As will be noted in Chapter 4, his account has often been held not to apply to unreflective human activities, to highly irrational actions, or to what people feel by contrast with what they do—limitations to which Collingwood himself often seemed to respond simply by banishing such things from the historian's proper subject-matter. As will be noted in Chapter 5, he has also been accused, because of the way he emphasizes the historian's concern with past 'thought', of ignoring the considerable role played by physical conditions in history, and of remaining strangely silent about how large-scale social processes are to be understood. The latter, say many of his critics, is scarcely surprising, since his theory, which was originally devised as an account of the way we are to understand individual actions, cannot be expected to have anything to say about these quite different and more important problems. I shall argue (as have Mink and some others) that Collingwood's true position on such issues has often been misunderstood, and that, although something may have to be conceded to his critics here, his theory of history is a good deal less restrictive than has frequently been thought, at any rate so far as its conception of the historian's subject-matter is concerned.

In Chapter 6, I shall ask about the relation between Collingwood's theory of understanding as re-enactment and his claim that historical work requires an exercise of imagination on the historian's part. An analysis of his conception of the historical imagination will lead to a consideration of his contention that, besides requiring, on the empirical side, the identification and interpretation of evidence, historical thinking has an important a priori dimension. Related matters to be touched on include Collingwood's idea of historical continuity, the sense in which he thinks historians deal with individuality, the extent to which he sees synthesis as well as analysis as involved in historical understanding, and his position on periodization, and on the need for universal history.

Chapters 7 and 8 will deal with the question of how far historians can claim, on Collingwood's theory of historical understanding, to set forth the objective truth about the past—the past 'as it actually was'. Chapter 7 will consider the significance for this problem of Collingwood's frequent reminders that the 'real' past no longer exists. Many critics have read into what he says in this connection the doctrine that what we normally call historical events are not past realities, but mere mental constructions, thoughts generated in the minds of historians by their own inquiries, the true object of historical knowledge therefore being present, not past—a position which has sometimes been called 'idealist'. Collingwood himself, although claiming to have repudiated the philosophical realism in which he was reared, denied that he was, in consequence, to be considered an idealist (*A* 56). Contrary to the stand taken by commentators like Goldstein, and perhaps also Nielsen, I shall argue that he was not one, at any rate in the constructionist sense just indicated. I shall maintain that his view of historical understanding as re-enactment is, by implication, objectivist, and that he often, if not always, accepted the implication. However, there is much confusion to be cleared up in this connection. In Chapter 8, I shall examine some other things which Collingwood had to say which have at times been interpreted as denying the objectivity of history. These include his maintaining that historians' conclusions are necessarily expressions of their own points of view; that what history offers is thus a view of the past from a present perspective; and that we can therefore expect it to be continually rewritten. His views on the nature of narrative in history will also be considered in this connection.

Finally, in a brief Epilogue, an attempt will be made to draw together some of the threads of the preceding discussion, and, more particularly, to summarize what has emerged with regard to both Collingwood's view of the nature of historical understanding as re-enactment, and the place which that doctrine should occupy in a broader Collingwoodian theory of historical understanding.

One more general comment might be made about the aims of the present book. It has been noted that discussions of Collingwood's views on history have tended to be rather specialized; they have also sometimes been rather technical; and they have frequently highlighted claims of his that seem no more than remotely connected with the actual practice of history. Such tendencies have sometimes raised difficulties for non-philosophers among Collingwood's readers, and especially for historians, many of whom look to his writings for illumination on the way they should conceive their own work. Indeed, Collingwood has been widely regarded as the historian's philosopher of history *par excellence*, and he would have welcomed the encomium. As Martin has put it, historians commonly 'glow' at the mention of his name (*HE* 16 n.). Yet *The Idea of History* is far from easy reading for the philosophically uninitiated; and historians have sometimes praised (and also criticized) what they have found Collingwood saying about history for questionable reasons. In determining what to discuss and how to discuss it, I shall try to keep in mind the possibility of an historical as well as a philosophical readership, taking note from time to time of what has been said about Collingwood's doctrines by historians as well as by philosophers, and periodically raising the question of the significance of those doctrines for the actual practice of history—

including their relevance to Collingwood's own practice as an historian.[11]

However, I shall not restrict myself to discussing only aspects of Collingwood's philosophy of history which seem to bear directly upon historical practice, and historians may therefore find some of the topics treated less relevant to their interests than others. I think it is plausible to regard the re-enactment theory itself, as I shall explicate it, as directly relevant to the practice of history, since it offers a justification for pursuing inquiry one way rather than another, and provides those who want to pursue it that way with some answers to recurring sorts of criticism. It is more difficult to represent as similarly relevant to historical practice the examination of arguments about whether the objects of historical thinking are 'real' or 'mere constructions'; for an historian who accepted one of these alternatives could be expected to continue with his own inquiries in much the same way as one who accepted the other. The difference would be in the epistemological status they would ascribe to their conclusions. Yet, in their own theoretical writings on history, historians have not failed to raise the question of the reality of what they take to be their objects of knowledge—Beard and Becker are among the best-known examples.[12] Perhaps a philosopher need offer little apology, therefore, for raising the same question.

§ 3. *Sources*

Until very recently, accounts of Collingwood's philosophy of history have been based chiefly upon *The Idea of History*, supplemented by the latter half of the *Autobiography*, which offers a brief description of how Collingwood arrived at his position, and further elaborates some aspects of it, including the idea of re-

[11] One fellow guildsman, Geoffrey Elton, has complained that Collingwood's practice fails to instantiate his own theory. Since Collingwood claimed to derive his philosophical conclusions at least partly from his own experience of historical research, this is an important, although I think questionable, criticism (*The Practice of History* (London, 1969), 79).

[12] Charles Beard, 'That Noble Dream', reprinted in Fritz Stern (ed.), *The Varieties of History* (New York, 1973), 323–4; Carl Becker, 'What are Historical Facts?', reprinted in Hans Meyerhoff (ed.), *The Philosophy of History in Our Time* (New York, 1959), 125.

enactment. In fact, most such accounts have been based almost entirely on a single part of *The Idea of History*, its Epilegomena, the collection of seven essays appended to Collingwood's extensive survey of changes which have taken place in the way history has been conceived over a period of more than two thousand years. It has been common to regard the Epilegomena as offering the nearest thing there is in his writings to a systematic statement of his own idea of history.

A number of authors have warned of the dangers of trying to reconstruct Collingwood's views about history on so narrow a base. Mink has emphasized the extent to which the issues discussed in the Epilegomena also receive attention from time to time in the earlier parts of *The Idea of History*, and sometimes in ways that require some revision of conclusions which might be drawn from the systematic writings alone (*HU* 223–4). He has argued also that certain 'recessive' Collingwoodian doctrines, such as the importance of notions like process or dialectic for an understanding of historical thinking, become more apparent when the base is broadened in this way. Mink maintains, further, as did Donagan before him, that one cannot fully understand what Collingwood says about history in *The Idea of History* and the *Autobiography* unless one sees it as a contribution to a developing Collingwoodian philosophy of mind. According to Donagan, this requires its being interpreted in close relationship to *The Principles of Art*, which sets forth such a theory in embryonic form, and *The New Leviathan*, which further elaborates it and applies it to philosophical problems of politics (*LPC* 220).[13] Rubinoff has similarly argued that Collingwood's philosophy of history, as expounded in all his later works, is not fully understandable without reference to *Speculum Mentis*, which he sees as having formulated something like a long-term plan, almost a blueprint, for the philosophical study of various forms of knowledge and experience, all with a view to amplifying and revising the philosophical system sketched in that volume.[14] A number of commentators have maintained also that students of Collingwood's ideas on history need

[13] The interpretation of Collingwood's writings on politics and their connection with his theory of history has been facilitated by the publication of *Essays in Political Philosophy: R. G. Collingwood* (Oxford, 1989), and a revised edition of *NL* in 1992, which includes lectures and a further essay of Collingwood's, both edited and introduced by David Boucher.

[14] Rubinoff, *Reform of Metaphysics*, 27.

to pay more attention to concepts and principles which are implicit in his own historical and archaeological work, two fields upon which he made a remarkable impact quite apart from his writings in philosophy, and between which he saw no radical distinction. Mink, especially, has called for a more deliberate attempt to relate Collingwood's theory to his practice in this way, and Donagan, if necessarily on a restricted scale, has shown how this can fruitfully be done, as have Goldstein, van der Dussen, and some others.[15] In what follows, I shall from time to time take into account both what Collingwood says in his other philosophical books and articles, where I think this has some bearing on his theory of history, and what he actually did as an historian and archaeologist, including what he sometimes did as an historian of ideas in the philosophical writings themselves.

The task of interpreting Collingwood's views on history has been greatly complicated since 1978 by the opening to scholarly study of a large collection of his unpublished manuscripts on history and related topics.[16] These manuscripts include well-developed notes for some of his Oxford lectures, the most striking being those prepared for delivery in 1926 and 1928. But there are also papers written for particular occasions and delivered orally, papers written simply with a view to getting something straight or to trying out an idea, drafts of papers which were eventually published but in a form which differed from the draft in interesting ways, and jottings on a host of topics bearing on his philosophy of history. Of special interest is a plan which Collingwood drew up in 1939 for his projected but never finished book to be called 'The Principles of History', which, with knowledge that he had not long to live, he poignantly described as the work for which his whole scholarly life had been a preparation (*HS* 61–2). In this book he intended to set forth in systematic form his mature thought both on the nature of historical thinking and on its general cultural significance. Van der Dussen has concluded, from

---

[15] Donagan, *LPC* 182 ff.; L. J. Goldstein, 'Collingwood on the Constitution of the Historical Past' (cited hereafter as 'Constitution'), in Michael Kransz (ed.), *Critical Essays on the Philosophy of R. G. Collingwood* (Oxford, 1972), 241–67 (cited hereafter as *Critical Essays*); van der Dussen, *HS* 201 ff.

[16] For an annotated list of most of those pertaining to philosophy of history, see D. S. Taylor, *R. G. Collingwood: A Bibliography* (New York, 1988) (cited hereafter as *Bibliography*). For a more extensive list and discussion of the manuscripts, see van der Dussen, *HS*, ch. 4.

evidence afforded by the manuscripts, that, had Collingwood lived, he would have published what we now call *The Idea of History*, without its Epilegomena, as a companion volume to 'The Principles', i.e. as a work in the history of ideas (*HS* 61). In conception, it would have been similar to *The Idea of Nature*, which traces the rise of modern ideas of physical nature without any cosmological epilegomena. Collingwood himself revised the historical part of his university lectures of 1936 with a view to this manner of publication, and gave it the name it now bears, *The Idea of History*.

Different judgments have been made about the importance of the manuscripts for the reconstruction of Collingwood's philosophy of history. Van der Dussen rates their importance very highly: Collingwood, he observes, 'will never be the same for us again', adding that 'the new Collingwood is more important than the old one was generally thought to be' (*HS* 127–8). Other close students of the manuscripts like those of Taylor and Nielsen have similarly stressed how much there is to be learned from them. By contrast, C. B. McCullagh, reviewing van der Dussen's *History as a Science*, reported that he found 'few surprises' in them.[17] I think myself that it would be a very prescient student of the published Collingwood who would not be surprised by them at all. They not only throw more light on the way Collingwood's ideas developed, illustrating his own account of the way he 'licked his ideas into shape' by writing and rewriting (*A* 116; NTM A-1*b*), but also touch on a number of matters that are either neglected entirely or are given more restricted treatment in the published writings. They contain passages, too, which are not easily reconciled with the latter, at any rate as they have generally been interpreted. A number of the manuscripts will be referred to in this book where they seem relevant. A list of the ones used is included in the Bibliography.

The kind of authority which should be ascribed to what is found in these sources is a further and difficult question. Donagan has questioned whether, in working out an author's position, anything should be accepted from an unpublished source which contradicts what the author himself chose to publish.[18] In the

[17] McCullagh, Review of *HS*, 221.
[18] In a lecture delivered at the Collingwood Centennial Conference at Pembroke College, Oxford, in 1989.

present case, there is the further difficulty that Collingwood himself put the authority of his unpublished manuscripts in question by forbidding their publication, except for a few which he designated, notably a completed fragment of 'The Principles of History' and the partially revised lectures of 1936 which were made the basis of *The Idea of History* by its editor, T. M. Knox. Yet it is now scarcely feasible to refuse to take Collingwood's manuscripts into consideration when interpreting his ideas, sizeable extracts from them having appeared in a number of recent books and articles, and the most interesting of them, the notes for his lectures of 1926 and 1928, having recently entered the public domain as appendices to a revised edition of *The Idea of History*.[19] Some may feel that, in view of the reservations which Collingwood himself expressed about most of these materials, I sometimes take the passages which I cite from them too seriously. I can only try to show that their content makes them (both for good and ill) too interesting to ignore.

One salutary consequence of the opening up of the manuscripts is an increased awareness on the part of students of Collingwood of how mixed is the claim of *The Idea of History* itself, as we have become familiar with it, to be treated as an authoritative source for its author's considered views. Two essays of the Epilegomena, the inaugural and the British Academy lectures, were public addresses delivered in such prestigious circumstances that they must be seen as very authoritative, although still not necessarily final, statements of Collingwood's ideas. The book's first four parts, the historical survey, save for certain minor editorial changes and the addition of materials from two reviews, were revised for publication by Collingwood towards the end of his life. The sections of the Epilegomena entitled 'Historical Evidence' and 'History and Freedom', fragments of Collingwood's 'Principles of History' which Knox chose to include, were also approved for publication by Collingwood, while, by a judgment that can now only be regretted, other fragments, similarly approved, were excluded (*HS* 63–4).[20] The rest of the Epilegomena,

[19] Published by the Oxford University Press in 1993, with a new preface by W. J. van der Dussen. Pagination of the original edition is retained.

[20] While the present book was going through the press, it was announced by Oxford University Press that the sections of Collingwood's 'Principles of History' which Knox excluded, and which have until now been thought lost, have been found in its archives, and will be made available to scholars in due course at the Bodleian Library.

'History as Re-enactment of Past Experience', 'The Subject-matter of History', and 'Progress as Created by Historical Thinking', originally formed a postscript to the lectures of 1936 and, as such, have no more authority than other lecture notes left by Collingwood. They were, of course, delivered publicly; but they were neither published nor approved for publication by him.

What a study of Collingwood's philosophy of history has to draw upon is thus quite a heterogenous collection of sources: writings composed at various times for various purposes or occasions. In this book, although sometimes pointing out that a source used is early or late, I have not tried in any systematic way to follow the development of his ideas through various writings, nor, except in the most general way, to judge their relative authority as sources where claims conflict. I have treated as of special importance what Collingwood had to say in his inaugural lecture, his lecture to the British Academy, the first four parts of *The Idea of History*, the *Autobiography*, and, despite their somewhat more questionable status, the other parts of Knox's Epilegomena. This gives priority to what Collingwood wrote in the years 1935–9, when he is generally regarded as having been at the height of his powers. I have also made some use of his other philosophical books of the 1930s and 1940s, especially the *Essay on Metaphysics*, and have drawn illustrations from his historical writings of various dates.

The published essays of the 1920s Collingwood himself described as 'work in progress'. They nevertheless contain indispensable Collingwoodian ideas, which were not always expressed as well in other works; and this could be said also of some unpublished manuscripts of the same years. I have made especially extensive use of the now published lectures of 1926 and 1928, the second set being the 'Martouret' manuscript which Collingwood described in the *Autobiography* as marking perhaps the most important watershed in his thought about history (*A* 107). When referring to these sources, I shall give page numbers from the new edition of *The Idea of History*, but I shall signalize their special status relative to the rest of that volume by using the abbreviations L26, L27, and L28 rather than *IH* (L27 designating the long introduction which Collingwood added to his lectures of 1926 in the following year). The unpublished manuscripts of the 1930s are not work in progress in quite the same sense: they might better be described as 'miscellaneous reflections'. But I have found them valuable for their occasional treatment of questions which are almost ignored in *The Idea of History* or the *Autobiography*, although puzzling, too, in apparently reverting, at times, to positions which Collingwood might be thought to have repudiated.

My concern, in what follows, will often be to make clearer just what Collingwood thought on various contentious issues. But I shall generally be quite as much concerned to elicit from his writings, to the extent to which it can be done, a coherent and persuasive philosophy of history employing his key ideas. With that end in view, the earlier writings, even if possessing less prima-facie authority, will still sometimes be worth stressing: latest is not necessarily best. My approach to the burgeoning expository and critical literature on Collingwood will be to exploit it wherever this seems useful, whether as containing viable interpretive ideas, or as expressions of criticism which need to be met, or as evidence of misunderstanding which needs to be cleared up. It will become evident as I proceed how much I owe to fellow students of Collingwood, even if I have not always learned from them the lessons they most wanted to convey.

§ 4. *Collingwood on Philosophy of History*

Before going on to examine various aspects of Collingwood's philosophy of history in detail, it may be useful to offer a preliminary sketch of his conception of philosophy in its relationship to history, and of his general idea of history and historical knowledge.

Whatever may have been the view of the relation between philosophy and history propounded in his later works—and that has been a matter of some controversy[21]—it is clear that Collingwood distinguishes the two sharply in *The Idea of History*. Philosophy, he says, is, by contrast with history, a second-order activity. History is thought about the past; philosophy of history

---

[21] See e.g. Lionel Rubinoff, 'Collingwood's Theory of the Relation between Philosophy and History: A New Interpretation', *Journal of the History of Philosophy*, 6 (1968), 363–80; Rex Martin, 'Collingwood's Claim that Metaphysics is a Historical Discipline', *Monist*, 72 (1989), 518 (cited hereafter as 'Collingwood's Claim'); Tariq Modood, 'The Later Collingwood's Alleged Historicism and Relativism', *Journal of the History of Philosophy*, 27 (1989), 117; van der Dussen, *HS* 181.

is thought about that thought about the past (*IH* 1–3). Given this conception of it, Collingwood rejects three senses borne by the term 'philosophy of history' since its invention by Voltaire in the eighteenth century. The first, which appears to have been what Voltaire himself meant by it, is simply history itself philosophically pursued: i.e. it is a critical rather than a credulous study of the human past. In Collingwood's view, all history ought to be philosophical in this sense. The second sense, which comes to us especially from Christian historiography in the Middle Ages, is a search for the overall pattern or plot of past events. This, properly conducted, is also, according to Collingwood, a form of history itself, since all history seeks, on some chosen scale, to determine the pattern of the past, and philosophy of history, so conceived, would seek to determine the pattern of the whole past, thus becoming universal history. The third sense, which Collingwood attributes especially to nineteenth-century positivists, is an inquiry into the laws, especially the large-scale laws, according to which the historical process is thought to develop, and by reference to which one may hope to make it intelligible. If such a study were viable (which Collingwood thinks it is not), it would be a type of science. Philosophy of history as second-order thought about the past must be different from all of these.

Collingwood sometimes phrases the philosopher of history's question as 'What is history?', insisting that, in attempting to answer it, he must take as his point of departure the existence of historical inquiry as an ongoing enterprise, a cultural achievement with a nature and significance to make clear.[22] We must ask what such inquiry is about, how it proceeds, and what it is for. This suggests that Collingwood's conception of the philosopher's task with regard to history is rather like that of contemporary analytic philosophers, many of whom have viewed his writings as addressing their own concerns, if not always using their language.[23] Thus R. F. Atkinson, author of one of the most substantial books on historical inquiry written in the analytic style,

[22] Mink has maintained that Collingwood never frames the philosopher's question in this way (*HU* 247–8), but see *IH* 7; PH 126; L27 348.

[23] In the introduction which he added to his lectures of 1926, Collingwood offers a list of what he considers typical philosophical problems about history (L27 348), which remarkably anticipates the kinds of questions which analytic philosophers of history were later to ask.

remarks on 'how much of the interest there is in the subject
derives from Collingwood' (*KEH*, p. x). And Rex Martin refers to
Collingwood not only as 'the intellectual founder' of analytic
philosophy of history, but as still one of its 'presiding geniuses'.[24]

Collingwood makes it clear, however, as some of the analysts
have been loath to do, that the task, as he conceives it, has a
metaphysical as well as an epistemological side (L28 429; *A* 77).
His attack on traditional philosophy of history is not an attack on
metaphysics of history as such. He does, certainly, assign to the
philosopher the task of elucidating historical modes of thought:
he must analyse the logical structure of historical arguments,
determine the degree of certainty attaching to historical conclusions, clarify basic historical concepts, and so on. But he must also
(and perhaps inevitably, in doing the former) ask questions about
the nature of the historian's subject-matter of a sort which can
only be called metaphysical: whether what is studied is the 'real'
past, for example, or how historical processes differ, if at all, from
natural ones. In addition, he envisages the philosopher of history's enterprise as having a second stage, which he calls the
construction of a complete philosophy from an historical point of
view, finding a model for this in the way philosophy of natural
science invaded and modified all regions of philosophical
thought following the analyses of scientific method that were
carried out by philosopher-scientists in the seventeenth and eighteenth centuries (NHV 21; RAH 35). However, he specifically excludes this further (and rather puzzling) stage from his concerns
in *The Idea of History* (*IH* 7), and little account will be taken of it in
this book.

There are two distinctions which it might be well to note
in even a brief and preliminary attempt to characterize Collingwood's approach to the philosophy of history. The first is
between prescriptive and descriptive conceptions of the way a
philosopher ought to undertake the philosophical analysis of a
discipline or a type of knowledge. Collingwood himself may
sometimes give the impression, especially when emphasizing
what he calls the 'autonomy' of the historian, that the philosopher
must take actual historical practice as a datum, treating this
as something to be clarified and explained, but not criticized

[24] Review of van der Dussen, *HS*, in *American Historical Review*, 88 (1983), 75.

(L27 341). Indeed, the objections he levels at rival philosophical accounts of historical inquiry may sometimes seem to amount chiefly to the claim that philosophers have gotten the datum wrong: they have based their theories, at best, on a kind of historical practice which has long been superseded; for history, like natural science, has not stood still, especially in the last hundred years, during which, according to Collingwood, it has been turning itself into a special kind of science quite different from the natural sciences (*IH* 208–9).

The notion that philosophers must accept what historians do rather than criticize it is reinforced when Collingwood, at times, phrases his overarching question Kantian style as 'How is history possible?' (*A* 77; *IH* 6). For this may suggest that the task of the philosopher is essentially to make clear what is in fact presupposed by accepting history as a genuine branch of knowledge— what its mere existence as a widely accepted type of inquiry shows to be the case. In fact, Collingwood is not at all uncritical of historical practice as he finds it: he arrogates to himself at least the privilege of deciding which practice is good and which is bad. However, if he is asked how good practice is to be distinguished from bad, his answer is often less helpful than one might have wished. The philosopher, he says, if he is to get the datum right, must himself be an historian, and must judge practice, as it were, from the inside (L28 495; *IH* 9). This is an approach which, in view of his own high reputation as historian and archaeologist, puts Collingwood very much in the driver's seat; and it too often encourages him to terminate philosophical arguments abruptly with advice to readers who are inclined to question his conclusions to test them by doing some history for themselves (*IH* 263).

The other distinction is between two senses of the word 'history' which Collingwood employs in *The Idea of History* and in some other works, a narrower and a broader one.[25] This is a distinction which it is important to note because, as Mink, especially, has pointed out (*HU* 255 ff.), Collingwood leaves it largely unexplained; and, to make matters worse, he generally

[25] The broad sense is more characteristic of *SM*, and the narrow sense of *IH*; but both can be found in both works. Still another way of distinguishing broad and narrow senses is proposed by Herman Simissen in 'On Understanding Disaster', *Philosophy of the Social Sciences*, 23 (1993), 354.

expects the reader to determine from the context which of the two senses he has in mind when making a given point. In the first sense, history is conceived as a special branch of inquiry, a discipline applying rules and strategies of research, something that goes on to a large extent nowadays in departments of history at universities, but which can also be recognized, at least in embryo, in the less professionalized activities of a Gibbon, or even a Herodotus. In the second sense, it is understood as including any drawing of conclusions about the past on the basis of what is here and now perceived, a kind of activity which is a commonplace of our practical life, and which some philosophers would call a fundamental 'mode of experience' or 'attitude of mind'.[26] When Collingwood says that history has increasingly abandoned the methods of compilation, which he denigrates as an activity of 'scissors and paste', it can be assumed that what he has in view is the narrow sense of the term (*IH* 257 ff.). When he tells us that all our knowledge of our past actions, once we no longer remember them, is historical, we can presume that he is using the word in its broader sense (*IH* 219).

Doubtless the two senses shade into each other; but they do not coincide; and failure to recognize this will sometimes make Collingwood's claims seem less reasonable than they really are. The broader sense, furthermore, is important for grasping one of Collingwood's wider philosophical concerns in *The Idea of History*. For although, on one level, and perhaps the level on which most readers will want to read it, Collingwood's aim in that book is to analyse the nature of history as a discipline, on another level, it is to show that all knowledge of human nature, indeed all knowledge of the human mind, strictly conceived, is historical in the sense of having to be obtained by methods more like those of professional historians than like those of professional scientists. When he says that history is the one true science of mind, he certainly does not mean to imply that only professional historians can reach the truth about human mentality. Provided they use analogous methods, students of the social sciences can do so too, and so can intelligent citizens in the course of their daily affairs.[27]

[26] 'Ruskin's Philosophy', reprinted in Alan Donagan (ed.), *Essays in the Philosophy of Art by R. G. Collingwood* (Bloomington, Ind., 1964), 14.

[27] Van der Dussen has drawn attention to Collingwood's claim to have studied folklore as a social phenomenon using historical methods (*HS* 183). Self-styled social science which uses historical methods while claiming not to do so, Collingwood calls 'crypto-history' (*NHV* 18).

A similar distinction might have been, but never was, drawn by Collingwood between natural science as a special discipline and scientific ways of thinking generally. Under the latter head might have been brought, for example, any attempt, in any context whatever, to make discoveries by inductive thinking, or to explain happenings as instances of regularities.

It is an unfortunate complication that the distinction just drawn needs itself to be distinguished from still another distinction between what could be called broader and narrower senses of 'history' which is also present in much of Collingwood's work, and which is also left in some obscurity. This is between history simply as a study of whatever is past and history as a study of the specifically human past, or even of the human past conceived in a special Collingwoodian way (this to be further clarified as we examine Collingwood's conception of historical thinking as a re-enactment of past thought). History simply as a study of the past would include natural history in the sense of a study of changes in nature; history in the narrower, essentially humanistic sense that Collingwood characteristically employs, would not. We shall consider this second distinction further in Chapter 2. What matters initially is that it not be confused with the distinction between history as a habit of mind and as a discipline. Collingwood goes on to argue that history as a habit of mind and as a discipline are in essential respects identical in their logical and conceptual structures, if not in their detailed procedures. He maintains, by contrast, that history of natural occurrences and history of human activities differ profoundly in their logical and conceptual structures—so much so, indeed, that he is sometimes unwilling to call the former history at all (A 109).

§ 5. *Collingwood on the Nature and Rise of History*

If we take the word in the narrower sense, in both dimensions, how, according to Collingwood, are we to answer the question 'What is history?'. First of all, he says, it is a type of research or inquiry, a way of finding out certain things, not, for example, simply a way of preserving memories or traditions, or of organizing knowledge which we possess already. Its subject-matter is 'humanistic': human activity in the past—the understanding of which, he goes on to argue, requires of one a re-thinking of past thought, or a re-enactment of past experience. Its mode of procedure is the interpretation of what is here and now perceptible as relics of past human activities, the latter being compendiously referred to as evidence, such interpretation requiring a characteristic mode of questioning and distinctive concepts and modes of argument. The ultimate goal of the inquiry, to put it shortly and in Collingwood's own words, is human 'self-knowledge': knowledge of human achievements and failures to date, and hence knowledge of what man is or has become, a knowledge which, although we are warned against interpreting this too simplistically, is said to be both valuable in itself, and useful for present human life (*IH* 9–10). Of these four features, the latter three, as conceived by Collingwood, entail a sharp distinction between history and natural science, the latter being concerned with abstract general features, not particular states of affairs, and employing a concept of understanding which misses the distinctiveness of human activities, and thus fails to provide human self-knowledge in the fullest sense. In *The Idea of History*, Collingwood describes his campaign for the recognition of a crucial distinction between historical and scientific modes of understanding as a 'running fight' with positivism (sometimes, and more appropriately, referred to as naturalism) in historical theory (*IH* 228).

Collingwood had not always contrasted history with natural science so sharply; and when he did contrast them, it was not always on these grounds. In *Speculum Mentis*, for example, which appeared some twelve years before most of *The Idea of History* was written, he had regarded a preoccupation with particular fact in all its concreteness as the feature of historical inquiry which marked it off from science (*SM* 211–12). For even when natural scientists concern themselves with particular occurrences, he held, they treat them only as 'abstract' particulars: i.e. as instances of generalities, not for their own sakes, and certainly not in all their concreteness. He had nevertheless maintained—for example, in 'Are History and Science Different Kinds of Knowledge?'—that the two types of inquiry are essentially the same in conceptual structure and subject-matter (HSD 23 ff.). There was said to be, at most, a difference of interest, scientists proceeding from knowledge of particular facts to knowledge of generalities, historians applying generalities in an attempt to understand, or even to ascertain, particular facts. Since what is thus asserted about history is the very doctrine which, by the time he wrote *The Idea of History*, Collingwood was identifying as the chief 'scientistic' error commonly made about the human studies, it is hard to agree with students of Collingwood like Debbins that there were no major shifts in the philosophical account which he gives of history in his earlier and later works.[28] However, as will appear in subsequent chapters, some of the earlier concerns, especially history's interest in the concrete, recur later as secondary themes.

As mentioned by Collingwood himself in his *Autobiography*, it seems to have been only in his lectures of 1928, after having experienced something like a philosophical 'illumination' at le Martouret in France, that he came to make central to his account of historical reconstruction the notion that, if the historian is to understand past human activities in a properly humanistic way, he must get 'inside' them by a process of re-thinking or re-enactment (*A* 107 ff.). Or, what is perhaps the same point, it is only thereafter that we find him insisting on a sharp distinction between human history and natural history, the latter—which he sometimes calls mere 'quasi-history' (*IH* 212), or even 'pseudo-history' (*NHV* 19)—including not only the pure generalizing sciences like physics and chemistry, but particularizing natural sciences like geology, which, in a way at least analogous to that of human history, set out to recover particular states of affairs that existed in the past.

But if the idea of history as Collingwood came eventually to expound it emerged in his own thought only over a period of time, no more, according to him, did it spring into existence fully-formed in the history of Western culture—and the idea of history which he is concerned to elucidate he regards as chiefly a Western achievement (*IH* 13–14). In fact, men's historical consciousness, and the historiographical practice which developed more or less in phase with it, are represented as themselves having had a long and rather uneven history, some of the major phases and turning-

---

[28] *EPH*, p. xxxi. For a more nuanced view, see Saari, *Re-enactment*, 20 ff. For contrary views, see Lionel Rubinoff, Review of *EPH*, in *Dialogue*, 5 (1966), 471–5; or Nathan Rotenstreich, 'From Facts to Thoughts: Collingwood's Views on the Nature of History', *Philosophy*, 35 (1960), 122–37 (cited hereafter as 'Facts to Thoughts').

points of which Collingwood relates with panache in the first fou:
sections of *The Idea of History*.[29]

It is in the writings of Herodotus, he says, that we first find a
recognizable ancestor of the modern idea of history. Not that the
researches of this fifth-century Greek proceeded in accordance
with all the sophisticated paraphernalia of present-day historical
scholarship; but the main elements of what the idea of history
subsequently became were already present embryonically in his
work: the emphasis on inquiry; the concern with human action;
the desire for human self-knowledge; the critical method—even if
the latter had not gone much beyond the cross-questioning of
eyewitnesses, this restricting the scope of historical inquiry to the
very recent past. Just how revolutionary the Herodotean idea of
history really was can only be appreciated, Collingwood maintains, if it is contrasted with what passed for historical consciousness in still earlier periods: a conception of things past which is
vague in its temporal reference, dogmatic in its assertions, and
more concerned with the doings of the gods than the doings of
men. Indeed, Collingwood draws the contrast so sharply that he
is in some danger of making the appearance of Herodotus seem
an inexplicable cultural miracle, the more so in view of the
strongly anti-historical tendency which he discerns in Greek
thought: more particularly, its static conception of human nature,
and an ideal of knowledge so abstract that it could be fully satisfied only by mathematics. This tendency, observes Collingwood,
ensured that Herodotus—or, at most, Herodotus and Thucydides
(in whom he finds the marks of decline already visible)—would
have no true successors. The general broadening of the Greek
vision of the world with the conquests of Alexander and the later
world empire of the Romans did induce historians like Polybius,
Livy, and Tacitus to expand both the spatial and the temporal
limits of their subject-matter. But this, at the same time, led to a

---

[29] A seldom noted peculiarity of Collingwood's survey is that roughly the first
half of it deals mainly with the idea of history that he finds implicit in the practice
of successive generations of historians, while most of the second half deals with
theories of history propounded by a succession of philosophers (the latter corresponding to the brief history of philosophies of history given in PH). This may be
because, on Collingwood's view, it was only at a certain stage of its development
that the idea of history was sufficiently established to become an explicit object of
philosophical reflection. It is nevertheless regrettable that he did not go on in *IH* to
trace changes in the idea of history as revealed in the practice of early modern and
recent historians.

regress in critical method, even if, perhaps, a necessary one, as a technique of compilation, or excerpting from authorities, came into vogue (*IH* 14 ff.).

It was not until the Christian Middle Ages that the next major advance in the idea of history occurred. Medieval historians are rightly charged with credulity, and, in general, their work betrays even lower critical standards than the later historiography of the ancient world—often, indeed, being virtually propagandistic. Christian theology nevertheless made certain contributions to the idea of history that were quite essential to its further advance. One of these, symbolized by the doctrine of original sin, was a more pessimistic, and hence more realistic, conception of human nature, along with which went the idea of a certain necessary blindness in human action, the good results of which could only be ascribed to 'grace' or to 'providence'. It is of the first importance, declares Collingwood, that Christianity should have promoted the salutary idea that what happens in history does not happen simply because men will it, even if, for the time being, it was only possible to exorcize illusions to the contrary by proclaiming that it happens because God wills it. Other important Christian influences were the undermining of static conceptions of historical process, and of human nature itself, through the doctrine of creation; the further challenging of Greco-Roman tendencies towards particularism by the ecumenical idea that all ages are equal in the sight of God; and the apocalyptic notion of history being divided into periods of darkness and light, this introducing an interpretive category, periodization, which was to be fundamental to later historical thinking (*IH* 46 ff.).

With the coming of the Renaissance, and the rise of modern physical science, while much that was valuable in medieval thought was retained, there was a return to a more secular focus of interest, typified by the work of Machiavelli, and, even more important, the beginning of a development in critical method which has continued to our own day. With an ingenuity which not all readers will find convincing, Collingwood finds an important role for Cartesian scepticism in the early stages of this movement (although not for Descartes himself, whose opinion of history was not high), speaking even of the 'Cartesian historiography' of seventeenth-century practitioners like Tillemont and the Bollandists. The rise of biblical criticism, the

sobering influence of British empiricism, the debunking on-
slaught of Enlightenment figures like Voltaire and Hume, all
made contributions to the rise of a new and more critical
historiography. But it is in the early eighteenth-century theorizing
of Vico, whom Collingwood clearly regards as the father of the
theory of history, that a thoroughly modern idea of historical
inquiry was first elaborated (*IH* 57 ff.).

The late eighteenth and early nineteenth centuries also wit-
nessed a movement in German philosophy from Herder to Hegel
which, for the first time, worked out clearly a fundamental distinction between nature and spirit, the proper subject-matters of
the natural and historical sciences, respectively; and the system of
Kant introduced the notion, later to be found indispensable in
historical theory, of human knowledge being perspectival, i.e.
relative to the knower. The positivism of the middle and later
nineteenth century, including the Marxism which in some ways
reacted against it, was, from this point of view, something of a
relapse, but only a temporary one. Pursuing, in the spirit of
von Ranke, the goal of recovering the past 'as it actually was',
historians themselves were gradually improving their methods.
Their more self-conscious approach to methodological problems
generated sets of rules for internal and external criticism of
sources, and led to the elaboration of auxiliary historical sciences
like epigraphy and numismatics (*IH* 86 ff.).

Collingwood brings his account of the rise of the idea of history
to a close with a review of recent developments in British, German, French, and Italian thought. While giving Bradley's single
paper on what constitutes the criterion of historical truth at least
its due, and ascribing to French philosophers like Bergson a certain importance for historical theory because of their emphasis on
human spirituality, it is clear that he sees the main developments
coming from the Germans and Italians. The German movement
culminated in Dilthey's abortive attempt to write a great critique
of historical reason that would do for history what the Kantian
critique did for Newtonian physics. The Italian movement issued
in Croce's philosophy of spirit, which, in holding that 'all history
is contemporary history' and 'all history is history of thought',
bears a close resemblance to the position taken by Collingwood
himself in his mature theory of history. Yet the critique of Croce's
theories which Collingwood offers, as well as the tougher and

more empirically-oriented content of his own writings on history, should give pause to anyone inclined to accept the common wisdom that he was little more than a popularizer of Italian ideas. Collingwood himself certainly claimed to be more. In fact, the rise of the idea of history, as he conceives it, is not just reported in his own philosophical and historical work: it is said to culminate in it—this exemplifying one of the senses (to be discussed in Chapters 7 and 8) in which, according to him, historical inquiry is, and ought to be, 'relative to the present' (*IH* 134 ff.).

§ 6. *Collingwood as Writer and Thinker*

A word might be added about special difficulties facing the interpreter of Collingwood's philosophy arising out of his character as a writer and thinker. Collingwood's writings have been justly praised for their apparent lucidity and general readability, even a relatively unfriendly critic like Arthur Marwick conceding that *The Idea of History* is often 'poetic in its sensibility'.[30] Collingwood's university lectures, too, appear to have been warmly received by those who heard them. Veronica Wedgwood recalls with gratitude the 'personality which, in the lecture hall, impressed itself indelibly on the rising generation of historians and philosophers';[31] and Max Beloff has remarked that to read *The Idea of History* is 'to recapture the thrill and stimulus' which he and so many of his Oxford contemporaries derived as undergraduates from Collingwood's public performances.[32]

It cannot be said, however, that Collingwood's writings, when carefully read, are easy to grasp. Although often graceful, they are not always careful. They do not exhibit that love of exact language which analytic philosophers have since made *de rigueur*—indeed, their author would have scorned the demand for it as putting improper pressure upon philosophy to become something like a technical discipline. In his *Essay on Philosophical Method*, Collingwood called upon philosophers 'to avoid the technical vocabulary proper to science', and to choose their words 'according to the rules of literature', the hall-marks of a literary rather

[30] *The Nature of History* (London, 1970), 80.
[31] Review of *IH*, in *Observer*, 8 September 1946.
[32] Review of *IH*, in *Time and Tide*, 28 September 1946.

than scientific style being expressiveness, flexibility, and dependence upon context (*EPM*, 207). He generally followed his own
precept, even the term 'history', as was noted above, sometimes
having to be interpreted by reference to the context in which it
appears. A term like 're-enactment' functions so little like a precisely defined technical term for Collingwood that there are up-
wards of a dozen apparent synonyms for it in his writings, not an
inconsequential matter, since some of them appear earlier than
the date at which he is supposed to have arrived at his view of
historical understanding as involving re-enactment.[33]

Not that Collingwood's own philosophical writings on history
are entirely free of what can only be described as a technical
terminology, this despite his stated view of what is appropriate in
philosophy. The technical terms which he does use, furthermore,
can sometimes raise problems, at any rate for readers who do not
share his particular philosophical background. Terms like 'tran-
scendentals' (L27 357), or 'ideality' (L28 440), or 'mediation' (*IH*
301), hardly belong to the stock-in-trade of even well-educated
general readers—the very readers to whom Collingwood often
claimed to be appealing over the heads of his philosophical
colleagues. And even when he uses more familiar philosophical
terms like 'subjective' or 'empirical', he often gives them meanings which have to be teased out of the way he employs them,
sometimes after initial misunderstanding. Thus, by 'subjective' he
often means something a good deal broader than what only
seems valid to particular persons (*IH* 292). And he often reserves
the term 'empirical' for what is directly perceived, an odd consequence of which is that much of natural science cannot then be
called empirical—although he clearly does not regard it as a priori
either (*IH* 176, 282).

Collingwood's work is characterized not only by problematic
pronouncements due to his use of language, but also by a proneness to exaggeration, paradox, and even apparent contradiction.
At various points, for example, he proclaims that all history is
history of thought (L28 444–5), or contemporary history (*IH* 202),
or prehistory (L26 372), or universal history (L26 420–1), or
tendentious history (L26 398), or history of history (L28 462),

---

[33] On this, see Margit H. Nielsen (now Grove), 'Re-enactment and Reconstruction in Collingwood's Philosophy of History', *History and Theory*, 20 (1981), 2 (cited
hereafter as 'Re-enactment and Reconstruction'); or Saari, *Re-enactment*, 32–3.

although it becomes clear, as one proceeds, that these stirring declarations are to be understood only in special senses. Again, although history is at a certain point said by Collingwood to be 'nothing but' the re-enactment of past thought in the historian's mind (*IH* 228), further acquaintance with his theory and practice shows that, in fact, he recognizes it to be much more than that, even if, in his view, re-enactment is one of its essential characteristics.[34] Collingwood also has an irritating habit, especially in his earlier work, of calling two things 'identical' when all he has really shown is that they are similar in some important respect. Thus history and science are said to be identical simply because both employ generalizations (HSD 32), and history and philosophy simply because both allegedly have mind for their object (*SM* 246). Small wonder that even a sympathetic commentator like Mink feels obliged to describe as 'provocative' the way Collingwood often states his doctrines (*MHD* 158), and that another, Taylor, charges him with 'rhetorical overkill'.[35]

Nor is Collingwood's work free from what often look like outright contradictions—contradictions not only between what he says in published and unpublished works, or in different published works, but even in different places in the same work, published or unpublished. At different points, for example, he maintains that historians do and do not apply generalizations (HSD 30; *IH* 223); that probability has no place in historical thinking and that it is all that historians ever discover (NHH, 60; NAPH, 43); that an historian must enter imaginatively into past forms of life and that his proper attitude to the past is that of a spectator (*IH* 218; NAPH 47); that only complete knowledge is really knowledge and that knowledge can be cumulative (*SM* 231; RAH 19); that thinking historically is not perception and that it is the highest form of perception (*IH* 222; NAPH 49). Such apparent contradictions may sometimes be resolvable by appealing from what Collingwood actually says to what he can be presumed to have meant. In other cases they are doubtless traceable to the fact that he was not afraid to change his mind—an admirable trait. Unfortunately, when he did, he didn't always concede that he had done so; and one sometimes finds him inveighing hotly against views which, as far as one can see, he had previously held

---

[34] For other problematic 'nothing buts', see CHBI 12; L26 422; *SM* 245.
[35] Taylor, *Bibliography*, 200.

himself. As he says, he often used his writing as a means of
'licking his thoughts into shape' (*A* 116), or even of trying out
ideas (the manuscripts give much evidence of this[36]). Collingwood was a probing, experimental thinker; and what he said
himself of philosophical systems generally might appropriately
be said of his own work, namely, that, at any particular point,
it offers no more than 'a temporary resting place for thought'
(L28 428). The citation of specific texts in support of given interpretations is therefore always somewhat chancy, even if it can
hardly be avoided.

Collingwood's writings are also sometimes disfigured by an
apparent arrogance or intransigence which shows itself in
brusque remarks addressed, not only to prospective philosophical opponents, but even to struggling readers. At one point he
bids farewell to all those whose judgment he has not carried with
the observation that they evidently know too little of the subject to
make it worth their while continuing to read him (*IH* 256). At
another, he snaps at an imaginary interlocutor bold enough to
demand supporting reasons for a position he has taken: 'I am not
arguing; I am telling him' (*IH* 263). Collingwood's stridency of
manner and unevenness of performance have sometimes been
blamed on failing health. However, there are traces of irritability
in the earlier works as well as in the later, and *The Idea of History*,
which comes from a relatively untroubled period, is not free of
them. Collingwood's failing health, which first became a problem
in 1931 and involved a series of debilitating strokes from 1938
until his death in 1943, has also been blamed by some critics,
notably Knox, for his having taken certain positions in his later
philosophical writings which they see as grossly misconceived:
for example, his apparent reduction of philosophy to history (*IH*
p. xxi). Van der Dussen has argued convincingly that, to a remarkable degree, Collingwood was able to rise above the problem of
bad health (*HS* 4). He shows, for example, that the *Essay on Philosophical Method* of 1933, which many, including Knox, rate as at
the pinnacle of his achievement, and which Collingwood himself
described as the only book that he had ever been able to complete
to his entire satisfaction (*A* 118), was in fact written just after a

---

[36] 'Reality as History' e.g. is described as 'an experimental essay' designed to
test how far its thesis can be maintained (RAH 1).

period of serious illness and not, as Knox had assumed, just before it.

It thus sometimes requires a certain amount of patience, and even of goodwill, to elicit a sensible and coherent doctrine from what Collingwood actually has to say. Perplexed students of his writings may nevertheless derive some comfort from the attitude which he himself adopted to the writings of Fichte. 'The chief difficulty which a reader finds in dealing with Fichte's view of history', Collingwood declares, 'is the difficulty of being patient with what appears so silly' (*IH* 108). He still managed to derive a remarkable amount of serious philosophy from his re- flections upon some of Fichte's dicta. This is in conformity with his own general conception of the proper role of a critic, which, he insists, is to reconstruct and to develop what his author says, not merely to dispose of it (*EPM* 218). I shall endeavour, in my own critique of Collingwood, to take a similar approach.

2

RE-ENACTMENT AND UNDERSTANDING

§ 1. *The Idea of Re-enactment*

The first task is to set out in a little detail what Collingwood means when he insists that historical understanding requires a re-enactment of past experience or a re-thinking of past thought. As noted already, commentators have differed about the importance of this idea for his whole theory of historical inquiry. But there have also been disagreements about the viability, and even the coherence, of the idea itself. Cebik has complained that it 'makes little if any sense';[1] A. R. Louch finds it 'extravagant and quasi-mystical';[2] Haskell Fain calls it a 'cryptic formula' (*BPH* 144); even Saari, who largely defends it, observes that it may be Collingwood's 'most difficult and controversial doctrine'.[3] By contrast, Donagan, Mink, and van der Dussen have not considered it especially problematic. My own position will be that the idea itself is basically sound; that it is indispensable, in some form or other, to any adequate account of historical understanding; that Collingwood states it clearly enough to make what he says about it a great improvement over older doctrines of *verstehen* or empathetic understanding in the human studies which some critics think it resembles; and that although the claims made for it may need some explication and development, both can be supplied. What Collingwood leaves most obscure is where he thinks the limits of its legitimate application lie. He often writes as if he thought that its scope was unlimited, *all* history being equally 'the re-enactment of past thought in the historian's own mind' (*IH* 215). I shall deal with the question of scope in Chapters 4 and 5,

[1] Cebik, 'Collingwood', 68.
[2] *Explanation and Human Action* (Oxford, 1966), 201.
[3] Saari, *Re-enactment*, 28.

and in this chapter ask only what can be said of the idea in the most favourable kinds of case.

Something like it appears as early as Collingwood's first book, *Religion and Philosophy*, published in 1916, in which, in considering how certain Christian heresies should be understood, he stresses the need to enter 'with some degree of sympathy into the problems which men wished to solve, and . . . to comprehend the motives which led them to offer their various answers' (*RP* 42). More explicit anticipations of his eventual view can be found in his critique of Croce's philosophy in 1921, in which, prefiguring also the later claim that in history past thought lives on in the present, he remarks that the very fact that an historian is 're-thinking [a dead man's] history proves that he is not dead' (CPH 15); and in a critique of Spengler's views in 1927, in which he maintains that we can understand other cultures only by 're-thinking for ourselves their thoughts', and by 'cherishing within us the fundamental ideas which frame their lives' (SHC 67, 71). There are no explicit references to the idea of re-enactment in *Speculum Mentis* or in the essays of the middle 1920s. However, as Nielsen and others have pointed out, we cannot conclude from this that the idea itself was entirely absent from Collingwood's thought at that stage, since near-synonyms like 're-create' or 'reconstruct in thought' occur in the earlier as well as the later writings.[4]

The re-enactment doctrine is expressly asserted for the first time in Collingwood's lectures of 1928. A peculiarity of his presentation of it at that point is his reporting that the idea first came to him while asking himself how one understands the present performance of a piece of music composed at some earlier time (L28 440–3). This, he says, requires that the auditor reconstruct it mentally, or, at least, follow a present performance of it actively, in that sense performing it again in imagination. He then came to see that the same idea applies to the way other sorts of human activities are understood—battles or revolts, for example—which are more central to the interests of historians. In fact, the idea of understanding artistic performances raises special problems, as Collingwood himself concedes later when, in *The Idea of History*, he excepts the history of art to some degree from his account of

---

[4] Nielsen, 'Re-enactment and Reconstruction', 3–4.

the way past military, political, and economic activities are to be understood (*IH* 313–14). I therefore postpone consideration of such examples until Chapter 4, § 5, and look at less problematic cases first.

As both van der Dussen and Nielsen have noted, Collingwood seems, as late as 1936, not to have been entirely satisfied with what is said in the 1928 lectures about the idea of understanding as re-enactment, remarking in a document of that year that 'the formula needs a good deal of clearing up' (NHH 19).[5] The doctrine is stated in as mature a form as he ever gave it, however, in three essays of the Epilegomena to *The Idea of History*: 'Human Nature and Human History', 'History as Re-enactment of Past Experience', and 'The Subject-matter of History'; and it also emerges from time to time in the historical survey which precedes them (e.g. *IH* 39, 97, 115). These sources can now be supplemented by what is found in relevant passages of Collingwood's manuscripts (e.g. NHH 19; CHBI 12; NHV 19). It is rather odd that the idea of re-enactment is not mentioned in the inaugural lecture, 'The Historical Imagination', in view of the common assumption that the ideas of re-enactment and imagination are closely linked in his thought.[6] Its absence also from those parts of 'The Principles of History' which were included in the Epilegomena, especially the one entitled 'Historical Evidence', may appear odder still. However, Knox has stated that re-enactment was the chief focus of the first seven sections of what was completed of that work;[7] and Collingwood's own outline of the book refers to it explicitly (NHV 20).

§ 2. *A Paradigm Case*

If there is anywhere in Collingwood's writings what might be considered a paradigmatic example of what he means by historical understanding as re-enactment, it is surely to be found in the

---

[5] On this, see Nielsen, ibid.; and van der Dussen's introduction to *IH*, rev. edn., p. xxxvii. In *IH* itself, Collingwood describes his account as correct in spite of 'ambiguities and shortcomings' and still requiring 'amplification and explanation' (*IH* 283).

[6] Taylor e.g. writes of Collingwood's idea of 'imaginative re-enactment' (*Bibliography*, 101); and Patrick Gardiner of his idea of 'imaginative understanding' (*The Nature of Historical Explanation* (Oxford, 1952), 132).

[7] In a conversation with Nielsen ('Re-enactment and Reconstruction', 2–3).

passage of his British Academy Lecture which outlines the way in which an historian would try to understand a past action like Caesar's crossing of the Rubicon (*IH* 213–15). There are, of course, other historical examples in his writings which have attracted critical attention: for example, what he says about the promulgation of the Theodosian Code (*IH* 283), or the invasion of Britain by Julius Caesar in 54 BC (*RBES* 32 ff.), or the incorporation of the earthwork called the Vallum into Hadrian's Wall (*RBES* 130 ff.).[8] And, as the manuscripts of the 1920s and 1930s become better known, historical examples drawn from them will doubtless become further points of reference for the discussion and appraisal of Collingwood's claims. However, it seems appropriate to begin here with what is probably Collingwood's best-known case, not only because of the prominent place it occupies in *The Idea of History*, but also because of the incisive and systematic way it is discussed there. It might be remarked that, although, in considering this example, Collingwood refers to what is required for 'understanding' rather than for 'explaining' a given action, he in fact recognizes no important difference between the concepts of understanding and explanation. It is true that, in *The Idea of History*, he seldom uses the latter term; but the way he uses it elsewhere makes it clear enough that, for him, the two terms are, for most purposes, interchangeable, understanding being what explanation typically yields, and explanation what understanding typically requires.[9] In what follows, I shall use them in the same way.

Two oddities about the way Collingwood prepares the ground for his example are worth initial notice. The first concerns the transition which he makes from representing history simply as a study of past happenings to representing it as a study of past human affairs.[10] He asks why historians invariably mean by 'history' the history of human affairs; and from the reply he gives it

---

[8] The second has been discussed at some length by Donagan, *LPC* 182 ff., and by Saari, *Re-enactment*, 117–21; the third by L. J. Goldstein, 'Collingwood's Theory of Historical Knowing', *History and Theory*, 9 (1970), 28 ff. (cited hereafter as 'Collingwood's Theory').

[9] See e.g. *IH* 176–7; *A* 111–12; *RAH* 14; also Saari, *Re-enactment*, 116. Collingwood also has a more troublesome tendency not to distinguish clearly between 'knowing' and 'understanding' with regard to an historical subject-matter (*L26* 422; *L28* 449; *IH* 115, 222–3).

[10] In his earliest writings on history (e.g. *SM* 211) Collingwood didn't even limit it to what is past.

could easily be concluded that he sees himself as offering a *proof* that only human affairs can have a history (*IH* 178, 212). But if that is what he is doing, the proof is clearly circular. For the reason that nature has no history, we are told, is that it cannot be understood in the distinctively historical way, i.e. by re-enacting its thoughts; and the reason that re-enactment is the method of history is that understanding a distinctively historical subject-matter, i.e. human affairs, requires it. Collingwood occasionally breaks out of this circle far enough to admit that nature, as studied, for example, in geology or evolutionary biology, may have a quasi-history or a pseudo-history, since the object of such studies is a process which may exhibit development, or even novelty—both said by Collingwood at other points to be features of historicity as such (*IH* 168; NHV 19). For present purposes, however, there is no need to challenge the circular 'proof'. What matters is Collingwood's claim that, to the extent that history is an attempt to understand past human affairs, it will require a kind of under-standing which is neither sought nor obtainable in natural history.

The second oddity is Collingwood's further identification of past human affairs with past human actions (*IH* 115, 178). This move is made without argument and may easily remain un-noticed. Yet it is a move which is clearly questionable, and which raises problems for Collingwood's theory later when the question becomes how much of what might normally be called human affairs is really open to a re-enactive kind of understanding.[11] In the present chapter, I shall leave Collingwood's identification of human affairs with human actions unchallenged, considering only what, according to him, is involved in understanding the latter.

What Collingwood has to say in setting forth his paradigm case is worth an initial summary, largely in his own words. 'The his-torian, investigating any event in the past', he declares, 'makes a distinction between what may be called the outside and the inside of an event.' By the outside is meant 'everything belonging to it which can be described in terms of bodies and their movements'; for example, 'the passage of Caesar, accompanied by certain men, across a river called the Rubicon' at a certain date. By the inside is

---

[11] I adopt this use of the adjective 're-enactive' from Martin (*HE* 82).

meant 'that in it which can only be described in terms of thought'; for example, 'Caesar's defiance of Republican law'. The historian 'is never concerned with either of these to the exclusion of the other'. 'His work may begin by discovering the outside of an event, but it can never end there; he must always remember that the event was an action, and that his main task is to think himself into this action, to discern the thought of the agent' (*IH* 213).

In carrying out such a programme, Collingwood continues, 'the historian is doing something which the scientist need not and cannot do.' For, in the case of nature, 'the distinction between the inside and outside of an event does not arise.' To be sure, the scientist, too, must seek to make what he studies intelligible. He does this, however, not by 'penetrating from the outside of the event to its inside', but by going 'beyond the event', observing 'its relations to others', and 'thus brings it under a general formula or law of nature'. The direction in which the historian proceeds is entirely different. It is impossible for him, without ceasing to be an historian, to 'emulate the scientist in searching for the causes or laws of events'. The relation which he seeks to grasp is not that of an action to other events, but that of an action to its own thought-side. 'To discover that thought is already to understand it. After the historian has ascertained the facts, there is no further process of inquiring into their causes. When the historian knows what happened, he already knows why it happened' (*IH* 214).

'But how does the historian discern the thoughts which he is trying to discover?', Collingwood goes on to ask, and replies: 'There is only one way in which it can be done: by re-thinking them in his own mind.' When 'the historian of politics or warfare, presented with an account of certain actions done by Julius Caesar, tries to understand these actions', this requires his 'envisaging for himself the situation in which Caesar stood and thinking for himself what Caesar thought about the situation and the possible ways of dealing with it'. To the natural scientist, the event to be explained is a mere phenomenon, a mere 'spectacle presented to his intelligent observation'. To an historian, the human actions studied are never 'spectacles', but always experiences which, in being understood, are lived thorough again in his imagination. Such re-enactment of past experience, Collingwood adds, is no 'passive surrender to the spell of another mind; it is a labour of active and therefore critical thinking.' It may require the

historian to bring to bear 'all the powers of his own mind' and all
his knowledge of the subject-matter—in this case Roman politics
(*IH* 215).

From this, Collingwood's own summary of his basic position,
three things seem to me worth singling out for special consideration. There is, first, the characterization of the historian's subject-
matter by means of the metaphor of 'inside' and 'outside'; second,
the attempt to contrast historical and scientific understanding
through the apparently paradoxical claim: 'When the historian
knows what happened, he already knows why it happened'; and
third, the requirement that the thought of the historical agent
which constitutes the 'inside' of an action not only be discovered,
but actually be re-thought or re-enacted by the historian, and
critically re-enacted at that. I shall argue that, although the metaphor of inside and outside may be misleading in some ways, it
need raise no serious problems for Collingwood's theory of historical understanding. By contrast, his declaration of the equivalence of the 'what' and the 'why', although accepted by many
of his apologists, I find quite indefensible, and I shall give reasons
for rejecting it. What Collingwood says about re-enactment having to be critical seems to me, on the whole, to be correct; but I
think it needs some interpretation and qualification, some of
which I shall try to provide.[12]

§ 3. *The Inside–Outside View of Action*

The inside–outside metaphor has bothered some critics of
Collingwood a great deal. It has been thought by some to fasten
upon history a view of thought as taking place in a private world
of consciousness, directly accessible only to the agent himself, this
leading either to scepticism about the possibility of historical
understanding at all, or to the ascription of extraordinary powers
to historians who claim to know what the thoughts of their subjects were. Patrick Gardiner, using a terminology which may now
seem somewhat dated, sees a Collingwoodian historian as required to postulate 'a peculiar entity' (a thought), 'a peculiar

[12] What follows derives from my 'Historical Understanding as Re-thinking',
University of Toronto Quarterly, 27 (1958), 200–15; and its further development in
Perspectives on History (London, 1980), ch. 1.

container in which this entity is to be "housed" ' (a mind), as well as 'a peculiar technique by which the "housing" may be achieved' (re-enactment).[13] And historians have often been as ready as philosophers to protest that Collingwood here makes a mystery of something which is not. As G. J. Renier puts it, he makes historical inference seem like a species of 'clairvoyance'.[14]

Certainly Collingwood carries the metaphor through relentlessly in the passages just noted, with his talk of outsides as things to be looked not 'at' but 'through', of historians as 'penetrating' the mere event in order to see what is 'inside', and of the impossibility of their ever actually 'perceiving' what they are looking for. Yet in much of what he says about understanding actions in *The Idea of History*, he uses an entirely different terminology which ought to put his metaphor in a more acceptable light.[15] Even in the passages summarized, actions are also described as *expressing* thoughts; and historians are assigned the task of interpreting their outsides as expressions. Nor should this be regarded as simply the addition of a causal dimension to the original quasi-spatial metaphor. By calling an action's outside an expression of the agent's thought, Collingwood doesn't mean that it was that thought's observable effect, furnishing the historian with a means of inferring the existence of an unobservable mental cause, the thought itself. It is true that he occasionally refers to thoughts as what 'made', 'caused', or even 'determined' people to act. But he is careful to add that, in all such cases, historians use causal language in a special sense, in which 'cause' is not to be identified with 'determining antecedent event'. According to Collingwood, the cause of an action, in a properly historical sense, is simply the thought which it expresses (*IH* 214–15).

Collingwood elaborated no full-scale theory of mind in *The Idea of History*. But, on the theory which he at least sketched, it is clear that, far from considering an agent's explanatory thoughts as

[13] 'The "Objects" of Historical Knowledge', *Philosophy*, 27 (1952), 213. Gardiner distances himself from this position in 'The Concept of Man as Presupposed by the Historical Studies', in G. N. A. Vesey *et al.*, *The Proper Study* (London, 1973), 19 ff. (cited hereafter as 'Concept of Man').

[14] *History: Its Purpose and Method* (London, 1950), 48 (cited hereafter as *Purpose and Method*).

[15] See *IH* 115, 118, 178, 212, 214, 216, 220; *A* 111, 128. What follows derives in part from my 'R. G. Collingwood and the Acquaintance Theory of Knowledge', *Revue internationale de philosophie*, 42 (1957), 420–32.

unobservable entities, he regarded them as having no existence at all apart from events in the agent's life which could be regarded as expressing them. On this question, his views are surprisingly close to those of his successor in the Chair of Metaphysics at Oxford, Gilbert Ryle.[16] Suggestive in this connection is his vigorous attack on what he calls the 'metaphysical' theory of mind—the conception of it as non-physical substance rather than as a complex of activities (*IH* 221), and his commendation of Hegel for opposing 'subjective idealism', the view that ideas exist 'only in people's heads' (*IH* 124).[17] Suggestive also is his denial that an acquaintance theory of knowledge has any application to the grasping of a person's thought—the very theory that so many of his critics accuse him of employing—and his labouring a distinction throughout *The Idea of History* between 'thought proper' and what he calls 'immediate experience' or 'flow of consciousness' (*IH* 294). The latter, on his view, is not thought at all, but mere psychic occurrence (*IH* 223, 231, 286–7).

In fact, so far is Collingwood from holding that explanatory thoughts are hidden, non-physical events, known directly to the agent himself, and only inferentially or indirectly to the historian, that he comes close at times to denying that, when it comes to gaining knowledge of his own thoughts, the historical agent has any advantage over the historian. A person's knowledge of his own thoughts, he insists, has to be obtained, as others have to obtain it, by placing interpretations upon his actions after the fact, i.e. by a kind of historical inquiry (*IH* 219). And he doesn't hesitate to ascribe to historians what is often ascribed to psychoanalysts: the capacity to discover in the record of what a person did various thoughts of which that person was quite unaware (*IH* 219). It is in this sense that I would interpret his claim that an historian may discover in past human affairs not only what has been entirely forgotten—by which he means something for which the documents afford no actual testimony—but also 'what, until he discovered it, no one ever knew to have happened at all' (*IH* 238).

---

[16] Collingwood's relation to Ryle is noted by Peter Skagestad (*Making Sense of History* (Oslo, 1975), 66—cited hereafter as *Making Sense*).

[17] Despite such considerations, Cebik characterizes him as a dualist ('Collingwood', 69), and Jonathan Cohen ascribes to him Ryle's 'dogma of the ghost in the machine' ('A Survey of Work in the Philosophy of History, 1946–1950', *Philosophical Quarterly*, 2 (1952), 173). Collingwood rejects mind–body dualism in his manuscripts on cosmology (NTM C-84).

Since, for Collingwood, what happened was human action, this implies that, at least sometimes, it may be the historian, not the agent, who first discovers what a given action really was, i.e. what thought a past event really expressed. This seems to me not only a legitimate conclusion to draw from Collingwood's stated doctrine, but also a correct assessment of the historian's powers.

Collingwood doesn't deny, however, that besides being expressed in his physical movements, an agent's thoughts can be expressed privately in his flow of consciousness.[18] This is apparent from his description of the relation between memory and autobiography, the latter being considered, rather restrictively perhaps, as an enterprise proceeding by strictly historical methods. The function of memory, Collingwood says, is to conjure up a 'vision' of past experience; the function of autobiography is to interpret the data thus provided, supplementing it, of course, with what can be found in old letters and the like (*IH* 295). But he seems not to have noticed a way in which the admission of private expressions of thought raises problems for the 'inside–outside' distinction as originally introduced. For, in his account of Caesar's crossing the Rubicon, he seems actually to have *defined* the 'outside' of an action in physical terms: it is that in it, he says, 'which can be described in terms of bodies and their movements'. If it was Collingwood's intention—as I think it was—that the distinction between 'inside' and 'outside' should mark the contrast between 'what is expressed' and 'what expresses it', this is clearly a mistake. The inadequacy of such a definition for his own purposes becomes the more apparent when he goes on, as he does later in *The Idea of History*, to talk of thinking as itself a form of activity, meaning by 'thinking' in this case a private activity of reflection which may have no physical expressions at all (*IH* 287). On Collingwood's general view of mind, if private reflection is action, it must be thought expressing itself in events; but *ex hypothesi*, these will be purely psychic, not physical, ones. For Collingwood, every action must have an outside. But in this case—to mix the metaphors—the outside will be entirely inside.

[18] On the dualist theory, of course, all thoughts are private. Some commentators who stress Collingwood's anti-dualism have attributed to him the opposite view that all thoughts are public, i.e. open to interpretation by anyone, their expressions then always having to be in the physical domain (see e.g. Skagestad, *Making Sense*, 65). Collingwood seems rather to take the more common-sense position that some thoughts are private, some public, and some both at once.

The admission of the possibility of private expressions and private acts of thought thus requires a revision of the common understanding of Collingwood's metaphor. By 'inside' must be meant 'whatever thought is expressed'; by 'outside', 'whatever event expresses it'. The same admission calls attention to a fact of historical inquiry which Collingwood's account often seems insufficiently to recognize, and which a view of the historian's task as interpreting expressions must not be allowed to obscure. This is the characteristic incompleteness of the historian's data, made worse by the unavailability in principle of private expressions of an agent's thought. From a practical point of view, this could perhaps be regarded as just an obvious limitation to which historical investigation is subject, and which no philosophical theory has any business trying to explain away. But if so, it is a limitation which Collingwood himself can hardly have had in mind when he claimed, to the later embarrassment of many of his apologists, that historical conclusions can be as certain as demonstrations in mathematics (*IH* 262).[19]

I have heard it argued that the sort of incompleteness which is envisaged here is of no real significance for a theory of history as inquiry. For a thought which lacks public expressions surely makes no difference to what we call 'the course of history'. It can therefore be of interest only to God and to the agent concerned, not to the historian; and the same might be said of private expressions of thoughts which also have public ones. The way this fails to be quite true points to a problem for 'inside–outside' accounts of historical reconstruction which may raise at least an echo of the philosophical worry expressed by Gardiner. For, at least occasionally, historians may want to assert, on the basis of later evidence, that an agent reached a certain decision at an earlier time, while keeping this entirely to himself. For example, an assertion to this effect might be made on the strength of a confession by someone considered in general to be honest.[20] In such a case, an historian, in arguing from the confession, will still be interpreting an expression of the agent's thought, namely, his confession—an expres-

---

[19] Mink has suggested that Collingwood does not mean by this that historical conclusions are incorrigible, or even that they follow with logical strictness from evidence, but only that there is a necessary connection between re-enacting and understanding (*HU* 280–2).

[20] Or, to use a Collingwoodian expression, someone whose 'personal coefficient' for truth-telling the historian considers high (L26 378).

sion of his claim to remember a past experience. But he will not, as Collingwood's theory would lead one to expect, be interpreting an expression of the thought which, in the end, he attributes to the agent, namely, his earlier decision: he will be interpreting the expression of a later thought, the claim to remember, as evidence for the earlier one.

Not that it would be necessary for the historian to infer that, at the time of the decision, any *particular* private events occurred in the agent's earlier stream of consciousness, and still less that a particular event occurred which was itself the private thought of the agent. What *would* have to be inferred is that some relevant private events occurred; and (here's the rub for Collingwood's theory) the historian would have to accept the agent's own interpretation of what thought those events expressed. A psychoanalytically-minded historian, for example, would presumably want to take account of Luther's actually having had a dreaded vision, not just his reporting that he had had one. Collingwood's own way with such examples would probably be short. What is in view here, he would say, is not history but belief upon testimony. This would be consistent with his general approach in *The Idea of History*, much of which is a polemic against opponents who allegedly fail to distinguish evidence from mere testimony, i.e. what we interpret on our own authority from what we accept on the authority of others (*IH* 256 ff.). But such a position is surely too restrictive. It is one thing to deny, as Collingwood so insistently does, that historians are dependent upon testimony, thus correcting a popular misconception of historical inquiry. It is quite another to contend that they could never have good reasons for accepting testimony at all.[21]

Before leaving the question of the sense in which Collingwood's metaphor should be understood, it may be of interest to note that Collingwood's own use of the notions 'inside' and 'outside' in *The Idea of History* is anything but strict. He sticks neither to the sense of 'mental' versus 'physical'—the sense exemplified in his discussion of Caesar's action, and the one which critics have

[21] For discussions of Collingwood's position on the acceptability of testimony in history, see C. A. J. Coady, 'Collingwood and Historical Testimony', *Philosophy*, 59 (1975), 409–24; or Gordon Couse, 'Historical Testimony in R. G. Collingwood's Theory and Practice', in David Carr *et al.* (eds.), *Philosophy of History and Contemporary Historiography* (Ottawa, 1982), 259–70.

generally had in mind when referring to his theory as the 'inside–outside' view of history—nor to the sense of 'what is expressed' versus 'what expresses it', which I have argued to be more in line with his broader intent. He charges Tacitus, for example, with having offered a merely 'external' view of Roman history, not because he represented actions as devoid of thought, but because he depicted his characters as 'exaggeratedly good' and 'exaggeratedly bad', and hence as 'mere spectacles of virtue or vice' (*IH* 39). He complains that nineteenth-century positivists reduced history to a succession of 'external events' because he found them, in their determination to consider only what they called 'the facts', not so much evaluating wrongly as refusing to evaluate the actions of historical agents at all (*IH* 132). He declares that some of his contemporaries—'scissors-and-paste' historians as he likes to call them—achieved only 'external' knowledge of the past because, instead of interpreting evidence on their own authority, they accepted and repeated what their authorities told them (*IH* 257). Clearly, in none of these cases does the historian's failure to present what is called the 'inside' of what happened mean that he has stressed unduly the agent's bodily movements, and still less that he has focused on his flow of consciousness as psychic event. It is unfortunately not untypical of Collingwood that he should have introduced the 'inside–outside' metaphor at a crucial point in his argument; given it the appearance there of being an important technical term; explained it in a way which, although a bit misleading, served his immediate purpose well enough; gone on then to use it very seldom when further elaborating his theory; and when he did so, to use it, more often than not, in a different sense.

§ 4. *Knowing What and Knowing Why*

Let me turn now from Collingwood's metaphor to what I called his paradox: what Donagan has described as his boldest and best-known saying about history (*LPC* 200). What sense can one make of the claim that, unlike the natural scientist, the historian, once he knows what happened, already knows why it happened—a claim which Collingwood thought important enough to make in the historical part of *The Idea of History* as well, and almost in the same words.[22] An interpretation offered by Walsh some years ago, although subsequently withdrawn, is that what Collingwood has primarily in mind here is the interest of historians in the thought-side of the actions they study, and that by contrast with 'mere events', he considers 'thoughts' to be *self*-explanatory.[23] This, if true, would indeed put the historian in a different position from that of the natural scientist. Yet even if his claim is more plausibly interpreted as being about understanding the action as a whole, it is hard entirely to get rid of the impression that, in equating the historian's 'what' with his 'why', *something* is being said to be self-explanatory.

Yet, in spite of such prima-facie difficulties, Collingwood's what–why paradox (as it might be called) has not lacked defenders; and among them are two of his most careful and critical commentators, Donagan and Mink.[24] Both concede that it seems to contradict an obvious truth about historical knowledge, namely, that at various stages of inquiry it will be known *what* various agents have done without knowing the reasons they had for doing it. Could a person not know, for example, that Caesar crossed the Rubicon without yet knowing what he hoped to achieve thereby? Two arguments have been offered against resting in such a common-sense position, both said to be at least implicit in Collingwood's conception of action and understanding.

The first is that, if it is knowledge through serious historical investigation we are talking about, and not just the acceptance of some claim about the past on authority, an alleged fact could not be grounded adequately in historical evidence without at the same time making clear why what happened came about. As Donagan has put it: 'An historian explains a fact in the very process of establishing it.'[25] The second argument turns on what it

22 *IH* 176–7; also *SM* 217–18, HUP 1. A difference between the what and the why is recognized in L27 348, and *NL* 33.

23 *IPH* 71; see also 'The Character of a Historical Explanation', *Aristotelian Society Supplementary Volume*, 21 (1947), 54 (cited hereafter as 'The Character'); or Rotenstreich, 'Facts to Thoughts', 135.

24 Others who accept the paradox include Cebik ('Collingwood', 88) and Rotenstreich ('Facts to Thoughts', 134–5). Mink thinks it more true of intellectual than of political or military history (*MHD* 188), this echoing Walsh's indefensible notion that, for Collingwood, thoughts, at least, are self-explanatory.

25 *LPC* 201; see also 'Explanation in History', reprinted in Patrick Gardiner (ed.), *Theories of History* (London, 1959), 432.

means, on Collingwood's theory, to know an historical fact fully. The fact, it must be remembered, is an action: a unity of inside and outside. One therefore cannot be said to know what an action really was until its thought-side has been discovered. An action's thought-side, however, is precisely what enables us to understand or explain it in the historically proper way. Thus, to know what an action is, both inside and outside, is at the same time to know its explanation—or, as Mink prefers to say, the full description of an action is at the same time its explanation (*MHD* 189). Something like this second argument seems to be widely accepted in the literature on Collingwood's philosophy of history. And those who accept it often regard it as pointing to a very distinctive feature of historical understanding.

The first argument seems to me to bear little examination. Doubtless an inquiry into whether a certain action was performed would often show why the agent performed it. But the precise evidence which would establish the 'whether' would not necessarily establish the 'why'; and nothing short of the claim that it would do so would support the paradox while keeping it interesting. The second argument is more slippery. In considering it critically, further distinctions need to be introduced into inside–outside accounts: distinctions between explaining why something happened and explaining what it was that happened; between what is to be explained and what is regarded as explaining it; between simply referring to an action and conceiving something as an action of a certain kind; between thoughts which explain an action and thoughts which render it an action of a kind to be explained. Let me look at the argument further, bringing these distinctions to bear where appropriate.

Defenders of the paradox insist that, on the inside–outside conception of an action, we cannot say that we know the 'nature' of an action until we know the thought which it expressed. And by this they tend to mean all the thought which it expressed. The search for understanding is thus seen as a rounding out of our knowledge of an action's thought-side. Mink represents this as a succession of responses to the question: 'What was the man really doing?' (*MHD* 189). Thus, an historian who already knew that Caesar crossed the Rubicon, might still ask: 'But what was he *doing*, crossing the river, when this was clearly contrary to Republican law?' In one sense, observes Mink, he already knows what

Caesar was doing; but in a sense that may matter to a Roman historian, he may not. He understands the action, say, as a river-crossing, but not yet as an assault upon enemies, and still less as a bid for supreme power in the state. This seems to me a perfectly good way of describing what an historian might be doing in setting out to explain Caesar's action. It even begins to make some sense of the claim that a full explanation, and perhaps also a full description, could somehow be self-explanatory. For if all the thought which was expressed in an action has been taken into account, there is clearly nothing more to understand the action as—at any rate, nothing that would represent it as an expression of thought.[26] This, however, still falls short of vindicating Collingwood's paradox. For that was explicitly stated in terms of knowing what things really were, not of knowing why they happened. The word 'why' drops too quickly out of many apologies for the paradox.

It is possible that Collingwood himself is in some confusion on this point. The longer passage in which reference to Caesar's crossing is embedded reads as if his concern, for the moment at least, is with historical understanding as the finding of answers to 'why' questions. Yet when he turns to his example to show what he means by an explanatory thought-side, what he mentions is 'Caesar's defiance of Republican law' (*IH* 213). This is hardly an answer to the question why Caesar crossed the Rubicon. It seems more like a logical—or perhaps legal—consequence of what Caesar did than one of the reasons he had for doing it, although a consequence of which he was certainly aware, and one the thought of which could also be said to have been expressed in his action. Caesar could, of course, have crossed the Rubicon *in order* to defy Republican law; but that is presumably not what Collingwood, as a Roman historian, believed. He seems, in fact, to have slipped here from asking why Caesar performed his action to asking what the significance of that action was, a question somewhat closer to Mink's 'What was the man really doing?'[27] I say 'slipped' because the shift is not acknowledged, and the rest of the passage is about knowing why something happened. It is a bit surprising to find Collingwood so oblivious at this point to

[26] As Mink observes, the 'complete description of an action already says everything about the thoughtfulness of that action that can be said' (*MHD* 190).
[27] Attributions of significance are considered further in Ch. 8.

what might be called the question-relativity of explanation in view of his well-known emphasis, not only in *The Idea of History*, but also in other works, on the primordial role of question and answer in inquiry (*IH* 273; *A* 29 ff.). However, since the paradox itself is stated in terms of the question why an historical agent acted as he did, it seems fair to insist on the distinction and to ask whether it can stand as stated.

The demanding and accepting of an answer to a 'why' question, I would argue, requires recognition of a distinction between what is to be explained and what explains it. When an historian claims to show, by referring to thought of the agent, why a certain action was done, one needs to ask precisely what is explained. Never, surely, the action conceived in such a way as to express *all* the thought which it in fact expressed, for that would leave no thought distinguishable from the action as conceived which could be regarded as explaining it. Not the mere event, either—the outside of the action considered by itself—although Collingwood himself, perhaps too much under the influence of his studies at the overlap of history and archaeology, did sometimes say that historical explanation is *of* an outside *by* an inside, as if what typically puzzled historians were sheer physical movements, or even sheer physical remains, like potsherds or Hadrian's Wall.[28] The inside–outside distinction, in fact, corresponds in neither of these ways to the distinction ordinarily drawn in history between what explains and what is to be explained. What is to be explained, as Collingwood himself says in his better moments, is action. To be conceived as an action at all, and hence as something to be explained, an event must already be conceived as expressing a certain thought, as does Caesar's crossing of the Rubicon, if only his intending to get to the other side. What explains the action so conceived is a thought which, to be explanatory, must also be expressed in the action. But at the same time, it must be a thought which, like Caesar's wanting to close with his enemies in Rome, does not belong to the conception or description of the action as it

---

[28] Debbins nevertheless represents this as Collingwood's standard case, the historian having first to reconstruct what happened in imagination, and then to discover through re-enactment what thoughts these happenings expressed (*EPH*, pp. xxviii–xxix). Such an interpretation is hardly borne out by Collingwood's paradigm case or by his general practice as an historian, but it may be encouraged by his talk of outsides being explained by insides, and by his reminders that historical thinking is grounded in the perception of present relics.

is to be explained. At no level of conception or description is something which can be referred to as 'the action' explained in terms of a thought which belongs to the same level of conception or description. But the contrary is exactly what the paradox seems to maintain.[29]

Still a shorter way with Collingwood's paradox would be to point out that, as stated, it really rests upon an equivocation. If we are told that, when the historian knows what happened, he already knows why it happened, we naturally assume that the same thing is being referred to by 'what' and 'it'. In fact, the assertion only makes sense if 'it' refers to the action as characterized before the explanation begins, and 'what' to the action as re-characterized when, as is always possible, the thought which is regarded as explanatory is incorporated into a re-description of it. If we adopt the latter, the equivocal, interpretation, Collingwood's claim that when the historian knows what happened he already knows why it happened, if applied to his Caesar example, yields the following statement: 'When the historian knows that Caesar was advancing against his enemies in Rome, he already knows why he crossed the Rubicon.' This is true, and not paradoxical, but seems less than Collingwood wants to say. To maintain the original thrust of his statement, and its air of paradox, we have to read Collingwood's 'what' as standing for the same thing as his 'it', this yielding instead the statement: 'When the historian knows that Caesar was advancing against his enemies in Rome, he already knows why Caesar was advancing against his enemies in Rome.' This, although more interesting, is obviously false. It might be added that, once Collingwood's paradox is seen to rest upon an equivocation, it will be seen to hold equally for the explanation of natural events. What happened on a certain occasion, someone might report, was a darkening of the sky. What really happened, he may learn later, was a solar eclipse. Evidently, when he knows what happened (meaning the eclipse)

---

[29] One thing missing from Collingwood's paradox is any recognition that explanation must be given relative to a description—that actions (and other things, too) can only be explained as described (or conceived). This principle has become a commonplace of critical philosophy of history since it was stressed by Arthur Danto (*Narration and Knowledge* (New York, 1985), 218). Saari believes that Collingwood recognizes it in *A* 131 (*Re-enactment*, 114), but it is not easy to find there. Martin recognizes the principle, but defends the paradox (*HE* 67 n. 2; 81).

he already knows why it happened (meaning the darkening of the sky). Since Collingwood's purpose in stating the what–why paradox was to sum up differences between history and natural science, and perhaps to dramatize them a little, this is scarcely a satisfactory result from his point of view.

But the differences between scientific and historical understanding which, in formulating the paradox, Collingwood was really concerned to establish, don't in any case need it for their elucidation. These he puts metaphorically in terms of the different 'directions' in which scientific and historical studies of an event might be said to proceed. The scientist, according to Collingwood, goes 'beyond' the event to other events related to it by law. The historian, by contrast, 'penetrates' to the inside of the event itself to discover the thought which it expresses. Put in other language, historical understanding of an action is said to be achieved without subsuming it under empirical generalizations or laws (see further Chapter 3, § 2). It is also said not to require reference to initial conditions in the sense in which a natural scientist could be expected to look for them—i.e. reference to other, and generally earlier, happenings.

By denying in this way that the historian needs to look beyond the action itself to initial or determining conditions—i.e. to further events—Collingwood is affirming the sufficiency of agents' reasons for the historical explanation of why actions were performed. Saying what those reasons were requires only a description of the agent's situation as he conceived it to be. The belief of Caesar that his enemies were vulnerable, for example, need not be true to be explanatory. In his concern to attack doctrines such as geographical determinism which might seem to deny such a claim, Collingwood sometimes says that the 'hard facts' of the situation in which any agent has to act consist entirely of 'thoughts', or denies that physical events and conditions can ever be historical causes of actions (*IH* 214, 316–17). There are certainly elements of overstatement in both of these formulations of his claims (see further Chapter 5, § 2). It would probably have been closer to what he really had in mind if he had said that, when deciding what to do, the situation an agent actually takes into account is constituted by his thoughts, or that actual physical conditions can be causes of actions only through agents' thoughts about them. What is overstated, however, is largely correct, and is of central importance for the philosophical analysis of historiography.

If Collingwood's residual claim here is from time to time denied, I think it is generally because it is misunderstood. Karl Popper appears to misunderstand it, for example, when he contrasts Collingwood's views with his own contention that historical actions are to be explained in terms of an objective 'logic of the situation'.[30] What history should be about, Popper insists, is situations as they really were, not as they were perhaps falsely envisaged by the agents. It is not easy to see, however, how objective facts of a situation could throw light on what historical agents decided to do in it if they believed their situation to be otherwise. Nor does the position which Collingwood was actually maintaining appear to be challenged by Popper's treatment of examples. One which he offers is the following. He found it initially surprising, he says, that Galileo should have refused to accept a lunar theory of the tides. While puzzling over this, he noted that Galileo rejected advances from Kepler, who held such a theory—failed to answer letters from him, for example. He noted also that Galileo rejected astrology; that astrology, as a theory about the influence of heavenly bodies on earthly events, was well-disposed towards a lunar theory; and that Kepler was an astrologer. These, he rightly observes, are all objective facts. The logic of Galileo's position, he goes on to say, called for his rejection of Kepler's advances—presumably to avoid intellectual contamination.

But what Popper has described looks exactly like what Collingwood would call a reconstruction of agents' thoughts. For one of the things which makes the cited facts explanatory is surely their being what Galileo believed. The 'initial conditions' which Collingwood wishes to exclude from historical explanation are not such 'objective facts' as that the agent believed certain things about his situation, but rather that the situation was a certain way whether he believed it or not. Should a further study show that astrological lore did not after all favour a lunar theory, the explanation which Popper gave would not be undermined in the least so long as it could be maintained that Galileo believed that it favoured it. Should it show rather that Galileo believed otherwise,

---

[30] 'A Pluralist Approach to the Philosophy of History', in E. Streisler (ed.), *Roads to Freedom: Essays in Honour of F. A. von Hayek* (London, 1969), 196 ff. (cited hereafter as 'Pluralist Approach').

no 'objective' connection between lore and theory could save the explanation.

§ 5. *Re-enactment as Critical*

Let us look now more directly at Collingwood's insistence that, in order to understand a past human action, the historian must not only discover the thought expressed in it, but must actually re-think or re-enact that thought in his own mind. Like the associated doctrines which I have been discussing, this claim has drawn critical fire. Gardiner sees it as making historical inference 'self-certifying';[31] Walsh as attributing to historians a power of 'intuition' (*IPH* 58); Elton as reducing history to whatever the historian 'dreams up'.[32] Remarks made by Collingwood himself do sometimes appear to justify such expressions of dissatisfaction. I think nevertheless that the re-thinking requirement, properly understood, points to features of historical understanding that no account of history as a mode of inquiry should ignore.

Many of the problems thought to be generated by Collingwood's requirement can be attributed to a widespread tendency to interpret it as promulgating a method for discovering historical facts. Collingwood's language does sometimes make it look as if what he is telling us is how to go about making discoveries, whether of the thoughts expressed in past actions, or of what constituted their 'outsides'. Even in the passage which I summarized earlier—and there are many more like it—Collingwood asks: 'But *how* does the historian discern the thoughts which he is trying to discover?', and replies: 'There is only one *way* in which it can be done: by re-thinking them in his own mind' (*IH* 215; emphasis added). With similar nuance, he says elsewhere: 'To discover what [an agent's] thought was, the historian must think it again for himself' (*IH* 283). Yet, if we take such pronouncements as methodological prescriptions, it is difficult to make much sense

[31] 'Historical Understanding and the Empiricist Tradition', in Bernard Williams and Alan Montefiori (eds.), *British Analytic Philosophy* (London, 1966), 276 (cited hereafter as 'Historical Understanding').

[32] *Political History: Principles and Practice* (London, 1970), 133. Arnold Toynbee takes Collingwood's doctrine to imply that an historian of Tamerlane who wished to re-enact his thoughts, would have to run amok in the streets (*A Study of History*, ix (Oxford, 1954), 733–4).

of them. How does someone who doesn't yet know what a past agent's thought was go about discovering what it was by re-thinking it? Small wonder that what Collingwood has often been taken to be offering is methodological advice which, although clearly suspect, does make literal sense, namely: first imagine yourself in the position of the agent, and then attribute to him whatever thought you find yourself thinking. Many have claimed to find a significant likeness between such an obviously unaccept-able prescription and such remarks of Collingwood's as that the historian must 'envisage for himself the situation in which Caesar stood, and think for himself what Caesar thought about the situation'. But the first is no more than a caricature of the second.[33] What Collingwood maintains is not that whatever the historian thinks, when he imagines himself in the agent's place, the agent can be assumed to have thought too. It is that whatever the agent thought, the historian who wishes to understand the way he acted must be sure to think too.

There are, in any case, two extensive sections of the Epile-gomena to *The Idea of History* which should throw immediate doubt upon any straightforwardly methodological interpretation of the demand that the historian re-think the thought of the his-torical agent. These are the sections specifically devoted to histori-cal evidence (*IH* 249 ff.) and to re-enactment of past experience (*IH* 282 ff.), the one comparing historical arguments to crime detec-tion, the other considering difficulties for the very idea that his-torians and historical agents might ever think the same thought.

Collingwood asserts constantly that history is inferential. As he puts it in the *Autobiography*: anyone who answers an historical question must renounce 'guesswork' and 'be able to show that his answer is the answer which the evidence demands' (*A* 128). The 'autonomy' which Collingwood ascribes to historians—a notion

---

[33] Elazar Weinryb offers the caricature when he represents an historian as positioning himself for re-enactment by putting the question: 'If I were in Caesar's place, what would have been my reasons for crossing the Rubicon?' ('Re-enact-ment in Retrospect', *Monist*, 72 (1989), 573). C. G. Hempel does the same in asserting that, on the 'empathetic' theory, the historian 'tries to realize how he himself would act under the given conditions, and under the particular motivations of his heroes' ('The Function of General Laws in History', 352–3— cited hereafter as 'General Laws'). Collingwood comes perilously close to the caricature himself when he imagines a historian asking 'what should I have done if I had been in Nelson's place' (*A* 113).

---

that has offended some critics almost as much as that of re-enactment—consists in being independent of testimony, not in being independent of evidence. Collingwood would have been astonished at the allegation of Fain that, in enunciating the re-enactment doctrine, he 'took the heroic path of attempting to dismiss historical evidence altogether'.[34]

This, of course, doesn't in itself dispose of the criticism, since what Collingwood says about evidence and about re-enactment might be in glaring contradiction; and he does tend to talk about the two in different places. It is therefore especially instructive, in considering the soundness of a methodological interpretation, to note the way in which re-enactment is discussed in the section of *The Idea of History* entitled 'History as Re-enactment of Past Experience'. Collingwood's aim here, it has often been assumed, is to show how the alleged method of re-enactment works; and if approached in this way it is positively spooky, with its suggestion of past thoughts hovering immaculately outside time, waiting to be re-thought by historians (*IH* 286). 'The peculiarity of thought', declares Collingwood, 'is that, in addition to occurring here and now in this context, it can sustain itself through a change of context and revive in a different one' (*IH* 297). Both the content of a thought and the act of thinking it, he insists, stand somehow 'outside time' (*IH* 287). In fact, what he says in such passages is more plausibly interpreted as an attempt to deal with a conceptual problem than with a methodological one—the problem of what it would mean to think the very same thought as another person. Collingwood asks, for example, *in what sense* the thoughts of the two persons would have to be the same—specific or numerical—*and what sort of thing* a thought would have to be to be re-thinkable at different times even by the same person. In trying to connect the idea of re-thinking a thought with that of understanding an action, Collingwood's concern appears to be of the same conceptual kind. In claiming that the only way the latter can be achieved is by doing the former, he is asserting what he takes to be a logical connection between these two notions (although he doesn't use this language). His thesis is that, in the sense of the term appropriate to understanding actions in history, understanding the action *is* (among other things) re-thinking the

---

[34] *BPH* 144. Cebik takes a similar position ('Collingwood', 77–8).

thought expressed in it. The thesis is about the goal, not about the procedures, of historical inquiry.[35]

Collingwood's explication of that goal, it must be acknowledged, is somewhat elusive. If we ask why the historian, in understanding an action, must actually re-think the thought said to explain it—why it wouldn't be enough, for example, simply to discover what it was—Collingwood's reply will be that thought is not 'mere object', not just a 'flow of consciousness', not something 'ready-made', not a mere 'spectacle' for contemplation (*IH* 214, 218, 292, 294).[36] It is an 'activity', he says, which is to be known as such only by engaging in it. Thus we *cannot* discover what a past thought was without at the same time re-thinking it. And the re-thinking will necessarily be critical. Seeing whether we can re-think the agent's thought as our own will raise for us the question of its cogency. Thus re-thinking another's thought is to be distinguished from merely duplicating another's experience. In Collingwood's phrase: re-thinking is never a 'passive surrender to the spell of another's mind'.

Such ways of talking are less puzzling if we remember that the thought which the historian would have to re-think, in trying to understand why an action was done, would take the form of a practical argument—a piece of reasoning about what to do in response to a perceived problem.[37] What would make Caesar's action understandable is the thought that, given a situation as he conceived his to be, and goals like the ones he wanted to pursue, faced with a barrier like the Rubicon, the thing to do would be to cross it. Such an argument will only render the action understandable, however, if its practical conclusions really do follow from the considerations which the agent is said to have taken into account. In other words, if the argument is to render the action understandable, it has to be seen as valid. And the only way to tell whether an argument is valid, Collingwood insists, is to try it out,

---

[35] This sort of interpretation was first advanced by Donagan ('The Verification of Historical Theses', *Philosophical Quarterly*, 6 (1956), 195). Van der Dussen records other versions of it, and himself supports a qualified one, in an excellent survey of the whole controversy over the methodological interpretation (*HS* 99 ff.).

[36] Collingwood's contention that history is not a spectacle, and cannot be understood by a mere spectator, is reiterated throughout his later work (*IH* 97, 163, 181; *A* 155), although flatly denied in his writings before 1928 (*SM* 204; NAPH 47).

[37] Here the interpretation of Collingwood's view of re-enactment makes contact with contemporary analyses of action explanation as the ascription of implicit practical arguments (to be discussed further in Ch. 3, § 3).

to test it, to see whether it can really be thought.[38] The insistence that re-enactment must be critical thus points to a quasi-normative dimension in historical understanding.[39] To understand an action in a properly historical way is in some degree to see it as having been appropriate to the circumstances as the agent saw them.

Arguments, of course, have generality. One recurring criticism of Collingwood which this consideration makes it difficult to sustain is that his theory of understanding assigns to historians the impossible task of explaining 'the unique and the particular'. According to E. H. Carr, for example, it was this which led him to deny the relevance of the scientific model of explanation to history (*WIH* 56). Yet Collingwood explicitly declares that 'the individuality of historical events and personages, if that means their uniqueness', falls outside the historian's concerns. It is 'just the universality of an event or character', he maintains, 'that makes it a proper and possible object of historical study, if by universality we mean something that oversteps the limits of merely local and temporal existence and possesses a significance valid for all men at all times' (*IH* 303). I take it that the 'universal significance' which is to be recognized in an action, when historically understood, resides in the validity of the practical argument which it expresses. This must surely be what Collingwood had in mind in the following, rather startling passage:

If the discovery of Pythagoras concerning the square on the hypotenuse is a thought which we can to-day think for ourselves, a thought that constitutes a permanent addition to mathematical knowledge, the discovery of Augustus that a monarchy could be grafted upon the Republican constitution of Rome by developing the implications of *proconsulare imperium* and *tribunicia potestas*, is equally a thought which the student of Roman history can think for himself, a permanent addition to political ideas. (*IH* 217–18)

---

[38] In a paragraph added to his 1928 lectures in 1935, Collingwood explicitly declares that 'the past thought which we re-enact is seen in re-thinking it as valid' (L28 470 n. 16); and the same doctrine is often at least implied in his published work (e.g. *A* 111). In the lectures of 1928, he maintains that to write the history of a battle, one must 'see the ground of the battlefield as the opposing commanders saw it, and draw from the topography the conclusions that they drew' (L28 441). The idea of drawing conclusions is inseparable from that of appraising arguments.

[39] I shall therefore refer to this view of Collingwood's meaning as the 'quasi-normative' interpretation when considering some others in Ch. 3, § 3.

When Collingwood talks, as he sometimes does, of the historian's task as the revival not of the thought, but of the experience of the historical agent (*IH* 283, 302), it is therefore important not to read this as implying that he can recapture the immediate experience, or flow of consciousness, of the agent. To use Collingwoodian language, the historian's re-thought thought and that of the agent must be identical in their 'mediation', not in their 'immediacy'. Martin seems to me to obscure this point when he observes that, for Collingwood, the understanding of actions, besides not requiring reference to generalizations, 'does not logically require any move to put actions under classificatory concepts' (*HE* 62–3). This, he says, makes his theory 'vulnerable', as indeed it would do if it were the position which he in fact held. What the quoted passage surely shows, however, is that Collingwood acknowledges that actions are necessarily understood—and that means re-enactively understood—as actions of a certain kind, i.e. as events expressing thoughts of a certain kind. As will be noted in § 7, Collingwood does not hold unwaveringly to this position. But he holds to it for the most part, and especially in contexts where re-enactive explanation is the issue.

§ 6. *Mis-statements of Re-enactment*

I have attributed to Collingwood the position that understanding an action by reference to the practical argument which it expresses requires the argument's having been appraised and found valid. If the historian fails to re-think it critically, or if the argument itself breaks down under criticism, then understanding fails. But if this is correct, Collingwood states both claims misleadingly from time to time. With a view to clarifying what is defensible in his doctrine further, let me look briefly at some examples of what seem to me such mis-statements.

Collingwood surely mis-states the claim that re-thinking must be critical when he says, in a part of the British Academy Lecture which was not quoted in § 2, that the historian, since he re-enacts past thought 'in the context of his own knowledge', therefore 'criticizes it, forms his own judgement of its value, corrects whatever errors he can discern in it' (*IH* 215). It may perhaps be suggested that all he means by this is that the historian will, as a matter of course, ask himself what the agent should have thought. But more extreme statements of the same claim suggest that he may have envisaged more. 'Nothing could be a completer error,' he declares, with the history of philosophy particularly in mind, 'than to suppose that the historian as such merely ascertains "what so-and-so thought", leaving it to someone else to decide "whether it was true"' (IH 215). He goes so far indeed as to call the idea of doing the one without doing the other 'self-contradictory' (IH 300). But it would surely be odd to say that understanding an action logically requires the historian's correction of errors of reasoning on the part of the agent. For if any were discovered, this would be equivalent to finding the agent's thought un-re-thinkable. And it is quite unnecessary for understanding an action that other sorts of errors on the part of the agent be corrected—factual ones, for example. If any were made, what is more likely to need correcting is the historian's initial conception of what the agent's argument was. What makes an elicited practical argument explanatory is not the truth of its conclusion but the argument's validity.

There are also times when Collingwood seems to misrepresent the sense in which a claim to understand an action must be based upon finding an expressed argument valid. A case in point is a remark which he makes about the importance of understanding Marx's philosophy as an attempt to solve a practical rather than a theoretical problem. What Marx wrote, he observes, 'would necessarily . . . appear nonsensical except to a person who, I will not say shared his desire to make the world better by means of a philosophy, but at least regarded that desire as a reasonable one' (A 152). The qualification which he adds here betrays at least a qualm about saying that the historian must actually agree with the purposes and principles of the agent if he is to understand his action. But for understanding, it is not even necessary that they be regarded as reasonable. They need only, if embraced, render the envisaged action a reasonable response.

Collingwood reaches for a slightly different qualification while trying to convey what would be involved in understanding Nelson's famous declaration at Trafalgar: 'In honour I won them, in honour I will die with them'—said in response to urgings that he remove his very visible decorations during battle. The thought which these words, said on this occasion, expressed, Collingwood concludes, is: 'This is not a time to take off my ornaments of honour for the sake of saving my life'—and he adds: 'Unless I were capable—perhaps only transiently—of thinking that for myself, Nelson's words would remain meaningless to me' (*A* 112). But this second qualification, if it means that only historians who accept Nelson's professional code can understand his acting as he did, will not do either. What the historian has to be able to think is that leaving one's decorations on in such a situation is indeed required by that code. And this not 'transiently', since the envisaged thought—the connection of ideas—must be seen (to use Collingwood's own phrase) as having a 'significance valid for all time'.

Collingwood sometimes mis-states in still another way the claim that understanding depends upon finding the agent's argument valid. This time it is with regard to certain attitudes which he seems, at some points, to be saying historians need to take up. As I have represented his doctrine, it might be said to make it a necessary condition of our understanding action in a properly historical way that the historian empathize with the agent concerned—meaning by this, however, no more than that in appraising the agent's practical argument, he will, at the same time, necessarily consider that agent's situation from the agent's own point of view. What Collingwood sometimes falls into saying, however, is that the historian needs to *sympathize* with the agent in attempting to understand him. He singles out the Romantics for special praise in this regard. The 'intense sympathy' which they brought to the study of the Middle Ages, he says, enabled them to recognize 'genuine and valuable human achievements' which the men of the Enlightenment missed (*IH* 87; see also *IH* 39, 105, 200, 326). Doubtless being completely out of sympathy with a way of life could prevent an historian from correctly interpreting actions performed in pursuit of it. But too much sympathy could be a problem, too. Collingwood cannot plausibly represent sympathy as either a logically or a psychologically necessary condition of historical understanding. But there is nothing in his original statement of it that requires him to do so.

Similar considerations apply to what Collingwood sometimes says about a need for historians to have an 'affinity' for what they study. The 'gulf of time', he says, must be 'bridged . . . from both ends. The object must be of such a kind that it can revive itself in the historian's mind; the historian's mind must be such as to offer a home for that revival' (*IH* 304). This, he adds, is not a matter of possessing a special 'historical temperament' or knowing a special 'historical technique'; it is simply the historian having to be 'the right man to study that object'. But the impression which may easily be given here is that Collingwood makes it a condition of attaining re-enactive understanding that historians come to their task equipped with mind-sets or experience resembling those of the agents whose actions they want to understand. He warns us, indeed, that if an historian tries to work 'against the grain of his own mind', he is likely to lapse into mere scissors and paste (*IH* 305; 329). But he cannot consistently regard affinity, so conceived, as a necessary condition of understanding, either logically or psychologically—which is fortunate for historians studying, say, the political methods of the Borgias or the treatment of the defeated Carthaginians by the Romans.

§ 7. *History as Knowledge of the Individual*

In the chapter to follow, I shall endeavour to explicate Collingwood's idea of historical understanding further by contrasting his view of it as re-enactment in a little more detail with his conception of explanation in the natural sciences. I shall also contrast the interpretation of re-enactment itself which I have outlined here with two somewhat different interpretations which have enjoyed some support. Before doing this, however, it may be useful to take a brief look at the quite different way in which Collingwood conceived specifically historical understanding before he arrived at his view of it as re-enactive, a way which, although incompatible with the latter, makes an occasional appearance in his writings long after the 'illumination' of Martouret.

In *Speculum Mentis*, and in some of the essays of the 1920s, what Collingwood took to be the essential characteristic of history was its being concerned with the concrete rather than the abstract, the individual rather than the general. 'The object of history', he tells us, 'is fact as such', this making historical knowledge more like sense perception than like natural science (*SM* 211; also *SM* 204, 217; NAPH 44). The historian, he says again in an essay of the 1920s, 'is concerned to discover the facts, the whole facts, and nothing but the facts'; what he deals with is 'the individual in all its individuality' (SHC 67).[40] As was noted earlier, Collingwood has sometimes been called an idealist philosopher of history because of his emphasis in his later work on historical understanding as the re-thinking or re-enactment of thoughts or 'ideas'. His earlier view of history as knowledge of the individual links him with still another tradition in philosophy of history which has sometimes been called idealist, one which conceives it as an idiographic or particularizing rather than a nomothetic or generalizing sort of inquiry. As Collingwood himself points out, this is a tradition represented in German thought especially by Wilhelm Windelband, and in English thought especially by Michael Oakeshott, although he finds rather more to praise in the latter than in the former (*IH* 155, 166).

It has sometimes been suggested that the idea of history as a study of the individual and the concrete belongs to a stage of Collingwood's thought on the subject when his chief interest was in history as a general form of experience or attitude of mind, rather than a discipline or type of inquiry, and that he moved away from this doctrine as his interests developed in the latter direction. Rotenstreich has maintained, for example, that Collingwood's early concern with history in a broader sense for some time 'blocked the way' towards a serious analysis of historical method, the thing for which he eventually became most noted.[41] But, although his writings of the middle 1920s, as just instanced, devote much less attention than his later ones do to the detailed characterization of history as inquiry, it seems clear that what he says in them about an essential connection between historicity and factuality, or particularity, or individuality, is intended to apply *pari passu* to history as historians understand it. Thus, in his Historical Association Leaflet of 1930, which sums up his findings of the previous decade for an historical readership, he characterizes the task of the historian simply as 'the study of the past', with no hint of restriction to any more particular type of subject-matter or inquiry. As Collingwood puts it there, 'to be an historian' is simply 'to know how things have come to be what they are' (PH 124). In Chapter 1, I drew attention to two different

---

[40] The sense in which history is here conceived as individualistic is to be distinguished from that considered in Ch. 4, §§ 3–5.
[41] Rotenstreich, 'Facts to Thoughts', 123.

ways in which Collingwood talked of history in broader and narrower senses: the first, history as a way of thinking or attitude of mind by contrast with history as a discipline; the second, history as (knowledge of) whatever happened in the past by contrast with history as (knowledge of) the specifically human past. Clearly, when he describes history in his earlier writings as concerned with what is individual, what he has in mind is the discipline as well as a general way of thinking, and the study of the human past as well as the study of the past as such.[42]

In his later philosophical writings on history, the idea that history is essentially concerned with factuality or knowledge of the individual recedes into the background, becoming what Mink might have called a 'recessive' doctrine, but it never entirely disappears.[43] It is present, for example, in his saying that evolutionary biology, with its attention to a particular strain of change, effects 'a partial reduction of nature to history' (*IH* 129); in his praise of Samuel Alexander for having defined the idea of historicity 'further' through the notion of the historicity of all things (RAH 1–2); in his criticism of Bury for failing to realize that individuality is 'the very substance of the historical process' (*IH* 150); in his remarking that history, like perception, 'has for its proper object something individual' (*IH* 233). The doctrine is softened somewhat in the Epilegomenon, 'The Subject-matter of History', where (as already noted) Collingwood warns that to call history knowledge of the individual 'claims for it a field at once too wide and too narrow', the historian not being able to apprehend a past act of thought 'just as it actually happened' but only as something possessing 'universal significance'—in other words, as a thought of a certain kind (*IH* 303). But it reappears in an extreme form in *The New Leviathan* in the affirmation that 'history is the science of the individual; the individual is the unique; the unique is the only one of its kind' (*NL* 221).

In contrasting Collingwood's conceptions of history as knowledge of the individual and as knowledge of the re-enactable, it

---

[42] So no significant distinction is drawn at this stage between human and natural history, the distinction between discipline and attitude of mind applying also to the latter.

[43] Walsh thus has some justification for observing that, for Collingwood, history is 'a special form of knowledge . . . whose distinguishing characteristic is that it gives us knowledge of the individual' ('The Character', 53); and Carr for saying that he conceives history as a study of 'the unique and particular' (*WIH* 56–7).

needs to be stressed that the earlier position is not just a characterization of the kind of subject-matter that supposedly interests
historians. For along with it goes a distinctive, if rather sketchily
worked out, idea of the way that subject-matter is to be understood. The individual, and even the unique, is said to be understandable 'in itself'. There are times, certainly, when Collingwood
seems to place such a notion in doubt, as when he appears to hold
(with the Greeks and against Windelband) that 'rational knowledge of the individual'—by which is presumably meant understanding it—is impossible (*IH* 167). But at other times, he seems to
assert precisely the opposite.[44] Thus he puts aside as 'positivist
prejudice' Bury's alleged belief that 'individuality as such is unintelligible' (*IH* 150); and he insists that, by contrast with attempts to
achieve understanding in science, there is an historical kind of
inquiry 'whose function is to understand the flux of events as they
actually happen, seeing them in their actual connexion with one
another' (RAH 21). Historical thought, we are told, 'follows the
movement of the events themselves, and in so doing finds them
intelligible' (RAH 5). Collingwood sometimes asserts further that
finding them intelligible is a matter of discerning their 'continuity', which, in history, by contrast with science, is said not to be
a matter of their succession instantiating laws. Collingwood applies this doctrine specifically to the analysis of causal judgment
in history. 'The cause of an event in history', he says, 'is its
intrinsic relation to other events in history, and the causal nexus is
not external to them but lies in their very nature' (*SM* 218). Again,
in rejecting positivist conceptions of causality for history, he
maintains that causal laws would not explain anything unless the
necessity of the particular connections to which they apply could
be recognized independently, this, of course, making the laws
redundant (RAH 18).[45]

Collingwood nowhere adequately explains what could plausibly be meant by understanding the individual as such, or grasping actual connections between events, or discerning continuity in
some sense which transcends law-instantiation. Rather strangely,

[44] Claiming e.g. that history is 'wholly a reasoned knowledge of what is tran-
sient and concrete' (*IH* 234).

[45] Here Collingwood's position curiously resembles that taken by Maurice
Mandelbaum in his *Anatomy of Historical Knowledge* (Baltimore, 1977), 68 ff. (cited
hereafter as *Anatomy*).

he sometimes gives the impression of regarding re-enactment as a way of grasping the individuality of past thoughts and actions. There is more than a hint of this in the approval he expresses of Croce's 'mature' doctrine that the distinctive feature of historical, by contrast with scientific, thought, is concern with the individual. The only reservation he voices is that 'individuality' without 'inwardness' is not enough—as if he thinks that to speak of grasping individuality inwardly, i.e. re-enactively, if not outwardly, makes perfectly good sense. And he specifically calls for 'apprehending the individuality of a thing by thinking oneself into it' (*IH* 199–200).[46] But if, as was argued above, the idea of understanding an action re-enactively implies, among other things, discovering a universal significance in its expressed idea, any claim that it can be understood 'in itself' is surely ruled out. Collingwood contrasts thinking oneself into a thing's individuality with 'analyzing or classifying it from an external point of view'; and this may be acceptable so long as the emphasis is on the idea of externality. But an action cannot be understood re-enactively if one refuses to analyse or classify it at all: and if Collingwood is here claiming the contrary, then his endemic hostility to 'abstraction' (cf. *IH* 234) has clearly overstepped the mark. There remains, in any case, the difficulty that the idea of the individual being understandable 'as such' is not intended to apply only to what is re-enactable: Collingwood offers illustrations from natural as well as from human history (RAH 12).[47]

That is not to say, of course, that one cannot properly claim re-enactive understanding of individual actions 'as individual' in the sense of recognizing them to be performed by specific, identifiable persons at specific places and dates. In other words, there is no question of their having to be understood as acts of persons

[46] Authors who have seen the later Collingwood as claiming to grasp individuality via re-enactment include van der Dussen, who sees his idea of continuity between individual things as a matter of rational necessity (*HS* 343); Rotenstreich, who holds that in the later work individuality gets a 'human meaning' (*PHP* 12); and Paul Conkin, who says that he envisages the historian as seeking 'knowledge of the particular by getting inside it' (*Heritage and Challenge of History* (New York, 1975), 93).

[47] Yet Collingwood makes it a matter of complaint against Croce that he represents history as 'no longer in any special sense knowledge of the human as opposed to the natural world. It is simply the knowledge of facts or events as they actually happen, in their concrete individuality' (*IH* 199)—the very position he sometimes asserts himself.

belonging to certain classes or kinds. Caesar's crossing of the Rubicon may be re-enactively understood as an action peculiar to Caesar the historical individual.[48] But so to be understood, it must still be seen as falling under some classification which reveals its 'universal significance': for example, as an attempt to close with enemies, or as a bid for supreme power in the state. Still another way in which claims to have achieved re-enactive understanding may be reconciled with a wish to take seriously the individuality of historical events is that actions which have themselves been re-enactively understood, may be seen as elements of some larger patterning of events which is too complex to be considered repeatable (see further Chapter 6, § 4).[49] But neither of these ways of relating re-enactive and individualistic conceptions of understanding legitimize the radical sense in which Collingwood sometimes holds individuality to be intelligible 'in itself'.

I have pointed out that Collingwood's radical doctrine lingers on anachronistically long after its applicability to human history has been put in question by the re-enactive theory of historical understanding embraced in the lectures of 1928. This is not just a matter of occasional lapses on Collingwood's part. A striking indication of how thoroughly the idea was entrenched in his thought is his including, in his plan for 'The Principles of History' (see his outline of Book Three), a version of the long-deferred project of elaborating a 'complete philosophy conceived from an historical point of view' (*IH* 7). For the idea of such a philosophy is that of projecting historical ways of thinking into our view of the world generally, i.e. coming to understand everything historically. However, if historical ways of thinking are to be projected into our view of the world of nature, this cannot coherently be taken to mean that we are to understand natural happenings re-enactively. Collingwood does seem a little tempted, at times, by the idea that, at some level of analysis, all that exists, including natural events and processes, may somehow be conceivable as an

---

[48] As Donagan puts it, the historian, in dealing with past human agents, makes 'a presupposition of individual choice' ('The Popper-Hempel Theory Reconsidered', reprinted in W. H. Dray (ed.), *Philosophical Analysis and History* (New York, 1966), 149—cited hereafter as 'Popper-Hempel').

[49] The view of David Thompson ('Colligation and History Teaching', in W. H. Burston and David Thompson (eds.), *Studies in the Nature and Teaching of History* (London, 1967), 87–8).

expression of thought, and thus be open to re-enactive understanding.[50] But that is not his considered position (see further Chapter 5, § 7). The sense in which natural things are to be understood historically must therefore be that they are to be grasped in their concrete individuality.

This makes the sense in which Collingwood could hope for a general adoption of an historical outlook by contemporary philosophers very different from the sense in which he himself represents philosophers of the seventeenth century as having adopted a scientific one. For, as he makes very clear, what was considered to be projectible into every field in the latter case was a way of thinking which had been developed by a special type of inquiry, positivistic natural science, for dealing with its own subject-matter, and, more particularly, for explaining it. Collingwood cannot plausibly contend that the way of thinking which, on his own showing, has been developed by those we call historians for dealing with their own subject-matter, and especially their idea of how that subject-matter is to be understood, should be followed in seeking knowledge of anything whatever.[51] Nor does he, in his better moments, contend this, as is evidenced by his rejection of the thesis of Alexander and Whitehead regarding the historicity of all things (*IH* 210 ff.; RAH 1). Yet the idea is clearly one which he found difficult to renounce.

---

[50] Murphy claims to find evidence of this in *IN* (Review of *IH*, in *Philosophical Review*, 56 (1947), 591).

[51] A far from promising sample of what such an approach might yield as applied to the field of ethics is the conception of dutiful action, offered in *The New Leviathan*, as something entirely concrete and particular, not falling under any 'kind', and thus an essentially 'historical' idea (*NL* 128).

3

RE-ENACTMENT AND LAWS

§ 1. *Collingwood on Scientific Explanation*

I have looked at what Collingwood has to say about a paradigmatic case of explanation in history in which an individual action is made intelligible by reference to the thought which it expresses; and I have contrasted the theory of explanation which he derives from it with an older Collingwoodian view of historical explanation as an immediate grasping of individuality. In this chapter, I want first to examine a little more closely than I did in Chapter 2, § 4, the kind of understanding which Collingwood himself more often contrasted with the re-enactive sort: understanding achieved through explanation in terms of laws. I shall then consider two views of re-enactive explanation itself which differ somewhat from the quasi-normative interpretation which I offered in Chapter 2, § 5, and then explore some implications of Collingwood's theory for some related questions, like the viability of assuming determinism in history, and the extent to which historians properly use generalizations.

The way Collingwood conceives scientific understanding appears clearly enough in the passage which I paraphrased from 'Human Nature and Human History'. What historians are there said to be bound to avoid, as a lapse into scientific ways of thinking, is seeking to make past actions understandable by bringing them under 'a general formula or law of nature', a procedure which, as Collingwood puts it, yields only an 'external' sort of understanding (*IH* 214). Scientific inquiry aims to make events intelligible by 'seeing how they fall into general types and how these general types are interrelated', i.e. by 'laws of nature' (*IH* 205). Similar statements of what scientific understanding consists in can be found in other writings, both published and unpublished (e.g. RAH 14).

As has sometimes been remarked, what Collingwood says

along these lines remarkably anticipates what later became known among analytic philosophers of history as the covering-law model of explanation.[1] This conception of it was given an influential formulation by C. G. Hempel in an article of 1942 entitled 'The Function of General Laws in History', which argued that, for the historian as much as for the scientist, it articulates the only acceptable conception of explanation. The general view of explanation which is there set forth, however, considerably ante-dates Hempel's challenging statement of it. Collingwood himself refers to something very like it as the nineteenth-century 'positivist' notion of explanation; but, in fact, it goes back at least to Hume, and Collingwood himself finds traces of it even in Thucydides (*IH* 29–30).[2] The idea of understanding things by bringing them under laws he sometimes describes as 'superficial', even as a theory of explanation for science (*IH* 126); and Donagan, attributing it to Comte, has called it 'jejune' (*LPC* 227).[3] However, the important consideration for present purposes is not how adequately it reflects the way explanations are sought in the sciences, but how acceptable it is, as stated, as a model for histori-cal studies. In what follows, I shall sometimes refer to it, as Collingwood does, as the 'scientific' theory of explanation, but also sometimes, following some current practice, as the 'nomological' or 'law-subsumption' theory.

The idea of explanation as law-subsumption can be found in Collingwood's earlier as well as later writings; but he doesn't always represent it in the early ones as a false ideal for historians. In 'Are History and Science Different Kinds of Knowledge?', for example, he argues that there is no difference between scientific and historical inquiry so far as logical structure or 'epistemolo-

[1] Margit H. Nielsen hesitates to describe Collingwood's position as anti-covering-law, since he 'wrote before the discussion of historical explanation which sprang from Hempel's paper' ('Making Sense of History: Skagestad on Popper and Collingwood', *Inquiry*, 22 (1979), 482—cited hereafter as 'Making Sense'). What came to be called the covering-law theory is nevertheless what he attacks, and he often uses its language.

[2] As Donagan observes, Collingwood might more accurately have called the model 'naturalist' (*LPC* 227–8), a term which he does sometimes use in a related way (NAPH 34).

[3] As van der Dussen notes, it has sometimes been criticized as ignoring the role of theories in scientific explanation (*HS* 169). But the basic contrast between scientific and re-enactive explanation would remain even if a more sophisticated view of scientific explanation were used.

gical analysis' is concerned. The true difference between them is one of 'interest' (HSD 28–32): both regard particular facts as exemplifying generalities; but, while scientists are interested in the particular only as instantiating the universal, historians are interested in the universal only as a means to gaining knowledge of the particulars falling under it.[4] Collingwood sometimes blurs the distinction between the two sorts of inquiry by denying that, even in science, what is sought is knowledge of the universal as such. Thus, a geologist, he says, is not someone who can recite geological generalities, but someone who can make geological sense of a perceived situation in nature—who can 'interpret particular facts in the light of these generalities' (HSD 27). His doctrine here may owe something to his having chosen an example from one of the 'historical' natural sciences, of which it can with some plausibility be said that, like human history, they 'record' (HSD 32). However, he goes on to apply the same analysis to what are sometimes called the theoretical natural sciences: physiology, chemistry, mechanics, and even mathematics. His claim here is curiously reinforced by the contention that, strictly speaking, we can never have genuine knowledge of either the particular or the general, since both are mere abstractions from what actually exists, the latter being a 'synthesis of universal and particular' (NAPH 40). Sometimes, however, only history is said to achieve concrete knowledge of the individual, so conceived, while science, with its fixation on the general, achieves only abstract knowledge (*SM* 203, 208, 225, 227).

In 'The Nature and Aims of a Philosophy of History', Collingwood goes on to declare the epistemological and logical equivalence of science and history in terms that would have won approval from most of those he later pilloried as 'positivists'. 'No historical fact', he avers, 'can be determined without the help of generalisations' (NAPH 36). The difference between the scientist and the historian is only that the scientist generalizes 'for the sake of generalising' whereas the historian does it 'for the sake of helping himself to determine historical fact' (NAPH 48). Here, at least, is dropped the earlier claim that neither the general nor the particular, being abstractions, can be known. In his Historical Association essay of 1930, Collingwood again says that, in

[4] Collingwood talks here of interpretation, not understanding or explanation, but he seems also to have the latter in view.

science, individual facts are important only as illustrations of laws, while, in history, laws are only important as facilitating the discovery of the facts (PH 132)—this suggesting that he had still to absorb some of the implications of the re-enactive view of historical understanding which he had formulated in his lectures of 1928. In an essay of 1935, the positivist theory of science, and the contrast with history, is again expressed in the claim that scientists, although studying unique things and occurrences, as historians also do, are simply not interested in them as such, taking account of them only as examples of their kinds (RAH 12–13; IH 167). In Chapter 2, we noted a 'recessive' Collingwoodian idea of understanding as grasping individuality, a conception which, although assigned to history, is not easily reconciled with the theory of historical understanding as re-enactment. Here, surprisingly, we find in Collingwood a second 'recessive' idea of understanding in history, in this case one logically identical to the one he assigns to natural science.

There are some oddities about Collingwood's discussion of scientific explanation itself which might be noted, if only to be put aside as diverging from his considered views. In the manuscript, 'Reality as History', the difference between explanation in history and in science is at one point described as a difference between explaining why *particular* events and processes occurred, and why certain *kinds* of events or processes occurred (RAH 13). Scientific explanation, Collingwood there maintains, since it brings things under laws which state relations between kinds of events, only explains why *some* B comes after an A, never why *this* B did (RAH 9).[5] This is said at a point where he is defending the idea that, in history, explanatory necessity can be found in individual developments, the intrinsically intelligible not being rendered more intelligible by being repeated; and if that notion is dropped, such an eccentric basis for contrasting history and science disappears too. But what Collingwood should in any case have said is not that scientific explanation is necessarily of kinds, but that, even when it is of particular occurrences, what it shows is that the thing explained is of a kind which is connected by law with events or conditions of the kinds said to explain it. Scientific

[5] This meshes with what he says later (in *NL* 108, 116, 122) about regularian (and hence utilitarian) explanation leaving something to caprice, something unexplained.

thought is not limited to explaining kinds of events; it can explain particular events, if only by showing them to exemplify certain kinds. Nor could Collingwood derive a distinction between scientific and historical explanation from his doctrine here. For, on his own mature account of historical understanding as re-enactive, as has already been noted, explanation in history will also necessarily be of something conceived as exemplifying relevant kinds—kinds of response to kinds of envisaged circumstances, for example. By parity of reasoning, therefore, Collingwood would have to say that, in historical cases, too, what is explained is only kinds.

A second and related oddity is the way, especially in his earlier writings, Collingwood sometimes obscures the difference between recognizing generality in the sense of finding something to instantiate a law and in the sense of finding something to fall under a concept. In 'Are History and Science Different Kinds of Knowledge?', he passes without remark from talking about the explanatory role of 'generalisations', to talking about that of 'general concepts' (HSD 27–9). In 'The Philosophy of History', he collapses this distinction in a similar way (PH 136). As late as his laudatory account of Croce's contribution to philosophy of history in *The Idea of History*, he still obscures the difference between concepts and laws when he hails the Crocean idea that historical knowledge is an 'identity of the universal and individual judgement' as somehow offering an escape from the errors of nineteenth-century positivist thinking about history (*IH* 140). It cannot be regarded as such an identity, at any rate, in any sense that supports the nomological theory of explanation; all that can legitimately be said is that, on Croce's account, historical knowledge involves generalization in the sense of applying concepts to what occurred. Collingwood does explicitly recognize the difference between the conceptual and the nomological levels of generality when, in *The Idea of History*, he describes explanation in science as 'classifying [events] and establishing relations between the classes thus defined' (*IH* 228; also *IH* 214; RAH 11). But he still leaves it less than entirely clear that, when historians offer explanations, they must generalize in the first way quite as much as scientists do, even if they need not, and on his own theory should not, generalize in the second.

A third point of clarification with regard to Collingwood's view of scientific explanation relates to both the foregoing issues. When he rejects the idea that historians explain by means of laws, he sometimes gives the impression that what he has chiefly in mind is large-scale laws: the overarching historical laws of great system builders like Comte, Marx, or Spengler, for example, or at least laws which apply directly and simply to large-scale historical events or processes like the French Revolution or the Hundred Years War (NAPH 34–5; IH 114, 144, 182). In seeking explanations, he says, historians are not concerned to show 'repetitions' in their subject-matter; for 'no explanation of the French Revolution can be the right one which will fit any other revolution' (RAH 11). A nomological theorist could agree with this, however, while still holding to the position that Collingwood really wants to undermine. He could say that, although it is unlikely that the kinds of circumstances and actions which together constituted the French Revolution will appear again in precisely the same combination, every aspect of that revolution is open, in principle, to being explained through subsumption under lower-order generalizations of various kinds, the whole event thus being shown, in the end, to be law-instantiating. Since Collingwood's position would certainly be that the latter is neither possible nor appropriate in history, it is unfortunate that he puts his case in terms of there being no repetitions of gross historical events like the French Revolution. Such an event could, of course, be said to be a repetition simply in the sense of being yet another revolution—in that sense, for example, 'repeating' the British Revolution. But a Collingwoodian historian is unlikely to be satisfied to explain an event as interesting as this one at such a gross level of description; he will also want to show why this revolution was distinctive in various ways, and in that sense not a repetition.[6] But scientists are no more obliged than historians are to offer explanations in terms of laws functioning only at a very general level of description.

§ 2. *Re-enactive Explanation and Completeness*

In his later writings, Collingwood generally distinguishes quite sharply between the nomological sort of explanation which he

---

[6] For a good discussion of this issue, see Skagestad, *Making Sense*, 49.

sees as characteristic of natural science and the re-enactive sort which he thinks normally offered by historians. However, some critics of his position have argued that, upon closer examination, this contrast turns out to be bogus. For, in spite of what Collingwood claims for explanations of actions in terms of agents' thoughts, they have maintained, these will only be truly explanatory to the degree that they approximate to explanation in terms of laws. Ascribing certain thoughts to an agent, the contention goes, will explain his performance of a certain action only if it is known that, in general, people who think in the indicated way act in the indicated way. As Hempel sometimes puts it, the goal of all well-conceived explanation is to exclude chance from a subject-matter: to show that whatever happened in it happened necessarily.[7] And the only way to do that, he insists, is to show that it falls under laws—in the historical case, laws linking thoughts to actions. There is thus 'no formal difference between motivational and causal explanation'.[8] Ascribed motives and beliefs, if they are to be considered explanatory, must be seen as nomologically sufficient 'antecedent conditions'.

Critics who argue in this fashion will usually admit that the explanations of actions actually given by historians seldom conform strictly to this requirement; for they almost never actually state laws linking what is supposed to be explained with what is supposed to explain it. According to Hempel, they must in consequence be regarded as either elliptical or incomplete. They can be said to be elliptical if the context is such that we can take the required laws for granted, perhaps because they are generalizations about human behaviour which are so well known that it would be tedious for historians to mention them. So understood, any action explanation offered will, of course, stand or fall by what it assumes as well as what it states. And Hempel suspects that most of those offered by historians will fall. If, on the other hand, they simply leave in limbo the generalization (or generalizations) supposed to justify the assertion of an explanatory connection between thoughts and actions, they must be considered incomplete. The important point is that they will be

[7] Hempel, 'General Laws', 348.
[8] C. G. Hempel, *Aspects of Scientific Explanation* (New York, 1965), 254 (cited hereafter as *Aspects*).

incomplete nomological explanations, not explanations of some different sort.[9]

Hempel is quite prepared to allow a role for re-enactment in all this. While finding the connection between ascribed thoughts and an action to be re-thinkable does not, in itself count as explaining the action, he maintains, an historian's imagining himself in the agent's place, and trying to make sense of what he did by re-thinking his thoughts, may sometimes be heuristically helpful. For it may suggest a connection between thought and action which can be generalized as an hypothesis for further verification. Thus an attempt at re-enactive understanding may function as a first step towards offering a real, law-instantiating explanation. If re-enactment is to be conceived in such a way, however, it clearly belongs to the strategy of historical inquiry, not to its epistemological characterization. For until an alleged re-enactment has been nomologically transformed, nothing will have been explained. Nor, according to Hempel, is re-enactment any more necessary for explaining actions by reference to thoughts than it is sufficient for it. For historians who already know viable laws which apply to the case have no need to ask, when offering an explanation, whether the connections between thoughts and action is re-thinkable.

Those who argue in some such way for regarding re-enactment as of purely heuristic significance use a vocabulary rather different from the one which Collingwood generally employs. It seems clear enough, however, that he would have denied that a proffered explanation of an action which depicted it as expressing re-thinkable thoughts would have to be judged incomplete until supplemented in a way which establishes the thought-action connection as law-instantiating.[10] What he says at several points in fact suggests a quite different idea of what would count as completeness in a re-enactive explanation.

[9] Hempel, 'General Laws', 352–3. Various proposals have been made as to how ostensibly non-nomological action explanations which refer to thoughts should be brought into line. One advanced by Hempel himself is that premisses need to be added to the effect that the agent was rational, and that, in the envisaged circumstances, rational agents always act in the way this one did ('Rational Action', *Proceedings and Addresses of the American Philosophical Association*, 35 (1952), 14).

[10] Collingwood occasionally seems to question whether complete explanation, re-enactive or otherwise, could ever be given (HUP 1–2). Yet, having set forth what he believes the emperor Claudius took into account in deciding to invade Britain, he is prepared to assert: 'the case for invasion was complete' (*RBES* 78).

He would agree with Hempel that the goal of scientific explanation is to show the necessity of what occurred, this requiring its subsumption under laws. He would agree also that it should be the goal of re-enactive explanation to show necessity. But he would maintain that the necessity in the latter case is of a different kind, a kind which he sometimes refers to as 'rational' (L27 349). There are indications of this doctrine in *The Idea of History* (*IH* 214, 316), but it appears even more explicitly in some of the manuscripts: for example, in the lectures of 1928, where the way actions are understood in history is compared to the way an onlooker would try to follow the moves of players in a game of chess (L28 475). Declares Collingwood: 'It is because White has moved in a particular way that Black replies with a particular move; and this again determines the next move of White.' But what is meant here by 'determines' must not be misunderstood. 'What happens is that White's move places Black in a certain situation, and in this situation there is only one move by which Black can avoid defeat: in order to avoid defeat, he therefore chooses to make that move, and this again creates a new situation for White.' In such cases, Collingwood maintains, action is explained as having been necessitated not in the sense of falling under laws, but in the sense of there having been only one rational way for the agent to deal with the problem which faced him. Re-enactive explanations are therefore complete when the thoughts attributed to the agent offer *compelling reasons* for performing the action—when the agent, like the chess player, has been shown to have been able to say, legitimately: 'I had to do it; I had no alternative.'[11] Concluding that an agent thus acted for compelling reasons has nothing to do with seeing that his action fell under laws. It requires a judgment from the 'inside', considering what the agent ought, in reason, to have done, not from 'outside', trying to infer what he would necessarily have done.

The position which Collingwood might be said to be advancing here is that historical inquiry, being more concerned with the point of actions than with their predictability, employs a different *concept* of explanation or understanding from the one which is

---

[11] It is a weakness of Collingwood's own use of the chess example that he appears to represent mere rules of a game as sufficient to render a player's moves rationally obligatory, forgetting that rules of strategy and other considerations would also be relevant to such a judgment.

appropriate in natural science.[12] This concept brings with it its own criteria of explanatory completeness. An explanation ascribing thoughts would be incomplete in a way which was relevant to its own aim if, for example, it cited only beliefs, or only motives, since that would incompletely show the rational necessity of acting as the agent did (*EM* 292). If what Collingwood says about understanding moves in chess is acceptable as a paradigm, the same might be said of any combination of beliefs and motives which failed to show the obligatory nature of what was done. The crucial point is that in neither case would completing the re-enactive explanation, if it could be done, convert it into a law-instantiating one. It would simply round out the thought-side of the action to the point where the ascribed thoughts were fully explanatory in the relevant sense.

In fact, the explanations which historians offer in terms of agents' thoughts are often incomplete even on this non-nomological criterion. Attributed beliefs and motives seldom render one and only one course of action rationally obligatory.[13] What they generally show is only that what was done was a more or less reasonable thing to have done under the circumstances.[14] However, the relationship of such weaker forms of re-enactive explanation to Collingwood's ideal case is not unlike that of many would-be law-instantiating explanations to the scientific ideal. For, as those who regard nomological explanation as the only legitimate kind commonly admit, even when what is to be explained is natural events, laws which are less than universal are often all that we can claim to know—mere statistical regularities, perhaps, which show only that what happened was in some degree probable. The explanation of actions by reference to agents' reasons is also often a matter of degree, in that the agent can only be shown to have had good, but less than compelling, reasons for

[12] A good example of the frequent failure to appreciate this is Robert Stover's assumption that re-enactment is a weak way of trying to achieve the same kind of understanding that is better achieved by a nomological approach (*The Nature of Historical Thinking* (Chapel Hill, NC, 1967), 106). As Martin aptly puts it, there is a 'logical discontinuity' between re-enactive and nomological explanation (*HE* 45).
[13] Donagan calls for a dissociation of the ideas of acting rationally and of doing the one and only rational thing ('Popper-Hempel', 155).
[14] Collingwood, *qua* historian, although sometimes citing considerations which 'demanded' a certain line of action ('Hadrian's Wall', *History*, 10 (1925), 202), is content at other times to note that an action was 'a reasonable move' (*Roman Eskdale* (Whitehaven, 1929), 38).

acting as he did. In still other cases, a re-enactive explanation may not even aim at showing that what was done was rationally required, but only at showing that it was rationally permissible under the circumstances. The analogue to this in the scientific case would be a nomological explanation which aimed only to show what made a given event possible, not predictable or even probable.[15] The Collingwoodian point would be that, in their weaker versions quite as much as in their stronger ones, the explanatory ideal is formally different in the re-enactive and scientific cases. Re-enactive explanations are never incomplete simply as such; and when judged incomplete, they should be so judged with reference to their own criteria and goals, not nomological ones.

We have been considering the criticism that explanation on Collingwood's re-enactive model is, by its very nature, *formally* incomplete. But dissatisfaction with that model has sometimes centred rather on the question whether mere formal completeness in explanation is enough—whether explanations of actions in terms of thoughts may not sometimes need to be supplemented for reasons other than their supposed logical inconclusiveness.

It has been claimed, for example, that although the premises of a re-enactive explanation may be accepted as true, and the explanation itself not judged logically incomplete, the nature of the premises may still leave the explanation open to question. Walsh puts the point as follows.[16] In seeking to understand your action, I may re-enact your thought 'without seeing fully why you thought as you did; what it was that gave those particular premises their special appeal for you'; and as long as this is so, I may surely say that I do not really understand you. The difficulty is particularly acute if you are 'a person whose principles of action diverge very markedly from my own'. It is natural, in such a case, 'that we should look for further enlightenment at a different

[15] For a general defence of such 'how-possibly' explanation, see my 'On Explaining How-Possibly', *Monist*, 52 (1968), 390–407; or G. H. von Wright, *Explanation and Understanding* (London, 1971), 135–6; for arguments against recognizing them, see Hempel, *Aspects*, 428–31.

[16] 'Collingwood and Metaphysical Neutralism', in Krausz (ed.), *Critical Essays*, 152–3. See also K. M. Martin, 'Caesar and Collingwood as Historians', *Latomus: Revue d'études latines*, 28 (1969), 167; and W. H. Walsh, 'The Constancy of Human Nature', in H. D. Lewis (ed.), *Contemporary British Philosophers* (4th series; London, 1976), 290.

level', asking 'whether there was anything about that type of man in that type of situation which made it natural for him to think in that way'. We may therefore find ourselves asking, in the end, for an explanation of a different kind—one that refers us to a generalization. Walsh thinks it unfortunate that Collingwood 'gave no consideration to this aspect of historical thought'. The allegation that satisfactory re-enactive explanations need to identify thoughts which are somehow 'acceptable' in themselves, as well as appropriately related to the actions performed, has been taken further by Leo Strauss.[17] An historian who tried to re-enact Plato's thought about political matters, he maintains, would find that he could not re-think it. For Plato genuinely believed in 'an unchanging ideal of political life'; and thinking that way entails criteria for action which a modern historian would simply be unable to 'take seriously'.

Such criticism might be dealt with by Collingwood in the following way. He might accept that there are two sorts of reasons why a re-enactive explanation could be judged unsatisfactory. On the one hand, it could be so judged because it lacked a premiss which was needed to make it formally sound in the sense appropriate to its explanation type. On the other hand, it could be rejected because, although formally complete of its kind, it did not (as we might say) probe 'deeply' enough. This, however, must not simply mean that it left something unexplained; for, as Collingwood himself points out, all explanations do that, and, more to the point, all leave their own premisses unexplained (RAH 19). It must mean rather that it left something unexplained that needed to be explained.

Walsh's complaint is presumably of the latter kind, and he makes a valid point in thus insisting that re-enactive explanations can suffer from a *material* as well as from a formal kind of incompleteness. But care must be taken about the sort of criticism which is derived from the ever-present possibility of responding to a formally satisfactory explanation with a further 'why?'. For one thing, as Collingwood himself observes, the same possibility holds for nomological explanation. Having been offered an explanation of the lake system of the Canadian Shield as a consequence of glacial melting, a person may still want to know, as part of a

---

[17] Leo Strauss, 'On Collingwood's Philosophy of History', *Review of Metaphysics*, 5 (1952), 575.

'deeper' explanation of the same thing, why the glacier was there in the first place. Nor need it be the case, as Walsh seems to assume, that if a premiss of a thought explanation is found puzzling, the explanation of this premiss, if pressed for, would turn out to be of a non-Collingwoodian kind. As noted in Chapter 2, § 4 (and discussed further in Chapter 4, § 3), lower-order reasons for acting are often explicable as following from higher-order ones together with further information about the circumstances. If we continue to ask 'why?', we may thus find ourselves ascending a hierarchy of explanations all of which are Collingwoodian. Suppose, for example, that someone who is by nature uncombative remains puzzled by Caesar's crossing of the Rubicon even after learning that he wanted to put down his enemies and saw his action as a necessary step towards achieving that goal. A 'deepening' of the explanation might then take the form of pointing to more general beliefs and aims of the agent which account for these more particular ones, not to antecedent conditions and laws.

As for Strauss's contention that ideas which we don't ourselves accept are not re-thinkable by us, this seems to ignore a crucial *formal* feature of re-enactive explanation which has already been stressed, namely, that what has to be re-enacted—what has to be found 'acceptable'—is not the ideas ascribed to the agent, but the connection between them and what was done. In order to understand an action, historians will need, at most, to accept the ideas of the agents 'hypothetically': to ask what action would be required if they *were* accepted, however bizarre or even repulsive the ideas may be in themselves.[18] To hold this to be impossible is at any rate to register a much lower opinion of the power of the historical imagination than Collingwood's own (*A* 55, 152).[19] A valid point nevertheless emerges from all this about the way terms like 'explanation' and 'understanding' are often used, and not only in history, for we do sometimes reject a proffered explanation as 'no explanation at all', in order to call attention to the fact that it leaves something unexplained that we think ought to

---

[18] Skagestad seems to ignore this in his otherwise illuminating analysis of possible re-enactive explanations of Stalin's purges (*Making Sense*, 99 ff.).

[19] For analogous arguments that the 'foreignness' of past thought makes it impossible to re-enact its thoughts, see H.-I. Marrou, *The Meaning of History*, tr. R. J. Olsen (Baltimore, 1966), 45–6; or Lorraine Code, 'Collingwood's Epistemological Individualism', *Monist*, 72 (1989), 556.

be explained. In other words, explanations can be judged unsatisfactory because trivial, or materially inadequate in some other way, as well as because untrue or formally incomplete. Nothing follows from this, however, about the legitimacy of regarding Collingwoodian explanations of actions as a distinctive and respectable logical genre.

§ 3. *The Logical Connection Analysis*

The interpretation of Collingwood's theory of historical understanding that I have been expounding represents the historian as aiming to show that, given what the agent believed and wanted to accomplish, the action he performed was one that he *ought* to have performed. The central idea is that we understand perfectly well a person's choosing to act in a certain way when we can see that, from that person's own standpoint, it was an appropriate (or reasonable) thing to have done. Since reaching that conclusion involves a degree of appraisal of the agent's behaviour, I have called this interpretation 'quasi-normative' by way of contrasting it with the nomological or law-instantiating conception of what it is to understand which is held by his positivist opponents.

The quasi-normative interpretation is not, however, the only alternative to the nomological view of re-enactive explanation which has been proposed by students of Collingwood. Another that has been widely considered (and which links the recent literature of philosophy of history at this point to that of philosophy of action) argues that the connection between explanatory thoughts and the actions which they explain is neither law-instantiating nor quasi-normative, but logical or conceptual. This position was advanced by Donagan in an exceptionally lucid and uncompromising way in the 1950s, both as an expression of his own view of what satisfactory explanation of action must consist in, and as an interpretation of what Collingwood himself meant, the latter claim impressively grounded in examples taken from Collingwood's historical work (*LPC* 182–209).[20] I shall outline Donagan's theory briefly and then express some reservations about it. Following that, I shall consider still another alternative,

[20] Donagan formulates it as his own position in 'Popper-Hempel', 132 ff.; also in 'Explanation in History', 428 ff.

an interpretation offered more recently by Rex Martin, which stakes out a middle ground between positions which, like both Donagan's and the quasi-normative interpretation, deny any role in re-enactive explanation for empirical generalizations or laws, and positions which hold reference to them to be a *sine qua non* of acceptable explanation (*HE* 39–57).

Donagan begins by accepting the principle that no explanation of the performance of an action can be considered complete which leaves open the possibility that the agent might have done something else instead. In other words, he accepts the contention, often associated with Collingwood's positivist opponents but rejected on the quasi-normative view, that an explanation is not complete until it indicates a sufficient condition of what is to be explained (*LPC* 201–2). He denies, however, that this commits one to the nomological theory of explanation where it is action which is to be explained, arguing that the thoughts of the agent can constitute a sufficient condition without the connection between thought and action instantiating any law.[21] For the sense in which the thought must be sufficient, he maintains, is conceptual, not empirical or normative. He illustrates this claim as follows.[22] If an historian explains Brutus's joining Cassius's conspiracy against Caesar by citing his intention to protect the Roman Republic at all costs and his belief that Caesar was a danger to it which could only be removed by ensuring his death, then it follows strictly from the ascription of that intention and belief that Brutus acted accordingly. For if Brutus had decided not to join the conspiracy, that in itself would have shown that he either did not after all have the intention attributed to him, or did not have the attributed belief. To say otherwise, maintains Donagan, would be self-contradictory.

That isn't to say, however, that no general claim of any kind is involved in, or presupposed by, the envisaged explanation. For we can only represent Brutus's action as following necessarily from the thoughts cited in the explanation if we hold that *anyone* who intends to achieve a certain result at all costs, and believes that a certain action is necessary to attain it, performs that action,

---

[21] A sufficient condition here means one, given which, what it is sufficient for necessarily occurs. As indicated earlier, a sufficient explanation will not necessarily identify such a condition.

[22] 'Popper-Hempel', 150 ff.

that being our warrant for saying it in Brutus's case. But although, the truth of some such 'covering' general statement is thus required for the valid assertion of the particular explanation, that statement does not affirm a genuine law. For, since no conceivable counter-instances could possibly falsify it, it makes no empirical claim. It is rather a logical truism, which partially explicates the meaning of the various concepts employed. Donagan's conceptual-analytic interpretation (as we might call it) thus concedes to positivist theory that an explanation must instantiate a generalizable connection, while at the same time retaining Collingwood's doctrine that re-enactive explanations do not use or presuppose empirical laws.

Donagan's analysis, which is a version of what has sometimes been called 'the logical connection argument', has been subjected to various kinds of criticism.[23] It seems clear enough, for example, that the explanatory connection, as he actually states his example, is less than logically tight. For it to be so, many further beliefs would need to be ascribed to Brutus: for example, that the conspiracy was a feasible way of doing away with Caesar, or that his joining it would significantly add to its chances of success, and so on. Donagan concedes the point, while at the same time arguing that any further thoughts of Brutus which might need to be added to the explanation in order to make the thought–action connection logically conclusive would bring it no closer to being law-instantiating. What such further 'thought' premises would do is simply establish, more and more clearly, a fully deductive *logical* connection between ascribed thoughts and the action.[24] If a thought explanation, as offered, is in fact less than deductive, what one needs to seek is thus a better (i.e. logically tighter) explanation of the same conceptual-analytic kind, not explanation of a different, i.e. nomological, kind.

The logical ideal for historical explanation which Donagan here sets forth may appear to be one which would seldom, if ever, be instantiated by the way past agents actually behaved. How often, for example, could historians expect to find themselves studying

---

[23] On this sort of analysis generally, see Frederick Stoutland, 'The Logical Connection Argument', in Nicholas Rescher (ed.), *Studies in Theory of Knowledge* (Oxford, 1970), 117–29. For a more detailed examination of Donagan's position, see my *On History and Philosophers of History* (Leiden, 1989), ch. 1.

[24] For a contrary view, see Michael Martin, 'Situational Logic and Covering Law Explanations in History', *Inquiry*, 11 (1968), 392–4.

the actions of agents who intended to accomplish their ends 'at all costs'? But even if it had to be allowed that the connection between ascribed thoughts and action would seldom be strictly deductive in explanations as normally given, something crucial to Donagan's position might still remain. As was noted in § 1, advocates of the nomological model have been obliged, with a view to showing the applicability of their theory to the actual practice of history, to allow that explanations turning upon laws which are less than universal may also deserve the name of explanation; and a somewhat analogous position was maintained with regard to explanation of the re-enactive sort, quasi-normatively conceived. Donagan could argue similarly that, although explanations in terms of thoughts which historians normally accept may fall short of strict deducibility, their acceptability will still turn upon the perception of a conceptual, not a nomological, connection between thinking in a certain way and acting in a certain way, although a looser one. It might be held, for example, that knowing that a person was at least favourably disposed towards attaining a certain goal, or intended to attain it provided that it did not cost too much, would also count as explaining his acting in a particular instance. It would not, of course, explain it deductively. But the explanation would not be found acceptable simply because the stated connection between thought and action was known to hold at least in most cases. It would be found acceptable because of what is conveyed by logically porous, but still serviceable, expressions like 'favourably disposed' or 'cost too much'.

There is a further way, however, in which Donagan's account, despite denying that re-enactive explanation can be assimilated to the nomological kind, might be said not quite to catch what Collingwood wanted to maintain about it. For, to a degree at least, it shares with the nomological account what might be called an 'external' approach to what happened. As Peter Munz has put it, Collingwood holds that, in trying to understand actions by re-enacting thoughts, we try 'to understand others as they understood themselves'.[25] And a person does not come to understand his own past actions by asking whether what he did follows deductively from his having had certain goals and beliefs. As the quasi-normative interpretation stresses, the standpoint of

[25] Peter Munz, *The Shapes of Time: A New Look at the Philosophy of History* (Middletown, Conn., 1977), 195.

re-enactive explanation is that of someone wondering what to do. What is needed to make a given action understandable, on Collingwood's view, is to show how choosable it was for the person who did it. And that is a matter of showing that, from that person's point of view, there were good reasons for doing it. On the conceptual-analytic model, re-enactive understanding is to some extent dissociated from this standpoint, if less so than on the nomological one. The historian is assigned the standpoint of a perceptive observer rather than that of a vicarious participant.

Martin begins roughly from where Donagan leaves off. He is more inclined than Donagan to concede that what he offers, although certainly inspired by what Collingwood himself had to say about understanding as re-enactment, aims less at a faithful interpretation of it than at a 'reconstructive analysis', which may go well beyond anything which Collingwood himself said or might have accepted (*HE* 66). Martin also sets himself the task of finding a viable 'middle ground' between the conceptual-analytic and the nomological-empirical interpretations, since he sees something of value in both of them.[26] His analysis is very complex, however, and it will not be possible to consider more than a few of its salient features here.

Following the lead of G. H. von Wright in *Explanation and Understanding*, Martin outlines a network of kinds of assertions or assumptions the ensemble of which he refers to as setting forth the ideal schema of an action explanation (*HE* 77–81). To the distinction which Collingwood himself draws between references to the purposes and the beliefs of the agent, he adds such considerations as his having been aware of alternative modes of action open to him and preferring the one which he chose; his having viewed the action performed as a better means to achieving his purpose than others which seemed open to him; his not having had any other purposes at the time which would override or cancel the purpose for which the action is said to be done, and so on. Donagan had already begun sophisticating Collingwood's more simply stated version by noting that a complete action explanation would need to indicate, besides the agent's goal, the conditions under which he was prepared to seek it—his

---

[26] I add 'empirical' to 'nomological' here to indicate that, in this case, the connecting generality is not conceptual or analytic.

scruples—and also his actually having seen that his goals and beliefs required the action he performed—or, as Donagan phrases it, his having performed 'an act of practical reasoning' (*LPC* 193).[27] Unlike Donagan, Martin is prepared to say, with those who accept the quasi-normative interpretation, that the explanatory force of the complicated set of considerations or 'thoughts' thus set forth resides in the fact that it represents the action under scrutiny as the 'most appropriate' one for the agent to have performed at that time and place. Like Donagan, however, he rejects the notion that the explanation must represent the action as a 'rational' choice. What it must do rather, he says, is show it to have been an 'intelligible' one (*HE* 115, 235).

The most important way in which Martin's analysis differs from both the quasi-normative and the conceptual-analytic views is in his insisting that empirically-based generalizations have a necessary role to play in action explanations, although a more minor, more auxiliary one than that assigned to them on the nomological theory. Martin denies that merely citing relevant thoughts of an agent, or even setting them forth completely, is quite enough to constitute a satisfactory action explanation. For, unlike Donagan, he denies that the connection between thought premisses and action conclusion is strictly deductive: a mere matter of logic. The explanatory premisses, he says, must require acceptance of the conclusion, but only because we normally consider the schema for action explanation as a rule for thinking about action—something like a presupposition brought to the study of it (*HE* 198). As with foundational claims like 'every event must have a cause', this schema is a priori, and in some sense necessary, but not analytically so. Martin hints that its status is best conceived by analogy with what Wittgenstein called the ground-form of a language game. This, however, is no more than a hint, which can be disregarded in assessing the cogency of his analysis of action explanation itself (*HE* 203).

The chief difficulty of that analysis is Martin's claim that we cannot legitimately bring an action under the general schema for action explanation, with a view to pronouncing it intelligible, unless we can at the same time cite at least a weak empirical generalization which affirms that people do sometimes act in the

---

[27] Collingwood himself gives a more extended analysis of what a thought explanation might involve in *IH* 283, than he does in *IH* 215.

indicated way (*HE* 121). To be regarded as explained, an action must not only be seen to follow appropriately from thoughts of the sort attributed to the agent, but must also be seen as 'plausible', empirically speaking. It would seem to follow that, according to Martin's conceptual-plausibilistic interpretation (as we might call it), if we lack prior experience of people acting for certain sorts of reasons, we cannot legitimately offer an explanation of an action which we have under study in terms of such reasons. To take one of Martin's examples: if someone belonging to another culture is found to clean a knife after being wounded by it, rather than cleaning the wound itself, then, unless this sort of thing has already been found to occur from time to time in that culture, our merely ascertaining that the purpose was cure, and that the agent believed that cures are achieved by treating the damaging object rather than the damaged part, would not count as a re-enactive explanation of his action (*HE* 88). Until the action can be seen as a way in which at least some relevant people sometimes behave, understanding is said to fail. Martin thus represents knowledge of weak empirical regularities as performing the second-order function of providing inductive support for 'general assertions of appropriateness' (*HE* 115). This contrasts significantly with the function assigned to empirical generalizations in nomological theory, that of grounding an estimate of the probability of what was done in the particular case, given the agent's thought.

Not surprisingly, there has been disagreement about the extent to which Martin can be read as interpreting Collingwood. Taylor thinks that his analysis takes him at least closer to Collingwood's position than to the nomological theory.[28] David Carr, by contrast, opines that, by the time he is finished, there is not much of Collingwood left.[29] Quite apart from the question of how much Martin's account explicates Collingwood's own views, however, it is not easy to see why one should accept his empirical addition to what is otherwise an impressive development of the Donaganian analytic-conceptual interpretation, with a marked affinity also to the quasi-normative one. If setting forth the agent's calculation of means and ends at the level of detail envisaged by Martin's account does not justify our saying that the agent acted *because* he thought those things, it is difficult to see how such a

---

[28] Taylor, *Bibliography*, 247.
[29] Review of *HE*, in *Southwestern Journal of Philosophy*, 10 (1979), 212.

conclusion is made any more justifiable by an assurance that people do in fact behave in the indicated way from time to time. It might be noted that an empirical claim which is as weak as that could also be taken to show that the action performed was a very improbable occurrence, which would surely not enhance either its plausibility or its appropriateness. There is the further puzzle of how it could be argued that we cannot know, in a particular case, that an agent acted in a certain way because of certain considerations, unless we know that other agents have acted in the same way because of the same considerations on at least some previous occasions. For if we claim to know the latter, we surely assume that in the previous cases it was possible, without benefit of a generalization of appropriateness, to make the very sort of 'because' statements which Martin's account proscribes in the case with which we began.

§ 4. *Re-enactive and Scientific Explanation*

We have been looking at three ways in which Collingwood's re-enactment doctrine has been interpreted: the quasi-normative, the conceptual-analytic, and the conceptual-plausibilistic.[30] All three try to clarify his central claims by transposing what he says from the rather phenomenological language which he often employs into an idiom which makes it easier to compare re-enactive explanation with explanation of the scientific kind.[31] All three depict historical and scientific explanation as fundamentally different. It is therefore of some interest to ask just how Collingwood thinks the two kinds of explanation are related to each other: whether, for example, he thinks that both can coherently be sought of the same thing; whether, if so, he would regard them simply as supplementing each other, or would consider one kind as intrinsically superior; and, if he thinks that they cannot both be sought of

---

[30] I pass over the interpretation of it as covertly, if incompletely, nomological (see § 2), since this is not generally offered as an explication of Collingwood's own position.

[31] Cohen accuses Collingwood of confusing the phenomenology of historical understanding with its logic ('Survey of Work in the Philosophy of History', 173). Collingwood's terminology (see e.g. *IH* 283) may seem to justify this; but he uses something closer to the analytical language of later British philosophy of history when listing the questions which he considers central to the field (*L27* 347–8).

the same thing, what his reasons are for seeing them as excluding each other.

There is no problem about the compatibility of the two explanation types, of course, where different sorts of things are to be explained. To the extent that, besides explaining actions in the re-enactive way, historians want from time to time to explain various natural events or conditions, they will necessarily do it in the nomological way. Collingwood sometimes comes close to denying that historians should ever be concerned with understanding the natural world—as if history were, in some very strict sense, the history only of thought. This Collingwoodian exaggeration will be considered further in Chapters 4 and 5. Here it might simply be remarked that, if Collingwood sometimes displays a strange reluctance to allow that the understanding of natural processes, and therefore, at times, even the findings of the natural sciences, may play some role in historical thinking, he at any rate implicitly concedes the point in his own historical practice. Thus he draws attention to differences in the geological formation and climate of contrasting regions of Britain in partial explanation of diverse settlement patterns (*RBES* 1–15), and to the relative efficiency of different types of plough, and the physical reasons for it, when comparing the agricultural systems of villa and village in Roman Britain (*RBES* 211–12). Oddly enough, he displays no comparable reluctance about maintaining that scientific inquiry makes some use of historical modes of thinking—for example, in dealing with its own records. Indeed, he tends to overstate the degree to which this makes science 'dependent' upon history, and history the 'logically prior' type of inquiry (*IN* 177; *A* 86–7). It seems closer to the truth to say that, in dealing with their respective subject-matters, the two modes of inquiry presuppose each other, if in different ways. On Collingwood's own showing, history presupposes science in the sense of sometimes needing to incorporate its results. Science, it seems, presupposes history only in the sense of sometimes needing to employ its modes of argument when marshalling its own data.

Collingwood occasionally appears to assert the compatibility of the two kinds of explanation in the stronger sense of there being no theoretical reason why they should not both be given of the same thing. More specifically, he sometimes appears to leave it open that a human action might be explicable in the nomological as well as in the re-enactive way. One might read such a position into his concession that a positivist science of human action is entirely possible, since regularities in human behaviour can in fact be found if one looks for them (*IH* 222). And sometimes he opposes bringing actions under laws only on the comparatively weak ground that it is unnecessary to do this, since perfectly satisfactory re-enactive explanations are generally available (*IH* 223). This suggests the position that, although historical explanations, once offered, leave nothing for scientific inquiry to add, it is quite proper for historians to look for nomological ones when the re-enactive kind are not available. To this Collingwood adds the observation that there are times when all we want to know about a person is something nomological: for example, whether a given man is capable of digging a garden, in which case we regard him in much the same way that we regard a razor blade when we ask whether it is sharp (RAH 12–13). Some of the difficulties about such a 'live and let live' approach will be considered presently. But let us ask first whether, if both kinds of explanation could in fact be given in a particular case, Collingwood would regard them as of equal value.

Donagan, in commenting on Collingwood's theory, has argued that the two forms of explanation cannot be accorded equal status as possible explanations of the same thing. If scientific explanations can be had, he says, they must be acknowledged to be superior because they are 'more powerful' (*LPC* 295). The implication seems to be that they should therefore be as welcome in history, whenever available, as they would be in any other form of inquiry. The reason why Donagan calls scientific explanation more powerful is presumably that explaining something nomologically shows, at the same time, how it could have been predicted. And if one's chief interest in a subject-matter is predictability and control, then judging nomological explanation to be superior will seem reasonable enough. If Donagan himself doesn't urge historians to seek nomological rather than re-enactive explanations, it is only because he sees no real hope of them coming to know the laws of human behaviour which would make the nomological explanations they might offer empirically respectable. Any hope that this situation might ever change he

dismisses as 'an infatuation'.[32] Historians should therefore be content to offer re-enactive explanations; but they will offer them
faute de mieux.

There is little evidence that Collingwood ever held such a view
of the relative worth of the two kinds of explanation. In fact, he
often reverses the relationship, insisting that understanding actions re-enactively is intrinsically superior to any understanding
that could be gained by subsuming them under laws. Scientific
explanation, since it affords only a view of what happened 'from
the outside', leaves what is to be understood still something of a
mystery. Collingwood is prepared, at times, to draw from this the
conclusion that, even in the study of nature, nomological understanding is inferior to the kind that re-enactive explanation would
confer if only it were obtainable. Even in this sphere, he sometimes implies, it can only be regarded as a regrettable second best.
Hence the touch of wistfulness with which he expounds Croce's
notion of how much better we should understand something like
a blade of grass if only we could get inside it, as we get inside
human actions, thereby grasping the object or point of its changes
(IH 199–200).

Collingwood even flirts, on occasion, with the view that what
we commonly call scientific explanation is not really explanatory
at all, and is not intended to be, the function of scientific thought
being essentially pragmatic: the discovery of ways to master nature, not to understand it. In his Essay on Metaphysics, he represents natural science as a cogent sort of inquiry only to the
extent that it remains true to its Baconian origins: a search for
ways of producing and preventing things. Attempts to move
from such a 'practical' view of scientific work to something more
'theoretical', he charges, only makes science anthropomorphic. A
prime example is what happens to the notion of law in abstraction
from the experience of social relations from which, according
to Collingwood, it is derived (EM 297, 320, 334). In part,
Collingwood's view here anticipates a view of scientific laws and
theories as formulating mere 'prediction mechanisms' which was
to achieve popularity some years after his death, although it was
strongly hinted at much earlier by Bacon (IH 84; A 90). His more
usual view, however, is simply that scientific explanation yields

[32] Donagan, 'Popper-Hempel', 157.

an inferior sort of understanding, which we have no alternative to accepting in physical inquiry, but should refuse in the human studies, where something better is available (*IH* 223). As Atkinson puts it, precisely reversing Donagan's position: for Collingwood, nomological explanation is, at best, 'something to fall back on when we cannot see the rationale of actions' (*KEH* 25).

Yet there are moments when, rather than holding the two forms of understanding to be compatible, each possible at least in principle with regard to any subject-matter, even though one may be judged superior to the other, Collingwood represents them as incompatible, so that giving one kind with regard to any particular thing excludes the possibility of giving the other. This is the position which he finally adopts about the possibility of explaining natural events in the re-enactive way. Such an enterprise, he says, is not impossible just because, when we try to find evidence for attributing purposes and beliefs to natural events and processes, we do not find it. It is impossible because, unlike certain of our ancestors and the members of some other cultures still extant, we operate under the *presupposition* that nature has no 'inside', and is thus open only to nomological explanation (*IH* 217). The impossibility of giving re-enactive explanations of natural events is thus logical or conceptual. Some philosophers friendly to Collingwood's general position (Winch is an example) have argued somewhat similarly in the other direction.[33] They have maintained that we cannot explain human actions as instantiations of genuine laws not only because, as Donagan insists, we do not in fact find the relevant laws, but, more fundamentally, because our very concept of action is of something not determined by laws. Action is not something which an agent simply finds himself undergoing; it is something which he engages in by choice, with chosen ends in view, even if guided by what he considers adequate reasons.

Collingwood, too, appears, in many passages, to accept the notion that an inquiry taking human action as its subject-matter operates under the presupposition that its object of inquiry cannot be explained scientifically. Or, to put it another way, that it cannot be so explained and still, with logical consistency, be considered action. His position, so conceived, is nowhere more

---

[33] Peter Winch, *Idea of a Social Science* (London, 1958), 94.

plainly signalled than in one of his most characteristic sayings about history, namely, that a positive, i.e. law-subsuming, science of human activities would 'dementalize' its subject-matter; it would treat expressions of mind as if they were merely natural events (*IH* 223; *A* 93).[34] The point is put more nearly as a point of conceptual logic in Collingwood's plan for 'The Principles of History', where he declares that history and science are 'not reducible' to each other (Book 2, § 1). P. H. Nowell-Smith, expressing Donagan's position less sharply, has maintained, in discussing Collingwood's views, that the inability of historians to give plausible nomological explanations of actions is due only to the 'contingent fact' that suitable laws are not to be found.[35] What Collingwood himself often says suggests something much stronger.

§ 5. *Re-enactive Explanation and Determinism*

The fact that Collingwood at least sometimes represents re-enactive explanation as logically excluding nomological explanation of the same thing raises the general question of where he stands on the issue of historical determinism, taking this (following Donagan) as the doctrine that 'all past actions can in principle be explained by subsuming them under general laws of nature' (*LPC* 228). A theory of what would count as understanding in a given field does not, by itself, of course, entail any particular view of the nature of the subject-matter. However, claims to find the theory applicable may do so, and the many re-enactive explanations which Collingwood offers or accepts may therefore be regarded as committing him to historical indeterminism. It is nevertheless of some interest to ask, independently of this, what his writings show about his own views on this question. As on some other issues, the evidence does not all point the same way.

Much of what he says does indicate an indeterminist position, quite consciously held. Thus he praises what he sees as the inde-

---

[34] The first prominent historian to try to do this, according to Collingwood, was Thucydides, whom he calls 'the father of psychological history' (*IH* 29).

[35] 'Are Historical Events Unique?', *Proceedings of the Aristotelian Society*, 42 (1957), 115.

terminism of the Greek view of history, and commends Christian historiography for treating determinism as an 'aberration' (IH 23, 54–5). He criticizes Montesquieu for depicting human institutions as 'the necessary effects of natural causes', and Spengler for failing to envisage 'a future which is undetermined' (IH 79; SHC 69). In an early work in which he still thinks of causation exclusively in terms of law-instantiation, he denies that actions have causes at all.[36] In a later one, after taking the position that actions do have causes, but only in the sense that agents perform them for reasons (IH 214), he insists that, when the term 'cause' is used in this, its properly historical sense, caused actions are ones which we freely make up our minds to perform (EM 290). In an essay of the 1930s, he holds that, although the past may be said to determine the human present, 'it only determines *possibilities* between which the present may choose. . . . The fall of a man's income may lead him to retrenchment or to bankruptcy': which it does depends on him (HUP 2–3). In another essay of the same period, the idea that history is determined is rejected in a different way when Collingwood maintains that the past only 'conditions' the present (RAH 6), and in still another when he says that it determines it only 'disjunctively'.[37] A striking expression of indeterminism occurs in his criticism of Dilthey for allegedly reducing differences between philosophers to 'differences in psychological structure or disposition' (IH 173). To treat a rational enterprise in this way 'makes nonsense of it', Collingwood objects, since it puts the question whether a given view is right or wrong completely out of court.

At some other points, Collingwood may appear, on the face of it, to indicate an acceptance of determinism. Thus, although he repeatedly denies that actions are determined by 'external' (for example, geographical) conditions, he often describes them as being done under 'internal' necessity. He assigns to the historian of the Roman Republic the task of finding out what Brutus thought which 'made' or 'determined' him stab Caesar (IH 214–15); and he frequently describes actions as 'forced' or 'compelled'.

[36] 'The Devil', in B. F. Streeter and others (eds.), Concerning Prayer: Its Nature, Its Difficulties and Its Value (London, 1916), reprinted in Lionel Rubinoff (ed.), Faith and Reason: Essays in the Philosophy of Religion by R. G. Collingwood (Chicago, 1968), 219.
[37] 'What Civilization Means', NL, rev. edn., 497.

'The rational activity which historians have to study', he declares, 'is never free from compulsion'; indeed, 'the more rational it is, the more completely it undergoes this compulsion' (*IH* 316). It seems clear, however, that what he envisages here is not the necessity of something happening because it falls under laws, but that of something being done because there are strong reasons for doing it. The 'force' of an agent's reasons, when we say that they 'made' or 'compelled' or even 'determined' him to act, is not measured by the predictability of his acting accordingly: it is a matter of rational, not natural, necessity, something to be judged from the standpoint of the agent. Similar considerations apply to remarks which Collingwood sometimes makes about 'dramatic' necessity in history. In an early work on Ruskin's philosophy, he describes history as 'a drama, the unfolding of a plot in which each situation leads necessarily to the next';[38] and in his inaugural lecture, he observes that a good historian, like a good novelist, aims to show that 'every character and every situation is so bound up with the rest that this character in this situation cannot but act in this way' (*IH* 245). But the phrase 'cannot but act in this way' need mean no more than 'had compelling reasons to act in this way'; and the apparent demand for 'complete' explanation can be satisfied by explanation of the re-enactive kind. Doubtless, to demand even this is to lay too heavy a burden upon historians; but it does not imply determinism.

There are still other points at which Collingwood may give the impression of being at least somewhat ambivalent about determinism. He concedes, for example, that people's actions are often to some extent determined by their established characters (RAH 22–4). But although he considers that what a person has done in the past can make it very difficult for him to act differently later on, he still contrasts this with the way in which the character (or 'nature') of a natural object determines how it will react in a new situation. Unlike natural objects, he maintains, we can act contrary to our established characters. For a person's character is, in part, an accumulation of past decisions, a 'deposit' left by the past, which, like a habit, may limit present choices, but leaves many possibilities open. And acting contrary to one's character begins to change that character, making it as true to say that our de-

---

[38] 'Ruskin's Philosophy', 19–20.

cisions determine our characters as that our characters determine our decisions. Collingwood makes no more than a start at working out what is distinctive about explanations which advert to agents' characters; but he clearly denies that they assume determinism.

The way in which he sometimes argues against the admissibility into historical accounts of chance, contingency, or accident may also give a false impression of support for determinism. As noted earlier, positivists like Hempel see it as a chief goal of nomological explanation to show that what happened did not happen by chance. And when Collingwood inveighs against an historian like Bury for asserting a role for contingency (said to mean chance) in human affairs, he may seem to be adopting a similar position (IH 151). Certainly a Hempelian would find very acceptable Collingwood's remarking that 'contingency means unintelligibility' (IH 151; SM 209), or his claiming that 'calling an event accidental means that it is not capable of being understood' (EM 289). But although for him, as for the positivists, terms like 'contingent' or 'accidental' evidently signify a gap in the historian's understanding, he generally sees the gap as a re-enactive, not a nomological one. Thus when he hails Hegel's dictum that historical events are never accidental, the contrast which he has in mind is with history as 'at bottom a logical process', i.e. one exhibiting rational necessity, not determination by laws (IH 117). In a manuscript of 1938–9, he takes a different but equally non-determinist line, arguing that by 'accidental' historians simply mean 'not intended'. It follows, he says, that the term has application only to the 'background or scenery' of history, its foreground, human action, being, by its very nature, intended (NHV 22–3). It is interesting to note that Collingwood here, like many whom he would regard as positivists, offers both subjective and objective accounts of the meaning of 'chance' and 'accident' in history.[39] On the one hand, it is something not understood (by the historian); on the other, it is something not intended (by the agent). In neither case, however, will disputes about the legitimate use of this idea turn upon the question whether what happened was nomologically determined.

[39] See e.g. Ernest Nagel's 'Determinism in History', reprinted in Dray (ed.), *Philosophical Analysis and History*, 371–3.

Collingwood occasionally makes more cryptic pronouncements about necessity in history which some may take as evidence of deterministic thinking. In the lectures of 1926, for
example, he observes that, while the present is the realm of the
actual, and the future that of the merely possible, the past is the
realm of the necessary (L26 412–13). The least problematic way of
interpreting such a way of characterizing the historical past is as
a reminder that what has happened cannot be changed (the Mov-
ing Finger has writ). The past, as we sometimes say, is 'fixed'; the
future is not. If this can coherently be said at all, it clearly has
nothing to do with determinism. Historians do themselves sometimes say, as if in echo of Collingwood's dictum, that, while it is
wrong to regard historical events as determined before they happen, they must be so regarded afterwards.[40] This, however, only
makes sense if 'determined' successively bears two different
meanings: first, 'was brought about by what preceded it'; and
then, 'is unchangeable once it has happened'.

A related sense in which the historical past might wrongly be
thought of as necessarily the way it is, and which some of
Collingwood's remarks also suggest, is that present evidence may
be taken to show how the past must have been (IH 110). The
necessitating relationship now runs from present to past, however, not from past to present, so that, even if it obtained, it would
be irrelevant to the truth of historical determinism. Collingwood
himself sometimes invites confusion on the latter point in other
ways. For example, in a manuscript of the 1930s, he illustrates his
claim that the past is a process exhibiting necessity by observing
that, had there not been a devaluation of the pound while he was
on vacation in France one summer, he would not have made the
profit in foreign exchange which he did upon his return (RAH 14).
But in pointing to this as an example of what he means by historical 'necessity', he confounds the ideas of necessary and sufficient
condition.[41] That the past was a certain way may be a necessary
condition of the present's being the way it is now, but that does
not make it a sufficient (i.e. determining) condition of it.

The fact that Collingwood occasionally refers to historical happenings as 'inevitable' may seem to raise more substantial prob-

[40] See e.g. E. H. Carr, WIH 90; or Lawrence Stone, The Causes of the English
Revolution 1529–1642 (London, 1972), 11.
[41] See also NTM A-60.

lems for regarding him as an indeterminist. It was inevitable, he says, that the science of human nature would be distorted by the success of natural science (*IH* 208); it was inevitable that, after Versailles, the have-not powers would turn to aggression (*NL* 151). And even when he abjures such strong language, he sometimes describes historical developments as predictable. Thus, having observed that Roman Britain had stronger enemies than Gaul, and had been Romanized to a lesser extent, he declares that, 'but for these facts, England would today be speaking a Latin tongue' (*RB* 13). And in some of his later writings, he comes close to predicting catastrophe for our civilization (*A* 155 ff.; *EM* 343). Something analogous to prediction is sometimes represented, too, as a normal technique of historical inquiry. An historian who is appropriately critical, Collingwood tells us, would ask, when presented with a commander's despatches claiming a victory: 'If it was a victory, why was it not followed up in this or that way?' (*IH* 237). And an historian studying a medieval ruin who possesses appropriate archaeological knowledge, might, he says, predict that certain kinds of artefacts, such as green-glaze pottery, will be found in it (HSD 32).

Yet, Collingwood often states or implies that any predictability which we can hope for in history must be very limited. 'The historian,' he declares, 'has no gift of prophecy'; he can 'neither foretell the future developments of human thought nor legislate for them, except so far as they must proceed—although in what direction we cannot tell—from the present as their starting point' (*IH* 220). And he maintains that, although 'we can certainly anticipate the future' by means of historical inquiry, 'all our anticipations are guesses, or mere statements of what so far as we can see may happen' (L26 412), or, as he also says, are mere 'conjectures' (SPAT 147). Not all Collingwood's pronouncements in this vein are such as to give determinists pause, however. In a passage which has often caught the attention of commentators, he ridicules the idea of an historian setting out to predict the future by comparing him with 'a tracker anxiously peering at a muddy road in order to descry the footsteps of the next person who is going to pass that way' (SHC 68; *IH* 120). But, as the context makes clear, Collingwood's 'tracker' is only debarred from discerning the future *qua* historian—i.e. *qua* investigator using specifically historical methods devised for the interpretation of relics, there being, of course, no relics of the future. The real question is whether a person may not be able to predict the human future (and to show certain past events to have been predictable) by arguing nomologically from what is (or was) perceived as reliable signs of what is (or was) in store. Similarly inconclusive is another argument on which Collingwood appears to place some weight. 'No one', he avers, 'can possibly forecast the course of European history, even in the next ten years, with anything approaching the certainty and precision with which even the least competent historian can reconstruct its course in the last ten or even in the last ten thousand' (L26 412). This may be so, but it is not difficult to think of other reasons for it than its not yet being determined what the next ten years will bring.

Collingwood has a good deal to say about the human actions studied by historians being free, the implication apparently being that they are not fully determined. It is not always clear, however, that the kind of freedom he ascribes to them is incompatible with the assumption that everything falls under laws. In discussing the Greek view of history, for example, he describes it as 'the very opposite of deterministic' because it represents what happened as 'open to salutary modification by the well-instructed human will' (*IH* 23). But this could be freedom simply in the sense of power—being able to accomplish one's purposes—which has no implications for determinism one way or the other. In another sense of 'free' often used by Collingwood, he virtually makes it a condition of actions being understandable in the distinctively historical way that they *not* be free. 'The rational activity which historians have to study', he declares, 'is never free from compulsion: the compulsion to face the facts of [the agent's] own situation' (*IH* 316). To put it in another way, actions will be found most fully understandable when they can be seen as responses to what was earlier called compelling reasons to act as the agent did. But the freedom which is incompatible with scientific determinism is neither that of not being prevented from doing what one wishes, nor that of being free from compulsion, i.e. from circumstances which rationally require one to act in a certain way. It is freedom in the sense of not being nomologically determined by antecedent conditions to choose to act in one way rather than in another—freedom of the will in a traditional sense.

It is not easy to find Collingwood arguing unmistakably for

human freedom in this sense, and sometimes he seems almost to be arguing against it. He appears to be arguing for it, when, having referred to the way an agent's situation may exert compulsion, he tells us that 'the freedom that there is in history consists in the fact that this compulsion is imposed upon the activity of human reason not by anything else, but by itself'—in other words, not by independently existing antecedent conditions (*IH* 317). He seems to be arguing to the same effect when he maintains, with Ravaisson, that the historical world is one 'whose laws are freely made by that same spirit which freely obeys them' (*IH* 184). However, it is difficult to understand similarly his describing a dutiful act as one 'which at that moment character and circumstance combine to make it inevitable, if he has a free will, that he should freely will to do'—for 'free will' itself now seems to mean a certain kind of predictability (*NL* 124). Collingwood clouds his own position further when, having said that history is about 'free acts', he asserts (following Dr Johnson) that we know 'immediately' that we are free, since we know that we can 'choose between alternatives' (*NL* 90–1).[42] For there is no question of our knowing immediately that our choices are not determined by antecedent conditions beyond our ken. It is thus left in some obscurity in the end whether Collingwood asserts human freedom in the traditional sense of an undetermined (or less than fully determined) power of choice. Donagan has argued on his behalf, with a perspicacity that would be difficult to match, that claims to offer re-enactive explanation do presuppose free will in this sense (*LPC* 227–36). On this point, at least, he seems to me entirely correct.

§ 6. *Collingwood's Generalizations*

If there is some ambiguity in Collingwood's stance with regard to historical determinism, it is hardly surprising that the same is true

[42] He clouds his position in a different way when he registers acceptance of something like a Spinozistic view of the mind–body relationship (*NL* 10–11), history and science then becoming just two different ways of studying the same (determined or undetermined?) thing. (The reader for OUP notes that Collingwood discusses the whole question of choice and action in relation to history further, if still not very satisfactorily, in his 1940 lectures on moral philosophy, now appended to *NL*, rev. edn.)

of what he says from time to time about the place of generalizations in historical thinking. I have argued that historical understanding, on his theory of it as re-enactive, does not require knowledge of, or commitment to, related laws or generalizations; indeed, that a claim to have achieved it rules such generalizations out. I have also maintained that the metaphysical position which Collingwood most often took is the one which his theory of historical understanding would lead one to expect: an indeterminist one, at any rate with regard to actions. Yet although he seems committed to maintaining that historians neither need to assert, nor could justifiably assert, generalizations about their subject-matter, generalizations do appear from time to time in his philosophical writings about history, and in his historical writings as well. Van der Dussen has welcomed this as showing that the criticism sometimes levelled at Collingwood for ignoring the evident use of generalizations by historians is unwarranted (*HS* 341).[43] The question, however, is whether he can accord them the place which he does without his overall position becoming incoherent. The best that can be said, I think, is that, although he does sometimes assert or accept generalizations of a kind, or in a way, which is difficult to square with both the metaphysical and epistemological positions which I have imputed to him, what he says, in most cases, raises less of a problem than might have been expected.

Since Collingwood's theory of re-enactive explanation and his indeterminist metaphysics are intended to apply only to human activities, there is, of course, no reason why he should not call upon generalizations or laws where what is to be understood is physical events and processes; and, as already noted, he does so. The same could be said of cases where the problem is not why human actions were undertaken, but why they succeeded or failed, this, as Donagan has observed (*LPC* 203), sometimes making generalizations of a technological sort relevant. Collingwood himself also frequently points to what he calls the auxiliary sciences of history—he lists numismatics, epigraphy, palaeography, archaeology, and sometimes includes generalizing social sciences like economics or sociology (L26 386; PH 132; RAH 11–12)—as sources of generalizations of one or other of these

[43] Such criticism is expressed e.g. by John Higham (with Leonard Krieger and Felix Gilbert, *History* (Englewood Cliffs, NJ, 1965), 143).

kinds, although he gives few examples. It is of interest to note that, in some such cases, the relevant generalizations have to be adopted by historians 'ready-made', this despite the hostility which Collingwood expresses towards the acceptance of anything like 'authorities' in history. However, they will not be called upon to explain 'on authority' why people acted in certain ways. The generalizations derived by historians from auxiliary disciplines may also take the form of maxims or rules of good investigative procedure rather than claims about what in fact generally happens (L26 386; L28 490).[44] This sometimes leads Collingwood to describe 'the archaeological sciences', i.e. all the auxiliary disciplines taken together, as 'the empirical methodology of history' (L28 491).

Even when the generalizations which he cites are factual rather than prescriptive, Collingwood often represents historians as using them not to ground explanations, but to suggest what further inquiry might establish in cases under study. They are conceived, in other words, as setting forth no more than explanatory hypotheses. As van der Dussen points out, Collingwood himself sometimes uses analogical argument to this purpose.[45] Having noted, for example, that the Emperor Commodus's frontier works on the Danube were responses to frontier raiding, he goes on to remark that 'the situation on the Solway is like enough to that on the Danube' to suggest that the same explanation may hold for Hadrian's Wall in Britain.[46] He makes similar use of analogical reasoning in pointing to the spontaneous rise of villas in Gaul as indicative of what may also have been true of villas in Britain (*RBES* 302–4).[47] Using a known case to suggest a possible

[44] These may seem to resemble what, in LHK, Collingwood calls 'rules of the game'; but the latter are rules which determine what shall count as historical inquiry at all, whereas these are rules for conducting it well: truly methodological, not constitutive principles.

[45] Collingwood blows hot and cold on the acceptability of analogical reasoning in history. He looks with kindly eye on Vico's arguing analogically from what was true in the Middle Ages to what was probably true in Homeric Greece, on the ground that both were heroic ages (*IH* 67). But he argues against Bradley that, where historical rather than natural events are at issue, conditions differ so much at different times that 'no argument from analogy will hold' (*IH* 239).

[46] 'Roman Signal-Stations on the Cumberland Coast', *Transactions of the Cumberland and Westmorland Antiquarian and Archaeological Society*, NS 29 (1929), 143. See also *A* 136.

[47] He even invokes the principle here: 'same cause, same effect', a surprisingly crude positivist lapse.

explanation of another one—i.e. using it heuristically rather than substantively—leaves Collingwood's anti-positivist metaphysics and explanatory theory intact, since he insists that any explanatory hypothesis so derived must be independently confirmed in the particular case.[48] In taking such a position, he turns upside down a concession which we found Hempel making to the idea of historical understanding as re-enactment, namely, that attempts to re-think the thoughts of agents may sometimes serve the heuristic function of suggesting relevant generalizations linking thought and action which may be worth further testing. Collingwood, by contrast, represents tentative generalizations based on knowledge of other cases as an occasional aid in re-thinking a given agent's thoughts, the generalization then falling away like scaffolding from a completed building. He does not, unfortunately, spell out in any detail what he considers the theoretical justification of such a heuristic use.

From time to time, Collingwood does call upon generalizations in order to support, not merely to suggest, certain conclusions. But when he does so, the ones he cites are often very loose and weak. As he puts it himself, in commending Bury for denying that historical events fall under laws: 'Uniformities, yes; laws, no' (*IH* 149). Sometimes the uniformities cited are no more than summative statements of fact: for example: 'all Roman silver of the third century is debased' (*IH* 166). Sometimes they incorporate qualifications or are expressed vaguely, as when Collingwood describes a certain kind of script merely as 'characteristic of English thirteenth-century writing' (L26 383). In still other cases, they are treated as having explanatory force but only in the sense of stating what *may* happen, as when he notes the way 'incapsulated' habits and desires can reappear in behaviour that is ostensibly quite different (*A* 141 ff.). Citing generalizations of the latter kind suggests an implicit, although never formally acknowledged, acceptance by Collingwood of a kind of explanation in history (mentioned in § 2) the aim of which is only to show the possibility of what happened. Such explanation—which is sometimes given of natural events as well as of human activities—is commonly offered of happenings which seemed quite unlikely under the circumstances, this raising the question not why they

---

[48] This heuristic use of generalizations is to be distinguished from their alleged use in helping to establish past facts (NAPH 48; *IH* 167, 223).

happened, but how they could possibly have happened. One might have expected explanations of this kind to be of special interest to Collingwood, since their concern is explicitly not with the predictability of what is to be explained. But although he does offer them, he never incorporates an account of their structure and use into his anti-positivist theory of history.

Some other kinds of less-than-universal generalizations which are sometimes cited or used by Collingwood pose more of a problem for his theoretical position. One of these asserts that a certain connection holds in a proportion of cases, its claim thus being essentially statistical in nature, even if not formulated in precise quantitative terms. Collingwood explicitly recognizes a role for statistical thinking in history, calling it 'a good servant', if 'a bad master' (*IH* 228). But he seems to see it as useful chiefly for characterizing backgrounds or for setting problems for further analysis, not for answering the sorts of questions which historians typically ask about why people lived and acted as they did. He employs statistical methods himself when dealing with demographic problems like estimating the size of the population of Roman Britain, or ascertaining the relative proportion of town-dwellers and country-dwellers in it (*A* 134–7). In the same spirit, he commends Mommsen for treating Roman military epitaphs statistically (*IH* 131). There are only occasional hints that he might see statistical generalizations as sometimes having an explanatory function: for example, when he observes that 'if the members of a certain society have been in the habit of acting or thinking in certain ways . . . the desire to go on thinking and acting in the old way will probably persist' (*A* 141), or when he warns that 'official documents tend to exaggerate successes and to minimize failures' (L26 383).

Most of Collingwood's positivist opponents would contend that statistical as well as universal generalizations have explanatory force, this deriving from their showing that the events to which they apply were probable to some degree. Donagan has denied that subsumption under a statistical law can ever explain a particular occurrence, since it is compatible with its non-occurrence;[49] and Collingwood appears to take much the same position in a manuscript of the 1930s, where he holds that statistical laws,

[49] Donagan, 'Popper-Hempel', 145.

even in natural science, 'tell us nothing' about any individual event or action falling under them (RAH 31). In another late manuscript, he distances himself from the positivist conception of statistical explanation in another way. Conceding that finding something to fall under a statistical law might lead one to see its occurrence as probable, he declares that judgments of probability are subjective, expressing only the degree of expectancy of those making them (NHH 59). He is not much more helpful on the question of the significance of assenting to statistical generalizations for a commitment to indeterminism, at any rate with regard to actions. He never asks, for example, whether they might be seen as entailing determinism (and allowing nomological explanation) at the level of overall trends, while not at the level of the individual events which constitute them. It is especially disappointing that such mysteries of statistical connection are not probed by Collingwood, since they are highly relevant to an issue which he does come back to from time to time: the relationship of history to the generalizing social sciences, the findings of which are largely statistical (PH 132; RAH 11–12; NHV 18).

Still a further kind of generalization which is often cited or used by Collingwood, and which also falls short of the universality envisaged by the nomological theory of explanation, is a kind which is understood to hold only for certain periods or geographical regions (NAPH 35; IH 223).[50] A case in point is his assertion that the Greeks and Romans exposed new-born children as a way of controlling the population—this, he observes, being something quite beyond the experience of contributors to the *Cambridge Ancient History* (IH 240). He sees the 'laws' of classical economics as basically of this kind, having no application beyond modern European society (NHV 18). Such spatio-temporally limited generalizations should not be confused with merely summative ones. They set forth 'what is characteristic of a certain date or origin'—in other words, they are true generalizations within their spatio-temporally restricted field of application, presumably holding for unexamined as well as for examined cases in

---

[50] By C. B. Joynt and Nicholas Rescher, these are called 'limited laws' ('The Problem of Uniqueness in History', *History and Theory*, 1 (1961), 156); by Rex Martin, 'historically localized generalizations' (*HE* 46); by Donagan, 'closed hypotheticals' (*LPC* 187); by Collingwood himself, 'a generalized description of certain phases in human history' (*IH* 224).

it, and thus warranting a degree of prediction (L28 490–1). Historians sometimes signal, without actually saying it, that any generalization suggested by an explanation which they are offering will only be a limited one. Collingwood does this himself when, in support of his denial that the growth of villas in Roman Britain was due to an influx from abroad, he stresses 'the improbability of foreign settlers at so early a date going anywhere except to the towns', thus directing attention to a generalization which he regards as true for the indicated time and place (*RBES* 215). As this particular example makes clear, spatio-temporally limited generalizations can also be less than universal in the further sense of being statistical, thus warranting no more than a probability judgment even within an already restricted field of application.

It is an important question, but not an easy one to answer, how Collingwood conceives the relationship between spatio-temporally limited generalizations and universal ones bearing upon the same subject-matter. In a number of passages, he seems to imply that, if an historian accepts generalizations of the limited kind, this commits him to there being related unlimited ones. Thus, at a point where he denies that the generalizations which historians can claim to know might 'transcend' particular times and places, Collingwood remarks that types of behaviour will doubtless recur 'so long as minds of the same kind are placed in the same kind of situations' (*IH* 223). He continues: 'The behaviour-patterns characteristic of a feudal baron were no doubt fairly constant so long as there were feudal barons living in a feudal society. But they will be sought in vain . . . in a world whose social structure is of another kind.' This is hardly an unambiguous rejection of the idea that there are universal as well as limited laws in history. The conclusion seems at least to be invited that, if limited laws obtain, they do so because they fall under universal ones which, together with changes in circumstances, explain why the limited ones hold for some times and places and not for others. It is difficult to see why Collingwood should feel obliged to make such a concession to the positivists. And he does, in fact, often cite or use limited laws as if he regards them to hold in their own right.[51]

[51] Two further questions of importance with regard to limited laws which Collingwood unfortunately leaves unconsidered are whether explanation by reference to them is any less 'external', and any less deterministic than is explanation by reference to universal laws.

I have maintained that the position taken by Collingwood on the place of generalizations in historical thinking cannot be decided without taking into account how logically various are the ones which he mentions or implies. Some are only summative; some are maxims or principles rather than factual claims; some have a heuristic rather than a substantive function; some are merely statistical and probabilistic; some are spatio-temporally limited. There are nevertheless occasions on which he does appear to appeal to generalizations conceived as statements of invariable connections in human affairs, including human actions, thus himself falling into what he calls 'pseudo-history' when he discerns it in the work of others.

For example, in support of his explanation of the revival of Celtic art, after the departure of the Romans, as the reappearance of a tradition that had only gone underground, he cites the generalization: 'a man who changes his habits, thoughts, etc., retains in the second phase some residue of the first' (*A* 141). In considering evidence that the Romans may have intended to reoccupy Britain early in the fifth century, he observes: 'Any government which had lost a frontier district, and had the smallest expectation of reclaiming it, would keep a record of its organization as a matter of course' (*RBES* 296).[52] In his manuscripts on folklore, he generalizes freely, almost recklessly. He asserts it to be 'a universal human feeling', for example, that 'to take off one's clothes in public' is 'to forfeit one's dignity'; and holds it to be transculturally true that 'marriage bulks larger in the emotional life of a woman than in that of a man'.[53] Perhaps with less serious intent, he declares in the *Autobiography* that there are only 'two reasons why people refrain from writing books: either they are conscious that they have nothing to say, or they are conscious that they are unable to say it' (*A* 19–20). Completely serious, however, is a piece of nomologically-tinged advice which he offers to historians in the same work: 'If you want to know why a certain kind of thing happened in a certain kind of case, you must begin by asking "What did you expect?" You must consider what the normal development is in cases of that kind' (*A* 140).

Collingwood's tendency thus to reach for even universal gener-

[52] For similarly universal generalizations in Collingwood's historical work, see *RB* 108–9; or *RBES* 8.
[53] 'Magic', 1936–7, Dep. 21/7, fos. 12, 24.

alizations when they seem useful (or provocative) might itself be taken by an unfriendly critic to exemplify still another exceptionless generalization which he himself enunciated, namely, that 'an intense polemic against a certain doctrine is an infallible sign that the doctrine in question . . . has a strong attraction for himself' (*IH* 21–2). As I have noted before, however, Collingwood was not a particularly careful writer, and he was not always consistent. His considered position must, I think, be taken to exclude the applicability of universal empirical generalizations to human action conceived as having a re-thinkable 'inside', and even of non-statistical limited laws to the extent that they are regarded as truly predictive of actions, if only within their own spatio-temporal field.

4

INTELLECT, RATIONALITY, FEELING

§ 1. *The Scope of Re-enactment*

I want to turn now from the question whether Collingwood offers a viable account of the way individual actions like Caesar's crossing of the Rubicon or Nelson's declaration at Trafalgar are understood in history to the question whether his account, even if correct for such cases, formulates a theory of historical understanding which is generally applicable to an historical subject-matter. Even those who have found much to admire in Collingwood's *Idea of History* and related writings have often complained that his idea of re-enactment is relevant only to a small part of what is normally regarded as history. His account of the way particular actions are to be explained has been said unduly to stress man's intellectual life; his emphasis on agents' reasons for acting has been criticized as ignoring the basic irrationality of human nature; his almost exclusive concern with what people did has been held to neglect other important aspects of human experience; his claim that all history is of thought has been challenged as ignoring the part played by natural events and conditions in the human past; and the stress which he places upon individuals has been said to put out of focus what is distinctively social in human life.

Collingwood's theory of understanding has thus been charged with being too intellectualistic, too rationalistic, too action-oriented, too mentalistic, and too individualistic, to be regarded as an acceptable general account of the nature of historical understanding. What even Collingwood's admirers have commonly seen it as offering is, at most, an account of one quite limited sort of understanding which finds a place from time to time in historical studies.

I shall concede that what Collingwood has to say about the way past actions are re-enactively understood does not, in itself, provide a satisfactory *overall* theory of historical understanding, this despite the fact that so many of his own remarks may seem to promise that it will. I think, however, that Collingwood himself anticipates, and to a considerable extent meets, many of the difficulties raised by those who complain about the unduly narrow scope of his theory, and that where he does not, it is often possible to sketch a plausible modification of what he actually says which leaves a more satisfactory, but still recognizably Collingwoodian, account. In this chapter, I shall consider and suggest ways of responding to the first three criticisms noted, and in the next, I shall similarly examine the other two. In doing this, I shall to a considerable extent be following in the footsteps of students of Collingwood like Donagan and Mink, although I think that Mink may attribute too much to what he sees as Collingwood's willingness to go beyond simply characterizing historical inquiry to prescribing a new 'conceptual system' for it (*HU* 265). In later chapters, I shall consider ways in which the idea of re-enactment may need not just some reformulation, but also some supplementation by notions of a different sort, even these, however, often being prefigured in what Collingwood himself has to say.

§ 2. *Collingwood's Supposed Intellectualism*

The first complaint cited is that Collingwood's approach imposes upon the historian a conception of human action which is far too self-conscious, far too calculating, to apply to more than a very small fraction of the past actions which ordinarily interest historians. As Walsh has observed, comparing him unfavourably with Dilthey in this connection, Collingwood seems to confine history to a study of man's 'intellectual operations' (*IPH* 50). Even as friendly a commentator as Winch has felt obliged to characterize the idea that the thoughts of the participants must be rethought by the historian as 'to some extent an intellectualistic distortion'.[1]

[1] *Idea of a Social Science*, 13. For similar views, see Fain, *BPH* 271; Peter McClelland, *Causal Explanation and Model Building in History* (Ithaca, NY, 1975), 90; Gardiner, 'Historical Understanding', 279.

Collingwood's writings do furnish some excuse for this complaint. In the section of the Epilegomena of *The Idea of History*
entitled 'The Subject-matter of History', having raised the question of how much or how little is meant to be included under the
term 'thought' when history is described as a re-thinking of past
thought, Collingwood states quite categorically that only 'reflective' thought can be re-thought. This, he says, means that only
reflective acts, i.e. those expressing reflective thoughts, can be the
proper concern of historians. A reflective act, he continues, is 'one
which is performed in the consciousness that it is being performed and is constituted what it is by that consciousness': it is
'one in which we know what it is that we are trying to do, so that
when it is done we know that it is done by seeing that it has
conformed to the standard or criterion which was our initial
conception of it' (*IH* 308). In a further elaboration which reads like
a provocation to the future author of *The Concept of Mind*,
Collingwood even describes it as something which proceeds in
'two stages', 'first conceiving the purpose, which is a theoretical
activity or act of pure thought, and then executing it, which is a
practical activity supervening on the theoretical' (*IH* 311). The
way he goes on to apply this doctrine has seemed to many critics
like sheer effrontery. For he claims to draw from it the conclusion
that politics, warfare, economic activity, science, religion, philosophy, and historiography itself, all fall well within the scope of
historical investigation. For what is a politician, he asks, but a
man with 'a plan of action conceived in advance of its performance'?—adding that, if a man 'did the first thing that came into his
head and merely waited to see the consequences, it would follow
that such a man was no politician' (*IH* 309–10).[2] Arnold Toynbee
probably speaks for many readers when, with such passages
in mind, he expresses surprise that Collingwood apparently
knew so little about the 'intellectually horrifying way' in which
politicians in fact behave.[3]

[2] Collingwood here ignores a vast range of possibilities between acting without thinking, and acting on a preconceived plan. A better contrast would have
been with acting deliberately or with full intent. Acting on a preconceived
plan really does have two parts, a theoretical and then a practical; but the theoretical is not the 'inside' of the act eventually performed; it is a prior act with
its own inside and outside, the outside not necessarily being physical (see Ch. 2,
§ 3).
[3] Toynbee, *A Study of History*, ix. 722.

What needs to be noted—and this is the first thing to be said in response to the charge of intellectualism—is that there is little trace of this quite unacceptable doctrine in other parts of *The Idea of History* or in Collingwood's other writings.[4] Generally he either says, or clearly enough implies, that actions which would never in any ordinary sense of the term be called reflective, and certainly not deliberate or planned, are quite open to the sort of understanding which his theory ascribes to historians. As was pointed out in Chapter 2, § 3, he even accepts the possibility of historians explaining actions by reference to thoughts of which the agent was quite unaware at the time of acting—thoughts which would ordinarily be called 'unconscious'. How else are we to take the observation that an historical-style inquiry into my own thoughts may 'surprise' me, or that even animals may have 'the beginnings of historical life', since some of their actions, at least, express their thoughts (*IH* 219, 227)?

There are passages throughout *The Idea of History*, furthermore, which directly contradict the strange position set forth in 'The Subject-matter of History'. Thus Vico is praised for recognizing that historical greatness is seldom associated with a 'reflective intellect', although it would clearly be impossible, on Collingwood's view of thought and action, to judge a person's greatness without knowledge of his thoughts (*IH* 69). Greco-Roman historiography is criticized for attributing 'far too much to the deliberate plan or policy of the agent', this drawing from Collingwood the remark that 'to a very great extent people do not know what they are doing until they have done it, if then' (*IH* 42). The changes which a new generation typically makes when succeeding an old one are said often to be effected 'in obedience to a blind impulse to destroy what it does not comprehend' (*IH* 326). The anti-intellectualistic strain in Collingwood's thought in fact goes back to *Religion and Philosophy*, in which he strongly resists the idea that 'first we think and then we act', declaring that 'the thinking goes on all through the act' (*RP* 30–1). On the question of the historian's being exclusively concerned with 'intellectual operations', Collingwood seems, indeed, to have anticipated and responded to many of the objections of his future critics.

[4] Contrast *IH* 308 with *IH* 219. However, the intellectualist doctrine is present in *SM* 84; *IH* 119; *A* 110.

Does he, then, simply contradict himself? Are we simply to opt, say, for the Collingwood of the British Academy lecture rather than for the Collingwood of 'The Subject-matter of History'? It would be convenient if there were some plausible external reason for distrusting the latter paper—some circumstance relating to its composition, for example—but I know of none that would make it more suspect than other parts of the Epilegomena which were delivered as lectures by Collingwood in 1936. I do think, however, that there are good internal reasons for distrusting it on the point in question. Indeed, I think that, if it is read closely, a reasonable speculation can be hazarded as to how the offending statements came to be made. The first half of 'The Subject-matter of History' offers a sketch of a theory of mind which Collingwood was to develop further in later works like *The New Leviathan*. In the light of this, he argues in that half of the paper that an historian's object of study must always be actions expressing reflective thoughts, but in a peculiar, technical sense of 'reflective' which he stipulates in constructing his theory. He goes on then, in the second half of the paper, to assert that historians are concerned exclusively with reflective thoughts, but in the ordinary sense of 'reflective'. The shift of meaning occurs in mid-paragraph and is carried through consistently thereafter (*IH* 308).

Since my contention is that Collingwood's position here rests inadvertently on an equivocation with regard to the term 'reflective', let me offer a little more support for what may seem otherwise a rather presumptuous claim.[5] Collingwood's account of mind employs the notion of 'levels' of consciousness, each generating a level higher than itself by becoming an object to itself.[6] To simplify a simplification, he recognizes a lowest level which he calls mere 'feeling' or 'immediate experience', and which he doesn't consider thinking at all; an intermediate level which has mere feeling, so conceived, for its object, and which he does consider thinking, although not yet reflective thinking (examples would be sense-perception and memory, these being interpretations of immediate experience); and finally, a level of reflection which has thinking rather than feeling for its object, this being

[5] The argument is stated more fully in my 'R. G. Collingwood on Reflective Thought', *Journal of Philosophy*, 57 (1960), 157–63.

[6] There are helpful summaries of Collingwood's philosophy of mind in Donagan, *LPC* 25 ff. and Mink, *MHD* 113 ff.

exemplified by the thinking of the historian, since what the historian thinks about is the thought of the historical agent (*IH* 306–8). In this scheme, the distinction between reflective and unreflective thought does not turn on how a thought is thought—for example, in words or only by gesture, attentively or inattentively—but rather on what kind of a thought it is: what it is about. A reflective thought is a thought about thought. Thus when Collingwood goes on to ask whether the thought of the historical agent, which the historian has the task of re-thinking, will be reflective or unreflective, he concludes, as he should, given his somewhat eccentric use of the term, that it will always be reflective. For it will have for its object, not the agent's immediate experience, but his unreflective thought about that experience, notably his perceptions and memories.

Collingwood's denial that the historian can re-think the agent's unreflective thought is thus one of his ways of denying that the historian can re-perceive or re-remember what the agent perceived and remembered. It is only thinking at the level of the agent's responses to what he perceived and remembered which can be recovered by interpreting his actions as expressions of his thought. Since what is re-thinkable about such expressions is the connection between the agent's reasons for acting and his choice of an action to perform, Collingwood's doctrine here is a further way of putting his claim that what the historian has to re-think is the practical argument which was expressed in the agent's action. But in the very paragraph in which he completes his own argument to this effect, he leaps to the entirely different conclusion that the first-order reflection of the historical agent must be reflective in the sense of being 'performed in the consciousness that it is being performed', and the door is open to all those intellectualistic dicta of the second half of his discussion upon which his critics naturally seize. The position finally adopted, however, is quite unwarranted by the analysis which precedes it; everything is owed to the fact that, at a crucial point of his exposition, Collingwood slips unwittingly from using 'reflective' in his technical sense into using it in its ordinary sense.

What I would maintain, therefore, is that the charge of intellectualism can be fully met, if not by everything which Collingwood says, then at any rate by his own theory of historical understanding when carefully stated. His account of how actions are to be understood does not require, and for the most part does not employ, an intellectualistic conception of the explanatory thoughts which are expressed in them. In a few cases he does fall into the contrary position—the most notorious being the passage cited from 'The Subject-matter of History'. But he can be seen in such cases to be drawing conclusions which, on his own theory, he should not have drawn.

It might be added that Collingwood's pronouncements in the second half of the flawed Epilegomenon are intellectualistic in varying degrees. Sometimes what he tells us is that all reflective actions are 'deliberate', and that the universal character of any act is its 'plan'.[7] At other times, he says only, and more acceptably, that historians study what people do 'on purpose'. Even this probably assumes an awareness by the agent of the whole thought which his action expresses, which goes far beyond the kind of thing required for action explanation as Collingwood envisages historians giving it. On the other hand, to say only, as he also does, that the actions which historians study must be 'purposive' (*A* 109), may not go far enough. For thought, according to Collingwood, is not just an activity, but an activity of consciousness. Thus, although he conceives of that activity as expressing itself in physical as well as in psychic events, it seems doubtful that he would have regarded a bodily movement of which the agent himself was quite unaware as an expression of that agent's thought. Although he considers unconscious thought in one familiar sense to be part of the subject-matter of history, he probably doesn't in another (see Chapter 2, § 3). He accepts the idea that an action might be understood as expressing thoughts of which the agent was unaware. What is more doubtful, is that he accepts the more troublesome idea that an action might be understood as expressing thoughts the *expressions* of which the agent was unaware.

---

[7] Action may be deliberate without being planned, or Collingwood could not, as he does, represent theorizing itself as a re-enactively understandable activity. Planning is not the inside of implementation, but an activity with its own outside. But actions need not even be deliberate to be understandable; e.g. they can be impulsive, or thoughtless (in an ordinary sense), and still express explanatory thoughts. Thus it is no criticism of Collingwood when Walsh points out that action of interest to historians is often done 'on the spur of the moment' ('The Character', 55).

§ 3. *The Assumption of Rationality*

If Collingwood, at his best, did not over-intellectualize the subject-matter of history, did he at any rate over-rationalize it? Finding a past action understandable, he tells us, requires the discovery of the agent's reasons for doing it (*IH* 19, 283). And these must really be reasons; the practical argument into which they enter, and which the action will be interpreted as expressing, must be re-thinkable, i.e. must be found to be sound. But if it is only upon this condition that historians can understand their subject-matter, say many of Collingwood's critics, then his theory of history is surely very inadequate.[8] For it either assumes that people act much more rationally than it is plausible to believe they do, or it excludes from the subject-matter of history much of what normally engages the attention of historians.

As in the case of his alleged intellectualism, Collingwood seems at times not quite to have made up his mind on the question of how far human rationality has to be assumed in claiming historical understanding. On the one hand, he commends Hegel for having applied the 'very fertile and valuable principle' that 'every historical character in every historical situation thinks and acts as rationally as that person in that situation *can* think and act'; and he brands the attitude of Enlightenment historians to the past as 'unhistorical' because they assumed the irrationality of all earlier times (*IH* 116, 77–8).[9] And having noted that 'certain historians, sometimes whole generations of historians, find in certain periods of history nothing intelligible, and call them dark ages', he observes that 'such phrases tell us nothing about those ages themselves, though they tell us a great deal about the persons who use them, namely, that they are unable to re-think the thoughts which were fundamental to their life' (*IH* 218).[10] On the other hand, in

---

[8] See e.g. Walsh, 'The Character', 55; Atkinson, *KEH* 26; C. K. Grant, 'Collingwood's Theory of Historical Knowledge', *Renaissance and Modern Studies*, 1 (1957), 69, 74. For contrary views, see D. A. White, 'Imagination and Description: Collingwood and the Historical Consciousness', *Clio*, 1 (1972), 16–17; Taylor, *Bibliography*, 235.

[9] Elsewhere Collingwood says that historians study 'rational activity' (*IH* 316) or 'rational life' (*IH* 115); or 'human reason' (*IH* 78), and that their aim is 'to show the rationality of that which is explained (*L26* 402).

[10] This position is prefigured in THC 87–8, and *L28* 470 n. 16; and is implicit in Collingwood's blaming historians, not the agents, for the difficulty of discovering the policies of certain early Roman emperors (*IH* 310).

comparing human and animal behaviour, Collingwood declares, after observing that rationality is 'a matter of degree', that it is 'only by fits and starts, in a flickering and dubious manner, that human beings are rational at all' (*IH* 227); and when discussing Kant's view of history, he warns that, while human rationality comes into existence in the course of history, human irrationality does not thereby disappear (*IH* 104). One of his chief criticisms of Greco-Roman historiography, a criticism over and above the charge that it is too intellectualistic, is that it is 'based on the idea of man as essentially a rational animal'. This, he says, is 'a naïve idea which takes no account of certain important regions in moral experience' (*IH* 41).[11]

Two distinctions need to be borne in mind in considering how such remarks should be interpreted, and in deciding how restrictive Collingwood's theory really is in this regard. The first is between what might be called objective and subjective rationality, the second between assuming an agent's rationality and discovering it.

With regard to the first distinction, the historian, in claiming to understand an action, necessarily claims to find it rational in the sense of viewing its implicit argument as sound. But since that argument derives its conclusions from beliefs of the agent which may have been quite erroneous, and takes account of whatever purposes the agent in fact had, no matter how foolish or even monstrous they may have been, the claim to understand the action by grasping the soundness of its argument is clearly compatible with the judgment that, objectively speaking, the action is very irrational indeed. There is no reason to think that Collingwood associates understanding actions with finding them objectively rational. On his view, historical understanding is always to be sought from the agent's point of view, and entails only the subjective rationality of the agent. Collingwood's insistence, in *The Idea of History*, on the historian's envisaging the situation as the agent saw it is conclusive on this point. And even in passages like the one which hails Hegel's 'fertile principle', there is a hint of the relevant limitation. Men are said to act only as rationally as it is possible for men *in their situation* to act. And since, according to

[11] Van der Dussen believes that Collingwood's reputation for excessive rationalism derives from his critics paying too much attention to what he said in *IH*; but if so, there seems to be much in it that ought to have given them pause (*HS* 259).

Collingwood, a person's situation, when deciding how to act, is the one he thinks he is in, the rationality involved would be of the subjective sort.[12]

It is something of a curiosity that a positivist like Hempel, who would not, in general, agree with Collingwood's account of historical understanding, should accept something like the present claim as true of at least a limited class of explanations, while Donagan, one of Collingwood's chief apologists, should at least seem to reject it. Hempel agrees that there is a special kind of action explanation which requires the citation of the agent's reasons for acting, stipulating only that an explanation of this kind remains incomplete unless the historian is prepared to include in it an assertion that the agent is rational.[13] By this he means that he has a disposition to do the rational thing, whatever that may be in the circumstances. One chief function of the explanation is therefore to make clear what was the rational thing to do in those circumstances. In 'The Popper-Hempel Theory Reconsidered', Donagan denies that an explanation need show the rationality of an action. It is enough for understanding, he says, that it be shown to be 'intelligible'.[14] I find this contention puzzling, the more so when taken in conjunction with Donagan's further claim that what has to be shown in explaining an action is not good reasons, but the reasons on which the agent actually chose to act. This suggests that an action might be made understandable by citing an agent's reasons for doing what he did even where he is conceded to have had, and knew that he had, better reasons for acting otherwise. I cannot give a sense to this possibility.

Turning to the other distinction which needs to be kept in mind, the distinction between assuming and discovering an agent's rationality, it has already been allowed that understanding an action, on Collingwood's theory, entails finding it subjectively rational. But that is not to *assume* that it is rational, even subjectively.[15] The vindication of a claim to have found an action

---

[12] 'Subjective' rationality does not mean whatever the agent happens to think is rational, but what is rational for him in view of his own beliefs and goals (his 'point of view'), this being something for the *historian* to judge.

[13] Hempel, 'Rational Action', 10, 12.

[14] Donagan, 'Popper-Hempel', 155. Rex Martin concurs (*HE* 235 n. 10).

[15] Both van der Dussen (*HS* 273) and Saari (*Re-enactment*, 19), clearly with some warrant, represent Collingwood as assuming rationality (see also *EPM* 226).

subjectively rational requires neither the assumption that all men are subjectively rational, nor the assumption that the particular agent under study is always subjectively rational. It is only if one adds to Collingwood's conceptual thesis that understanding involves recognizing rationality, the metaphysical thesis that all actions are, in principle, understandable in this sense, that one can speak of making an assumption of rationality. The first position doesn't require the second; and the second is dubious, to say the least.

It isn't easy, however, to determine exactly where Collingwood stands on this matter. His saying from time to time that historians study rational activity could simply mean that they study it wherever they find it. But he does sometimes appear to assert the metaphysical thesis. It is hard to interpret in any other way, for example, his assault on historians who claim to discover dark ages: 'It is the historian himself who stands at the bar of judgement', he says, 'and there reveals his own mind in its strength and weakness, its virtues and its vices' (*IH* 219). (Incongruously, he seems to allow that *historians*, if not historical agents, may sometimes be subjectively irrational.) What he says about Hegel's fertile principle could perhaps be interpreted as enunciating no more than a heuristic principle.[16] But it is unlikely that he intends only the admonition that, no matter how unpromising an action may seem at the outset, it is always worth looking for subjective rationality in it. I offer this as a criticism of Collingwood; but many of those who object to what they see as his overly rationalistic view of human nature might find that it puts them on his side. For it is unlikely that many of those who charge him with excessive rationalism want to deny that people generally see good reasons from their own point of view for doing what they do. When Collingwood is called too rationalistic, it is more often in the mistaken belief that he assumes objective rationality, or that he takes much too calculating a view of human decision (a charge already dealt with in § 2), or that he neglects human emotions (a question to be considered in § 4).

What kinds of case might the metaphysical assumption of subjective rationality improperly rule out? The following four

---

[16] This principle might be supported by Collingwood's even weaker rationalist claim that 'every individual human being is an animal *capable* of reason' (*IH* 42)— emphasis added.

kinds (by no means an exhaustive list) might be seen as raising difficulties at any rate for any claim to explain something done in a straightforwardly Collingwoodian way.

The first kind of case might be called confused action. Collingwoodian understanding depends upon interpreting what someone does as expressing a sound practical argument. If the agent was so confused that he failed to act in accordance with such an argument, then, *ex hypothesi*, his action cannot be understood in the re-enactive way. Making a logical error—miscalculating the course of action that one's own purposes and beliefs required—would be a case in point. For one cannot re-enactively understand an action as an expression of an invalid argument. However, it is easy to exaggerate the extent to which this sort of possibility reduces the scope of Collingwood's theory. For even when an action is done in error, there will probably be something in it which is rationally explicable from the agent's point of view.[17] An illustration might be my own attempt to account for Collingwood's apparently falling into a radically intellectualist view of action explanation which is incompatible with his basic position. I identified his error as wrongly treating the term 'reflective' as if it were being used consistently in the technical sense which he began by assigning to it. This could be regarded, at the same time, as finding subjective rationality in what is said in the latter half of 'The Subject-matter of History'. Much depends on how what is to be explained is characterized. If what Collingwood did is described as 'mistakenly conflating two senses of the term reflective', for example, then no explanation in terms of agent's reasons is possible, for one cannot have a good reason for making a mistake. If what was done is explicable at all under that description, it will have to be explained in another, and perhaps nomological, way.[18] Whether it would then count as an action for Collingwood is perhaps questionable, since one does not commit

[17] This seems to be Debbins's point in maintaining that 'all so-called irrational actions contain an element of reason' (*EPH*, p. xxiii); and perhaps Collingwood's, too, when he insists that 'there must be a "reason" for an error', any action applying 'a positive principle', it being erroneous only in failing 'to apply also some further principle' (L26 345).

[18] An example might be Knox's explaining Collingwood's alleged lapse into extreme historicism after 1936 by reference to his deteriorating health—although, as van der Dussen rightly observes, bad health would hardly explain why he lapsed into this rather than into some other erroneous view (*HS* 4–5).

an error 'on purpose'. The objection to his position might then be to his apparently limiting the concerns of historians to confusion-free activities.

A second kind of case that raises some problems for Collingwood's theory I'll call an inadvertency. By this I mean a kind in which there is a discrepancy between what the agent was trying to do and what he succeeded in doing. Let us suppose that a back-bencher on the Government side of the House of Commons gives a maiden speech in support of his party's policies which is so ill-conceived that the Government in consequence falls. What the unfortunate member did could be described, and will doubtless be described by many of his colleagues, as 'bringing down the Government'. However, one can hardly ask for an explanation of his action in the sense of making clear his reasons for bringing down the Government, since that is not at all what he was trying to accomplish. Yet, even more obviously than in the first case, there is something in what he did that may be quite explicable in the Collingwoodian way: for example, his giving the kind of speech he did. The member may even complain that giving that speech is what he actually did, the fall of the Government being no more than an unintended consequence of it.[19] But it is normal practice for historians, as well as for parliamentarians, to incorporate into their characterizations of actions what, if the latter were characterized differently, but still truly, might instead be called consequences of what was done. Since the appropriateness of such incorporation sometimes derives from the degree to which the agents can be held responsible for what eventuated, one might have expected this aspect of the concept of human action to have caught Collingwood's interest more than it seems to have done. What is important here, however, is that, although there may always be something about an inadvertency which can be explained in the Collingwoodian way, what was done may have no Collingwoodian explanation under the description which historians are most likely to apply to it.

Inadvertencies are actions which are characterized in such a way as to include unintended consequences of what the agent did, conceived under another description. Achievements—a third, if related, kind of case—present similar problems for

[19] See § 6 for a related kind of case: unintended 'emergent' qualities of works of art.

any straightforward application of the Collingwoodian view of understanding, since these are (generally) actions which may be characterized in ways which incorporate intended consequences. Collingwood leaves no doubt that he considers it part of the historian's task to explain both successes and failures, conceived as such (*IH* 237; *A* 128).[20] 'What lunatic idea of history is this', he exclaims in the *Autobiography*, 'which would imply that it is history that Phormio rowed around the Corinthians, but not that he beat the Corinthians by doing it' (*A* 72). But Phormio's *beating* the Corinthians, if that is what he is said to have done, cannot be explained by reference to his reasons for acting. It may perhaps be possible, in special circumstances, to ask for a person's reasons for winning—for example, when a jockey wins a race which he has been instructed to lose. And it may often be possible to explain, at least in part, why people achieved certain things by offering Collingwoodian explanations of actions of other agents which helped to make the achievements possible—in Phormio's case, perhaps the tactics of the Corinthians. Something analogous could often be said, however, of the non-rational behaviour of other agents, or of physical circumstances like the storm which helped the English defeat the Spanish Armada, in which case the explanation will go beyond even the reasons attributable to other agents. It thus seems unlikely that a purely Collingwoodian explanation of an achievement, characterized as such, would often be possible. One kind of response to this problem might be to concede (although thereby departing radically from the ordinary usage of historians) that what can be explained in the re-enactive way is never an agent's actual performance, but only his decision to act. Collingwood himself occasionally seems prepared to adopt this position, as when he observes that, if a chess player's move is 'due to an oversight', then 'the best you can do is to understand what he meant, but failed to achieve' (L28 475).

Still a fourth kind of case that to some extent escapes the Collingwoodian model, as stated, is that of arbitrary action,

[20] In the *Autobiography*, Collingwood argues, dubiously, that only successful action can be understood by historians, because what an agent tried but failed to achieve cannot be reconstructed from evidence (*A* 69–70). The discussion of this claim, initiated by J. W. N. Watkins ('On Explaining Disaster', *Listener*, 10 January 1963, 69–70), has been taken further recently by Simissen ('On Understanding Disaster').

where by this I mean action for no reason, or for insufficient reason.[21] *Ex hypothesi*, if someone chooses to do what he did for no reason, or for insufficient reason, there is no valid practical argument to be reconstructed which will explain why he did it. As in the previous cases, a Collingwoodian explanation might sometimes be given of an action which is arbitrary under one description but not arbitrary under another. For example, although a general may have had no reasons for sending in the particular cavalry unit he did at a certain point in a battle, he may have had very good reasons for sending in cavalry at all. Collingwood himself notes that a person cannot set out to perform an action characterized down to its last detail (*NL* 96, 108).[22] But that still falls short of recognizing the present problem, which is that historians may raise 'why' questions about past actions characterized in such a way that there are no agents' reasons to be discovered, the agents having had no reasons for performing them as characterized. In commenting on Collingwood's view of action, Donagan has maintained that the explanation of an agent's purposes in terms of higher purposes eventually comes to an end (*LPC* 230).[23] If that is so, an action characterized in terms of the highest purpose an agent had in performing it would also necessarily be inexplicable in the Collingwoodian way because it would necessarily be arbitrary as characterized. And as Donagan points out, a 'highest purpose' might sometimes be as low as a decision to play a game of golf. Donagan prefers to say that action so conceived can only be explained by saying: 'That is what he chose to do.'[24] But that comes to much the same thing as saying that it has no Collingwoodian explanation.[25]

[21] Collingwood accepts the possibility of such action when he observes that, if we write history 'on authority', 'we merely decide to follow A and ignore B for no reason except that we decide to do so', or we give 'an irrelevant reason' (L26 375).

[22] Collingwood applies this doctrine only to utilitarian actions, in all of which he finds an element of 'caprice' (*NL* 108); but the actions which interest historians will generally be of this kind.

[23] See the hierarchy of purposes considered in Ch. 2, § 4.

[24] The same idea is generalized by Collingwood in an early work, when he says that 'an act of will is its own explanation' ('The Devil', 219).

[25] Further cases which raise problems for a Collingwoodian analysis, but which I have not been able to consider here, include systematically deceitful actions (cf. RNI 16), actions done for too many reasons (cf. *A* 120), 'quasi-actions' like neglecting or failing to do something (cf. *IN* 42; *HU* 67), or actions with explanations citing both reasons and natural tendencies (cf. *IH* 227).

§ 4. *Perception, Appetite, Emotion*

The objections to Collingwood's theory of historical understanding as too intellectualistic and too rationalistic charge it with limiting the historian's concerns unjustifiably to actions of certain restricted kinds. The third objection represents it as too narrow in limiting them to human actions at all. In the British Academy lecture, as was pointed out in Chapter 2, Collingwood moves directly from saying that history is about past human affairs to saying that it is about past human actions. And the connected themes that history is a study of actions, and is concerned with thought as expressed in actions, are reiterated throughout *The Idea of History* from the point at which Herodotus is praised for first having made of history, by this emphasis, a truly humanistic study (*IH* 19).

When Collingwood insists that the subject-matter of history is human actions, what sorts of past human experience is he trying to exclude? At one point he mentions 'feeling, sensation, and emotion'; at another, 'immediate experience'; at still another, man's 'animal nature' or his 'natural appetites'; at still another, 'blind forces' in human life (*IH* 205, 216, 231, 306). Such things he is happy to relinquish to the psychologist, the student of 'psyche', not rational mind (*IH* 231). To keep the present discussion manageable, I shall look mainly at what he says about perception, appetite, and emotion, since it is his apparent exclusion of these that has bothered his critics most. As Walsh has observed, it is puzzling that Collingwood should have been willing to admit, as he did, that actions take place 'against a background of feeling and emotion', and still maintain that the historian ought not to be occupied with that background (*IPH* 50). I shall concede that a more serious problem is raised here for Collingwood's view of history than is raised by the first two objections. But I think that, even here, his position can be shown to be less restrictive than his critics often make it out to be.

Collingwood's official reason for excluding perception, appetite, and emotion from the proper subject-matter of history is stated in the following passage, itself so evocative as immediately to raise resistance to the idea that all history is concerned only with thought. 'We shall never know how the flowers smelt in the garden of Epicurus,' he writes, 'or how Nietzsche felt the wind in his hair as he walked on the mountains; we cannot relive the triumph of Archimedes or the bitterness of Marius; but the evidence of what these men thought is in our hands' (*IH* 296). The reason that human experiences of the indicated kinds are to be excluded, it seems, is that they are not re-thinkable. On Collingwood's view, when a past action is to be understood, the historian must literally think what the agent thought, since he must grasp and find valid the practical argument which his action expressed. It makes little sense, however, to speak of grasping the argument expressed by a person's perceptions or feelings; and it hardly seems a necessary condition of understanding them that they be re-perceived or re-felt.

Should we conclude from this, then, that Collingwood categorically excludes such things as perception, appetite, and emotion from the proper concerns of historians? Let us look first at the case of perception. Knowing that Nietzsche felt the wind in his hair cannot mean grasping the argument expressed by his having had that feeling, and need not involve the historian's having a wind-blown feeling too. But that does not mean that it couldn't be discovered, by examining evidence, that Nietzsche felt the wind in his hair; and it is clear that Collingwood himself intends no such thing. He claims constantly to possess evidential knowledge of what past agents perceived through their senses (*RBES* 43; *IN* 176–7); and it would be disastrous for his own theory of historical understanding if he did not, since the practical arguments which historians attribute to agents commonly employ perceptual premisses. Understanding actions by reference to such arguments does not, of course, require the historian's affirmation of the agent's premisses; it requires only his judgment that the latter's practical conclusion follows from them. Attributing the premisses, however, entails claiming to know how the agent perceived his situation. And even as elementary a perceptual experience as Nietzsche's feeling the wind in his hair could be what such a premiss reports. More likely ones might be Caesar's perception of the state of the English Channel on the eve of his invasion of Britain, or the perceptions of Roman road builders of the contours of the British landscape.

One of Collingwood's objects in the passage cited is doubtless to warn readers (as he does at other points) against thinking that historical reasoning from evidence can recapture the immediacy of past experiences, the private mental process which an agent actually went through.[26] And this is acceptable enough. However, when he contrasts thought with other aspects of mentality as alone being of historical interest, he may often give the impression of maintaining more. Troublesome in this connection is a certain looseness in the way he uses the term 'feeling'. He often uses it in a technical sense of his own to mean simply a flow of uninterpreted experience, something to be 'enjoyed' but not 'known' (*IH* 293, 306). But he also means by it, as ordinary English permits, having determinate sensations, experiencing determinate desires, suffering determinate emotions, or even thinking that something is the case.[27] Clearly, what will be relevant to a re-enactive understanding of something done is not an immediate awareness of the agent's feelings in Collingwood's primitive sense, but knowledge that he had a feeling of a certain kind—a point which Collingwood sometimes puts rather awkwardly by saying that what historians can recover is not past experiences, but only propositions about them (*NL* 34). What he means by excluding 'feeling' from the subject-matter of history is also made more obscure, at times, by his tendency (noted in Chapter 2, note 9) to talk about what can be known, when what he really has in mind is what can be re-enactively understood.

Sense perception is therefore admitted by Collingwood to the subject-matter of history at least in the sense that knowledge of what agents perceived may be a necessary ingredient in a re-enactive understanding of what they did. A different set of questions is raised when he maintains that perception is not what historical inquiry is *about*, although the central issue is much the same. Collingwood insists that anyone who set out to write a history of human perception 'would find nothing to write about' (*IH* 307). He supports this contention by observing that if different peoples in the past have in fact perceived in different ways—he offers 'second sight or the power of seeing ghosts' as conceivable examples (*IH* 308)—no historical accounts of such things will be

---

[26] Collingwood speaks loosely when he describes a diary or memoir as a 'record of immediate experience with its flow of sensations and feelings, faithfully preserved' (*IH* 304). Sensations could be recorded only as conceptualized or interpreted, not as immediate experiences.

[27] He mentions a need to understand what people 'felt' about the religion they practised (*IH* 132), and criticizes Spengler for not knowing what classical man 'felt' about his life (*SHC* 71).

possible because we shall be unable to re-enact the relevant experiences at will. It is a little strange to find Collingwood talking here of a subject-matter being provided for history by different ways of perceiving rather than by the perceiving of different things by different people at different times. But either way, the denial that perception could be the focus of historical interest rests upon a denial that it is re-enactable.

That denial has been questioned by some commentators on the ground that, although Collingwood sometimes contrasts perception with thought, he also shows perception to be itself an elementary form of thought, this raising the question whether it might not be re-enactable after all (*IH* 283; *L28* 444–5). Mink has argued that, on Collingwood's view of mind, anything above the level of sheer sentience is in fact re-enactable (*HU* 234).[28] However, it is not very plausible to maintain that perception itself is re-enactable, unless we have in mind a sense in which it shades into interpretation—as when Collingwood speaks of a present object being 'perceived' (by virtue of historical thinking) as a thirteenth-century charter (*NAPH* 50), or when historians write, say, of the perception of certain women in colonial New England as witches. It may be suspected, furthermore, that the idea that perception is re-enactable owes something to a confusion between regarding something as itself re-enactable and holding it to be an element— a premiss—in a re-enactment. If perceptions are not themselves re-enactable, however, and if some of them are of interest to historians, then any explanations which are offered of them will have to be nomological. To that extent, at least, a limit has to be recognized here to the applicability of Collingwood's theory of understanding as re-enactment, a limit which many of his pronouncements certainly give the appearance of ignoring.

Like perceptions, human appetites will presumably be relevant to historians' concerns, on Collingwood's theory, whenever reference to them is required for the re-enactment of explanatory thoughts expressed in actions. But Collingwood's apparent contention that such things are of no interest to historians in themselves is much more difficult to make plausible than was his similar claim with regard to perception. In a notorious statement

[28] Mark Olsen makes a similar claim in 'The Re-thinking of History: Comments on Collingwood's Theory of Historical Understanding', *Register*, 6 (1985), 10 (cited hereafter as 'Rethinking of History').

of his position that 'natural appetites' form no part of history's subject-matter, Collingwood declares roundly that 'the historian is not interested in the fact that men eat and sleep and make love' (*IH* 216). Not just philosophers, but historians, too—for example, D. H. Fischer—have complained that Collingwood here gets the interests of historians seriously wrong.[29] In developing this theme, he sometimes manages, furthermore, to make the study of history appear a rather callous affair. Thus, in a passage which Marwick has called 'absolute rubbish', he contends that what military history is about is not 'weary marches in heat or cold, or the thrills and chills of battle or the long agony of wounded men', but 'plans and counter-plans', issues of strategy and tactics (*A* 110).[30] The impression of withdrawal from genuine human concerns which this is bound to give is reinforced when, in another context, Collingwood provocatively maintains that it 'makes no difference to an historian, as an historian, that there should be no food in a poor man's house', or that his children should suffer 'unsatisfied hunger' or have 'empty bellies and wizened limbs' (*IH* 315–16). What is relevant, he says, is only what people thought and did about such things.

In fact, the question what history is, or should be, chiefly about is one on which Collingwood could hardly have expected complete agreement, even on his own principles. As he points out in the 'Preliminary Discussion' to his lectures of 1926, successive generations of historians (and he might as well have said historians of the same generation) have differed substantially about which aspects of past human affairs are most worthy of their consideration, adding that decisions on such matters follow 'arbitrary conventions' (L27 356). He might better have said, and does implicitly say elsewhere, that they involve value judgments (*IH* 180; CHBI 11). It seems apposite, therefore, to remark that his own pronouncements about history's proper subject-matter have appeared to many to betray an overvaluation of those aspects of human life which have been the traditional focus of interest in political, military, and diplomatic history.[31] It seems

---

[29] *Historians' Fallacies* (London, 1971), 196.

[30] Marwick, *Nature of History*, 83.

[31] Yet Collingwood himself made significant contributions to the cultural, economic, social, and demographic history of Roman Britain (see e.g. *RBES* 175 ff.; *A* 134 ff.; 'Roman Britain' in Tenney Frank (ed.), *An Economic Survey of Ancient Rome*, iii (London, 1937), 1–118).

fair to say, too, with W. B. Gallie, that Collingwood's views on
what should be considered subject-matter for history often
suggest an excessively 'activist' attitude to human life generally—
as if problem-solving were the only kind of human experience
that really mattered—a tendency which Gallie sees reflected
also in his insistence that problem-solving (perhaps by contrast
with narrative-following) is the essence of historical thinking.[32]
But, to the extent that this emphasis is rejected—to the extent that
human appetites, and perhaps also human sufferings and
endurings, are conceded to be, in their own right, appropriate
subject-matter for history—a further limit to the applicability
of Collingwood's theory of historical understanding has to be
recognized.[33]

Collingwood's apparent exclusion of emotions from the subject-matter of history raises similar, but also further, questions. As
Mink has noted, he frequently talks of emotion as if it were a kind
of feeling or sensation (*MHD* 164).[34] Even as such, he ought to
have seen it as belonging to history's subject-matter to the extent
that it enters into the explanation of actions. But if, by emotions,
he means something like the triumph of Archimedes or the bitterness of Marius, he ought also, on his own principles, to have
considered expressions of emotion as deserving of study by historians in their own right. For behind his identification of human
actions as subject-matter for history is a larger claim: that history
is the study, and the only proper study, of rational mind. And it
appears that, unlike perception and the grosser forms of human
appetite, we have to understand such things as triumph, bitterness, anger, love, jealousy, as we do actions, at least partly by
reference to their rationale. It makes sense, for example, to ask
why a person was triumphant or bitter, expecting in reply, not a

[32] Gallie, *PHU* 17. As Collingwood puts it: 'The business of the historian is to
discover what problems confronted men in the past, and how they solved them'
(THC 85), an emphasis seen by Gardiner as recommending a certain 'conceptual
framework' to historians ('Historical Understanding', 277–8).

[33] As will be noted with regard to emotions, a more extended treatment might
require recognition of a scale (as Collingwood himself points out) ranging from
the grossest of bodily appetites, through various levels of desire, to something like
decision and will, a scale on which reason increasingly appears.

[34] Collingwood lumps emotion with feeling and sensation (*IH* 205), contrasts it
with reason and thought (*IH* 297; *EM* 167), specifically excludes it from history as
bound up with bodily life (*IH* 304), and consigns it, with sensation, to the atten-
tions of psychologists (*EM* 141).

set of antecedent conditions and laws under which the occurrence of the emotion can be subsumed, but a reason for being triumphant or bitter, with reference to which the appropriateness of the agent's being so can be judged.

Curiously enough, as Donagan has noted, Collingwood himself makes essentially this point in one of his earlier works when criticizing William James's *Varieties of Religious Experience* (*LPC* 161–2). He charges that James, in his comparative study of various sorts of religious states and occurrences, tries to treat his subject-matter, including what he calls the religious emotions, as if they were natural facts. When he considers a specifically religious kind of happiness, for example, he takes no account of what makes it specifically religious—i.e. of what it is happiness in. To study mind in this way, complains Collingwood, is not to treat it as mind. We might therefore expect him similarly to insist that the triumph of Archimedes was not just a state of triumph, but a rationally comprehensible response to a scientific experience, as the bitterness of Marius was to a political one. But he often gives a contrary impression by the way he refers to the emotions. Thus, in 'History as Re-enactment of Past Experience', when contrasting the re-enactability of thought with the non-re-enactability of immediate experience, and needing an illustration, he seizes upon the emotion of anger. When I now 'think of the anger I once felt', he says, 'the actual past anger of which I am thinking is past and gone; that does not reappear, the stream of immediate experience has carried it away for ever' (*IH* 293). This could perhaps be interpreted as meaning only that past anger, like any other human experience, including thinking itself, cannot be recovered in its immediacy. But one would scarcely conclude from anything which Collingwood says at this point that, on his view, anger could in any sense or degree be re-enacted.

There are a number of other passages in which Collingwood seems on the verge of saying that emotions are re-enactable. He gets close to doing so in discussing the dual emphasis on reason and passion in Hegel's view of history. He writes: 'To prove, therefore, that someone acted in a certain way from passion—e.g. a judge sentencing a criminal in a fit of anger or a statesman overriding opposition from motives of ambition—is not to prove that he did not act rationally; for the judge's sentence or the statesman's policy may be a just or wise one notwithstanding this passionate element in its execution' (*IH* 116). However, this still doesn't go much beyond saying that the presence of anger is *compatible* with an action's being understood by reference to reasons of the agent apart from the anger itself. Collingwood goes somewhat further in a passage criticizing Dilthey for holding that emotions require psychological explanation in the end. Suppose, he says, that I am now 'experiencing an immediate feeling of discomfort', and I 'ask myself why I have this feeling. I may answer that question by reflecting that this morning I received a letter criticizing my conduct in what seems to me a valid and unanswerable manner. Here I am not making psychological generalizations; I am recognizing in its detail a certain individual event or series of events, which are already present to my consciousness as a feeling of discomfort or dissatisfaction with myself.'[35] He continues: 'To understand that feeling is to recognize it as the outcome of a certain historical process. Here the self-understanding of my mind is nothing else than historical knowledge' (*IH* 174). Since, for Collingwood, an historical process is a rational process, a thought process, this is tantamount to asserting the re-thinkability of the emotion of chagrin.[36] Unfortunately, the way in which actions expressing emotion should be explained in historical inquiry is not further clarified.

The main difficulty about declaring emotions to be re-enactable, if our model is the way we understand something like Caesar's crossing of the Rubicon, is the following. When reasons for acting are attributed to an agent, what is explained includes his decision to act in a certain way. When reasons for someone being angry or jealous are cited, there is no decision to do anything; there is simply the fact that the agent experiences the emotion. The element of will is missing. A person may, of course, express anger or jealousy by actions which are done on purpose—Collingwood instances a person expressing hatred of another by damaging something which he has made in the belief that this will hurt him.[37] One does not, however, become angry or jealous

---

[35] A feeling of discomfort suggests something non-rational; a feeling of dissatisfaction something that could be experienced only by a rational agent.

[36] One can say 'I have a good reason to be chagrined' (or angry, or bitter, or dissatisfied, or even thrilled), but not 'I have a good reason to perceive a chair before me', and probably not 'I have a good reason to be in a blind passion'.

[37] 'Magic', 9.

'on purpose'.[38] Yet explaining the experiencing of an emotion is not like explaining someone's being in a certain bodily state by reference to antecedent conditions and laws. The explanation of emotion thus seems to fall somewhere between the fully re-enactive and the nomological.[39] To make things even more difficult, different emotions appear to occupy different points on a scale, with some, like fear, often being explicable almost entirely by reference to natural causes (such as a loud noise), while others, like jealousy, may be incomprehensible, in most cases, without reference to quite sophisticated rational considerations.

There are problems, too, about saying, without qualification, that reference to emotions can be elements in re-enactive explanations of actions. When beliefs or desires are said to explain actions, they are formulable as premisses of a practical argument attributable to the agent. But the fact that an agent was experiencing a certain emotion cannot be transmuted so easily into a premiss of such an argument. 'He hated him' may suggest 'He wanted him dead', which could function as such a premiss, but the two assertions are not equivalent. Collingwood sometimes complicates things further by speaking of actions not as expressing emotion, but as carrying an emotional 'charge' (*PA* 266–7) or as done with emotional 'heat' (L28 447). This suggests that explanations referring to emotions can be 'mixed' in the puzzling sense of conflating two kinds of thinking which are not obviously compatible, for it is difficult to see any difference, so far as implied practical argument is concerned, between, say, killing someone cold-bloodedly for gain and doing the same thing, for the same reason, while taking great satisfaction in it, i.e. doing it with emotion. Historians do give such 'mixed' explanations, however; and Collingwood himself appears to have a possible one in view when he speaks of an historian having to decide, with regard to

[38] We can, it is true, to some degree cultivate or evoke emotions, but what is then re-enactively explicable will be the cultivating or evoking. On this, see C. B. McCullagh, 'The Rationality of Emotions and of Emotional Behaviour', *Australasian Journal of Philosophy*, 68 (1990), 47 ff.

[39] The nomological is at least suggested when Collingwood refers to one person 'infecting' another with fear (*NL* 143). And we often speak of being 'overcome' by emotions. Small wonder therefore that there have been disagreements over Collingwood's views on the re-enactability of the emotions, Mink and Taylor holding that, as aspects of thought, they are fully re-enactable (*HU* 226; *Bibliography*, 205), and Walsh and Saari that, as forms of immediate experience, they are not re-enactable at all ('Collingwood's Philosophy of History', 157; *Re-enactment*, 42).

the rise of nationalism, 'how much was due to popular emotion, how much to economic forces, how much to deliberate policy' (*IH* 132).

The problems that arise in connection with explanation both of and by the emotions thus suggest, even more than does what was said about perception and appetite, a need not only to supplement the Collingwoodian account of historical understanding as exclusively re-enactive, but also to revise it to some extent. Since some emotions which are of interest to historians, like fear or anger, may be explicable, or partially explicable, by reference to what Collingwood would call natural causation, a place has again to be accorded to some nomological explanation in history (although, again, what is explained will not be action). And since the idea of re-enactment as applied to the explanation of action does not fit very well what it seems necessary to say about rationally comprehensible emotional states, some revision of the idea of re-enactive understanding itself also seems to be called for. Perhaps, following Saari, we may have to regard that idea as having a 'family' of related but not identical meanings (further reasons for saying this will appear in § 6).[40] But Collingwood himself offers little guidance on these matters. This is the more unfortunate because, as he seems not to have noticed, some of the same problems arise with regard to the explanation of beliefs (*IH* 215, 283). For beliefs, too, can sometimes be explained rationally and sometimes not, and no more than emotions can they be regarded, at any rate straightforwardly, as expressions of will.

§ 5. *The History of Art*

I have argued that, although Collingwood's re-enactment theory fails to apply to some of the things which historians claim to understand, it is not, as some have maintained, completely inapplicable to non-reflective, irrational, and emotional actions. In Chapter 5, I shall go on to consider the charges that it ignores the role played by physical conditions in the historical process, and that it insufficiently recognizes the social dimension of the past.

[40] Saari, *Re-enactment*, 33.

But before doing that, I should like to look briefly, at two problems of a different but related sort which have sometimes been raised for Collingwood's theory, and on which he himself had some interesting, if controversial, things to say. In the present section, I shall ask how far the idea of re-enactment, as I have explicated it, can plausibly be thought to apply to history of art, given the account which Collingwood himself offers of special problems which arise for this branch of history. In the final section, I shall ask about the relevance of that idea to the history of philosophy, and more particularly to the history of metaphysics as Collingwood conceived the latter.[41]

A crucial problem for any attempt to apply the idea of re-enactive understanding to the history of art is stated by Collingwood himself in 'The Subject-matter of History' as follows. He notes that, although art, like politics, warfare, economics, science, or religion, is a problem-solving activity, it is not one whose problems can be expressed before their solutions are discovered (*IH* 314; *PA* 29). For art, he holds, is the expression of the artist's immediate experience; and if it were known what that experience amounted to in advance of the expression given to it in the work of art, the artistic task would already be accomplished. It would seem to follow from this not only that a work of art cannot be seen as a solution to a problem which could have been articulated in advance, but that it cannot be seen, even in retrospect, as the solution of an independently articulable problem at all. The conclusion which Collingwood draws is that the history of art can only be a history of artistic achievements, not of artistic problems. And this appears equivalent to saying that it cannot be an account which makes understandable the way successive artistic problems have been resolved. In consequence, it seems impossible to bring the history of art under the general conception of history as a re-enactment of past thought, at any rate as we have been conceiving it. It cannot be represented as the discerning of valid practical arguments, implicit in the performance of actions, which link something done with agents' reasons for doing it.

---

[41] Collingwood makes these issues the more important for an appraisal of his position by criticizing Hegel for limiting history to 'objective mind', i.e. to past politics, when its true subject-matter, as Hegel's own practice shows, is 'absolute mind', i.e. history of art, religion, and philosophy (*IH* 121).

It therefore comes as a surprise that, neither in the indicated section of *The Idea of History*, nor at any other point, does Collingwood draw the further conclusion that the history of art is either a defective form of history, judged by his own theory of what constitutes historical understanding, or that art is a human activity of such vital concern to historians that the original conception of such understanding must be expanded to accommodate it. The first alternative may seem the more plausible one. This would amount to saying that all we can hope for in history of art is a description of selected works, supplemented perhaps by some background information about the circumstances of their production and how they were regarded in their own day or subsequently—perhaps all that many would in fact expect of a history of art. Yet Collingwood frequently talks as if he is quite willing to assign to the art historian the task of explaining re-enactively why particular works of art were produced by particular individuals or groups at certain times and places.[42]

Thus, in a paper of 1929, he tells us that the development of architecture from Roman to Romanesque to Gothic has a 'logical and rational character', this illustrating the thesis that in history 'every change occurs for a sufficient reason' (PP 111). In comparing Michelangelo and Thorwaldsen as sculptors, he observes that their work cannot be properly understood until we grasp the fact that they were 'not trying to do the same thing', this at least suggesting that we should understand their works by reference to their differing intentions, just as we understand the practical activities of generals and statesmen by reference to their intentions (THC 82). Of Smollett he remarks that he 'knew enough about the Middle Ages to know that they had a taste in buildings very different from his own [but] not enough to see why they had that taste' (THC 88), this implying that the aim of an historian of architecture should be to understand taste, presumably from the 'inside'.[43] And he explicitly associates re-enactive understanding with art history when he laments that, although we may believe

[42] What we get out of both music and thought, he says, is 'something which we have to reconstruct in our own minds' (PA 141). And the function of an artist's audience (he might as well have said 'of his historian') 'is not passively to accept his work, but to do it over again for themselves' (PA 315).

[43] Olsen contends, in criticism of Collingwood, that, in art history, 'the distinction between the inside and the outside of an action dissolves, for the idea of the painting and the painting itself is the same thing' ('Re-thinking of History', 16).

(on testimony) that there were great painters among the ancient Greeks, this cannot be called historical knowledge because, their works having perished, 'we have no means of reliving in our own minds their artistic experience' (*IH* 202). He adds that we have such means in the case of Greek sculptors because their works have survived and can become objects of present aesthetic appreciation. It is not easy to see how Collingwood can think it justifiable to make claims like these, given what he says about the impossibility of articulating artistic problems.

It is noticeable that, in his allusions to the possibility of explanation in art history, Collingwood seldom points to specific reasons why he thinks the artists he mentions produced just the works of art they did. And when he does state or hint at such reasons, they are frequently of the wrong kind to make what was done understandable as an *aesthetic* activity. In the case of the architectural transition which he cites, for example, he observes that 'the reason why people stopped building Norman and began building Gothic' was that they 'wanted a more favourable ratio of strength to weight', this offering what he himself characterizes as an engineering rather than an aesthetic reason (PP 109).[44] He records his puzzlement about Scott's motives in designing the Albert Memorial, which, judged aesthetically, he finds positively 'verminous' (*A* 29); but he apparently concludes that it was not really intended as a work of art, but rather as something to stir patriotic emotions—what he elsewhere calls a work of 'magic' (*PA* 65 ff.). And his well-known account of the survival of Celtic art under the Romans, which may seem to have implications for his view of art history, does not in fact try to make it understandable why Celtic artists produced the kind of works they did, but only how it was possible for their creative traditions to survive underground during an alien occupation (*A* 137 ff.).

Even when Collingwood depicts artists as having had problems and as having responded to them, the problems are characterized in such general terms as to be unhelpful for our present

---

[44] Collingwood warns against confusing truly aesthetic problems with problems of aesthetic technique—technique being something which one artist can learn from another (e.g. Beethoven from Mozart). The artistic task is not 'mastering technical processes' but 'using them to express the artist's experience and give it reflective form' (*IH* 330–1). Mink nevertheless interprets Collingwood as holding that there can only be a history of problems of artistic technique, not of artistic expression (*MHD* 166).

concern.[45] Thus the problem of Roman artists in the Romano-British period is contrasted with that of Celtic ones by remarking that, because the aesthetic imagination of the Romans was outward-looking, their aim in art was to represent things, while because that of the Celts was inward-looking, it sought to express itself in symbolic, non-representational ways (*RBES* 259). But such a view of two groups of artists working within two quite different styles, these placing opposite limitations on their creativity, hardly begins to explain why they produced the particular works of art they did: why the Romans, for example, produced heads of emperors, and the Celts the Bath Gorgon. In fact, in discussing cases, Collingwood sometimes falls back upon vaguely nomological explanation or naturalistic metaphor. For example, he remarks 'a constant tendency in the mind of the Celtic artist that pushes him in the direction of the S-shaped or serpentine curve' (*RB* 113). He attributes the 'dull and clumsy' imitation of Roman traditions by some Celtic artists to a cultural 'vortex' into which 'fragments' of alien traditions were 'sucked' during the occupation (*RBES* 260). And, switching from physical to biological images, he calls the Bath Gorgon the 'first cross' between imported approaches to stone-cutting in Britain and a native tradition of decorative design, the 'hybrid' eventually proving 'infertile' (*RB* 118).[46]

Some commentators have seen no great difficulty for Collingwood's theory of understanding as re-enactment in what he says about the distinctiveness of history of art. Saari, for example, accepts it that the thoughts expressed by an artist in his works can be understood simply by studying those works, there being no need, he says, to express the thoughts propositionally.[47] Taylor somewhat similarly holds that, although 'expressiveness' cannot be 'inferentially demonstrated' or even 'described', it can be re-enacted. 'Re-enactment', he says, 'takes place where the work of

---

[45] Collingwood does claim to explain the 'badness' of Romanizing British art, which he connects with the Celtic revival (*A* 144). Closer to offering aesthetic reasons are remarks about Celtic art in *RBES* 247, 254.

[46] Collingwood comes closer to genuinely aesthetic explanation when he observes that the 'positive principle' of pre-Roman British art was 'to create a harmonious design made up entirely of curves', while the 'negative principle' was that 'this must be wholly abstract, a picture that is not a picture of anything' (*RBES* 258). This, however, is rather a small step in the desired direction. See also *PA* 55.

[47] Saari, *Re-enactment*, 39.

art takes place—in the mind. We understand Rembrandt by "reading" his paintings to reach that imagined emotion for which the painting was and is the sensuous means of discovery.'[48] But if this view is to be attributed to Collingwood, it must be stressed how large a departure it is from what he says elsewhere about the need to base claims to re-enactive understanding not only upon a critical study of evidence, but upon a critical analysis of the thought which an action allegedly expresses, this being required if it is to be seen as a rational response to a problem. Collingwood's own claim is that, although, in history of art, we cannot reconstruct the artist's problem, meaning by this a truly aesthetic problem, not a merely technical or utilitarian one, we can nevertheless recognize aesthetic achievements after the fact. But how can a work of art be judged an achievement except by seeing it as a successful response to a statable problem? The only way around this difficulty would surely be to claim for historians an intuitive grasp of art works as solutions to inexpressible problems, the view that Saari and Taylor give the impression of accepting. Collingwood himself does sometimes talk as if he believed that some kind of direct empathetic understanding of works of art is feasible. Against this, however, must be set his repeated insistence that historical understanding is ratiocinative, not intuitive.

Michael Krausz has put the problem in a different, and I think helpful, way. Collingwood's theory of understanding as re-enactment, he observes, simply will not stretch to cover human activities to the extent that they are creative, creativity being characteristic of more than art, of course, but especially characteristic of it.[49] A work of art, Krausz avers, normally has an 'emergent' quality which is 'structurally related to the activity'. The finished work typically transcends the explicit intention of the artist; and this is often what we find of special value in it. Since the emergent quality goes beyond anything which the agent intended, however, it cannot *ex hypothesi* be understood in the

[48] Taylor, *Bibliography*, 261; also Review of van der Dussen, *HS*, in *History and Theory*, 20 (1981), 181 n. 12.
[49] 'Historical Explanation, Re-enactment, and Practical Inference', *Metaphilosophy*, 2 (1980), 152 ff. (cited hereafter as 'Historical Explanation'). Krausz also points to the creativity of theories, and even to the creativity of the invention of odd and even numbers, despite their being an unintended product of inventing natural numbers.

Collingwoodian way. Krausz doesn't say how an occurrence with this elusive quality may otherwise be understood. There is some analogy with what was called, in § 3, inadvertent action; but the creativity of an artist is presumably not to be seen simply as accidental, a mere unintended consequence of what the artist deliberately did, such as lay pigments on canvas or chip away pieces of marble. Krausz himself offers an amusing example of genuine inadvertency in artistic creation. A friend of Braque who visited him in his studio one day pointed out that he had inadvertently painted a squirrel into the canvas he was working on. Embarrassed, Braque undertook to paint it out, but the squirrel repeatedly came back no matter how he altered the structure, the light, or the composition. It was eight to ten days before the squirrel was finally eliminated (so far as Braque or the friend could see). Any attempt to show that art history can be truly Collingwoodian might usefully begin by showing how such accidental emergence differs from emergence of the creative kind.

In view of the difficulty of bringing what Collingwood has to say about history of art into a comfortable relationship with his account of historical understanding as re-enactment, it is somewhat ironical that, in his lectures of 1928, when stating for the first time the nature of the idea of re-enactment and its importance for the elucidation of the idea of history, he claims to have arrived at this idea through reflection upon how we understand musical compositions which have come down to us from the past. The implication is that, having considered the musical case, he came to see that the same sort of understanding can be sought with regard to mainstream historical concerns like the decisions of opposing commanders on a battlefield (L28 441).

But, in fact, what Collingwood has to say about a need for re-enactment in the history of music scarcely touches our present concern. He passes quickly from his musical case to a consideration of the need for re-enactment in cases where the idea of grasping the force of an attributed practical argument has much clearer applicability. For example, he stresses the need of an historian of Hellenistic science, trying to understand the discovery of the principle of specific gravity by Archimedes, to be able to draw the conclusion which Archimedes drew from the same data; and the need of a military historian, writing the history of a battle, to be able to imagine the battlefield as the opposing commanders saw it, and to respond as they did to the tactical problems which they faced. But he does not spell out an analogous need for an historian of music to be able to appreciate the reasons which Beethoven, Mozart, or Palestrina had for continuing a melody or for introducing just the harmonies they did. In fact, the music example functions for him as little more than a convenient point of entry into a general discussion of the role of re-enactment in history. He does say that it is a *'sine qua non* of writing the history of past music' (or, he adds, of poetry, or painting, or other arts) that in one way or another what is understood be 're-enacted in the present' (L28 441). But he never explains what such aesthetic re-enactment must, or indeed can, consist in, beyond remarking that a person's present performance of a past work can serve as 'a medium through which he sees to the original experience of the composer and his first performers and first audiences' (L28 442 n. 8).

It is difficult to avoid the conclusion that, although Collingwood rejects an intuitive conception of re-enactive understanding for most of what historians do, he somewhat casually falls back upon just such a conception of it when discussing history of the arts. The way he characterizes art makes it impossible for him to represent the understanding of a work of art as a matter of seeing it as a rational response to a problem, so that, if something is 're-enacted', it cannot be an argument, but only some non-rational or pre-rational form of experience. We are left with something like a view of understanding as an emotional identification with the artist or the art work, an idea which Collingwood rejects when he claims to find it in Dilthey (*IH* 174), or as an intuitive vision of individuality, which, when he believes he finds it in Windelband, he says extrudes history from the sphere of knowledge (*IH* 168). Collingwood roundly criticizes the positivist view of history for its alleged inability to deal with history of art (or religion or science) (*IH* 132). Yet his failure to give a clear sense to the idea of re-enactive understanding as it might apply to the history of art leaves his own position open to the same criticism. And that may have larger implications for the Collingwoodian view of history than at first appears. For, at least in a broad sense, a sense analogous to the broad sense in which he sometimes also speaks of history itself, Collingwood holds that all human activity has an artistic dimension or aspect (L26 353)—the building of the Albert Memorial or the Randolph Hotel not excluded.

§ 6. *The History of Metaphysics*

Just as the way Collingwood characterizes art raises special problems for the application of his idea of re-enactive understanding to history of art, so the way he sometimes characterizes philosophy raises special problems for the application of this idea to history of philosophy. In fact, the problem is less one for history of philosophy generally than for metaphysics as Collingwood rather idiosyncratically conceives it, namely, as a study of absolute presuppositions made by human thought at various times and places in the past.[50] This view of it is expounded chiefly, and sometimes rather provocatively, in the *Essay on Metaphysics* and the *Autobiography*, although it is anticipated in *The Idea of History* and elsewhere (*IH* 229–30).[51]

Collingwood's theory of the nature and functioning of absolute presuppositions has been much discussed, and not all of the tangled issues raised by it can be considered here.[52] For present purposes, the main points are as follows (*EM* 40 ff.). According to Collingwood, all thinking, and especially all systematic, serious thinking, is an attempt to answer questions. Underlying every question is a presupposition which gives it purchase, itself possibly an answer to a prior question, behind which may lie some more fundamental presupposition. The chain of presuppositions, however, comes to an end in an absolute presupposition, behind

[50] Collingwood does sometimes claim that all philosophy, not just metaphysics, 'is liquidated by being converted into history' (NHV 11). This appears to conflict with what he says about philosophy in *EPM*, and is contradicted by his declaration, in a letter to Knox of 1936, that philosophy (including metaphysics) 'cannot be resolved into the history of itself except by a vicious circle' (Taylor, *Bibliography*, 95).

[51] Van der Dussen finds it anticipated in lectures given by Collingwood in 1934 (*HS* 192–6).

[52] See e.g. Michael Krausz, 'The Logic of Absolute Presuppositions', in Krausz (ed.), *Critical Essays*, 222–40; J. E. Llewelyn, 'Collingwood's Doctrine of Absolute Presuppositions', *Philosophical Quarterly*, 11 (1961), 49–60; David Rynin, 'Donagan on Collingwood: Absolute Presuppositions, Truth, and Metaphysics', *Review of Metaphysics*, 18 (1964), 301–33; Stephen Toulmin, 'Conceptual Change and the Problem of Relativity', in Krausz (ed.), *Critical Essays*, 201–21; and works by Donagan, Mink, and Martin cited below.

which no more ultimate one can be found. Absolute presuppositions Collingwood equates with those most general claims about the nature of things which philosophy has traditionally been thought to have the special task of examining: for example, that there is a single world of nature, or that everything has an explanation. Presuppositions which are really absolute are said not to be open to further inquiry, if by that is meant inquiry into their validity or truth (*EM* 162). They are unverifiable in principle, since to verify them would involve deriving them from something still more ultimate—a doctrine which Collingwood sometimes puts by denying that they state propositions, or that the distinction between truth and falsity applies to them.[53] The only kind of study to which they are open is one which identifies those which have been made at determinate times and places, and which traces the way they have changed through time. The task of the metaphysician, according to Collingwood, is 'to follow the historical process by which one set of presuppositions has turned into another' (*A* 66).

The upshot is that metaphysical inquiry is reduced (or elevated) to the status of a branch of the history of ideas. But if one of its tasks is to study the way absolute presuppositions have changed, in what way could it hope to represent the changes as understandable? Would it make sense, for example, for the historian of absolute presuppositions to try to make them understandable in the re-enactive way which Collingwood repeatedly says is alone appropriate in historical studies? The view of them as non-propositional, non-verifiable, neither true nor false, seems to rule out the possibility that anyone might have reasons either for retaining or changing them. Indeed, as Collingwood remarks, absolute presuppositions will themselves, at least in part, determine what is to count as a reason. The only attitude which one can sensibly adopt towards one's own absolute presuppositions, he declares, is one of 'unquestioning acceptance' (*EM* 173); and the only attitude which an historian can sensibly adopt towards those made by the human agents whose life and thought he is studying

---

[53] Collingwood does not consistently maintain the odd position that what metaphysicians study is not expressible as propositions. In claiming Newton as a covert metaphysician, for example, he describes him as having put forward 'metaphysical 'propositions' (*EM* 90), by which he evidently means that he himself made absolute presuppositions, not simply statements about them. For similar statements, see *PA* 131, 255; *RAH* 7.

is to try to determine what they were. In neither case is there any question of the presuppositions themselves being examined in a critical way.[54] Indeed, if one ever succeeded in bringing an absolute presupposition of one's own under critical scrutiny, it would *ipso facto* lose its status as an absolute presupposition; and if an historian ever represented an historical agent as right or wrong, reasonable or unreasonable, in making the absolute presuppositions he did, he would necessarily do this from his own standpoint—the standpoint of his own absolute presuppositions—not from the standpoint of the agent, as re-enactive understanding requires. As long as an absolute presupposition is conceived as such, it appears to be impossible to consider it as something held or changed for reasons.

Collingwood shows awareness of this problem, but his attempts to deal with it go little beyond the offering of suggestive metaphors. The absolute presuppositions which a person makes at a particular time, he maintains, will generally be in 'unstable equilibrium'; they will be subject to 'internal strains', which will eventually lead to their modification, upon which new 'strains' will manifest themselves, leading to still further changes. Groups, or 'constellations', of absolute presuppositions thus have 'seeds of change' within them (*EM* 74). An interpretation of this which is supported by some of what Collingwood says is that strains are eased by the elimination, or at any rate reduction, of contradictions existing between concurrently held absolute presuppositions, these, in consequence, not being 'consupponible' (*EM* 66). In fact, it is far from clear how really ultimate principles ever could contradict each other. But even if they did, the need to eliminate the contradiction would provide no more than a negative reason for changing at least one of them. Although reference to such a need might enter into a re-enactive explanation of absolute presuppositions having changed at all, it would do little to show why the changes took the particular form they did (a problem which also arose in connection with Collingwood's view of history of art). Collingwood maintains that changes in absolute

---

[54] As Code has pointed out ('Collingwood's Epistemological Individualism', 545), Collingwood himself hardly renounces such critical appraisal, calling the eighteenth-century presupposition of physical causation in history an 'illusion' (*EM* 98), and what Kant presupposed about causation an 'error of the past' (*EM* 341).

presuppositions are historical, not natural, processes, presumably to be understood therefore in the way which historical processes are properly understood (*EM* 75). On his own showing, however, changes of this kind do not constitute historical processes in the sense which he gives this term elsewhere: that of being composed of transitions each of which was rationally appropriate, in view of its antecedents.

Collingwood's failure to deal satisfactorily with the problem of how changes of absolute presuppositions are made intelligible manifests itself not only in rather lame theoretical remarks which he makes about the way they change, but also in the descriptions which he offers of historical developments which could be expected to illustrate his claim that presuppositional changes are understandable. As Skagestad has noted, the account he gives of successive cosmologies in *The Idea of Nature* shows a good deal of continuity and rationally comprehensible change within each major phase—the Greek, the Renaissance, the Modern—during which the agents were operating largely within shared presuppositions; but it fails to show this in the movement from phase to phase, when the presuppositions themselves were changing. What we get is 'the merely temporal succession of three apparently discontinuous "ideas of nature"'.[55] No more can Collingwood be said to have shown, in *The Idea of History*, why the Greek view of history was succeeded by the Christian, and that by the approaches of Romanticism and the Enlightenment, and those in their turn by modern historical idealism, if by this is meant making clear the reasons why each conception of the general nature of the historical world was repudiated by those who held the next (see also *EM* 98).[56]

The sketch offered by Collingwood, in the *Essay on Metaphysics*, of the way ideas of causation have succeeded each other over several centuries hardly exemplifies any better his own idea of a comprehensible historical transition, although it is supposed to be a demonstration of how metaphysical analysis should proceed (*EM* 285 ff.). He distinguishes three senses of 'cause' in order of

[55] Skagestad, *Making Sense*, 82. See also Lorraine Code, 'Collingwood: A Philosopher of Ambivalence', *History of Philosophy Quarterly*, 3 (1986), 113 ff.

[56] Collingwood does represent the move from positivism to idealism in historiography, apparently a change of absolute presuppositions, as effected partly by criticism of positivistic principles from within by authors like Bradley, Bury, and Oakeshott (*IH* 138, 148, 155).

their historical appearance, the first being an essentially humanistic sense, the second reflecting the interests of what he calls
practical science, and the third intended for use in theoretical
natural science. But he makes no attempt to show that the second
has developed rationally out of the first in order to resolve strains;
or that the third has similarly arisen out of a rejection of the
second.[57] Each is presented as an idea which pertains to a different
kind of subject-matter, to be used with different purposes in view.
The only strains which Collingwood identifies in fact appear
within the third sense, which is not represented as leading to
anything (*EM* 287). And strains apart, the later senses are not, in
any case, represented as superseding the earlier ones. According
to Collingwood, the first two remain operative today in their
proper spheres, the most ancient, indeed, being precisely the
sense which he regards as alone acceptable in modern 'scientific'
historical studies.

What Collingwood has to say about the way the idea of history
has changed over time is also problematic in sometimes directing
attention to changes which seem to be of the wrong kind to be
understood re-enactively. For example, he contends that what
inclined the Hellenistic mind towards an ecumenical view of
history and away from an earlier particularism was the conquests
of Alexander (*IH* 37). Just how the latter is supposed to have had
this effect is not made very clear; but the example immediately
calls to mind Collingwood's remark in the *Essay on Metaphysics*
that, although changes of absolute presuppositions are not
usually effected by an effort of will, they can sometimes occur as
a result (presumably a nomological result) of powerful influences
or pressures (*EM* 194). At one point, he attributes to 'mass-
suggestion' or to 'neurosis' the way people characteristically resist acknowledging their absolute presuppositions (*EM* 43, 46);
and he sometimes appears to commit himself to similar explanations of their adopting or retaining them.[58] We are nevertheless

[57] This despite Collingwood explicitly maintaining that a study of the process
by which one sense of cause has been replaced by another will show why each was
held (*IH* 230), and criticizing Kant for not realizing this when he undertook to
vindicate the causal category a priori. The term 'absolute presupposition' is not
used here, but it might as well have been.

[58] More consistently, he observes that, when absolute presuppositions change,
each historical phase 'gives place to another, not because one is violently des-
troyed by alien forces impinging on its fabric from without by war or from within

warned that absolute presuppositions do not change as inconsequentially as fashions do (*EM* 48).[59] Collingwood seems occasionally on the verge of conceding that changes of absolute presuppositions may be rational at any rate in a pragmatic sense. Thus the conflict between mechanism and vitalism in biology, or between accepting statistical laws and demanding universal ones in physics, he pictures as one in which the winner will be the view found most rewarding in practice (*EM* 255).[60] This is a far cry from the idea that presuppositional change arises out of a need to resolve internal strains.

Given Collingwood's account of the nature of absolute presuppositions, it therefore seems reasonable to question whether the view of metaphysics as a branch of history propounded in the *Essay on Metaphysics* and the *Autobiography* can be reconciled with what is said about historical understanding as re-enactment in *The Idea of History*, the lectures of 1928, other parts of the *Autobiography*, and the extant fragment of 'The Principles of History'. Should we then, like Knox, regard Collingwood's reduction of metaphysics to history simply as an aberration, an inconsistency in his thought, perhaps an indication of failing powers in his later years?

Some have maintained that there is more to be said for his analysis than that. Thus Martin has argued, with some persuasiveness, that when Collingwood represents accounts of changing absolute presuppositions as history, it would be a mistake to think that what he has in mind is history in the full-blown disciplinary sense which he analyses in works like *The Idea of History*. More particularly, we should not expect a history of absolute presuppositions to exemplify the re-enactment theory.[61] What it exemplifies is Collingwood's idea of an inquiry based upon evidence, one which eschews what he calls the method of scissors

by revolution, but because each of them while it lives is working at turning itself into the next' (*EM* 73).

[59] Donagan argues that Collingwood is in fact committed to holding that changes of absolute presuppositions *are* like changes of fashion (*LPC* 276)—a view challenged by Grant (Review of *LPC*, in *Philosophical Books*, 4 (1963), 4). Elsewhere, oddly enough, Collingwood asserts that fashion changes for reasons (*SM* 227).

[60] With reference to the presupposition 'that natural science is essentially an applied mathematics', Collingwood imagines someone saying: 'See what noble results have come from its being accepted for the last three hundred years! One must surely admit that it works; and that is sufficient justification' (*EM* 254).

[61] Rex Martin, 'Collingwood's Claim', 524 n. 33.

and paste (*EM* 59). A history of absolute presuppositions will also conform to his idea of history as an inquiry concerned with thought—one that penetrates to an 'inside'—even though, in this case, the thought can only be identified, not re-enactively understood.[62] Support for Martin's view can be found in many of Collingwood's own pronouncements. He affirms, for example, that, since it is the metaphysician's task 'to prove that somebody has made or has not made a certain absolute presupposition', what he must do is 'analyze the records of his thought and find out' (*EM* 60). He maintains, further, that discovering absolute presuppositions, simply finding out what they were, 'is already an historical inquiry' (*EM* 57)—which it clearly is, at any rate in the more general sense of 'finding out what happened' which lurks in the background of so much of what Collingwood wrote on the subject. The view propounded in the *Essay on Metaphysics* also falls comfortably under Collingwood's characterization of history as a 'study at once critical and constructive, whose field is the human past in its entirety, and whose method is the reconstruction of that past from documents written and unwritten, critically analysed and interpreted' (*IH* 209).

Martin usefully goes on to stress the fact that, even if absolute presuppositions are not themselves re-enactable in the special sense of being shown to be appropriate responses to problems, the knowledge that they were held may, like knowledge of thoughts of other kinds (for example, beliefs) enter into the re-enactive understanding of actions the full statement of whose implicit practical arguments may require reference to them.[63] Such reference, he opines, is most likely be required when the problem is to understand what was done by members of another culture.

Yet what Martin has to say is more plausibly read as a revision of Collingwood's own view than as an explication, or even an interpretation, of it. Collingwood himself often writes as if he considers metaphysics an historical discipline in his full-blown

[62] Rex Martin, 'Collingwood's Doctrine of Absolute Presuppositions and the Possibility of Historical Knowledge', in Leon Pompa and W. H. Dray (eds.), *Substance and Form in History* (Edinburgh, 1981), 100 ff. As Taylor happily phrases it, the Collingwoodian historian 'does not rethink absolute presuppositions—he reasons toward them' (*Bibliography*, 246).

[63] Rex Martin, 'Collingwood's Claim', 499–500. Like beliefs, insists Martin, they 'may be used in a re-enactment but are not the object of a re-enactment'.

sense, which would require that absolute presuppositions be themselves re-enactable, not just possible elements in the re-enactive explanation of actions. He says explicitly, for example, not only that 'the problems of metaphysics are historical problems', and its methods 'historical methods' (*EM* 62), but also that, as 'an historical science', it 'shares the presuppositions of all history' (*EM* 63). And, as Donagan does, Martin takes the latter to include the presupposition that its subject-matter is re-enactable.[64] Quite telling in this connection is Collingwood's maintaining (as noted already) that the historian-metaphysician attempts 'to follow the historical process by which one set of presuppositions has turned into another' (*A* 66). Still more telling is his saying, in criticism of Kant, that the metaphysical task is not just to identify the presuppositions of modern science, but to show 'how they have been built up in the historical development of thought' (*IH* 230). It is clear that by 'how' here is also meant 'why'. Again, according to Collingwood, the holding of an absolute presupposition is to be explained by indicating the 'process of change' by which it came into being (*EM* 151). Thus the sense in which he holds metaphysics to be an historical discipline in the *Essay on Metaphysics* appears to be much closer to the one set forth in *The Idea of History* than Martin's apology allows.

Other students of Collingwood have dealt differently with the problems raised by what he says about history of absolute presuppositions. Some have located the problem in the alleged fact that absolutely presupposing is not action, Collingwood's theory of understanding claiming only to apply to action. Martin sometimes seems to accept this view, too, of the reason why absolute presuppositions cannot be regarded as re-enactable.[65] But, as was noted in § 5, lower-order beliefs are not actions either, nor are emotions. And, whether or not justifiably, Collingwood claims to offer re-enactive explanations of them.

Another view of where the main difficulty lies is suggested by Donagan's contention that, strictly speaking, absolutely presupposing is not 'thinking'. An absolute presupposition, he holds, is

[64] Ibid. 521 n. 13. For Donagan's view, see *LPC* 213.

[65] Rex Martin, 'Collingwood's Claim', 499. Collingwood himself sometimes talks as if he regards presupposing as acting, as when he describes Hegel as having favoured replacing the presuppositions of nineteenth-century physics by something closer to what now exists (*EM* 271).

only a logical implication of what an agent thinks, a 'logical cor-
relate' of it (*LPC* 273). This might well debar it not only from being
itself explained in a re-enactive way, but also from functioning as
an element of such an explanation. The same consideration would
surely raise doubts about whether presuppositions or assumptions of any kind, not just absolute ones, can be reasons for acting,
and thus provide premises for Collingwoodian explanations. Yet
Donagan's objection here does have some force. One would not
want to say that everything which is logically entailed by what a
person admittedly thinks can be ascribed to him also as his
thought—the whole of mathematics, for example, as entailed by
his thinking '1 plus 1 equals 2'. But the line to be drawn in this
connection may be somewhat arbitrary.

Still other critics, like David Boucher, have seen the problem for
applying re-enactment theory to absolute presuppositions as
residing not in their being non-thoughts, but in their being 'unconscious' thoughts.[66] On the question of whether we are ever
conscious of our own absolute presuppositions Collingwood is, in
fact, somewhat ambivalent. He does say that we are seldom
aware of them: they usually function, he says, 'in darkness' (*EM*
43). Yet he admits cases in which people are brought to confront
their own presuppositions, generally reacting testily, or at least
defensively, when this is done (*EM* 43). And his thesis that metaphysical analysis, in his own special sense, is essential to our own,
or our society's, mental health would seem to require that absolute presuppositions can be brought from darkness into light.
Besides which an agent's not ordinarily being aware of what he
absolutely presupposes ought surely to raise no more of a problem for re-enactive explanation than is raised by unconscious
motives, which Collingwood regards as both explanatory and
explicable.

A more radical way with the problem is taken by Skagestad.
Presuppositional analysis, he maintains—the eliciting of what

[66] See Rex Martin, 'Collingwood's Claim', 496–7, 521 n. 12. Boucher shifts a little
from this position in his introduction to the new edition of *NL*, pp. xxvii–xxx, but
the idea is still there. Even Martin ascribes to Collingwood the view that absolute
presuppositions cannot be changed 'directly' because they are held unconsciously
('Collingwood's Claim', 494); and Knox, too, seems to assume that, for
Collingwood, they are always unconscious (original preface to *IH*, p. xiv). Against
this might be set Collingwood's own declaration: 'If a man did not know that he
was making certain presuppositions he would not be a scientist' (NHV 11).

people presupposed by analysing what they said and did—is itself what Collingwood meant by re-enactment. 'Re-enactment' and 're-construction' are just different ways of characterizing the same intellectual operation.[67] But although the two ideas may be closely related in Collingwood's account of history, they can hardly be considered identical. Other things besides thoughts, for example, can be reconstructed by historians from evidence; and a past agent's thought might conceivably be re-enacted on occasion without evidence, or despite the weakness of available evidence.

It thus seems to me that Martin is correct in maintaining that metaphysics, as inquiry into the history of absolute presuppositions, is not, and cannot be, history in the sense in which understanding Caesar's crossing the Rubicon is history. The problem of saying otherwise is put too gently by Saari when he remarks that 'the relation between Collingwood's theory of absolute presuppositions and re-enactment remains unclear in many respects'.[68] I think that relation is clear enough to warrant the conclusion that, if metaphysics, as conceived by Collingwood, is to be called history, it must, on his own theory of history, be judged a defective form of it.

---

[67] Skagestad, *Making Sense*, 91. Nielsen similarly regards 're-enactment of past experience' as synonymous with 'reconstruction by the interpretation of evidence' ('Re-enactment and Reconstruction', 24).

[68] Saari, *Re-enactment*, 125. The same could be said of Nielsen's assurance that there is no 'need' to interpret Collingwood's re-enactment doctrine in terms of his theory of absolute presuppositions ('Re-enactment and Reconstruction', 16–19). See also Nielsen, 'Making Sense', 485.

5

THE PHYSICAL AND
THE SOCIAL

§ 1. *Objective Conditions*

In the last chapter, we looked at some problems which arise for Collingwood's claim that all history is a re-enactment of past thought as expressed in past action. Some of these problems were found to be dismissible, others to require some modification of his position as generally stated. It was argued that the common criticism that his doctrine is too intellectualistic or too rationalistic largely dissolves upon analysis, and that the complaint that it rules out other forms of human experience, such as perception, appetite, or emotion, needs at any rate to be taken with caution. It was noted also that what Collingwood says about historical understanding as re-enactive is only marginally applicable, without substantial change, to some aspects of the history of art and of philosophy. Collingwood himself sometimes phrases his claims in ways which suggest that he expects to have to qualify them. For example, although maintaining that 'there is nothing else except thought that can be the object of historical knowledge' (*A* 110), he also says that history is nothing 'in itself' but the re-enactment of past thought (*IH* 228), and that the historian is concerned 'at bottom' with thoughts alone (*IH* 217). Such statements suggest that his true doctrine may be closer to holding that past expressions of human thought are the primary focus of interest for historians, their interest in other things always being in some way relative to, or conditional upon, that. In other words, one might, with Winch, regard the slogan 'all history is history of thought' as just one of Collingwood's many exaggerations.[1]

With this possibility in mind, and in any case with a view to making clearer just how restrictive Collingwood's position really

---

[1] Winch, *Idea of a Social Science*, 131.

needs to be in this regard, I want to consider, in this chapter, kinds of difficulties which are often thought to be raised by Collingwood's allegedly ignoring the role played by 'objective conditions' in history. By these I mean the natural environment in which people lived and acted, and the social groups to which they belonged, or which were in some way relevant to their lives.[2] More systematically than I did in considering the cases discussed in Chapter 4, I shall ask first whether, for Collingwood, such things are of concern to historians in the sense of being what their studies are at least partly about, and then whether they are in any case essential to them in an explanatory, and even a causally explanatory, way. The answers for natural and social conditions will be found to be different in important respects, although there are considerations in common. In §§ 2–3, I shall look at what Collingwood says about the place of physical conditions in history, and then, in the rest of the chapter, at his view of the role of social events, conditions, and structures.

§ 2. *The Physical Background*

Little needs to be said about the extent to which the inquiries of historians should be conceived as being *about* natural events and conditions. Once a distinction has been drawn between human history and natural history, and Collingwood often draws it, it is clear that what we generally call history will not be about such a subject-matter considered simply in itself. If the natural world enters into human history, it will necessarily be in derivative and secondary ways. The question to be asked, therefore, is how it legitimately does so, and how adequately Collingwood's theory takes this into account.

As Debbins has aptly remarked, when studying Collingwood, 'one must not overlook the obvious' (*EPH*, p. xvii). And one obvious way in which the physical enters into human history, a way which, although directly implied by Collingwood's charac-

---

[2] The expression 'objective conditions' is used by both van der Dussen (*HS* 329 ff.) and Rotenstreich ('Facts to Thoughts', 133), the latter complaining that Collingwood's neglect of them places actions 'in a vacuum'. Collingwood has been similarly criticized by Renier (*Purpose and Method*, 46–8), and Murphy (Review of *IH*, 590). Atkinson charges him with neglecting the 'non-willed social environment' (*KEH* 26).

terization of its subject-matter, still sometimes manages to escape
notice, is that it is required to constitute the outsides of actions.
Collingwood may conceive history as a study of mind; but he
never gets close to conceiving it as a study of *disembodied* mind.
Action, as we saw, he defines as a unity of an inside and an
outside; and, while the inside will consist of thoughts, at any rate
in some broad sense, the outside, in the vast majority of cases, will
consist of physical events.[3] In Collingwood's own summary of his
position, the historian's work is said to 'begin by discovering the
outside of an event' (*IH* 213)—an aspect of his basic theory which
a critic like Gardiner cannot have had in mind when he attributes
to him the view that historians are 'concerned with thoughts and
not with the physical "manifestations" of those thoughts'.[4] Nor
has the potential extent of a Collingwoodian outside always been
fully appreciated. If what we are to call historical actions includes
such things as sailing a ship into the Mediterranean, or levying
war, or even crossing the Rubicon (where this means not just the
passage of a single man across it, but also that of the army he is
leading, along with its supplies, transport, equipment, and so on),
the physical world will clearly be heavily involved. An even more
extensive role is assigned to the physical when Collingwood insists that the concerns of the historian include the success and
failure of actions: the actual sinking of an enemy fleet, for
example, not just the issuing of relevant battle orders. But even
the issuing of the orders is not just a commander's 'thought'; it has
a physical outside.

Collingwood does sometimes make statements which may appear to deny a place to the 'real' physical world in history. He
says, for example, that 'when an historian says that a man is in a
certain situation this is the same as saying that he thinks he is in
this situation' (*IH* 317). But such overstatements are corrected at
other points, as when he declares that the Roman invaders of
Britain were successful 'because they grasped the character of the
country to which they had come';[5] and when he calls attention to
what he describes as the ever-present element of 'brute force' in
human affairs (RNI 40). This he illustrates from a story by Joseph
Conrad in which a derelict boat just happened to be available

---

[3] See Ch. 2, § 3, for an exception.
[4] Gardiner, *Nature of Historical Explanation*, 47.
[5] 'Rome in Britain', *Home-Reading Magazine*, 36 (1924–5), 71.

when the story needed it—a real boat, it seems, one which could actually be rowed, not just an envisaged one. The relevance of the real physical world to historical process is also quite directly implied by much of what Collingwood says about the interpretation of evidence, to which, he observes, an historian must 'bring everything he knows', including all his 'knowledge of nature and man' (*IH* 248).

Sometimes attention is directed to the historical relevance of the natural world in a broader sense. As noted in Chapter 3, § 5, Collingwood sometimes describes nature as the 'scenery' of history: the 'stage' upon which, or the 'background' against which, historical action takes place (NHV 23; RNI 40). This theme is prominent in his historical writings, long passages being routinely devoted to descriptions of the geographical setting, knowledge of which is said to be essential for any adequate understanding of the historical developments which took place. In the opening pages of his most substantial work on Roman Britain, he observes that the 'relief, soil, and climate' of the island's two main geographical regions 'have deeply affected the life of their respective inhabitants' (*RBES* 3–4).[6] He is even prepared (presumably with tongue in cheek) to make a guess at characteristics of the British upon which such geographical factors may throw light: 'resistance to new ideas . . . blind devotion to lost causes, deficiency in logic, proneness to half measures and hypocrisy.' In the *Autobiography*, the eruption of Vesuvius is cited as a natural occurrence which became an historical event by virtue of the way those 'affected' by it 'reacted to this affection by actions of various kinds' (*A* 128 n.). It might be noted that Collingwood here concedes something which he strenuously denies when discussing his paradigm case of historical understanding, namely, that, at least sometimes, historians are concerned with 'mere' events, not just with events which are 'the outward expression of thoughts' (*IH* 217). For no matter how much climatic changes or volcanic eruptions may owe their place in history to their relation to human affairs, they are not themselves the outsides of any actions, and are thus 'mere' events on Collingwood's own definition of the term.

---

[6] See also *RB* 48, and the detailed survey of geographical factors in 'Roman Britain', 7 ff.

It is already clear from the first example that Collingwood not only concedes a place to natural conditions in history, but also allows them at least a vaguely indicated causal role. And it is clear from the second that, although he is inclined to deny historical status to such conditions where the agents 'affected' by them made no response, he recognizes the fact of 'affection', and its historical relevance when a response was forthcoming. I shall leave until § 3 the question whether he allows that physical (or biological, or other natural) conditions can cause specific actions to be performed. But already we have the admission that physical events can at any rate cause human states, and that these (as argued in Chapter 4, § 4) may sometimes be of interest to historians. It follows that, at least in the shape of flood, plague, fire, drought, and a host of other such things, Collingwood accords the physical world some causal role in history. Nor is what is involved here just the causation of bodily states like pain or lassitude, or bodily conditions like infection or malnutrition. For, as was indicated in Chapter 4, Collingwood sometimes admits, as he should, that human emotions and beliefs can also be caused by natural conditions. This is a far cry from his rash declaration that the historian is only interested in natural events 'which are the outward expression of thoughts, and is only concerned with these in so far as they express thoughts' (*IH* 217).

Still putting aside the question whether natural conditions can cause actions, but bearing in mind the Collingwoodian principle that the interests of historians are relative to actions, it should be noted that natural conditions can sometimes cause a lack of action. The eruption of Vesuvius is to some extent a case in point, since for many of its victims there was no question of 'responding' to the way they were 'affected': they were either killed or incapacitated. Collingwood thus surely overstates what he would presumably want to maintain when he declares that natural events belong to history 'only' to the extent that agents responded to them. Less lurid examples of natural conditions attaining historical status by rendering certain kinds of action impossible might be the contrary wind which, according to Collingwood, delayed the embarkation of Caesar's cavalry in support of his invasion of Britain (*RBES* 37), or the bitter winter which, as some historians maintain, made the orderly retreat of Napoleon's army from Moscow impossible. In such cases, the Collingwoodian requirement that the focus of historical inquiry be upon action is met at least in the negative sense of showing why action which might have been expected was not forthcoming. It is true that, in many such cases, what is said to have been beyond the powers of the agents is so judged only relative to the state of their technology, or even to their ingenuity or powers of perseverance. However, within limits which it might be difficult to specify precisely, conditions like the ones cited could be said to have made certain responses impossible for all practical purposes. Collingwood appears to have such a case in view, although one involving human rather than natural assault, when he remarks of the First World War that 'fighting ended because one side was fought to a standstill' (*A* 93).

We go quite beyond such cases, of course, where an absence of action in the face of natural disaster takes the form of acceptance, or resignation, or in some other way a refusal to act, as might be common, say, in a medieval population afflicted by plague or drought. Here non-action becomes itself a form of action, to which the analysis of action causation sketched in § 3 would apply. Also beyond the range of cases just considered would be actions described as 'impossible', where this only means that they were 'rationally unacceptable'.

There are still other kinds of cases in which, although what the historian explains is not human states or non-actions of various kinds, but actions as Collingwood ordinarily conceives them, and the explanation is in terms of natural conditions, the conditions cited are not represented as what caused the agents to act. As was noted in Chapter 3, § 6, there is a kind of explanation, frequently given both in ordinary life and in history, which seeks to show not why someone did something, but what enabled him to do it. An historian might, for example, point to the presence of coal and iron in the British Isles as a *sine qua non* of the development of the Industrial Revolution there; and Collingwood would seem to have the possibility of giving the same kind of explanation in mind when he declares that 'England is a country designed by nature to be invaded from the mainland of Europe'.[7] Rotenstreich has called attention to the fact that physiological or biological as well as physical conditions in the narrow sense have a role to play

[7] 'The Roman Signal Station', in Arthur Rowntree (ed.), *The History of Scarborough* (London, 1931), 40.

in history: conditions like 'the stamina and endurance of a people or a society which is called upon to act'; and he complains that Collingwood's theory offers them no place.[8] But, in fact, they could easily be accommodated as enabling conditions of action. Natural conditions may also sometimes be said to explain actions in the slightly stronger sense of having invited or encouraged them, while still not actually having caused them. It is true that both conditions which merely permit and conditions which merely invite are sometimes called causes by historians. But that is not their usual practice.

There is still a further way in which natural conditions sometimes enter history, short of being considered causes of actions, namely, as explanations of other natural conditions whose place in an historical account is already secure (perhaps for one of the reasons just reviewed). Donagan has argued that, whenever historians concern themselves with explaining natural conditions themselves, they leave historical thinking behind—and Collingwood would doubtless have concurred.[9] But it might surely be said to be the historian's business, on occasion, to indicate, say, the causes of the rapid spread of a flu epidemic or of the varying regional incidence of a disease like tuberculosis. What the agents themselves thought about such things, rightly or wrongly, will certainly be of historical interest; but the true nature of the phenomenon may also need to be known, if only with a view to fully appreciating the possibilities and impossibilities of action in the circumstances. As was noted in Chapter 3, § 6, Collingwood himself, in his own historical work, sometimes makes explanatory remarks about natural processes and mechanisms. Perhaps a critic like Cebik will seem to go too far when he maintains, ostensibly against Collingwood, that an historian of early modern Italy might need to understand the mechanism of the eruption of Vesuvius.[10] But even that could not be ruled out a priori. A celebrated case, cited by G. J. Renier, in which historians have in fact accepted the obligation to explain a puzzling natural condition is the attribution of a shift of the herring 'pastures' off the Low Countries in the fifteenth century, a matter vital to Dutch

[8] Rotenstreich, 'Facts to Thoughts', 133–4.
[9] Donagan, 'Verification of Historical Theses', 201 n. However, Donagan does not absolutely forbid this, offering examples in which he thinks it justified.
[10] Cebik, 'Collingwood', 83.

fishermen of the time, to changes in the course of the Gulf Stream.[11] This is surely just the kind of case in which, if an historian simply reported a significant natural fact and left it at that, he would be considered not to have finished his job.

§ 3. *Physical Causes of Actions*

It seems therefore that, although Collingwood denies that natural events and conditions are what historical inquiry is about, he ascribes an important role to the physical world in history in a number of ways: as constituting the outsides of actions; as affording a general background to human activities; as causing human experiences other than actions; as enabling, preventing, or otherwise conditioning actions themselves; and as furnishing explanations for natural occurrences which, for one reason or another, have caught the interest of historians. That, however, still leaves untouched what bothers Collingwood's critics most: his apparent rejection of the idea that natural conditions could ever enter history as causes of actions.

In his earliest writings, as both van der Dussen and Donagan have remarked (*HS* 330; *LPC* 231), Collingwood denies that actions have causes at all. In an essay of 1916, he says that by action we mean 'precisely that which is not caused'.[12] In his lectures of 1928, he insists correspondingly, that a thought (and therefore the action expressing it) can never be an effect (L28 474). In some of his later work, he expresses much the same idea in a different way. He maintains that, although actions can have causes, these will invariably be the agents' beliefs about their situation, not the actual situation they were in. Thus, in *The Idea of History*, he declares that the mere fact that people live on an island 'has in itself no effect on their history; what has an effect is the way they conceive that insular position; whether for example they regard the sea as a barrier or as a highway to traffic' (*IH* 200). In the same work, he tells us that the 'hard facts' which explain why an agent acts in a certain way are the 'hard facts of the way he conceives his situation' (*IH* 317). Even more explicitly, he asserts that what historians call causes of actions is 'the thought in the mind of the

---

[11] Renier, *Purpose and Method*, 47.   [12] 'The Devil' (1916), 218–19.

person by whose agency the event came about', this being a 'special sense' which the term 'cause' takes on in historical studies (*IH* 214). The same position is expressed in a manuscript of 1936, in which Collingwood maintains, apparently in illustration of a general principle, that when a person runs out of ink, what causes him to buy more is not the lack of ink, but his resolve to remedy the deficiency (NHH 49).

Both Donagan and Mink have found this position quite acceptable. Donagan states, approvingly, that it is 'a fundamental principle for Collingwood that no physical fact can *per se* be the cause of any act' (*LPC* 193). Mink, with similar approval, formulates Collingwood's view as follows: 'Strictly speaking, the geographical location and configuration of the Alps have not been the cause of anything in history. It is men's awareness of and beliefs about the Alps which have been the constraining and effective factors in human events' (*MHD* 171). Yet it is surely paradoxical to maintain that what causes a person to act is always his conception of his situation, never the situation itself. Nor is this the way in which historians usually talk about past actions: they commonly refer to physical events and conditions themselves as their causes. And so does Collingwood, when he writes as an historian. It is actual 'differences of soil and climate' that he points to in explanation of cultural differences (which include ways of acting) between the south-east of England and the rest of the country (*RB* 48); and it is actual physical elevations and depressions—'the *force majeure* of geography', as he calls it—which he represents as having induced Roman engineers to lay out the British road system in the way they did.[13] Surely something has gone wrong here. I shall try to show what it is, arguing at the same time that Collingwood's doctrine can be emended in ways that resolve the problem without surrendering anything which he need consider crucial for his overall position.

First, it is worth taking a closer look at what he says about the eruption of Vesuvius. His description of those who experienced it (and lived to tell the tale) as having 'reacted' in various ways may seem to conform strictly to his principle that actions are never caused by physical events. For he says quite explicitly that what the victims reacted to was the way they were 'affected' by the

---

[13] 'Britain', *Cambridge Ancient History*, xi (Cambridge, 1936), 520.

eruption. Their response, in other words, was to a certain experience they had, not to the event itself. But we must not lose sight of the fact that what caused them to have the experience was the eruption. The full Collingwoodian account would thus be that the eruption caused the agents to experience in certain ways, and that this, in turn, caused them to react in certain ways. And if the causal relation is transitive, which it is generally taken to be, this surely means that the eruption can be said to have caused the reaction at second remove. The fact that the connection between eruption and reaction is indirect surely does not warrant our denying that the action was caused by the event. If Collingwood did deny causal transitivity in such a case, it would presumably be on the ground that those affected still had to decide what response to make to the way in which the event affected them— whether to stay or flee, for example—this eliminating anything that could properly be called a causal connection between what did the affecting and what was eventually done. And there is this much to be said for such a view. The sense in which the eruption can be described as having caused the agents' 'affections' is presumably nomological, instantiating what Collingwood would call a scientific sense of cause. The sense in which the agents' reactions could be said to have been caused by their 'affections' is presumably specifically historical or rational. It might be held that the shift of sense invalidates any claim that the three-term causal series is transitive in such a case. Yet there is no indication that Collingwood bases his position upon any such consideration. Nor does he appear to have any objection to the idea of causal transitivity itself. In a manuscript of 1933, for example, he accepts two-stage and transitive causation with regard to feelings and emotions, these, he says, having causes proximately in 'bodily states and processes of which the mind is conscious', and secondarily in 'external forces' impinging upon our bodies.[14]

The problem is both clarified and rendered more complex if we compare what is said in *The Idea of History* about a special historical sense of cause with what is said on the same subject at greater

[14] 'Outline of a Theory of Primitive Mind', 1933, Dep. 16/8, fo. 2. Van der Dussen prefers in such cases to speak of two levels of causation rather than two stages in a causal series (*HS* 92–3). But the notion of levels surely applies better in cases where, say, causes at one level are considered to be constituted by causes at the other level—as social causes are considered by methodological individualists to be constituted by individual causes (see § 5).

length in *An Essay on Metaphysics* (*EM* 285 ff.).[15] It is often assumed that Collingwood's doctrine in the two works is the same. But although there are similarities, there are also important differences. In both cases, attention is directed to a sense of cause which is called specifically historical because it is regarded as incorporating a re-enactive view of historical understanding. But in the *Essay*, what is called the cause of an action in the specifically historical sense is not what the agent thinks, but what affords him a motive for acting: not a thought, but something thought about (*EM* 285–6). Among Collingwood's illustrations are a speech given by Mr Baldwin in the House of Commons causing the Speaker to adjourn the proceedings, and a solicitor's letter causing someone to pay a debt (*EM* 290). Such examples comport well with his repeated claim that only an historical fact (in this case an action) can be a cause of another historical fact (NHV 5).[16] But if the cause of an action in history can be the action of another agent which afforded the first one a motive for acting, a three-term analysis could once again be offered. There is, once again, a happening (the speech) affecting an agent (the Speaker) in a certain way (hearing it), and the agent responding rationally to the affection. What is now called the historical sense of cause incorporates both the non-re-enactive first stage and the re-enactive second stage of the relation of speech to eventual action. It thus includes within it what, in *The Idea of History* Collingwood calls the historical sense of cause, while going beyond it.

The way it goes beyond it is significant for our present concern. For in the *Essay* version of Collingwood's position, something is singled out as the cause of a subsequent action which was not a thought, but an occurrence in the physical world (a speech may

---

[15] Van der Dussen notes that Collingwood abandoned his earlier view on action causation in a manuscript of 1933–4 in which he writes: 'An historical cause is a fact or assembly of facts which, when an agent is aware that he stands in them as his circumstances, determine him through this awareness to act in a certain way' (*HS* 330). This is the position which Collingwood was to take in *EM*.

[16] Collingwood reverts in the same manuscript to the position taken in *IH*, remarking that 'what causes a development [in history] is not the geographical facts in question but the way in which people think of these facts and of themselves in relation to them' (NHV 5–6). He is ambivalent on the point in *IH* 316, and again in EM where, in introducing what he calls '*causa quod*' as one element in his special historical sense of cause, he says: 'The *causa quod* is a situation or state of things existing' which is 'known or believed by the agent in question to exist' (*EM* 292). 'Believed' hints at a reversion to the *IH* sense.

express thoughts, but is not itself anyone's thought). And if the fact that Mr Baldwin's speech was, among other things, a physical event does not invalidate its claim to be called the cause of the Speaker's adjournment, it is difficult to see why the fact that the eruption of Vesuvius took place in the physical world disqualifies it as cause of what was done by the responding agents. Of course, when actions are caused by other actions, the causal connection goes 'through the mind'; responses will be to what one agent did as another conceived it. But the same can be said of cases where the causes of action are said to be natural events; here equally the connection goes 'through the mind'. It is thus simply irrelevant, and is potentially misleading that, in the *Essay*, Collingwood explicates his historical sense of cause in terms of a re-enactive response to actions: physical events would have done just as well. Oddly enough, he implicitly concedes the point by including among his examples of judgments using the (new) historical sense of cause (although without remarking its difference from the other two senses which I cited) one in which the cause is a physical state of affairs, namely, bad weather causing someone to return from an expedition (*EM* 290).[17]

Yet, although what historians regard as having caused agents to act will most often be the actual situation they were in, something 'outside the mind', they do sometimes regard it as more appropriate to identify the agent's thought about the situation as cause. This may seem at first just an inconsistency on their part. But a further look at cases suggests that there is more to it than that—and also that much more needs to be said in clarification of the causal concept typically employed by historians than is said in either *The Idea of History* or in the *Essay on Metaphysics*.

In the *Essay*, Collingwood takes a step in the right direction in the analysis which he offers of causal judgments as they are made in what he calls the 'practical' sciences of nature, and in daily-life situations where people's concerns are essentially practical (*EM* 296 ff.). To put his position briefly: he points out that, where practical concerns are uppermost, causal explanations, although

---

[17] According to van der Dussen, Collingwood's admitting cases in which a physical event rather than another action can be called the cause of a given action introduces a further sense of cause into the historian's vocabulary. However, since the relationship of cause to effect is the same in both cases (that of being a reason for acting), there seems to me no need to speak here of a further sense of cause.

identifying a number of conditions without which the result would not have occurred, seldom represent all of them as causes. They generally select one or a few to which alone causal status is ascribed. To take one of Collingwood's own examples: one may judge the cause of a highway accident to have been the excessive speed at which a car was driven, even while conceding that the accident would not have occurred had the surface of the road not happened to be wet. According to Collingwood, the criterion employed to distinguish causes from merely relevant conditions in such cases is anthropocentric. The conditions considered as causal are those which give one a 'handle' on the situation (one can do nothing about the rain, but a good deal about bad driving habits). What Collingwood fails to say, and seems not to have noticed, is that the causal judgments which historians ordinarily make are selective in an analogous way. The cause of the outbreak of a war, for example, may be said to be a country's aggressive foreign policy rather than the fact that its armies were willing to follow their leaders, although the latter was no less a necessary condition of it. The cause of a political defection may similarly be seen as a person's ideological commitments rather than the fact, also relevant, that he felt unable to satisfy them by remaining loyal.

Like practical men, therefore, historians implicitly recognize a distinction between causes and merely relevant conditions. But this can hardly be on the principle that causal conditions are the ones which offer them 'handles' for dealing with situations of the kind studied. On what alternative principle or principles, then, do they select what they regard as specifically causal conditions? Since Collingwood ignores the selectivity of causal judgment in history, he cannot ask this question. Yet, without an answer to it, we still lack a satisfactory account of a special historian's sense of cause.

I do not pretend to be in possession of a definitive list of the principles used by historians in selecting specifically causal conditions. But a principle which has been helpfully discussed by H. L. A. Hart and A. M. Honoré as it applies to causal judgment in the law gives some indication, I think, of what sometimes lies behind the selective practices of historians as well.[18] In tracing a chain of explanatory conditions back to a point of causal origin,

[18] *Causation in the Law* (Oxford, 1959), 31 ff.

they point out, links which are considered normal in the envisaged context tend to be passed over, and the cause found in some earlier circumstance or conjunction of circumstances which is relevantly abnormal. It seems plausible to suggest that, in typical contexts of historical inquiry, an agent's mistaking his situation in certain ways, or his having illusions about it, would be regarded as a more abnormal possibility than his perceiving it correctly.[19] Thus, to revert to the example used by Mink: if the Alps are correctly regarded as a barrier to travel by men at a low level of technology, it will be the Alps themselves, not their thought about them, which will be regarded as the cause of their staying where they are. But if the Alps are regarded as the way to heaven and people start climbing them, it is more likely to be their 'thought' which will be said to cause them to act, their misconception about the object rather than the object itself. Thus, although the two-stage, two-sense account of causal connection may be applicable in such cases, it tells a good deal less than the whole story. For what historians regard as cause is sometimes located at the first stage, and sometimes at the second.[20] And the judgment as to where it should be located is not made arbitrarily, but on principle, in accordance with the historian's idea of what constitutes a satisfactory cause.

It turns out, therefore, that what Collingwood says in *The Idea of History* about a special historical sense of 'cause', in which what causes a person to act is what he thinks, and not the actual state of his environment, is true only of a special case, not of the usual one. And what he says about such a sense in the *Essay on Metaphysics*, although true of most cases, is not true of all.[21] Causes of actions in history will sometimes be thoughts, and sometimes be

[19] There are cases where the relationship might be reversed, e.g. where it would be normal for people to be misled, but some agent nevertheless managed to discover how things really were, and acted accordingly, his correct perception, because of its abnormality, then being regarded as the cause of his acting. Similar reversals can be expected in the historical examples offered above, where judgments of abnormality change. This aspect of causal judgment is dealt with further in my *Perspectives on History*, ch. 4; and in Raymond Martin's *The Past within Us: An Empirical Approach to Philosophy of History* (Princeton, 1989), ch. 4.

[20] Morton White, no doubt misled by Collingwood's saying in *IH* that historical causes are always thoughts, wrongly attributes to him the view that, when wishing to contrast specifically causal conditions with merely relevant conditions, historians should always select thoughts as causes (M. G. White, *The Foundations of Historical Knowledge* (New York, 1965), 147–8—cited hereafter as *Foundations*).

[21] It is only the position of *IH*, not that of *EM*, which might expose Collingwood to a criticism like Rotenstreich's that his theory places action 'in a

events. Yet it ought to be enough for Collingwood that, although
the physical world can cause an agent to act in a certain way, it
can do this only by being thought of in a certain way. Perhaps that
is all that Mink had in mind when he denied that physical events
can cause actions 'strictly speaking', and Donagan when he insisted that such events cannot be causes of actions *per se*. However, if by *per se* is meant 'in themselves', in a sense different
from 'by themselves', the dictum is clearly false, since the event
itself is sometimes the cause. And if it means 'by themselves', i.e.
in the absence of other relevant conditions, what is claimed, although true, would be true of all causes which were themselves
less than sufficient conditions of their effects, which almost all
causes are.[22]

It should be clear that admitting that physical conditions can
cause actions in the indicated sense concedes nothing to the doctrine of physical determinism, which Collingwood's whole account of the idea of cause in history often seems chiefly intended
to outflank. For if external conditions like the Alps are to produce
effects in the form of human actions, their ability to do this will
still be conditional upon appropriate decisions being made by the
agents involved. Or, to put it another way, the two-stage causal
series into which all causation of action by physical things can be
analysed, leaves room at its second stage for an intrusion of
human free will—a point which Collingwood characteristically
overstates by declaring that 'on hearing Mr. Baldwin's speech the
Speaker freely made up his mind to adjourn' (*EM* 290). To put it
in still another way, what Collingwood's position excludes from
history, so far as human action is concerned, is natural causation,
not causes which happen to be natural conditions.

§ 4. *Social Events and Conditions*

We turn now to consider what Collingwood had to say about the
place of social events, states, and processes in history, the other

vacuum' (*PHP* 13–14), or like Walsh's that it ignores the the background of
actions.

[22] Even when physical effects are attributed to physical causes, causal judgment
is normally selective, the cause of an avalanche, say, being heavy rains rather than
the equally relevant presence of moveable materials. Or vice versa.

category of 'objective' conditions. With regard to physical conditions, it was plausible to say that they are not what historical
studies are really about, and at least initially plausible to deny
that they have any explanatory function in them. It is not in the
least plausible to take either position with regard to social conditions. Yet Collingwood has been accused, by both historians
and philosophers, of completely excluding the latter from history's proper concerns, and of advancing a theory of understanding which has no relevance to them. E. H. Carr, for example, has
called it a 'serious error' for Collingwood to have restricted history to 'the thought of the individual actor'; Gardiner has stressed
how much even knowledge of particular individuals requires a
grasp of 'the wider setting of accepted belief and social convention which (very often) gave point and meaning to their behaviour'; Fischer has maintained that it should have been obvious to
Collingwood that historians cannot 'rethink the thought of a
collectivity'; and Mink has observed (although ultimately denying that this is Collingwood's own view) that history cannot be
seen as 'the incomprehensible sum of innumerable biographies'.[23]
Other critics have regarded Collingwood's theory of re-enactment
as having relevance mainly to special branches of historical inquiry: Walsh to political and military history; Morris Ginsberg
to diplomatic history;[24] and still others have considered well-
established branches of the discipline to be quite beyond its
scope: Morton White, social history; Leff, economic history; Rex
Martin, institutional or ecological history.[25]

Given such a chorus of dissatisfaction from both sides of the
Atlantic, it is more than a little curious that Collingwood himself
writes for the most part as if the fact that the historian's subject-
matter has a social dimension posed no serious problem for his
account of historical understanding. At no point in *The Idea of
History*, or in any of his other writings, does he isolate and confront in any systematic way the theoretical question of the relation
of individual to group in historical study.[26] He also leaves in some

[23] *WIH* 46; Gardiner; 'Historical Understanding', 279; Fischer, *Historians'
Fallacies*, 197; *MHD* 159.
[24] *IPH* 53; 'The Character of a Historical Explanation', *Aristotelian Society Supplementary Volume*, 21 (1947), 70 (cited hereafter as 'The Character').
[25] Morton White, *Foundations*, 148; Leff, *History and Social Theory*, 33; *HE* 15.
[26] This is made the more puzzling by his having included on his list of philosophical problems about history of 1927 the question whether history should

obscurity the extent to which he thinks that historians should concern themselves with group phenomena at all. Both his critics and his defenders are thus reduced to scrutinizing passing remarks which seem relevant, drawing out implications of what he says on related questions, noting attitudes he displays towards positions supposedly held by others, and remarking features of his own historical practice. Using gleanings of this kind, I think that something like a Collingwoodian position on the place of the social in historical studies can be discerned. Among those who have written extensively about his work, only Donagan and Mink have made much attempt to elaborate such a position. What follows is in their debt; but the interpretation which I shall defend falls somewhere between the opposed conclusions which they have drawn.

Let us ask first to what extent Collingwood actually defines or describes the subject-matter of history in an excessively individualistic way. Certainly when it comes to selecting examples of historical thinking for philosophical analysis, what he chooses often turns out to be actions of particular agents. The kind of thing he discusses most memorably is Nelson giving orders at Trafalgar, or Theodosius promulgating a legal code, or Caesar crossing the Rubicon. And when he undertakes to illustrate his claim that historical thought 'has for its proper object something individual', what he mentions is not social individuals like capitalism or the Lutheran Church, but two named persons, Elizabeth and Marlborough, the policy of two others, Ferdinand and Isabella, and a happening, the Peloponnesian War, traditional historical accounts of which have stressed the exploits of certain political and military leaders (*IH* 233). If Collingwood was ever going to give the social dimension of history its due, one would expect to find him doing it in the section of *The Idea of History* entitled 'The Subject-matter of History'. In fact, what he presents there is a list of subjects whose claims to historicity seem to derive entirely from their involving the plans, policies, and decisions of human individuals.[27] 'Human Nature and Human History' begins more

stress 'the biographical element' or be about 'movements whose magnitude transcends the individual' (L27 347).

[27] When he wants to undermine Spengler's attempt to 'predetermine' history, he similarly calls attention to unpredictable human individuals, not to unpredictable social ones (SHC 69).

promisingly, or at any rate less restrictively, with the declaration that history proper, unlike natural history, is about 'human affairs' (*IH* 212). But within a few sentences this dissolves into what, in an early section of *The Idea of History*, is said to be the only proper focus of an historian's interest, namely, 'actions of human beings which have been done in the past' (*IH* 9); and we are launched upon an analysis of what is involved in understanding the initiative of a military commander.

Yet, as Mink, especially, has noted, Collingwood often speaks with sympathy of both historians and philosophers whose theory or whose practice displays rather holistic tendencies. Thus his objection to Livy's concern with 'characteristic Roman institutions' and 'the typical Roman character' is not that he gave these central place, but only that he conceived them as static rather than as developing (*IH* 43). His objection to the way Montesquieu focused on changes in human institutions is not that he exaggerated their importance, but only that he regarded them as 'the necessary effects of natural causes' (*IH* 79). Historians of the Enlightenment, although criticized on other grounds, are congratulated for having given a new prominence to 'the history of the arts and sciences, industry, trade, and culture in general' (*IH* 81). And when reservations are expressed about the emphasis placed by Hegel and Marx on large-scale political and economic processes respectively, this is not because they neglected, in consequence, the actions of individual agents, but because they failed sufficiently to recognize the historical importance of human culture in an even more general sense (*IH* 122, 311). Especially significant is Collingwood's praise of Vico for having achieved for the first time 'a completely modern idea of what the subject-matter of history is', namely, 'the genesis and development of human societies and their institutions', the 'process whereby human beings build up systems of language, customs, law, government, etc.' (*IH* 65).[28] Remarks such as these suggest that Mink may be correct in maintaining that critics have read too much into Collingwood's frequent employment of examples dealing with actions of individuals (*HU* 244). These, as he says, may indeed have been chosen

---

[28] Another relevant passage is Collingwood's criticism of Hume and Voltaire for failing to see history as concerned with developing institutions (*IH* 78). In the Martouret manuscript, however, Voltaire receives praise for encouraging historians to turn towards 'social and economic questions' (L28 433).

more for the ease with which they illustrate the central notions of re-enactment and re-thinking, and perhaps also those of particularity and individuality, than for the degree to which they exemplify, in themselves, Collingwood's view of the historian's ultimate interests.[29]

Besides showing sympathy for holistically inclined views of others, Collingwood also, from time to time, makes at least quasi-holistic theoretical pronouncements of his own about the nature of the historian's subject-matter. Thus, while denying that historians properly concern themselves with the gratification or frustration of human appetites as such ('the fact that men eat and sleep and make love'), he insists, as critics like Fain appear not to notice, that they must study 'the social customs' which provide 'a framework within which these appetites find satisfaction in ways sanctioned by convention and morality' (*IH* 216). And, having made his provocative remark that it 'makes no difference to the historian, as an historian, that there should be no food in a poor man's house', he adds that the student of history must nevertheless be 'intensely concerned with the shifts by which other men have contrived to bring about this state of things in order that they should be rich and the men who take wages from them poor' (*IH* 315)—in other words, with political, economic, and social structures. At still another point, he puts down with irony those who regard industry and commerce as 'low matters' into which 'an historian with the instincts of a gentleman would not inquire' (*IH* 277).[30] He would surely have been astonished to find Fischer describing a book which (he alleges) disparages topics like 'ships, trade routes, currency, property, agriculture, town government, and military tactics', as the kind of historical work which would have 'warmed the cockles of Collingwood's heart'.[31]

---

[29] Yet, in a manuscript of 1936, after observing that 'history is knowledge of the individual', he adds 'e.g. the Norman Conquest' (NHH 16).

[30] Collingwood also represents the study of 'specific types of human organization, the city state, the feudal system, representative government, capitalistic industry' as characteristic of modern approaches to history (*IH* 211); expresses a personal interest in economic and demographic history (*A* 134–5); notes that, whereas formerly, history's assumed subject-matter was chiefly 'the names and dates of kings and battles', it is now a 'description of social and economic conditions' (L27 356); and contrasts 'the world of nature' not with the world of human action, but with 'the world of human institutions' (L26 408). What is discussed in *NL* is mainly social units as comprehensive as civilizations.

[31] Fischer, *Historians' Fallacies*, 197.

Nor is Collingwood's interest in the social, holistic aspect of history expressed only at the theoretical level; it shows itself even more clearly in his practice as an historian. The long chapter which he contributed to Tenney Frank's *Economic Survey of Ancient Rome* scarcely mentions an individual agent; and the same could be said of most of his archaeological studies, which he viewed as continuous with his history: his excavations of Roman forts and camps; his study of the general characteristics of Roman roads; his inquiry into the purpose of the Roman Wall; his controversial inference from an inscription on a gravestone at Silchester to the presence of an Irish colony there late in the Roman period. Even his two general histories of the Roman period in Britain, *Roman Britain* and *Roman Britain and the English Settlements*, although giving some space to political and military narrative and recounting the exploits of prominent individuals like Suetonius or Boudicca, are notable as much as anything for the brilliant fashion in which they trace changes in patterns of town and country life, the independent functioning of the agricultural systems centred upon villa and village, the survival of the Celtic style of art by contrast with the Romanization of Celtic religious cults, and the role played by provincial Britain in the imperial political and economic systems.

Some who have criticized what they take to be Collingwood's excessively individualistic conception of the historian's subject-matter would not think it enough merely to be shown that his work takes account of social events and conditions *as well as* individual actions. Thus Maurice Mandelbaum has contended that to say, without serious qualification, that history is about individual human actions at all is to invite misunderstanding.[32] For, as we normally conceive it, at any rate, history is about individual actions only to the extent that they relate to social structures and changes. To become subject-matter for history, Mandelbaum insists, an action must have 'societal significance'; and what history is primarily about is what provides that significance.[33] Yet Collingwood makes this point himself, thereby also to some extent answering the criticism of Gardiner noted above. Even in setting forth his paradigm case, he represents historians

---

[32] Review of *IH*, in *Journal of Philosophy*, 44 (1947), 186–7.
[33] *The Problem of Historical Knowledge* (New York, 1967), 9, 14.

as interested in Caesar's crossing of the Rubicon 'only in its relation to Republican law', and in the spilling of blood on the Senate
floor 'only in its relation to a constitutional conflict' (*IH* 213). The
same consideration appears when he discusses the relation of
history to biography. Biography, he says, takes as its framework
an individual life; and through this framework the currents of
history 'flow cross-wise . . . like sea-water through a stranded
wreck' (*IH* 304). If anything, the contrast between history and
biography is overdrawn, no mention being made, for example, of
hybrids like political or institutional biographies of figures chosen
by reason of their historical importance.

   One can certainly find statements which seem to imply a contrary view of the historicity of individual actions considered in
themselves. A famous one, to which Mandelbaum takes strong
exception, is Collingwood's remarking, in his Historical Association Pamphlet of 1930: 'To know who played centre-forward for
Aston Villa last year is just as much historical knowledge as to
know who won the battle of Cannae' (*PH* 124)—as if, comments
Mandelbaum, 'any action, no matter how trivial, can be the object
of the kind of inquiry carried on by an historian'.[34] However, as
Mink has argued, the distinction which Collingwood sometimes
draws between broader and narrower senses of the word 'history'
may be called upon here (*HU* 225–6). The quoted remark occurs
at a point where he is maintaining that 'everything has a past;
everything has somehow come to be what it is', so that 'the
historical aspect of things is a universal and necessary aspect of
them'. It appears, therefore, that the trivial action mentioned is to
be conceived as belonging to history only in the sense of a general
mode of thought, not in the sense of the special discipline practised by historians. One can interpret in the same broad way
Collingwood's claim, in *The Idea of History* itself, that the discovery of what someone was thinking even five minutes ago is an
historical discovery (*IH* 219). For this is only a way of saying that,
if what is envisaged is a warrantable claim to knowledge, there
will have to be an appeal to evidence and an employment of

----

[34] Mandelbaum, *Anatomy*, 206 n. 4. Collingwood himself says that history is not
'the mere determination of any and every past event', but only of those of which
knowledge is required to solve problems which have arisen for historians (NAPH
53), which he appears to think would relate, much of the time at least, to social
conditions and structures.

methods of inquiry which are at least analogous to those used by historians.

§ 5. *Social Reductionism*

It seems clear enough that Collingwood sees history as a study of an essentially social subject-matter. Many of his critics, however, have felt that he still conceives that subject-matter in an excessively individualistic way. For although he may accept it that the primary task of the historian is to understand social events and processes, he often seems to regard those events and processes as themselves just agglomerations of individual human beings acting and reacting, to be understood as such piecemeal. With this in mind, Donagan has described him as a 'methodological individualist, in the strongest sense of the term' (*LPC* 206); and Saari has found at least 'close affinities with methodological individualism' in his writings.[35] Mink, by contrast, has dismissed such a view of him as a 'caricature' and a 'fiction' (*HU* 225), and van der Dussen has also questioned it (*HS* 324). We must try to see what might lie behind such differences of judgment, and, indeed, what reasons there are for calling Collingwood a methodological individualist at all.

Certainly he often talks in ways which philosophers who have been so described—J. W. N. Watkins, for example—would find very acceptable.[36] In 'A Philosophy of Progress', he warns against the idea that society is 'a mythical superhuman being' rather than 'just individuals themselves in their mutual relations' (*PP* 119). In the *Autobiography*, he describes the British Constitution as 'a single complex of contemporaneous fact' exhibiting 'the beliefs of a given set of people at a given time' (*A* 67). In *Speculum Mentis*, he declares that, apart from its members, society is a mere 'abstraction' (*SM* 229).[37] In *The Idea of History*, he links this rejection of social 'reification' to his theory of re-enactive understanding with

---

[35] Saari, *Re-enactment*, 120.

[36] For some of the more important writings on this topic by Watkins and others, see John O'Neill (ed.), *Modes of Individualism and Collectivism* (London, 1973).

[37] In other writings he maintains that society 'consists of Tom, Dick and Harry' ('The Devil', 226 n. 4); that the actions of a society are the actions of the people in it ('Political Action', reprinted in Boucher (ed.), *Essays in Political Philosophy*, 102–3); that a society consists of the 'common way of life' of its members (*PA* 96).

the observation: 'If we are told that there was a strike at the factory or a run on the bank, we can reconstruct in our minds the purposes of the people whose collective action took those forms' (*IH* 310). The idea which is stressed is that social events and processes are, in some important sense, *constituted* by the actions, beliefs, attitudes, etc., of relevant human individuals. Collingwood doesn't put this position in the linguistic or conceptual form favoured by many contemporary methodological individualists, namely, that statements about social groups should be translatable without remainder into statements about their component individuals. He generally puts it ontologically, as a claim about what social groups really are. Whether that makes him a methodological individualist 'in the strongest sense of the term' will depend upon what one thinks of considerations like the following.

First, as Donagan has underlined, Collingwood is, at any rate, no advocate of what Popper calls the conspiracy theory of society (*LPC* 207). That is, he does not regard governmental failures, economic depressions, wars, and the like, as things which have to be seen as deliberately brought about by any or all of the individuals concerned if they are to be understood in a distinctively historical way. To think that this is the way historical events typically come about, Collingwood observes, was the mistake of the historians of the Enlightenment, with their view of institutions as 'inventions' or 'artifices' imposed by a powerful and intelligent élite on the weak and stupid masses, a view well exemplified by Voltaire's conception of religion as maintained by priestcraft (*IH* 78). The antidote to this 'error' he finds *par excellence* in medieval historiography, with its notion of events proceeding under God's providence, to a large extent over men's heads. For it is 'an indispensable precondition of understanding any historical process', he says, that we recognize that 'what happens in history need not happen through anyone deliberately wishing it to happen' (*IH* 48).[38] Not that he entirely denies the applicability of the contrary model. He represents the colonization of New England, for example, as 'a deliberate attempt on the part of the Pilgrim Fathers to carry out in terms of practice a Protestant idea of life' (*IH* 119).

---

[38] He also says that, when people act, they generally find that 'something has taken shape as the actions went on which was certainly not present to . . . the mind of any one when the actions which brought it into existence began' (*IH* 42).

And he sometimes adopts a stance which at least leans towards the conspiratorial, as when he represents history as 'a drama . . . co-operatively extemporised by its own performers' (NAPH 36).[39] More characteristic, however, is his view of the coming of the First World War, which, he says, occurred in spite of the desire of almost everyone to avoid it, basically because 'a situation got out of hand' (A 90). Gardiner points out, meaning it as a criticism of Collingwood, that 'what occurs in history often bears little or no relation to the intentions and expectations of the agents concerned'.[40] But this is very much Collingwood's own view. He typically represents what happened in history as largely a resultant of what individuals willed, the human past, on his view, being largely a story of unintended consequences.

It needs to be stressed, secondly, that, despite the interest which Collingwood shows personally in the exploits of the Caesars and Nelsons of history, he does not expect historians to be able to reduce the social phenomena they study, in more than a fraction of cases, to the actions of identifiable, named individuals. Like most contemporary individualists, he thinks it ordinarily sufficient that they be able to reduce them to what was done by unspecified or 'anonymous' individuals—a point underlined by Mink (MHD 174). Thus, when a critic like Leff complains that Collingwood's theory of understanding is inapplicable to something like the three-field system in agriculture, this because it would require us quite gratuitously to 'interpolate our own image of men ploughing', he misconceives Collingwood's position in an important way (HST 33). To be sure, it is no part of the historian's task, when reporting the operation of a three-field system, to interpolate imaginary ploughmen at particular times and places as writers of historical novels do (thus calling upon what Collingwood calls the artistic, not the historical, imagination). But any evidence for the operation of such an agricultural system would have to be considered, at the same time, as evidence for there having been men ploughing, this having implications for what would count as further verification of the original claim. In

---

[39] Much more modest is his remark that a sensible person well knows that the seemingly 'empty space in front of him' which he proposes 'to fill up with his activities' will be 'crowded with other people all pursuing activities of their own' by the time he steps into it, leaving no room for his own, 'unless he can so design this that it will fit into the interstices of the rest' (IH 316).

[40] Gardiner, 'Concept of Man', 17.

his philosophical pronouncements about history, Collingwood
often stresses its concern with the anonymous, as when he observes that 'in the last resort' what military history is about is
'what the men in the ranks thought about the battle' (*A* 110). In his
historical writing, too, he makes frequent reference to the actions
of anonymous individuals, as when he attributes the building of
Hardknot Castle to unknown Romans, to whom he is nevertheless quite prepared to attribute reasons for building it.[41]

Individualists who have considered themselves Collingwoodians have sometimes seemed to draw more extreme methodological conclusions than this from the thesis that the
social dimension of history is constituted by the activities of individuals. Thus A. M. MacIver has said that, since 'the ultimate stuff
of history is the countless individual doings of individual human
beings through the ages', any statements made by historians
about a past event like the battle of Hastings must be generalizations from their knowledge of what the particular individuals
did: 'this man shooting this arrow, that man avoiding it or being
hit by it', and so on.[42] Goldstein has very properly objected that
the ontological thesis of reducibility to individuals has no such
methodological implications—that justifiable statements about
the battle presuppose no such independent knowledge of a sufficient number of specific actions.[43] For the historian may infer the
occurrence of the battle from evidence which provides no information at all about particular cases of shooting; and even when
some such cases are known, inferences about the battle would
generally go well beyond them. If there is a sense of methodological individualism which denies this, then so much the worse for
it. What remains true is that evidence for the battle will at the
same time be evidence for there having been actions of a sort
which were characteristic of battles at the time, and that what is
claimed about the battle can be put in question by asking whether
sufficient numbers of such actions took place.

[41] *Roman Eskdale*, 38. No individuals could be more anonymous than the ones
assumed by Collingwood to have formed the alleged Irish colony at Silchester
(*RBES* 316), or the 'anyone' to whom he refers in explaining the replacement of the
Norman by the Gothic arch (PP 110). There are also mixed cases, like the following: 'Furious at this breach of faith . . . the Iceni rose at Boudicca's call' (*RBES* 99).
[42] 'The Character of a Historical Explanation', *Aristotelian Society Supplementary
Volume*, 21 (1947), 38 (cited hereafter as 'The Character').
[43] Goldstein, 'Collingwood's Theory', 19–20.

A third consideration which needs to be kept in mind in assessing the nature of Collingwood's individualism is that he is not among those who think that the reducibility of social events and processes to individual actions implies that they have no characteristics not possessed by the constituent actions considered in themselves.[44] He makes it clear, in fact, that he regards social phenomena as, at least sometimes, possessing characteristics that *could not* be possessed by any of the individual actions composing them. In *The New Leviathan*, for example, he insists that 'civilization' is something that can happen to people only collectively, not individually (*NL* 283).[45] He would presumably say the same of 'being at war', or 'populating the West', or 'maintaining the monarchy'.[46] It makes no sense to predicate any of these things of the individuals involved, taking them individually rather than collectively. There is thus no question, for Collingwood, of historians being able to eliminate distinctively social concepts from their descriptions and explanations: this possibility does not follow from their regarding what they describe and explain as reducible to the actions of individuals. Donagan leaves room for such considerations when he says, more exactly, that group phenomena are reducible to 'the acts of individuals *and the relations between them*' (*LPC* 206; emphasis added). For the relations in question may be distinctively social ones. Donagan may seem to deviate from this position when he observes, with apparent approval, that, for Collingwood, 'the theory of the simplest case is the theory of all cases; for complex interactions have no elements that cannot be found in the simplest act' (*LPC* 209). However, to claim that social phenomena are reducible without remainder to individual actions is to make a claim about what constitutes

[44] He is in danger of falling into the contrary position when he observes that 'any increase in freedom, intelligence, and self-reliance in individuals is automatically reflected in society', since society is just those individuals 'in their mutual relations' (PP 119).

[45] He also points out that certain types of human activity require a minimum number of people: that 'it takes two to make a quarrel, three to make a case of jealousy, four or five . . . to make a civil society, and so on' (*IN* 19–20). In the first two cases, the concept used to characterize the relationship can also be used to characterize the individuals: all the parties in a quarrel e.g. may be said to be quarrelling. But it would only be a joke to say that each farmer who went West was settling it, or that each of Nelson's sailors was making war.

[46] Social concepts (like 'cohesive' but not 'literate') may sometimes be said to express characteristics which are emergent relative to those possessed by the individuals concerned. See Ch. 4, § 5, on emergence in art.

them, not about the kinds of concepts needed for studying them. Collingwood may be an ontological individualist, and perhaps also a methodological one, but he is not a conceptual individualist.

In fact, it is an oversimplification to say that social phenomena are reducible to the *actions* of human beings, even if we take account also of their relations to each other. For, as Collingwood's theory and practice both make clear, human beliefs, attitudes, tendencies, and the like also enter significantly into the composition of the social world. At one point, Collingwood himself specifically mentions human 'passivities' as well as human 'activities' as constitutive of a social entity like the state (SPAT 136). And there are other ways in which the reduction of the social to the individual may be far from simple. Donagan distinguishes between three kinds of social phenomena, each reducible to what is individual in a different way (*LPC* 207–8). In a run on a bank, for example, the relevant individuals all do roughly the same thing; in an election campaign, different individuals and groups of individuals do different but interlocking and mutually supporting things; and in a declaration of war, certain individuals who are authorized to act for the group do certain things with at least the tacit consent of the rest. Mink sees institutions, which he contrasts with mere collective actions, as posing a special problem for the reducibility of the social to the individual (*MHD* 175). However, it is not clear that the way institutions are constituted introduces any new principle of importance for our present concerns (but see § 6). Collingwood himself distinguishes between the way individuals are related to each other in mere classes, namely, by resemblance (as when we speak of 'the monied class') and the way they are related in societies (he might as well have said institutions), namely, by participation (*NL* 134).

A point worth stressing about the historian's use of social concepts is that their applicability may often go quite beyond the awareness of the individuals whose activities jointly instantiate them. A social concept like 'electing a president' cannot be applied unless the relevant agents know that their own activities and those of others jointly instantiate it. But there are other social concepts, like 'depleting natural resources' or 'increasing the deficit', of which this is not true. Collingwood sometimes makes observations which could obscure this important point. Thus, with a view to illustrating his recurring claim that anything properly belonging to the historian's subject-matter will be an expression of human consciousness, he attributes approvingly to Vico the contention: 'The Italian language is exactly what the people who use it think it is' (*IH* 66). He would surely have to agree that there are many things about that language which almost certainly remained quite unknown to many who have spoken it, such as its having cases, a smaller vocabulary than English, and few guttural sounds. Mink seems close to repeating Collingwood's error when he declares: 'Institutions are constituted by the way in which they are thought of by the people living under them' (*MHD* 181). He nevertheless defends Collingwood effectively against the general charge that he is required by his re-enactment theory to maintain that historians can know human activities only as they were known to the original agents, a view which he associates with methodological individualism 'in the strongest sense of the term' (*HU* 231 ff.). Collingwood is certainly not, on balance, a methodological individualist in this most implausible sense, even if he sometimes talks as if he were. In his better moments, he would say, with Mink, that historians often study 'processes of change of which no participant could have given the account which historical inquiry can give' (*HU* 226).

§ 6. Social Causes and Effects

If methodological individualism is the claim that social phenomena are reducible (with the caveats noted) to individual human actions and the relations between them, it seems fair to say that Collingwood was, to a substantial degree, a methodological individualist. As we have considered it so far, however, his individualism is chiefly an ontological position, its main claim being that social events and conditions simply *are* individuals acting and reacting. But methodological individualism has also, and perhaps more often, meant a theory of what counts as acceptable explanation in history. We must therefore ask whether Collingwood can also be considered a methodological individualist in this further sense, and if so, how this meshes with his conception of historical understanding as re-enactment.

The question can be put somewhat out of focus by the fact that

claiming social events and conditions to be reducible to the actions of individuals can itself be regarded as advancing a theory
of historical explanation in one important sense of the term. For
one way of putting that claim would be to say that social events
and conditions can be explained *as* individuals acting and inter-
acting in various ways. It might be said, conversely, that actions of
individuals, taken together, can sometimes be explained *as* a
social phenomenon of some kind—for example, as an outbreak of
war, or as an economic recovery. In this sense, reducibility is
already explicability. Of course, explaining one thing as another
does not explain why anything happened. It does not explain
'why' at all: it explains 'what'—what something really was, or
what it amounted to. Some authors have described this very
common way of making historical materials intelligible as 'verti-
cal' interpretation, by contrast with the 'horizontal' kind instanced by explanation why.[47] Walsh, borrowing a term from
William Whewell, has called it 'colligation under appropriate
conceptions' (*IPH* 59–64). A claim to have achieved historical
understanding of this sort will often be signalized by the use of
distinctive social concepts, sometimes concepts invented for the
occasion, like 'bourgeois revolution' (Marx), or 'Time of Troubles'
(Toynbee). Collingwood offers no analysis of this sort of thing,
and, indeed, scarcely seems to recognize that historians might
explain what things really were as well as why or how they
happened, although his own historical practice provides examples of it (*RB* 32, 92, 143).

But methodological individualism, often in conjunction with
something like Collingwood's idea of re-enactment, has generally
been regarded as a theory of how historians can and should
explain why things happened as they did, including what caused
them to happen so. Three kinds of cases might be distinguished:
first, ones in which individual actions are explained by reference
to social causes; second, ones in which the causes of social
phenomena are found in other social phenomena; and third, ones
in which social phenomena are said to be caused by the actions of
individuals. Let us look at each of these possibilities in turn.

Philosophers well disposed towards Collingwood's view of
history have generally seen little difficulty in the idea that indi-

[47] See Lincoln Reis and P. O. Kristellar, 'Some Remarks on the Method of
History', *Journal of Philosophy*, 40 (1943), 240 ff.

vidual actions may be caused by social events and conditions. Indeed, as Mink has suggested, one reason why Collingwood may have felt so little need to discuss the explanatory role of social conditions in history could well be that, where such conditions are said to explain what most interests historians, i.e. past actions, they are seen as doing this in the same way that physical conditions do: by the agents becoming conscious of them and taking them as reasons to act in certain ways (*MHD* 175).[48] Donagan has made much the same point by calling attention to the fact that a person's *causa quod*, where this means his conception of the situation he faces, will frequently make reference to 'some group or institution to which he belonged' (*LPC* 208).[49] Indeed, one might go so far as to say that social considerations will typically enter into the explanation of actions in history, since it will seldom be possible to characterize, and thus show the force of, the reasons for which people acted without making use of social concepts. Van der Dussen has wondered whether Collingwood can properly be called a methodological individualist if he accepts the idea that 'holistic ideas play a role in the actions of individuals', and thus enter into their historical explanation (*HS* 325). But it is not a necessary condition of an historian understanding a past action in a methodologically individualistic way that the agent, too, have been a methodological individualist. The thought of an agent who conceived his situation holistically is just as open to being re-enacted by an individualist historian as is the thought of any agent whose beliefs the historian himself may regard as dubious. An historian might, for example, come to understand Charles de Gaulle's policy of promoting the grandeur of France as inspired by a holistic conception of his country as always right and good (even if most Frenchmen are not), without in the least seeing this as a sensible idea to act upon.

Clearly, the explanation of actions by social conditions will invite the same three-term analysis, and the same contrast between direct and indirect causation, which was found applicable in cases where the causes of actions were physical. Here, too, the

---

[48] According to Atkinson, Collingwood failed to make this point (*KEH* 26), but it seems to be implicit in many passages.

[49] There is unfortunately some ambiguity in the way Collingwood uses his term of art 'causa quod': it sometimes means a motivating situation, and sometimes an agent's conception of one, this reflecting his ambivalence as between the *IH* and *EM* senses of historical cause.

causation will (at some stage) go 'through the mind'. And where an agent misperceived a situation, this time a social one, we can again expect it to be his thought rather than the situation itself which will be said to have caused him to act. As in the case of physical conditions, it will also be necessary to distinguish between conditions which caused actions to be performed and conditions which caused them to be successful or unsuccessful, or even, in some cases, not to be undertaken at all—as when Collingwood reports that troubles in Gaul prevented Augustus from pursuing his policies there (RBES 72). Even a claim of the latter sort, however, is open to two kinds of interpretation, only one involving a connection 'through the mind'. It could mean, as Collingwood seems in this case to mean, that there were social circumstances which made it out of the question, rationally speaking, to undertake the action; or it could mean that such circumstances rendered a certain course of action impossible in something closer to a nomological sense. The latter alternative is suggested when Collingwood remarks (with the depredations of Picts, Scots, and Saxons in mind) that the reason why the Britons, unlike their neighbours, the Gauls, did not for long retain Roman culture after the Romans left, was that they had 'more and deadlier enemies' (RB 24). People, as well as volcanic eruptions, can maim and kill.

The sort of case where one set of social events and conditions is said to cause another—the second case to be considered—has sometimes evoked the rather strange objection from individualists like J. W. N. Watkins that, since social phenomena are, strictly speaking, 'nonentities' (SPAT 136), they are ontologically incapable of causing anything.[50] Others, like Paul Weiss, have denied that the idea of re-enactment applies to them, on the ground that 'the parts of history which are produced by uncontrolled masses of men' are not open to being understood that way.[51] In the face of such criticism, as Donagan has remarked, Collingwood is frequently less than helpful (LPC 209). At one point, having outlined how he thinks a rather simple act of mathematical calcu-

---

[50] See his 'Ideal Types and Historical Explanation', reprinted in Herbert Feigl and May Brodbeck (eds.), Readings in the Philosophy of Science (New York, 1953), 729.

[51] History: Written and Lived (Carbondale, Ill., 1962), 43 (cited hereafter as History).

lation could be re-enactively understood, and having noted the possibility of a critic questioning whether he could explain something like a battle in the same way, he responds impatiently in advance with the remark: 'I could, and so could you, Reader, if you tried' (A 111–12). But he does not tell us how.

In fact, what he says about historical causation as a matter of affording people motives for acting offers quite a satisfactory basis for claiming that, at least sometimes, large-scale social conditions may properly be regarded as having caused other such conditions. Both cause and effect in such cases must be reducible to what is individual, the cause as a conjunction of individual actions, most of them anonymous, and perhaps none of them aimed at producing the social condition that resulted, and the effect similarly conceived. As Donagan has put it, historians 'must explain processes in groups by explaining the individual acts of which they are composed' (LPC 207). In other words, they must explain them piecemeal—although it is important to remember again that social conditions will not be reducible without remainder simply to actions.

Some methodological individualists—Watkins could again be mentioned—have thought it illuminating in this connection to take note of the analogous causal reductions which are carried out in some regions of physical science.[52] When a source of heat is applied to a gas, for example, and this is said to cause it to expand, although cause and effect are both macroscopic physical events, the connection between them is conceived as consisting of detailed causal connections between their microscopic constituents. The chief difference between such cases and typical historical ones is that, in the physical case, the detailed explanatory connections will be nomological, while in the historical case they will generally be re-enactive. It may also be expected that the detailed tracings of connection in the historical case will be more complex, since the human constituents, unlike the particles of physics, may be quite heterogeneous. However, most methodological individualists would concede, and Collingwood in his historical writings implicitly concedes, that, in their ordinary practice, historians will only occasionally try to trace out human microconnections in all their detail. They will generally operate in what

[52] 'Historical Explanation in the Social Sciences', reprinted in Gardiner (ed.), Theories of History, 504.

might be called a practical holistic mode, considering full individualistic reduction (what Watkins calls 'rock-bottom' explanation) as something required of them only 'in principle' or 'on demand'. Collingwood's main point remains, however: that individual re-enactments function as the ultimate court of appeal in social explanation in history.

The third sort of case, one in which individuals or individual actions are said to be causes of social events or conditions, may sometimes seem to be placed in doubt by Collingwood himself. In a critique of Bury's view of history, for example, with the causal role which Bury assigns to identifiable individuals especially in mind, he castigates historians who, lacking a 'satisfactory theory of historical causation', acquiesce 'in most trivial causes for the vastest effects' (*IH* 80–1). He cites, as a typical expression of this 'grotesque' view, Pascal's famous aphorism: 'if Cleopatra's nose had been longer the whole history of the world would have been different.' It is rather ironical that an author who has so often been accused of ascribing too much to individuals, and even of embracing something like a Great Man theory of history, should have lashed out at others in this way for wrongly thinking that 'large' (i.e. social) events could have 'small' (i.e. individual) causes.

But what Collingwood himself says about historical causation as involving re-enactable motivations, taken in conjunction, this time, with what he almost says about the way specifically causal conditions are to be distinguished from merely relevant ones (see § 3), again points to a resolution of the problem. It should be noted, first, that satisfactory explanations of many social results which are of interest to historians require reference to both social states of affairs and to the actions of particular individuals. One of the circumstances cited by Collingwood when explaining the invasion of Britain by the Romans is the fact that the British tribes, at any rate as Caesar saw it, posed a threat to the political and economic stability of Gaul; but another is the fact that Caesar was ambitious. In such cases, it is sometimes appropriate for an historian to select the social condition as the specifically causal one, perhaps on the ground of its relative abnormality, and sometimes, perhaps on the same ground, to select the contributions of individuals. Doing the latter from time to time hardly amounts to ignoring the social dimension of historical causation. Nor does it fasten upon Collingwood a Great Man theory of history in any familiar sense of the term. For what would ordinarily be considered the 'greatness' of an individual in history does not derive simply from the fact that his actions are appropriately selected as causes of significant social results. To take a well-worn example: Charles I of England has sometimes been said to have caused the English Civil War by his misguided policies in Church and State; but he is usually represented, at the same time, as a blunderer, a victim more than a master of events, certainly not a 'great man' in any ordinary sense. What counts in such cases is not an individual's powers, intelligence, or virtue, but his actions happening to be indispensable for an envisaged result, and being selectable as the cause of it on something like the abnormality criterion.

With regard to cases where it is social events and conditions which are said to be causes, a remark should perhaps be added about the extent to which an acceptance of social causation commits Collingwood to some form of social determinism. The ideas of causation at the social level and of social determinism are sometimes virtually equated. It should be clear, however, that no such equation holds for Collingwood, any more than his acceptance of physical factors as causes can be equated with an acceptance of physical determinism. It is true that he sometimes talks of social change (as illustrated in Chapter 3) using language which may suggest social determinism. But when he does so it is usually not difficult to reduce what he says in the methodological individualist way. And he sometimes talks quite otherwise, reminding us, for example, that social orders are just 'historical facts' (*IH* 223), and repeatedly rejecting any idea that historical inquiry is about forces, structures, and movements, nomologically conceived. It should be equally clear that no argument for social determinism is derivable from Collingwood's admission that holistic social concepts will be needed if historians are to offer adequate characterizations and explanations of human activities. To recognize, for example, the applicability of concepts which attribute to groups what cannot be attributed to their members is still only to recognize resultants of what individuals, for their own purposes, do. How historical agents act is not determined by the applicability of social concepts; the applicability of social concepts is determined by how the agents act.

Some authors, like Mink, have thought that the fact that the historian's subject-matter includes institutions poses a special

threat to Collingwood's methodological individualism and conse-
quent social indeterminism. For institutions, as Mink remarks,
often seem to have 'a life of their own' (*MHD* 175).[53] In relation
to individual actions, they often appear change-resistant, even
coercive: not just social facts, but social forces—this despite
Collingwood's description of them as 'free inventions of human
reason' (*IH* 79). Such considerations, however, hardly raise an
insuperable problem for a Collingwood who has already allowed
that historical agents can be forced (but not determined) to act by
the actions of other individuals, or even by physical conditions.
Like the latter, social phenomena will be coercive when they offer
the individuals concerned urgent reasons to do what they would
otherwise prefer not to do. As long as being forced to act does not
mean being nomologically determined to act, Collingwood's
theory will claim to accommodate it. As for the claim that institutional developments are (even relatively) unchangeable, one
surely needs to ask: 'By whom?' The Collingwoodian position is
not that something like the Anglican Church or the American
Congress can in fact be changed by any particular person or
group. The contention is only that, given their ontological character, such institutions can be changed by an indeterminate but
sufficient number of their members deciding to act in new ways.

§ 7. *The Corporate Mind*

I have argued that, by and large, Collingwood reconciles quite
satisfactorily his acceptance of the idea that social events and
conditions are the principal subject-matter of history with his
theory of historical understanding as re-enactive. He does this by
accepting the reducibility of that subject-matter to the actions of at
least anonymous human individuals, and holding the understanding of the social phenomena to require (at least in principle)
the re-thinking of the thoughts expressed severally by the latter.
But there is another way in which he might have tried to bring the
two doctrines together: he might have seen it as the task of historians to re-think thoughts which were expressed by the social

[53] Historians themselves sometimes talk this way (see e.g. Veronica Wedgwood,
The King's War (London, 1966), 140).

events and conditions considered as such, these thoughts in many cases not being ascribable at all to the individuals involved. In other words, Collingwood might have adopted some form of group mind theory.[54] And there are critics who apparently believe that this is what he ultimately does. Thus the reason given by Morton White for denying that Collingwood's theory applies to social history is that the social historian 'can hardly be described as someone who seeks the thoughts in the mind of *society*'.[55] And the danger seen by Fischer in what he takes to be Collingwood's search for thought in the behaviour of 'collectivities' is that of 'conjuring up the fiction of a "corporate mind" '.[56]

It must be conceded that Collingwood often talks as if he finds nothing unacceptable about the notion of a corporate mind. He calls the body of human thought 'a corporate possession' (*IH* 226), and he characterizes progress as 'the corporate life of mankind remembering and learning by its own past' (THC 84). He praises as an advance in historical thinking the way the Roman historians focused on 'the continuing and corporate spirit of a people' (*IH* 34). Against Toynbee he argues that Western civilization formed itself 'by reconstructing within its own mind the mind of the Hellenic world' (*IH* 163). Against Marx he sets Fichte's alleged principle that the 'framework' of history is 'ideas' internally related to one another, the latter not to be thought of as lodged 'in people's heads' on pain of falling into 'subjective idealism' (*IH* 117–18, 124). Collingwood also speaks without disapproval of Hegel's doctrine of 'the cunning of reason' (*IH* 116) and of Ranke's 'conception of historical movements or periods as the realization of a concept or idea such as Protestantism' (*IH* 122). Perhaps none of these dicta are incapable of individualistic reduction. But, in their context, many of them can scarcely be said to invite it.

There are certainly remarks which could be cited on the other side; but these do not always present themselves as unambiguous denunciations of talk about superhuman minds or apparently

[54] Donagan states bluntly: 'since there is no such thing as a group mind, historians must explain processes in groups by explaining the individual acts of which they are composed' (*LPC* 207). But what we need to know is whether Collingwood's theory of understanding rules out such a theory (I do not see that it does) and how close he got to accepting such a theory himself (I think, at times, quite close).

[55] Morton White, *Foundations*, 148.   [56] Fischer, *Historians' Fallacies*, 197.

unattached ideas at work in society at large. In 'Human Nature and Human History', for example, having examined two cases of re-enactive explanations of individual actions, Collingwood observes, rather obscurely, that the same kind of understanding is the only one available to historians who wish to deal with 'the corporate mind . . . of a community or age'—adding, unhelpfully: 'whatever exactly that phrase means' (*IH* 219). He continues: 'to study the mind of the Victorian age or the English political spirit is simply to study the history of Victorian thought or English political activity.' At another point he observes, with a hint of individualistic nuance, that we can 'compare the seventeenth-century mind, in its general orientation, with that of to-day, by comparing the subjects dealt with in their literature' (*IH* 232). In neither case, however, is it made entirely clear whether the indicated thought, activity, or ideas should be considered to have been expressed by the relevant agents individually or collectively. And, in fact, the second case is uncomfortably similar to an actual one cited by Fischer to illustrate holistic misbehaviour, one in which an historian deliberately treated a number of literary works as if they were the work of 'a single intelligence' (the historian's own description of what he was doing), selecting *ad hoc* from them on this assumption.[57] To Fischer, not surprisingly, this is hypostatizing a non-existent entity.

From the standpoint of most methodological individualists, perhaps Collingwood's most disturbing passage is one in which he discusses the contribution of Kant to the development of the idea of history (*IH* 95 ff.). Here he expresses sympathy for the notion, which he attributes to Kant, that historians, in dealing with human collectivities, are driven to use 'teleological metaphors' in order to describe them adequately. For example, they need to use notions like 'the conquest of the Mediterranean world by Rome', even though the developments to which they refer may have taken several generations to work themselves through, and were not implementations of the policy of any one person. The particular notion cited is presumably called teleological because it is a description of something done, an 'action', which (on the face of it, at any rate) ascribes purposes and beliefs to a subject, 'Rome'. It is presumably called a metaphor because it can be

---

[57] Fischer, *Historians' Fallacies*, 197.

assumed that those who use it will believe that only individual human agents can, in a literal sense, have purposes and beliefs. Collingwood takes the opportunity, in this connection, to repeat his reducibility thesis in a particularly rigorous form, insisting that 'what we mean by Rome is only this and that individual Roman, and what we mean by the conquest of the Mediterranean world is only the sum of this and that individual piece of warfare or administration which these men carried out'. But he adds that, although no individual Roman actually said (i.e. thought) to himself: 'I am playing my part in a great movement, the conquest of the Mediterranean world by Rome', the fact that many Romans acted 'as if' that was what they thought they were doing makes the metaphor virtually indispensable methodologically.

If Collingwood nevertheless rejects the notion that something like a group mind is at work in such cases, he must do this on principles different from those suggested by his rejection, at two points in *The Idea of History*, of a corresponding hypothesis that mind is at work in the natural world. In discussing Croce's views, towards the end of his survey of the rise of the idea of history, he shows himself more than a little intrigued by the latter's challenge: 'Do you wish to understand the true history of a blade of grass? Try to become a blade of grass' (*IH* 199–200)—this following similar advice about the way one would have to understand a neolithic Ligurian or Sicilian. He confesses, however, that his scepticism 'reaches the point of rebellion' when he is asked to regard changes in a physical object like a crystal or a stalactite as 'an expression of its own spiritual life'. Here, he says, 'we look in vain for any expression of thought.' In 'Human Nature and Human History' he goes further. 'There is only one hypothesis', he declares, 'on which natural processes could be regarded as ultimately historical in character: namely, that these processes are in reality . . . expressions of thoughts, whether the thoughts of God, or of angelic or demonic finite intelligences, or of minds somewhat like our own.' He goes on: 'such an hypothesis could claim our serious attention only if it led to a better understanding of the natural world. In fact, however, the scientist can reasonably say of it, "je n'ai pas eu besoin de cette hypothèse" ' (*IH* 217). Yet, in his comments on Kant's teleological metaphors, Collingwood more than half concedes that the hypothesis of a group mind which transcends individual human minds does in fact lead to 'a better understanding' of the subject-matter. And he seems to hold that historians have need of it at least in the sense of having to talk 'as if' they accepted it.

Given the general theory of mind sketched in *The Idea of History*, the question arises with what propriety Collingwood can speak of people acting consistently and systematically 'as if' their collective actions expressed the thoughts of a group mind, while denying that they really do so. Fischer feared that a Collingwoodian approach to the understanding of social groups would conjure up a non-existing entity of a mental sort. But Collingwood doesn't regard even individual minds as 'entities': he conceives them as complexes of activities, the 'outsides' of which (generally) consist of events in the physical world (*IH* 213, 221–2). He insists that one cannot ask what a mind is apart from what it does. He is willing to press this view to the point of saying that if an historian ever succeeded in re-thinking all the thoughts of Becket and refrained from thinking others, then he would become Becket (*IH* 297). Why, then, on his theory, if there are group activities which can be interpreted as expressing collective thoughts, couldn't there be said to be a group mind consisting of such thoughts? Why would one have to say only that what happened is 'as if' there were such a mind with such thoughts? Collingwood's saying 'as if' in this connection is made the more problematic by the fact that, besides denying that minds are entities, he also (like Ryle after him) denies that they are known by introspection. In reacting against Collingwood's view, Ginsberg has raised the objection that 'if recourse be had to the extremely dubious notion of a group mind over and above individual minds it would still be necessary to show how this mind could ever be accessible to the individual mind'.[58] The 'inner side' of institutions, argues Ginsberg, 'is not in any one mind but in thousands of minds in interaction and it certainly cannot be ascertained by direct introspection or self-observation'. But as a criticism of Collingwood, this quite misses the mark. For Collingwood insists that even one's knowledge of one's own mind is achieved by interpreting one's activities as expressions of thoughts: that is, he denies 'privileged access'. It would thus seem that, on his theory, a group mind, if it existed,

----

[58] Ginsberg, 'The Character', 71.

would be 'accessible' to historians in precisely the same way that any mind is accessible to them.

Collingwoodians might perhaps want to argue that the problem raised by accepting the methodological necessity of using holistic teleological metaphors, while refusing to draw corresponding ontological conclusions, is not really Collingwood's, but Kant's. They might contend that, in his discussion of Kant's own views, he is simply doing what his own theory of historical understanding requires him to do, and what he does repeatedly in his survey of ideas of history from Herodotus to Croce, namely, entering empathetically into a given author's point of view and showing why, in the light of his own questions, assumptions, and beliefs, he said what he said. Yet it would be hard to make this contention entirely convincing. Most of the thinkers who find a place in Collingwood's survey enter it *honoris causa* (the few who do not, like Spencer and Comte, get very short shrift): most of them are there because they are seen as having contributed to the gradual emergence of 'scientific history'. It is true that, as a dialectical thinker, Collingwood often hails the appearance of ideas, not because he thinks them acceptable in themselves, but because he sees them as needed at the time for the advance of the intellectual tradition he is tracing—for example, the historical Pyrrhonism of Descartes, or the racial theories attributed to Herder (*IH* 60, 92). But he normally takes care to distinguish, in each case, what he thinks of permanent value and what he sees as due to be superseded; and it is notable that, in the case of Kant, his reservations are not about the holistic teleological approach itself, but centre upon its alleged failure, in Kant's hands, to free itself entirely from the analogy of searching out 'a plan of nature'—that is, from remnants of historical positivism. Thus Collingwood very much gives the impression that he regards what Kant said about the use of teleological metaphors as a promising move towards solving a problem for which he himself is unable to propose any better solution.

In other words, he seems to have been willing, at least in some moods, neither to deny the appearance of purposive pattern in history at the social level, nor to lapse into the easiest way of eliminating the problem this poses, namely, the acceptance of some form of conspiracy theory which would attribute the pattern to the intentions of the individuals concerned. He does, at times, make gingerly moves in the latter direction: for example, when he says, in an essay of the 1920s, that although 'history is a drama', its plot 'does not pre-exist to its own revelation', but is 'co-operatively extemporised by its own performers' (NAPH 36). This appears to be an attempt to walk a middle road so far as the problem of attributing purpose is concerned, but one which hardly does justice even to such a simple case of apparently teleological movement as the conquest of the Mediterranean world by Rome. It seems fair to say that Collingwood at least flirts, at times, with the group mind alternative. For this reason, as well as for some others mentioned earlier, he can hardly be said to be a methodological individualist 'in the strongest sense of the term'. One is tempted to say rather that, in response chiefly to what he regarded as certain exigencies of actual historical inquiry, he sometimes accepts a form of methodological holism, while clinging still to an ontological individualism, the precise warrant for which, in the context of his own thought about minds, he leaves unclear. However, it doesn't seem to me that anyone wishing to derive a coherent and plausible theory from Collingwood's writings need follow him in this direction. As earlier sections have shown, he is for the most part a methodological individualist, and in a way which jibes quite satisfactorily with his overall position on history.

6

THE HISTORICAL IMAGINATION

§ 1. *Re-enactment and Imagination*

In the preceding chapters, I have offered an interpretation of Collingwood's contention that historical understanding requires a re-enactment of past experience, and considered various limits, or supposed limits, to the applicability of this idea to what would ordinarily be regarded as history. I want to turn now to consider a Collingwoodian doctrine which has often been seen as closely related to that of re-enactment: the claim that historical inquiry requires an exercise of the historian's imagination.

Both friendly and unfriendly critics of Collingwood have often associated these two ideas. Taylor conjoins them in describing the Collingwoodian view of history as involving an 'imaginative re-enactment of past thoughts'; Rubinoff sees the idea of re-thinking as 'further explicated in terms of the *a priori* imagination'; Winch regards it as characteristic of idealist philosophy of history to connect the two ideas; Cebik considers the alleged connection as a good reason for rejecting both.[1] To others, Collingwood's notion that historical thinking requires imagination has seemed to reflect all too well certain weaknesses which they find in his work as an historian. In a review of *Roman Britain and the English Settlements*, R. E. M. Wheeler observes that Collingwood 'interpolates motives, builds characters, constructs episodes with a liberality or even licence that is great fun, but is liable to shock the pedant. Fact and speculation stand shoulder to shoulder.'[2] Philip Bagby

---

[1] Taylor, Review of van der Dussen *HS*, 175; Rubinoff, Review of *EPH*, 473; Winch, *Idea of a Social Science*, 90; Cebik, 'Collingwood', 79. Cebik holds that Collingwood 'viewed his notion of re-enactment as fundamentally an extension of creative reconstruction', which is a matter of imagination. By contrast, Leff dissociates the two ideas (*HST* 114–19, 127–8).

[2] Review of *RBES*, in *Journal of Roman Studies*, 29 (1939), 87–8. S. Kracauer

complains similarly of 'extensive flights of the imagination' in Collingwood's historical writings, this, in his view, exhibiting 'defects inherent in his idealistic theories'. A notorious example, he avers, is Collingwood's treatment of King Arthur, in which, 'out of a minimum of facts, he creates a new Arthurian Legend, worthy to stand beside the inventions of Tennyson and Geoffrey of Monmouth'.[3] Ironically enough, this is much the way in which Collingwood himself responds to certain passages in Thucydides. He agrees with Grote, for example, that the Melian dialogue 'contains more imagination than history', setting forth, indeed, less what the historian knows was said than what, in his view, it would have been appropriate to the occasion to have said (*IH* 30).

I shall argue that Collingwood's account of the way imagination does, and should, enter into historical work cannot be interpreted as simply another way of putting his re-enactment theory. The ideas of re-enactment and of imagination are certainly connected in important ways; but what is said about imagination requires independent consideration, at any rate in some of its aspects. I shall also maintain that, whatever truth there may be in the charge that, as an historian, Collingwood sometimes lets his imagination run away with him—a charge which others besides Wheeler and Bagby have made—there is at any rate nothing in his *theory* of the place of imagination in history to justify this: indeed, quite the contrary. I shall begin by examining, and to some extent criticizing, his best-known statement of that theory, the one offered in his inaugural lecture, 'The Historical Imagination', going on then to explore some connections between what he says there and certain ideas which interpreters of Collingwood have discussed less frequently: ideas like continuity, wholes, patterns, synthesis, periodization, and universality as applied to history. As in some of the cases already considered, an examination of what Collingwood has to say in connection with this group of

compares Collingwood's a priori imagination with the 'miraculous' ability of Poirot to solve problems in the absence of real clues (*History: The Last Things before the Last* (New York, 1969), 70–1—cited hereafter as *History*), and G. Buchdahl sees it similarly as obviating a need for 'hard data' ('Logic and History: An Assessment of R. G. Collingwood's *Idea of History*', *Australasian Journal of Philosophy*, 26 (1948), 106).

[3] *Culture and History: Prolegomena to the Comparative Study of Civilizations* (London, 1958), 68–9. See also Coady, 'Collingwood and Historical Testimony', 421.

ideas will be found to suggest certain ways in which the theory of historical understanding so far attributed to him in this book needs some revision. What will be found to be required, however, is less a rejection of Collingwood's official doctrine than a broadening of it to include some further notions which go well beyond re-enactment, but are compatible with it, and indeed supportive of it.

§ 2. *The A Priori Imagination*

In 'The Historical Imagination', Collingwood begins by asking how, in general, historians arrive at conclusions about what happened in the past (*IH* 231 ff.).[4] He points out that, far from accepting what their authorities, and even alleged eyewitnesses, tell them, they adopt a critical or 'autonomous' attitude to their sources in at least three ways. First, they select, restricting their attention to what they find especially interesting or important; second, they interpolate, adding statements of their own which go beyond anything which their authorities themselves say happened; and, third, they criticize, assessing the credibility of what is in fact said by the authorities, accepting some of it and rejecting the rest. All these are features of what Collingwood calls the intermediate or 'critical' stage in the development of modern historical inquiry, which, in its beginnings, was a mere activity of compilation—mere 'scissors and paste', as Collingwood likes to say.[5] The question arises by what right the historian acts 'autonomously' in such ways, especially in the third. Or, as Collingwood also puts it, on what criterion he goes beyond the mere organization and repetition of what his authorities tell him to elaborate an account which he advances on his own authority.[6]

The answer which he gives aims to show how critical history must in the end give way to fully-fledged 'scientific' history. He proceeds via an examination of F. H. Bradley's doctrine that, from

[4] Since he puts some of his points more clearly in his notes than he does in the published text, RNI will sometimes be cited below.
[5] Collingwood sometimes calls the 'constructive' phase a 'higher branch' of history than the merely 'critical' (RNI 9).
[6] Although Collingwood talks in this connection of the historian's criterion of truth, his concern seems not to have been with the meaning of 'truth' in history, but with what would constitute an acceptable historical account.

a body of evidence, the historian can only derive conclusions which bear an analogy with what he or his contemporaries find happening around them (*IH* 134 ff., 238–40). According to Bradley, the criterion of historical reconstruction which is taken to the evidence is thus an experience of the present world, this being summarized and systematized by the general laws of the natural sciences. As Collingwood points out, this is a doctrine which is prefigured in Hume's account of how reports of miracles should be assessed by historians, an essential element of which is the denial that there can ever be good evidence for a violation of a law of nature. And he allows that this doctrine has some application in history: for example, when a modern historian of Rome passes over in silence certain portents described by Livy (RNI 8). Considered as formulating a general criterion for historical reconstruction, Collingwood nevertheless rejects it for two reasons. He objects, first, that it is merely negative; at most, it allows the historian to set aside what cannot possibly have happened, despite what his authorities may say to the contrary, leaving it still to be determined what did occur. Second, he refuses it as inappropriately naturalistic; it assumes that the subject-matter of history is determined by laws, and thus that the experience which must be taken to the interpretation of the evidence is essentially scientific experience.

Collingwood's first response is curiously weak. Perhaps, as stated, the criterion enunciated by Bradley is purely negative, and, as Collingwood complains, entirely ignores the interpolative or constructive side of historical thinking. But the idea of conformity to law can easily be given a positive application, as would in fact be done by those positivist philosophers of history against whose views Collingwood describes his whole account of history as a 'running fight' (*IH* 228). That is, it could be claimed that historians go legitimately beyond what their authorities tell them to the extent that they can draw further conclusions from it in accordance with general laws. The same opponents would doubtless argue, too, that the general credibility of putative authorities might be established by applying to whatever they say generalizations about the kinds of witnesses whose reports can and cannot be believed, this leading, once again, to the making of positive assertions about the past. Collingwood himself seems to find something like the first of these possibilities acceptable enough in natural history (*IH* 239); and he sometimes appears to allow a marginal role for the second even in human history.[7] Collingwood has other reasons, of course, for questioning whether human actions, including those of past agents whom historians may now be inclined to treat as authorities, fall under laws at all. But the immediate point is whether laws, even if available, would yield only a negative criterion of what to believe; and there seems to be no good reason to say that they would.

Collingwood's second response—that Bradley's criterion is inappropriately naturalistic—is more apposite. He had denied at various points that there are any universal laws of human behaviour, whether individual or social in scope; and he reinforces his objection to any idea of acceptable testimony which implies the contrary by observing that the assertion that the Greeks and Romans exposed new-born infants as a way of controlling their population is made none the less believable by the fact that this practice is 'unlike anything that happens in the experience of the contributors to the *Cambridge Ancient History*' (*IH* 240). Collingwood can hardly object, of course, if historians appeal to laws of the physical sciences when interpreting evidence of the natural environment within which some past human action took place—and the more so if they are to be used only in the negative, eliminative way envisaged by Bradley's criterion. He concedes this explicitly when he writes: 'General laws play a great part in history but in themselves are not historical: they only determine limits within which historical facts can happen (possibilities)' (*NHH* 44). His present point, however, is that, if the notion of appealing to laws is to mean no more than that, then applying Bradley's criterion would leave almost everything of real importance in historical reconstruction still to be done.

Yet Collingwood does not want to deny that historians need to bring 'experience' to their interpretation of evidence. His objection, so far as human affairs is concerned, is to their bringing 'ready-made' experience, i.e. experience other than that gained in the course of historical inquiry itself (*IH* 139–40). As his remark about infanticide among the ancients suggests, his position would

[7] He says e.g. that, before accepting a statement of an authority, the historian must determine 'whether the alleged event could have happened; how trustworthy the writer is; and in what directions he is prejudiced or misinformed' (RNI 24).

be that, if an historian wishes to draw conclusions about what a Greek or a Roman is likely to have done on a certain occasion, what he will need to appeal to is not general sociological or psychological theories of how people of various sorts behave, but prior historical study of the beliefs, goals, and habits of Greeks or Romans, or even of particular Greeks or Romans.[8] More than once, he declares that historical knowledge grows (indeed, that it 'can only grow') from historical knowledge. 'The more historical knowledge we have', he avers, 'the more we can learn from any given piece of evidence; if we had none we could learn nothing' (*IH* 247). Thus, 'the printed marks on paper which represent Greek letters . . . are evidence of the activity of the printing-press only to a person who knows about printing, and evidence about Greek history only to a person who knows Greek' (RNI 43; *IH* 244). On the other hand, relatively small scraps of evidence may reveal much to someone who already possesses a great deal of historical knowledge. A striking example, to which Goldstein and others have drawn attention, is Collingwood's claim, on the sole authority of a tombstone on which there appears an otherwise inexplicable inscription 'written in the Irish, as distinct from the British, form of Celtic', that an Irish colony must have existed at Silchester in the middle of the fifth century (*RBES* 316).[9]

It might be remarked, in passing, that Collingwood's doctrine here offers a pertinent response to a criticism of his theory of history made by Gallie, especially when taken in conjunction with the stress which he places upon the question-relativity of historical thinking (PH 137). As Gallie sees it, Collingwood, in effect, represents historians as solitary thinkers, whose work begins with reflection upon discrete problems raised from scratch, whereas most of the problems which catch their interest do so at least partly because of dissatisfaction felt with the attempts of predecessors to solve them (*PHU* 60).[10] This, however, is precisely what Collingwood himself maintains. If anything, he overstates the extent to which historians unavoidably involve themselves in a critical examination of the way their predecessors treated their questions (see Chapter 8, § 4). To the extent that they do so,

---

[8] What was called limited laws in Ch. 3, § 6.

[9] Goldstein, 'Constitution', 262–3.

[10] Similar complaints are made by Renier (*Purpose and Method*, 88–9); and Atkinson (*KEH* 25).

however, a further sense emerges in which historical knowledge can be said characteristically to arise out of prior historical knowledge, and in which historical inquiry can be considered 'autonomous'. For, if the acquisition of historical knowledge requires the possession of some such knowledge already, it follows that, at any particular time, historians will have to regard some problems as settled, at least provisionally, so that they can get on with the investigation of others (*IH* 244). In that sense, the findings of predecessors could even be said to function to some extent, and quite legitimately, as 'authorities' (*RNI* 27; *IH* 244).[11] Of course, treating them as such, in this modified sense, could never preclude the possibility of their acceptability having to be reconsidered at some later time.[12]

Collingwood sees the interpolative, constructive aspect of historical thinking, working from selected sources and proceeding in accordance with certain principles of inquiry, as gradually elaborating a 'web' of accepted fact, an increasingly plausible and detailed 'picture' of a portion of the past, composed of assertions made in the sources which have survived criticism, and inferences from them. It is natural, he says, to conceive this at first as a construction which is 'pegged down' to 'fixed points' derived from the documents and other sources. But no points are really fixed: the historian is just as responsible for the points from which the web is woven as he is for the web itself (*IH* 244). In historical inquiry of any sophistication, furthermore—in what Collingwood calls 'scientific' as opposed to merely 'critical' history—it will be realized that the apparently fixed points depend on the web as much as the web depends on them. In fact, the web, Collingwood declares, is 'the touchstone by which we decide whether alleged facts are genuine'—a striking reversal of roles. Since 'any source may be tainted', the criterion of acceptability of an alleged new fact becomes whether 'the picture of the past' to which its acceptance leads is 'a coherent and continuous picture, one which makes sense' (*IH* 245).[13] The elaboration of the web, so conceived,

[11] For uses of the term 'authority' by Collingwood in this sense, see *RBES* 287, 291, 294.

[12] For a strong argument against this claim, see Leon Pompa, 'The Possibility of Historical Knowledge', *Aristotelian Society Supplementary Volume*, 67 (1993), 7 ff.

[13] The search for a criterion of acceptable historical reconstruction, thus passes from (1) agreement with the authorities, through (2) conformity to our experience

Collingwood describes as a work of 'the historical imagination', and the web itself as an 'imaginative reconstruction' of the past (*IH* 247). And he hails the achievement of this view of the nature of the historian's task, largely in the nineteenth century, as 'a Copernican revolution' in historical studies (*IH* 236).

Since some of Collingwood's critics have reacted so negatively to his holding that historical thinking requires an exercise of the imagination, it is important to see just what he means by it. Mink states the prima-facie problem thus: if imagination is a criterion of acceptability for historical accounts, surely this destroys the distinction between history and fiction, and legitimizes 'subjectivity and idiosyncrasy' (*MHD* 159–60). At an earlier point, Collingwood himself resists the idea that historical thinking is imagining on the ground that 'imagining knows nothing of the difference between truth and error' (LHK 102); and in his lectures of 1928, he warns that gaps between fragments of knowledge which cannot be filled by legitimate inference 'must not be filled by imagination' (L28 483). However, what he has in mind in such cases is clearly imagination as pure fancy—what, in *The Idea of History*, he calls the 'arbitrary' or 'capricious' imagination (*IH* 241–2).[14] There is no need to associate with this his contention that imagination has a structural role to play in history. He is more friendly towards what he describes as the 'ornamental' imagination—the power of making an historical account 'affecting and picturesque', a power so demonstrably possessed by historians like Macaulay (*IH* 241). But this, too, is not to be equated with the workaday, structural enterprise of constructing an imaginary web or picture which is in a satisfactory symbiotic relationship with what the historian considers as evidence justifying its assertion. Collingwood does, on occasion, find a respectable, if marginal, role for the fanciful imagination in history: for example, when he observes that quite uncritical, popular 'history', like the story of King Alfred and the cakes relayed to us by medieval historians, may serve the useful function of drawing those intrigued by it into more serious inquiry into the past (L26 373). Besides which,

of what in general happens, to (3) incorporability into a continuous and coherent imaginative web. Saari refines (3) by noting differing degrees to which various kinds of further 'facts' resist incorporation into existing webs.

[14] 'Imagine' is used in this sense in L26 385, 403; *IH* 70, 136; and in L26 347, is equated with 'conjecture'.

of course, such imaginings may bequeath to us 'imperishable gems of literature' (*IH* 52).

The constructive imagination, to which Collingwood assigns 'the whole task' of elaborating an acceptable 'imaginary picture of the past', is, by contrast, a 'disciplined' imagination—disciplined by evidence and by rules of inquiry, and 'subordinated to the pursuit of truth' (*NAPH* 48). The reiterated claim that the historian acts 'on his own authority' does not mean that he has authority to say what he likes. Walsh is surely on the right track when he maintains that, for Collingwood, 'the historical imagination' is 'only another name for the historical judgment',[15] and Donagan when he observes, conversely, that to think is 'to put the imagination to work'.[16] Collingwood himself sometimes associates the idea of imagination in history with that of inference; and such an association is, of course, sanctioned by ordinary usage. It is exemplified, amusingly, in his rueful account of an exchange he once had with some uncomprehending colleagues. 'I imagined, foolishly enough', he says of his own remarks, 'that so lucid and cogent a piece of reasoning must convince any hearer' (*IH* 253 n. 1).[17] The two notions are explicitly connected when, below the table of contents of his 1928 lectures, Collingwood lists as a topic still to be 'worked in': 'Historical imagination (i.e. closer study of the nature of historical inference).'[18] He does stress, however, that the inferences required of historians are of 'a peculiar kind'. An historian does not simply ask what a piece of evidence proves; he asks how it helps him 'to build up his imaginary picture of the past' (*RNI* 44).

But Collingwood has further, and more startling, assertions to make about the way he sees imagination functioning in historical reconstruction—assertions which have greatly reinforced criticism of his assigning a serious role to imagination in historical thinking at all. Even the fact that historians must ground their conclusions in prior historical knowledge, even the requirement that they reach them in accordance with 'autonomous' principles of interpretation, even the idea that they should elaborate a

---

[15] Walsh, 'Collingwood's Philosophy of History', 158.
[16] *Essays in the Philosophy of Art by R. G. Collingwood* (Bloomington, Ind., 1964), p. xii.
[17] 'Imagine' means 'think' also in RAH 2, 18; L26 392.
[18] An addition to L28 not included in *IH*, rev. edn. See also L28 483.

picture of the past in a mutually supportive relationship with what they regard as evidence, do not, he says, 'give the historian his criterion of historical truth'. That criterion 'is provided by the idea of history itself: the idea of an imaginary picture of the past' (*IH* 248). This idea, Collingwood goes on to say, is, 'in Cartesian language, innate; in Kantian language, *a priori*'; and, apparently in amplification of this astonishing claim, he describes history as a 'self-explanatory', 'self-determining', 'self-dependent', 'self-authorizing', and 'self-justifying' form of thought, 'an original and fundamental activity of the human mind', an idea of which is part of the 'furniture' of every mind (*IH* 246–9).[19] What can he possibly mean by such claims, which, to say the least, seem abruptly to renounce much of what he had previously said about historical inquiry being limited to discovering what the evidence obliges one to believe, and which, furthermore, carry us so far beyond the Bradleian starting-point that we seem no longer to be pursuing the same inquiry? I shall concede that Collingwood's doctrine at this point is not only obscure, but is in some important respects unacceptable. Yet, as I shall go on to argue, I think that it includes ideas which are both defensible and of the first importance for a theory of historical inquiry.

§ 3. *Coherence, Continuity, Necessity*

An important clue to what Collingwood has in mind, in saying that historians work with an a priori idea of history, is furnished by a contrast which he draws between the way he sees an a priori imagination functioning in history and the way he conceives something analogous to it to function in sense perception and artistic representation. A good deal of what we claim to perceive through our senses, he reminds us, is really imagined: the unbroken line of a hill when our view of it is interrupted by a tree; or the three-dimensional bulk of a box when we cannot in fact see its back (RNI 47). In artistic representation, too, we often cannot but imagine what cannot but be there: the expression on a face, perhaps; or the expanse of a room. In historical reconstruction, we

---

[19] Collingwood already refers to the idea of history in L26 422, as 'one of the necessary and transcendental modes of mind's activity', and in L27 357, as 'a universal and necessary form of mental activity'.

similarly imagine more than is directly conveyed by the evidence. Collingwood instances a journey taken by Caesar from Rome to Gaul where, although we do not doubt that he was in various locations between these centres at successive times, no direct evidence of his journey is available (*IH* 241). Such imaginings Collingwood calls a priori not only because they go beyond the evidence, but because (obverting Bradley's point about why miracle stories must be rejected) we will allow no evidence to count against them.

The special function of the a priori imagination in historical work, according to Collingwood, is to imagine the past. Perhaps that is something which could also be said of the work of novelists in some cases. But there are three 'rules of method', Collingwood maintains, which apply to the imaginative reconstructions of historians but not to the creations of novelists (*IH* 246). First, the picture of the past which an historian elaborates must be 'localized in space and time', every detail having a unique place and date, whereas the details of novels may be located anywhere and anywhen.[20] Pressing his Kantian analogy further, Collingwood calls this 'the first axiom of intuition for history' (*IH* 109). Second, in order to be deemed acceptable, the imaginary picture which an historian constructs must be consistent with all other pictures of the past elaborated by historians which are also found acceptable. There can be only one historical world, with a single system of relations, beginning with topographical and chronological ones. And third, the historian's picture must have that reciprocally supportive relationship to evidence which is illustrated by Collingwood's account of the extrapolation and growth of the historian's web of accepted fact, and which even those novels which we call historical largely lack.

Perhaps none of this will seem particularly controversial. It may seem obvious that historians take it for granted that whatever happened in the past happened at unique places and times in a definite relationship to whatever else happened, and that, as Collingwood maintains, this is not an empirical idea, not an idea which historians derive *from* their studies, but one which they take *to* them as a set of demands which must be met by any action,

---

[20] Or, more accurately, events are localized in novels only in an imaginary space and time, which is not necessarily connected to the space and time of any other novel.

development or state of affairs for which they claim to find evidence (L28 486).[21] The problem is how such contentions relate to some of the other statements which Collingwood makes about the a priori imagination of the historian—for example, that it does 'the entire work' of historical reconstruction (IH 241), or that it affords a 'criterion of historical truth' (IH 248), presumably the one which Bradley failed to discern. If this is not at all easy to determine, the difficulty owes something to Collingwood's tendency to blur three important distinctions in setting forth his doctrine, as well as to overstate his point on some important issues.

First, he fails to distinguish at all clearly between two senses in which he wants to maintain that historians work with an a priori or imaginary picture of the past.[22] One of these, which is exemplified by his three 'rules of method', is purely formal. It is an idea of the past as having to satisfy certain general demands, but without specific features: a mere notion of an empty grid which may be filled out in conformity with stated requirements, a mere idea of 'latitude and longitude' for history, to use an expression employed in one of the manuscripts (CHBI 10–11). But this can hardly be what he has in mind when he describes the historical imagination as doing the whole work of reconstruction, or the historian's a priori idea of the past as affording him a criterion of historical truth. For the idea of a past which is formally structured in certain ways is compatible with an indefinite number of quite different accounts of what in fact happened in it, just as the idea of a natural world structured by the causal relationship is compatible with an indefinite number of quite different views of what in fact causes what.[23] As Gallie has usefully put it, Collingwood's a priori idea of history (and he clearly means the formal one) is only an 'intellectual ideal or device' with no 'definite descriptive content': only a 'regulative' idea (PHU 59). What actual historical

---

[21] Jack Meiland denies that historians have or need an a priori idea of the past (Scepticism and Historical Knowledge (New York, 1965), 156, 172—cited hereafter as Scepticism. Donagan notes, in reply, the 'disastrous' consequences of assuming that the idea of the past is empirical (Review of Scepticism, in Philosophical Quarterly, 17 (1967), 85).

[22] On this, see Rotenstreich, PHP 56.

[23] As Donagan says, we must distinguish the idea of an imaginary picture of the past 'from any particular imaginary picture of it' (LPC 210). See also T. M. Knox, 'Notes on Collingwood's Philosophical Work', Proceedings of the British Academy, 19 (1944), 471.

inquiry does—as Collingwood himself says (*IH* 247)—is give this idea content, thereby elaborating an imaginary picture of the past which is *not* merely formal, but which, although conforming to a priori requirements, is substantive, or concrete, in a way justified by its relationship to evidence.

The formal idea of history could not possibly give the historian his 'criterion of truth'. For what it articulates is no more than a set of purely negative conditions (quite as negative as Bradley's candidate), failure to meet which disqualifies an historian's claims to know what happened. If an imaginary picture of the past is to be conceived as guiding historical inquiry as it proceeds, it will have to be a partly filled-out one: one which has substantive implications for the acceptability of further facts. But since the concrete, rather than merely formal, picture is at every stage open to empirical modification, new facts sometimes being incorporated into it at a cost of changing it, we cannot without qualification call it a priori. It could be considered a priori only in the secondary sense of instantiating the formal conception of the historical past, which is a priori in a primary sense.

It is of interest to note that even the historian's formal idea of the past is sometimes represented by Collingwood as including a good deal more than the three rules of method which he sets forth in his inaugural lecture. At a number of points, he refers to various more specific principles which are also said to be taken to historical inquiry, not derived from it—presumably further aspects of the a priori idea of history (*IH* 110). A striking example is the principle that the past will be divisible into periods, the idea of a period, often recognized as fundamental to historical thinking, thus gaining the status of an a priori historical concept (L26 415; L31 11).[24] In the *Autobiography*, as Donagan has pointed out (*LPC* 212–13), what historians are taken to know a priori about their subject-matter is extended to include its being composed of actions, conceived as events expressing thoughts, the thoughts being in principle re-enactable by historians (*A* 110ff.). Still another claim accorded such status is that the past, so conceived, is not dead, but lives on in the present,[25] this apparently being a development of Collingwood's third 'rule', i.e. that the present contains (or perhaps consists of) relics of the past, ripe for

---

[24] See further § 4 below.   [25] See further Ch. 7, § 5.

interpretation.[26] Almost certainly also part of Collingwood's a priori idea of history, understood in the formal sense, is the requirement that whatever is said to have happened in the past—whatever fills out the formal idea of history—must be 'coherent and continuous' (of which, more below). In the addendum to the table of contents of his 1928 lectures, Collingwood also maintains it to be an '*a priori* element' in historical thinking that the past can only be understood from a perspective.[27]

A second large distinction which Collingwood tends to blur when discussing the way an a priori imagination supposedly functions in historical thought is one between having an idea simply of the past, and having an idea of a specifically historical past. Collingwood moves back and forth between these two ideas without notice, as I have done myself up to this point. Yet much of what we might claim to know a priori about the past, and the most plausible part of it, is in fact about the past as such, not about a past which would be of special interest to historians. When it is affirmed, for example, that our idea of history requires that everything which is said to have happened be locatable in a single space and time, this is a requirement which applies as much to the natural as to the human past. Even the idea of the past as something recoverable from present relics is not one which applies specifically to the human past—unless the ideas of being recoverable and of being relics are given meanings which link them stipulatively to being re-enactable.

The point at which Collingwood begins to touch on what is specific to human history is precisely the point at which the a priori status of the formal idea of the past which he says we possess becomes more controversial. One might perhaps claim to know a priori that, no matter how far back one goes, there was a physical world which underwent changes in accordance with the laws of nature. But one can hardly claim to know in a similar way that, no matter how far back one goes, there were human beings

---

[26] This claim needs some qualification: Collingwood can hardly consider it an a priori principle for historians that there exists here and now evidence for everything that happened in the past, the only problem being to locate and interpret it. Such a claim would in any case mesh badly with his own lamentations about wanton destruction of evidence by public authorities (L26 369). For a more nuanced position, see L28 485.

[27] See further Ch. 8.

acting in ways which expressed re-enactable thoughts: indeed, it would generally be held that, at some not so very remote past time, no human beings existed at all. Even with regard to a past assumed to have been humanly populated, we surely cannot claim to know a priori that its denizens acted in ways expressing re-enactable thoughts. Maintaining that would in any case be difficult to reconcile with Collingwood's admission (see Chapter 4, § 3) that one can never simply assume that past agents acted rationally, even from their own points of view, this being something which inquiry has to discover in particular cases. Yet, if the claim with regard to the specifically human past is in consequence reduced to the mere affirmation that we can know a priori that what was done in it is re-enactively recoverable to the extent that people thought and acted rationally, the claim to have a priori knowledge of the historical past becomes little more than a tautology.

One way of trying to resolve the problem on Collingwood's behalf might be to divide the historian's reconstructive enterprise, as Debbins does, into two phases: first, discovering the outsides of past actions, and then discovering the insides (*EPH*, pp. xvi–xvii). Debbins apparently sees Collingwood as assigning to the constructive historical imagination only the task of 'filling gaps' in outsides, about which, assuming them to be physical, we can have some a priori knowledge. Some support for ascribing this more modest position to Collingwood may perhaps be derived from his having described the interpolation of a ship's unobserved positions between two observed ones as 'already an example of historical thinking' (*IH* 241). But here, surely, Collingwood slips back momentarily, as he does also at some other points, into the view of historicity expounded in *Speculum Mentis*: that of sheer concreteness, factuality, individuality, which is as well exemplified in physical events and processes as it is in human actions. At least sometimes, he talks of the extrapolative or constructive imagination as if he considered it to be exemplified also in the attribution of re-enactable thoughts to past agents. For example, when he points to an historian's account of the ride of Suetonius to London in response to Boudicca's rebellion, as an illustration of the historical imagination at work (RNI 13), what he reports is not just the displacement of his body, but also what his motivations and calculations were in so acting. Precisely what, in such cases, the historical imagination is supposed to discern a priori, however, he does not make very clear.

A third, and even more troublesome problem arises in connection with Collingwood's frequent talk of 'necessity' when explicating the way an a priori picture of the past is supposedly brought to bear in historical work. For he sometimes conflates two notions: that of each element of the picture being 'what the evidence obliges us to believe', and that of each, ideally at least, being related to other elements in a necessary way.[28] We might speak of these as the external and internal necessity of historical accounts, respectively. Collingwood sometimes leaves it uncertain which of these radically different relationships he means to assert. It could be either, for example, when he observes that, in the work of both novelist and historian, 'nothing is admissible except what is necessary, and the judge of this necessity is in both cases the imagination' (*IH* 245), or when he declares that what goes into the historian's picture is in every case what the historian's imagination 'actively demands' (*IH* 246).[29] The two come apart when he tells us that the historian, unlike the novelist, has a 'double task'. His picture, he says, like that of the novelist, must constitute 'a coherent whole where every character and every situation is so bound up with the rest that this character in this situation cannot but act in this way' (*IH* 245), but, unlike that of the novelist, it must also be necessitated by evidence.[30] Yet Collingwood passes with disconcerting ease from the first to the second of these ideas at the very point where he first introduces the notion of an a priori idea of history.

---

[28] The second notion reflects a view ascribed by Collingwood (sympathetically, it seems) to Hegel (*IH* 118). Debbins notes a further ambiguity between the first and the necessity of historians having a formal idea of history (*EPH*, pp. xviii–xix).

[29] Collingwood also leaves open the kind of necessity he has in mind when, in anticipation of his *IH* doctrine, he says: 'the past . . . can be the object of critical and rigorous inferential thinking, for everything that it contains it contains necessarily, and there is in the study of it no room for imagination or caprice or any kind of assertion which cannot justify itself by the production of valid reasons' (L26 413).

[30] In sum, Collingwood holds that: (1) the concrete picture is necessitated by evidence; (2) the concrete picture is necessarily connected internally; (3) we necessarily think of the past in terms of (1) and (2), i.e. we have an a priori idea of history. Or, as one might also put the Collingwoodian view: history is necessarily a system of necessary relations necessitated by the evidence.

Confusion is compounded when he goes on to argue, in defending Fichte against the charge of having believed the course of history to be discoverable a priori, that an historian's account must at every point be a necessary one because of the way he reconstructs the past from evidence. Collingwood insists that, historical thinking being a matter of arguing from present to past, it is 'based on the assumption . . . that there is an internal or necessary connexion between the events of a time-series such that one event leads necessarily to another and we can argue back from the second to the first' (*IH* 110). But, in saying this, he surely confuses the relations of necessary and sufficient condition (as he does at some other points: see Chapter 3, § 5). It is one thing to say, in support of some evidential argument, that since a past occurrence was necessary for the existence of something now in view, the latter's presence is sufficient for the earlier event or condition having occurred (Collingwood's evidential relationship). It is quite another to say that some earlier happening was sufficient for what is now in view (or for any intervening event), which can then be said to have occurred necessarily (Collingwood's 'cannot but act accordingly'). The same confusion would be implied if an historian were to argue, on grounds of 'historical necessity', from the observation of a present relic to the occurrence of some earlier event or condition, without making it clear whether by 'historical necessity' was meant earlier events necessitating later ones or being necessary for them.

Still further problems arise with regard to the internal necessity which Collingwood often insists must characterize satisfactory historical accounts. To say the least, he greatly overstates the extent to which such necessity can plausibly be ascribed, not only in view of the actual performances of historians, but also in view of his own theory of historical inquiry. Despite having repeatedly rejected the doctrine of historical determinism, he declares it to be the goal of history to show characters so acting and situations so developing that each element 'of necessity leads on to or arises out of the rest' (RNI 39). As a model for historians in this connection, he points to the way a novelist like Dostoevsky depicts his murderer as someone who 'cannot but confess his crime' (RNI 38). Collingwood also signals agreement with Fiche and Hegel that history is 'at bottom a logical process', instantiating 'a chain of logically connected concepts' (*IH* 117–18). He does sometimes say, more plausibly, that what is known a priori about the historical past is that it must 'make sense'—or, more particularly, that it must be 'coherent and continuous' (*IH* 245). One might perhaps interpret the call for coherence as demanding no more than logical consistency, which would go little beyond Collingwood's second a priori rule that there must be a single historical world. But the call for continuity, with its suggestion of some kind of internal connectedness, seems to envisage more, and, as Collingwood uses the terms, it often carries the idea of coherence along with it (*IH* 245).

Collingwood offers no systematic analysis of what he means by historical continuity, but there are indications from time to time of how he thinks of it. Sometimes what he seems to have in view is a kind of cumulativeness in human activities, this suggested by his observation, in criticism of Spengler, that Western civilization does not just succeed Hellenic civilization, but builds upon it (*IH* 182–3). Pointing in much the same direction is his doctrine that the historical past is 'incapsulated' in the present (*A* 100), an example being the way traditions may be inherited and preserved (*IH* 34). Sometimes continuity is seen as manifested with especial clarity in problem-solving activities, where 'the solution of one problem is itself the rise of the next' (THC 86). In this stronger and more explicit sense, Collingwood appears to see the requirement of continuity as eminently met by the history of philosophy, each philosopher being said to learn from predecessors and then to improve upon them (*EPM* 194). Yet he is often prepared to go beyond even this, maintaining that the continuity of a satisfactory historical account would consist in its elements forming a series of necessary connections.[31]

There are at least two reasons for resisting Collingwood's claim in the latter form, both considerations which we have noted in other connections. One is that, even when continuity is achieved

---

[31] Collingwood's discussion might have benefited from an analysis of what historians ordinarily count as continuity and discontinuity. A good point of departure would have been his own criticism of a fellow historian, R. E. Zachrisson, for asserting 'some kind of continuity' in the case of a Saxon town built on the site of a Roman predecessor. Collingwood's response: 'A handful of de-Romanized Britons squatting among the ruins of a Roman town, represent a continuity of race and to some extent a continuity of language. But from the point of view of the social, economic and political historian they are discontinuity incarnate' (Review of *Romans, Kelts and Saxons in Ancient Britain*, in *Journal of Roman Studies*, 18 (1928), 118).

by historical accounts in such a sense, it is only achieved, as Collingwood himself acknowledges, 'within certain limits' (RNI 40). For in all historical developments, he allows, there are elements which, to the historian, are 'as inexplicable as the length of Cleopatra's nose'. This is notably so where nature intrudes into human affairs; but even when only human actions are involved, one can hardly expect historical accounts to display very often the kind of continuity which Collingwood somewhat optimistically ascribes to history of philosophy. Strauss voices the same objection more concretely when he points out that, although, as Collingwood maintains, something like Hellenic civilization may be to a considerable extent continuous with Western civilization in the required way, the same incorporative relationship, the same pattern of one culture learning from another, will hardly be found to hold between, say, Chinese and Western civilizations.[32] An equally important reason why it is not plausible to make continuity, understood as internal necessity, a general requirement for historical accounts, is that the historical past can often be seen to 'make sense'—Collingwood's general requirement— without being analysable into serial *necessities*. As was noted at some earlier points, to make the responses of relevant agents intelligible, often all that needs to be shown is that they were sensible, or permissible, or even possible. And even when they are represented as having been necessitated by what preceded them, this need mean no more than that there were compelling reasons for making them. The essential consideration, however, is that, whether historians conceive continuity strongly or weakly, they can hardly claim to know a priori that what they study will exhibit it. At most, this is something which it may be worth their while looking for.

A problem which remains is how far Collingwood wants to press the claim that the a priori idea of history, as he understands it, is a truly universal one: an idea which we all necessarily have. The claim that it is such appears as early as the writings of the 1920s, where history is described as 'a necessary form of human experience . . . common to all thinking beings at all times' (L28 432); and it is given eloquent expression in the inaugural lecture, where the idea of history is said to be one 'which every man

[32] Strauss, 'On Collingwood's Philosophy of History', 563.

possesses as part of the furniture of his mind, and discovers himself to possess in so far as he becomes conscious of what it is to have a mind' (*IH* 248). This, however, is quite an impossible position for Collingwood to take, on any natural understanding of what he says. As Donagan has pointed out, he says himself that, before Herodotus, there were people—for example, the ancient Sumerians (*IH* 12)—who thought of the past in ways quite inconsistent with even the minimal demands expressed by the three a priori rules of method, and we should hardly want, in consequence, to deny that they had minds (*LPC* 211). It may be somewhat more plausible to associate having a mind with having an a priori idea of a past at all. But what Collingwood is supposed to be considering is an idea of the historical past.

Mink has suggested that the doctrine which Collingwood formulates in 'The Historical Imagination', using the language of 'innate' or '*a priori*' ideas, might be more acceptable if expressed in the language of absolute presuppositions which he adopts later on (*MHD* 185). The claim might then be that the basic content of what Collingwood calls the a priori idea of history has in fact been absolutely presupposed (or taken for granted) by those generally called historians since the fifth century in Greece. Even then, however, it could be questioned how closely what was generally accepted throughout that period approximated to Collingwood's a priori idea of history. The notion of having a 'necessary relation to evidence', for example, seems not to have been thoroughly grasped until quite recently, at any rate in Collingwood's strict way of conceiving it. To the original Greek historians, who were essentially reporters, evidence chiefly meant the evidence of one's eyes; and in the Middle Ages, some verificatory role may have been ascribed to revelation. As for our predecessors having presupposed the re-enactability of the historical past, Collingwood himself seems committed to holding that this is an idea of quite recent emergence, having been absent, for example, from the thought of positivists and Marxists. The most that it may be plausible to say is that various elements of the Collingwoodian idea of history have become increasingly accepted in recent European culture—and quite early in *The Idea of History*, Collingwood concedes, in effect, that he is expounding a European idea. To this Strauss adds the powerful consideration that Collingwood can hardly maintain that the idea of history, as he understands it, is native to the human mind, while at the same time rejecting, as he does, the whole notion of an unchanging human nature.

§ 4. *Historical Understanding as Synthesis*

I have argued that Collingwood leaves the idea of continuity, so central to his notion of the web or picture which the historical imagination reconstructs, in some obscurity in the end. Critics like Cebik are surely justified in complaining that it is difficult to grasp what he meant by it.[33] Explicating it as necessary connections in series seems too strong, quite apart from problems which arise out of the way Collingwood treats the idea of necessity in history. Explicating it as cumulative human responses to the actions of predecessors, although in some ways an improvement, also seems too strong, at any rate as an account of what historians can realistically hope to find.

However, what Collingwood has to say about the elaboration of imaginative webs and pictures by historians is of independent interest; for it brings into focus a characteristic concern of historical inquiry which is often next to invisible when his attention is fixed on historical understanding as re-enactment. The task which we now find him assigning to the historian is that of using the evidence available to elaborate accounts of the human past which are structured, concrete, and oriented towards the delineation of wholes. This emphasis is reminiscent of the approach taken by Collingwood in *Speculum Mentis*, before he had begun to think of history as involving re-enactment, where he describes the object of historical thought as 'organized individuality' or a 'concrete universal' (*SM* 220). What the historian is there said to investigate is 'the whole of what exists . . . concretely articulated into parts each of which is again individual', Collingwood adding that 'the historical spirit moves freely in all directions, never finding anything that is not individual and unique' (*SM* 119). That his preoccupation with other matters in *The Idea of History* has not led him to abandon the essentials of this earlier view is evident in a passage which contrasts the interest of historians in the particular with the interest of scientists in the general in the following way.

[33] Cebik, 'Collingwood', 78.

If an historian is found studying the Hundred Years War or the Revolution of 1688, he remarks, 'you cannot infer that he is in the preliminary stages of an inquiry whose ultimate aim is to reach conclusions about wars or revolutions as such. If he is in the preliminary stages of any inquiry, it is more likely to be a general study of the Middle Ages or the seventeenth century.' For 'in the organization of history, the ulterior value of what is known about the Hundred Years War is conditioned, not by its relation to what is known about other wars, but by its relation to what is known about other things that people did in the Middle Ages' (*IH* 250).

There are many other passages in which Collingwood places similar stress on what might be called the 'whole-istic' aspect of historical inquiry.[34] The past, he declares in his lectures of 1928, 'is not a plurality of atomic incidents, any one of which may be "known" in an adequate way without the rest, but a whole in which parts are so related as to explain one another and render one another intelligible' (L28 483). In the same work, he says that an historical monograph should be an 'organized system of parts' in which each part makes a 'proper contribution to the whole' (L28 473). In writing about Hadrian's Wall, he represents the task of the historian-archaeologist as that of seeing 'a tangle of human facts' as a 'luminous whole'.[35] In *The Idea of History*, in criticism of Hegel, he maintains that the historian should aim at 'a history of man in his concrete actuality', in which developments of a political sort are 'integrated with economic, artistic, religious, and philosophical developments'. And he congratulates certain of Hegel's successors for taking note of elements which Hegel had neglected, and for 'working them into a solid whole', while expressing regret that they stopped short of displaying the various elements as 'an organic unity in which every thread of the developing process preserved its own continuity as well as its intimate connexion with the others' (*IH* 122–3). In repeatedly stressing the need for a 'limited objective' in historical inquiry, Collingwood may give the impression, at times, of advising historians to stick to discrete and small-scale problems (*NL* 254; *A* 39). Yet he criti-

---

[34] Saari refers to Collingwood's 'holism' in this connection (*Re-enactment*, 18); but I think this term is better reserved for the position rejected by methodological individualists, who do not usually deny that historians concern themselves with wholes of various kinds (see Ch. 5, § 4).

[35] 'Hadrian's Wall: 1921–30', *Journal of Roman Studies*, 21 (1931), 62–3. See also L28 434.

cizes nineteenth-century positivists for promoting the idea that the 'field of the historically knowable was cut up into an infinity of minute facts each to be separately considered', the unhappy consequence of this being, he says, 'a combination of unprecedented mastery over small-scale problems with unprecedented weakness in dealing with large-scale problems' (*IH* 131–2).[36]

Later in *The Idea of History*, Collingwood does talk of the impossibility of historians 'judging the value of a certain way of life taken in its entirety' on the ground that 'no such a thing in its entirely is ever a possible object of historical knowledge' (*IH* 327). Such pronouncements, however, can plausibly be read simply as repudiations of any notion that historical inquiry can give us exhaustive knowledge of anything. Knowing something 'as a whole' might mean knowing 'the whole truth' about it; but it could also mean, and in the present context may be taken to mean, knowing what one does know about it as an organization or system of parts, rather than as a sum of discrete details (NTM E-110).[37]

What Collingwood has to say about the interest of historians in wholes is important not only for an adequate grasp of his conception of history's proper subject-matter, but also for a further appreciation of what he thinks counts as historical understanding. What emerges from his discussion is an idea of understanding as achieved through synthesis: through relating particular to particular to discern a larger whole of fact. Understanding becomes seeing things together, seeing them in their manifold interrelationships, whether in space, as in cross-sectional histories, or in time, as in narrative. The relationship of part to whole is thus placed alongside that of cause to effect, or reason to action, as a fundamental category of historical thinking.[38] One of Collingwood's own examples of the way this category may be applied is that of an historian coming to regard two events like the

---

[36] He observes similarly, using an expression later used by Mink (*MHD* 3), that the techniques of critical historiography have not 'taught us how to see what Henry James called the pattern in the carpet' (CHBI 7*a*).

[37] Collingwood says far too little about how he thinks historical wholes of various kinds are organized (he says most about wholes which can be delineated by narratives). As will appear in Ch. 8, he also sometimes puts the idea of studying structured wholes out of focus by maintaining that, in history, everything is as important as everything else.

[38] I consider here chiefly synthesis of the first kind, since Collingwood's view of narrative will be considered in Ch. 8.

murder of Caesar and the battle of Actium as 'forming parts of one event, the fall of the Roman Republic' (SPAT 137). His doctrine at this point is really a further, and more acceptable, development of the idea that historical understanding is idiographic (*IH* 166–7).[39] At one level, an idiographic approach to the human past could mean viewing it as a welter of discrete facts, each to be understood individually—the view which Collingwood reproaches nineteenth-century positivist historians for having held. But, at another level, it could mean an interest in large-scale historical units—unique concatenations of conditions and events—as vehicles of the individuality which Collingwood often points to as an essential feature of history's subject-matter.[40]

To say that all this forms part of Collingwood's *theory* of historical understanding is perhaps to put it too strongly, since he does not explicitly offer it as such, as he does the idea of re-enactment. Yet what he has to say about the elaboration and use of webs and pictures by historians implies it clearly enough to warrant its being regarded at least as one of his 'recessive' doctrines. The idea, especially, of constructing a 'picture' of a portion of the past conveys more than a concern simply to find coherence and continuity in a subject-matter: it suggests a search for wholeness.

Some students of Collingwood—David Thompson is an example—have seen a 'tension' between the ideas of viewing something in its individuality and seeing it as part of a whole.[41] And there is indeed a sense in which a thing loses individuality when it is understood as a part of something else. To understand it thus is nevertheless very different from understanding it as exemplifying a type of thing which recurs; for it is to incorporate the individuality of the part into the individuality of the whole, not to ignore it by treating it as a mere instance. A different kind of difficulty is raised by Leff, who asks how the idea of synthetic understanding can be reconciled with Collingwood's theory of historical understanding as re-enactment. The historian who engages in 'imaginative reconstruction' along the lines here envisaged, he observes, must go well beyond what is re-enactively understandable. For what is said to be reconstructed 'was never

---

[39] See Ch. 2, § 7.
[40] Although the concatenations may be unique, the relationships composing them will, of course, as indicated earlier, fall under general concepts.
[41] Thompson, 'Colligation and History Teaching', 88.

actual, but was rather contained in individual events' (*HST* 18). In other words, the wholes which historians identify were often not themselves objects of consciousness to the agents concerned. But Collingwood makes this point himself. 'The historian who sketches the economic history of the Roman Empire', he declares, 'depicts a state of things which no contemporary saw as a whole' (NTM E-110).[42] The point of importance is that, although synthetic understanding would normally go beyond what the agents were aware of, and thus beyond what can be re-enacted, it can include, and ordinarily would include, re-enactments. To revert to another Collingwoodian example: it is only when the actions of Caesar's assassins are understood as expressing certain beliefs and intentions that they can be incorporated into the larger historical whole described as a 'constitutional conflict'—or even 'murder'. The two kinds of understanding are thus complementary, not in competition, and certainly not incompatible.

The aspects of Collingwood's view of history which have just been noted call to mind attempts by philosophers of history like Walsh and Mink to do justice to the synthetic aspect of historical work. Introducing a term which has since become entrenched in the vocabulary of philosophers of history, Walsh (as noted in Ch. 5, § 6) has described historians as 'colligating' events under 'appropriate conceptions' (*IPH* 61–2). What he means by 'colligating', however, is only a special case of the understanding through synthesis which Collingwood envisages. According to Walsh, the historian seeks to make 'a coherent whole' out of what he studies by finding 'certain dominant concepts or leading ideas by which to illuminate his facts': ideas like 'Romantic movement' or 'Hitlerian policy of expansion'. But an historian's synthesis need not employ any idea of a 'whole' which is more specific than the idea of a multi-dimensional interrelation of parts. There is no necessity that what is thus delineated be brought under a colligatory concept; it is sufficient for understanding that the interconnections be shown. Collingwood himself criticizes Hegel for discounting 'the individuality, the concreteness and uniqueness', of certain historical periods by 'characterizing these periods by means of abstract concepts' (L29 16–18)—although he does not hesitate to do the same thing on occasion himself, when writing as

---

[42] See also Ch. 5, § 5, on the application of social concepts.

an historian, as when he describes the early years of Romano-British history as 'The Age of Conquest' (*RBES* 76).[43] The minimal position, the idea of discerning interrelationships without going on to overall conceptualization, is what Mink has in view when he represents the typical approach of historians to their subject-matter as 'configurational' rather than 'categoreal' (*HU* 51). And the fundamental idea here is, in fact, a cliché of working historians, namely, that if we wish to understand things 'historically', we must consider them 'in context'. This idea is implicit in Collingwood's claim, already noted, that it would be characteristic of historians, when studying a given war, to try to relate it not to other wars, but to other things which happened in the same period, and it is explicit in his observation that the reason why scientific explanation fails to engender historical understanding is that it removes things from their context (RAH 11; L28 452).

The colligating of historical events and conditions into periods is a logical half-way house between conceptualizing larger-scale historical wholes as movements, enterprises, structures, states of affairs, styles, institutional changes, and the like, and merely configurating them. Collingwood makes only scattered comments with regard to the conceptualization of configurated wholes as such. But he has some interesting theses to advance about periodization, if sometimes rather controversial ones.

He criticizes Spengler and Toynbee, for example, for dividing human history into periods which are mere 'arbitrary fabrications'. But what he says in support of this charge sometimes has the appearance of being an attack on the whole idea of discerning periods. A major problem raised by the periodizations which these authors offer, Collingwood says, is that they obscure important continuities which obtained between what their periodizing represents as discontinuous. He finds Spengler especially open to criticism on this score, failing as he allegedly does to see that even something as apparently distinctive as Western mathematics is not entirely new, but a development out of a Classical predecessor (SHC 71). This evokes from him the obser-

[43] Collingwood conceptualizes periods with abandon when he says that there have been four 'great constructive ages of European history': a mathematics-centred one in ancient Greece, a theology-centred one in the Middle Ages, a natural science-centred one in the sixteenth to nineteenth centuries, and a history-centred one which, having begun just before the nineteenth century, is still emerging in our own time (*IH* 4–5).

vation that every historical change must be seen as 'the growth of what comes after, and the decay of what comes before' (L28 472). But if the latter is to be taken as a general argument for the conclusion that periods can display no more than a 'fictitious unity'—and it is easy to read it as such—it comes rather surprisingly from an author who, in other contexts, strongly affirms the capacity of thought to 'arrest' a flux (for example, the flux of feeling) by bringing it under concepts (*IH* 303). One would have expected Collingwood to see the task of historical thought as, similarly, to arrest the flux of past events by bringing it under concepts—or, to change the metaphor, to do whatever is required to avoid falling into a view of the historical past as a seamless web, or a 'homogeneous flow' (L26 414).

An associated problem for claims to discern periods in history which Collingwood underlines, is the fact that periodization may be relative to a point of view, or even to interests. A stretch of the past which may plausibly be periodized in one way if an historian's interest is in the development of technology, for example, may have to be periodized in quite another if his interest is in the development of art or political institutions. As Collingwood points out, the 'decline of Hellas' after the fifth century in Greece, can be regarded as, at the same time, the rise of the Hellenistic world (SHC 75). But although such a consideration may raise a special problem for the great historical system-builders, like Spengler, who tend to see all the elements of their periods as interlocked and as changing together—as, indeed, Collingwood occasionally does himself (L28 472)—it is hard to see why it should put in question periodization as such. Periods which are identified in relation to different concerns may certainly be out of phase, and may also overlap, as when Collingwood, in criticism of Spengler, characterizes the style of the Roman Pantheon as neither Classical nor Magian, but as Classical turning into Magian (THC 74). That, however, scarcely requires that we regard either the Classical or Magian periods as 'fictitious'.

A third kind of reservation about periodization which Collingwood sometimes expresses is typified by the welcome which he gives to Lord Acton's famous advice to historians: 'Study problems, not periods' (*IH* 281). He sees an important connection between this precept and his own doctrine that serious historical inquiry proceeds not by assembling a body of evidence, to see what will come of it, but by seeking answers to specific questions. It is surely a mistake, however, to regard the contrast between studying problems and studying periods as similar to that between being guided by specific questions and collecting data aimlessly. For, as Oakeshott answered Acton long ago, periods can themselves be problems, what periods should be recognized and how they should be characterized being one of the many kinds of question which historians legitimately raise.[44] Nor does Collingwood refuse such questions in his own historical work. At the beginning of *Roman Britain*, for example, he asks how the Roman period in Britain should be interpreted, and, more particularly, whether it should be regarded as an 'isolated episode' (*RB* 2). He evidently thinks this question not only legitimate, but worth trying to answer by detailed historical inquiry— although, piling a priori argument upon empirical, he does suggest that an adequate philosophical analysis of the idea of a period would show that no historical period can properly be conceived as isolated.

In sometimes appearing to resist the idea that periods can be problems, Collingwood perhaps takes too much to heart a lesson which he claims to have learned early in his archaeological studies, namely, that little comes of excavating a site without knowing what one is looking for—this prompting him to offer, as an archaeological equivalent of Acton's precept: 'Study problems, not sites' (*A* 125). However, interpreting such precepts as properly limiting either historical or archaeological inquiry to questions on points of detail, would gratuitously ignore the synthetic dimension of inquiry in both fields.

But there is much in what Collingwood has to say about periodization which puts his view of its nature and legitimacy in better balance—if not, indeed, in overbalance. In *The Idea of History*, for example, he welcomes the notion of dividing the human past into periods, each 'with peculiar characteristics of its own', as a valuable contribution made by the Christian world-view to historiography—valuable because 'the attempt to distinguish periods in history is a mark of advanced and mature historical thought, not afraid to interpret facts instead of merely ascertaining them' (*IH* 49, 53). And he makes it clear that, along with the notion of periodization, comes that of subdividing peri-

[44] Michael Oakeshott, *Experience and Its Modes* (Cambridge, 1933), 143 n.

ods into stages or phases, periods within periods, generating a whole way of structuring an historical subject-matter which can be carried through on various scales and in varying detail.

At other points he goes further. In a manuscript of 1931, he declares that 'the distinction of periods and their fundamental characteristics is not a merely empirical matter', but is 'logically prior to the detailed investigation of the facts'. It springs, he says, 'from the historian's general outlook on the past' (L31 11). In his lectures of 1926, he maintains that, so long as we think of the past at all, 'we must think of it as possessing that kind of determinate structure which consists in a sequence of more or less clearly-defined periods . . . each possessing precisely those characteristics which would necessitate their turning into the next' (L26 415). He takes as an example the distinction between ancient, medieval, and modern history, the most elementary of all periodizations. This is a distinction, he insists, which 'is necessarily implied in our own point of view towards history. For the past is that which has turned into the present; but every past time was a present when it existed, and is now thought of by the historian as . . . having its own past; and therefore all historical thought necessarily generates a distinction between the past and the past of the past.'[45] It is thus a matter of sheer logic that 'there must be a broad general difference of character between . . . modern history, regarded as that which has immediately produced the present, and ancient history, regarded as that which produced the recent or modern past, and therefore produced the present mediately'. 'Within the recent past and the remote past', similar distinctions will reappear, 'so that these two main periods will reveal an internal structure reduplicating in principle their relation to each other' (L26 414).[46]

[45] Collingwood associates this claim with his view of the historical past as purely ideal, and thus necessarily the way we conceive it, an issue to be considered in Ch. 7. What he says about the necessary relativity of the ancient/modern distinction to a present standpoint raises the general question of perspective in history, an issue to be considered in Ch. 8.
[46] Collingwood concedes that, 'if this search for distinctions were pushed *ad infinitum*', the distinction ancient/modern would disappear. He puts this consideration aside on the ground that 'we are concerned with history as actually studied by actual historians'—a strange thing for him to say in view of having held earlier that philosophy of history is not based on empirical considerations, and deals only with what is necessarily and universally true of its subject-matter (L26 414).

Two observations might be made on this large shift from representing periodization as a dubious option in history to representing it as an unavoidable feature of it—to representing it, in effect, as an aspect of the a priori idea of history. It should be noted, first, that what Collingwood is saying here applies only to one kind of periodizing, and not the most interesting or even the most common kind. For, if one can know a priori that history falls into ancient, medieval, and modern periods, one certainly cannot know in a similar way that it was characterized by a feudal period, or a Romantic period, or an industrial period, or a period of imperialism—and still less, in the case of British history, by a period of Roman occupation. Whether there were such periods, or whether there were even such kinds of periods, is something to be discovered by examining evidence, i.e. empirically. That there were periods of this latter sort is not something which is 'incidental to our point of view' in the sense in which this can be said of the examples cited by Collingwood.[47] Furthermore, while Collingwood very properly asserts that from his 'a priori formula' about the existence of periods in history no historical facts can be deduced, some facts of at least a very general nature can be deduced from a claim to have identified a feudal or an industrial period.

The other observation is that, even where periodization implies only a division into something like ancient, medieval, and modern, no claim that the human past in fact manifests such a pattern can be completely a priori. For, as Collingwood himself appears to concede, the applicability of such a scheme presupposes an ability to discover plausible points of transition, changes which were sufficiently definite and sufficiently important to justify drawing a line between one historical state of affairs (or way of life, as Collingwood also sometimes says) and what is sufficiently different from it to count as its relevant antecedent. That we know such plausible points of transition—in fact, too many of them—is scarcely open to question. But our knowledge of them, or even our knowledge that there are some, is hardly a priori.

---

[47] They may, however, be relative to a point of view in further senses considered in Ch. 8.

§ 5. *Universal History*

Collingwood's emphasis on the historian's obligation to trace out detailed, concrete 'pictures' of the past, and on all histories having to be mutually consistent, raises the question of how far he conceives all historical inquiry as committed to some conception of universal history. It seems fair to say, as Cebik does, that he 'had no practical interest in universal history'—at any rate if this means the sort of thing done by authors like Spengler or Toynbee, or even H. G. Wells or William McNeil.[48] Certainly his own historical work on what was a rather remote corner of the Roman world was at the opposite end of the scale. Yet he often seems, at least in theory, to accept the legitimacy of inquiries at a universal level, and sometimes even to represent some notion of them as indispensable to a correct understanding of historical thinking.

Thus, in *Speculum Mentis*, he declares: 'Take away the conception of a universal history in which every special history finds its place and its justification, and you have committed the first and deepest sin against history' (*SM* 235), a claim which he summarizes, with typical exaggeration, in the aphorism: 'history is essentially universal history' (*SM* 231). He expresses a similar view at various points in *The Idea of History*. The 'modern conception of history', he avers, is of an inquiry 'whose field is the human past in its entirety' (*IH* 209); the historian's aim is, 'in principle' at least, 'to use the entire perceptible here-and-now as evidence for the entire past through whose process it has come into being' (*IH* 247); particular historical works are to be conceived 'as ideally forming parts of a universal history' (*IH* 27). One of the main weaknesses of the original Greek historians, according to Collingwood, was that their method made it 'impossible for the various particular histories to be gathered up into one all-embracing history' (*IH* 27). The Hellenistic historians, on the other hand, are commended for having achieved 'oecumenical history', this making the unity of the world for them, as it was not for Herodotus and Thucydides, a truly historical, not just a geographical, idea (*IH* 31). The Christian approach to history is seen as a further development in the same direction. One of its

---

[48] Cebik, 'Collingwood', 78.

strengths, Collingwood says, was its universality, its conception of the historian's subject-matter as 'in principle the history of the world', a symbol of this being its 'adoption of a single chronological framework' (*IH* 51). And when, later, he criticizes a practising world-historian like Marx, it is chiefly on the ground that he views the human past as having 'only one continuous thread', an economic one, when, in fact, it is an 'organic unity' with political, artistic, religious, and other dimensions as well (*IH* 123; L28 477).

Collingwood does, at times, express himself in ways which may seem hostile to the construction of anything like a universal history or history of the world. Such an attitude might be read, for example, into his doctrine, noted in other connections, that 'scientific' history is a matter of specific questions and answers (*A* 37 ff.); and the same might be said of observations like: 'All history is the history of something, something definite and particular; the history of everything is the history of nothing'—this in support of a contention that a world history 'claims a kind of universality which by its nature history can never possess' (PH 130).

Yet the burden of one of Collingwood's complaints against the nineteenth-century positivists was precisely that they wrongly encouraged the belief that only 'microscopic problems' could be adequately dealt with by historians, a natural fruit of this approach, he observes, being the failure of Mommsen's *History of Rome* to get beyond the battle of Actium (*IH* 131). At some stages of his thought, too, he throws doubt upon the ultimate viability of discrete and minute problems as such, on the ground that the solution of a new problem may affect the answers already given to old ones. Thus Bury is criticized for trying to bring Gibbon 'up to date by means of footnotes', which Collingwood describes as 'not unlike adding a saxaphone obbligato to an Elizabethan madrigal' (*IH* 147). Such considerations are significant for Collingwood's view of historical understanding as a grasping of the connectedness of things; but they suggest, further, that universal history could be expected to grow naturally, almost inexorably, out of the starting-point furnished by any particular historical inquiry. In fact, it was precisely an increasing realization that 'historical facts are what they are only in relation to other facts', he says, which led eighteenth-century writers to attempt the composition of universal histories (L28 453).

Collingwood thus often appears open to the idea that universal history will be, and perhaps should be, attempted. But he also stresses its difficulties, representing it as virtually an impossible enterprise in practice. In *The Idea of History*, even while stating it as an ideal, he concedes that the aim of using the entire present as evidence for the entire past is one that 'can never be achieved' (*IH* 247). In 'The Philosophy of History', he maintains that there exists no 'total body of past facts' which the historian, 'if he had time', might 'know in its totality', so that 'the attempt at a universal history is foredoomed to failure' (PH 138). When rejecting the possibility of judging overall progress in history, he uses the similar argument that 'the historian can never take any period as a whole' because there are always 'large tracts of its life for which he has either no data, or no data that he is in a position to interpret' (*IH* 329). And, in *Speculum Mentis*, it was precisely the impossibility of ever giving an account of the whole world of particular fact that was said to justify historical scepticism (*SM* 234). Collingwood occasionally blunts the edge of such doubts about the viability of universal history in ways that can only be called eccentric. Thus, in his 1926 lectures, he observes that any competent historical monograph is, in effect, itself a universal history 'in the sense that it is an attempt to give an account, as complete as possible, of the present world'—meaning the present world conceived as relics of the past (L26 421). At another point, he tells us that any historical inquiry can be viewed as a universal history since, for the historian working on it, it is 'the whole of history' at that moment (L28 459). Neither consideration really addresses the problem as originally raised, and Collingwood himself admits, in effect, that the first only shifts it to another point, since the present world, as an object of knowledge, is also 'inexhaustible'.[49]

There are considerations present in Collingwood's own discussion, however, which mitigate the problem raised about universal history in a more acceptable way. For if the difficulty is the necessary incompleteness, or lack of finality, of anything offered as a universal history, this, he allows, is a problem by no means peculiar to it. There is no more possibility of a complete and final account of something like the Peasants' Revolt, for example, than

---

[49] Both considerations are related to Collingwood's doctrine that history is only ideal (to be questioned in Ch. 7). See e.g. L26 419; L28 456.

there is of the human past in general (L26 420).[50] There may be a
sense in which a putative universal history would have to be even
more selective than a particular, monographic, one; but if incompleteness is the problem, it will arise as much for the one as for the
other. Collingwood does say that 'the essence of the error' of
those who call for universal history derives from the belief that
the historical past, taken as a whole, has 'a structure of its own'
which only needs discovering (L28 456). But this hardly differs in
principle from the belief that there is a structure to be discovered
in some more limited portion of the human past: for example,
European history in the nineteenth century, or British history in
the Roman period, the main lines of which Collingwood himself
tries to sketch.[51] Collingwood argues further that, 'because the
whole of history is too large a matter for anyone to bring together
into a single literary work', a 'so-called universal history' can be
no more than 'a mere selection of the facts which the writer
happens to think important or interesting'; and along similar
lines, he holds that the universality of a universal history can
only consist in 'the unity of the point of view from which it is
envisaged' (L28 454–5). Once again, however, the problem is not
peculiar to universal history.

Sometimes Collingwood seems implicitly to deny that any difficulty which arises in this connection is of much theoretical importance. Thus, with regard to the impossibility of a universal
history achieving full universality, he observes that 'this separation between what is attempted in principle and what is
achieved in practice is the lot of mankind, not a peculiarity of
historical thinking' (*IH* 247). Perhaps his most considered judgment, however, and one which changes the focus in an interesting
way, is expressed in the course of a critical commentary on Kant.
He writes: 'If universal history means a history of everything that
has happened, it is impossible. If particular history means a par-

[50] Collingwood writes: 'not only is there an infinity of facts concerning the
Peasants' Revolt that simply cannot now be discovered, but even if they could,
the Peasants' Revolt would remain unintelligible when torn from its context in the
history of the world' (L26 420).

[51] It is therefore strange that Collingwood should try to reinforce his point by
saying that the only thing likely to be wrong with a serious attempt at universal
history will be its title. Rather than being called a history of the whole human past,
it will be something better called, e.g. 'The Oppression of the Proletariat in the last
Twenty-five Centuries' or 'The Growth of the Modern Conception of Liberty'
(L28 459).

ticular study which does not involve a definite conception of the nature and significance of history as a whole, that too is impossible' (*IH* 103). The new idea which emerges in the second statement is reinforced when Collingwood adds: 'Particular history is only a name for history itself in its detail; universal history is only a name for the historian's conception of history as such' (*IH* 103–4). In other words, although universal history may not be a very promising undertaking in practice, Collingwood regards it as so far from being dismissible in principle that he sees all historical inquiry as presupposing it. At least the *conception* of universal history, and of every particular piece of historical thinking as aimed at making a contribution to it, is alleged to be essential to the idea of scientific historiography. As Gallie puts it, the idea of universal history—the idea of one historical world in which everything discovered by historical thinking must find a place—is, for Collingwood, 'an intellectual ideal or device', not a 'quasi-substantive whole' (*PHU* 59).[52] Or, as Rotenstreich prefers to say, the universality of universal history is 'the concrete materialization of the all-embracing coherence' which is required by Collingwood's three a priori principles of history (*PHP* 44).

There is still another way in which Collingwood sometimes takes issue with what he *calls* universal history. He frequently attacks those who, allegedly under positivist influence, and with a view to 'raising history to the rank of a science', engage in an enterprise which he refers to derisively as 'pigeon-holing'. These authors, he says, look for overall patterns in the past, 'extrapolate these patterns into a theory of universal history', and project them into the future (*IH* 264–5). In Collingwood's view, the idea of universal history which is thus applied 'claims a kind of universality which by its nature history can never possess' (PH 130). Those who apply it don't 'take facts seriously enough'; they fail to 'realise that every fact is unique'; they treat facts as mere 'instances' (PH 132). Clearly, what Collingwood has in mind when he speaks of 'patterns' here is 'laws'—those macroscopic laws (or assertions of 'historical cycles' as he sometimes says) which speculative philosophers of history like Comte, Spencer, Spengler, or Toynbee have claimed to discover. Even to look for such laws he regards as betraying 'a confusion between history

---

[52] Collingwood himself says that historical thinking aims at knowledge 'ideally forming parts of a universal history' (*IH* 27).

and science' (PH 131). In other words, he sees the thought processes of the speculative philosophers as repeating on a grander
scale the errors of the workaday positivist approach to historical
understanding. Not that he considers the search for large-scale
laws of history, which was mainly an interest of the eighteenth
and nineteenth centuries, to have been entirely without value. He
concedes that it 'fostered, in especial, the tendency towards research into obscure and little-known periods'; it 'broke down
parochialism in history much as the Newtonian theory of universal gravitation finally broke down parochialism in astronomy'
(L28 453).

But Collingwood also frequently characterizes universal
history, and even the work of these same speculative philosophers, as a search for patterns in the different sense of plots or
plans. If he shows greater indulgence towards this, it is because
here, at least, the individuality of history is fully recognized.
There is no question of regarding past happenings as mere instances; the aim is to represent each incident as 'an irreplaceable
and unique element in an irreplaceable and unique whole'
(NAPH 40). It is made clear, however, that terms like 'plot' and
'plan' are used here somewhat metaphorically. 'The plan which is
revealed in history', Collingwood writes, 'is a plan which does
not pre-exist to its own revelation' (NAPH 36). And even this he
seems ultimately to reduce to little more than the ideas of continuity, coherence, and synthesis, which we have already noted. Exhibiting a plot, for example, he equates with being 'coherent,
significant, intelligible' (PP 111), or with being a sequence in
which 'each situation leads necessarily to the next'.[53] Collingwood
does himself sometimes seem half-seduced by the idea of history
as a drama, this, on occasion, showing itself in surprising ways, as
when he remarks, in *Speculum Mentis*, that changes of fashion in
dress are 'as inevitable as the plot of a drama' (*SM* 227). Yet, as
early as that work, he tries to strike a balance, remarking that
anyone unable to see the dramatic force of history 'will never be
an historian', while at the same time warning that 'the historian
who handles history as if it were mere drama is in a state of
deadly sin' (*SM* 210). It might be noted, in this connection, that he

[53] 'Ruskin's Philosophy', 19.

is prepared, somewhat surprisingly, to say that Thucydides was a greater tragedian than he was an historian (*SM* 215–16).

Apart from his doubts about its practicality, all this may seem to leave Collingwood rather favourably disposed towards universal history conceived as a search not for laws, but for individual patterns in the human past taken as a whole. But he raises one further concern about it, and a curious one, which, if valid, would put pattern-drawing or synthetic understanding in history in question generally. He contrasts discerning patterns with making clear the actual details of past events in their myriad interrelationships, and stresses that the former is no substitute for the latter. In 'The Nature and Aims of a Philosophy of History', he puts the point this way. 'The real plot of history', he says, 'is coincident with universal history in all its extent and with all its profusion of detail. Omit any part, truncate the course of history or eviscerate some of its detail, and you mutilate the plot, imparting to it a false emphasis and misrepresenting its general significance' (NAPH 39). This declaration is somewhat softened by his adding that such mutilation and misrepresentation are nevertheless 'inevitable', and may sometimes even be heuristically valuable as a way of organizing research on the details. However, his claim still needs to be challenged at a theoretical level. For it makes little sense to *identify* the pattern of history with its details; a pattern is something derived from, or discerned in, a mass of details. To adopt one of Collingwood's own similes: it is supposed to display the skeleton of history, not its flesh. Collingwood insists that no true historian could be satisfied merely with the skeleton. Yet he might surely, in his quest for understanding, want to know what it was. Collingwood seems here to have allowed the endemic hostility to abstraction, which surfaces periodically in his thought, to carry him to an unproductive extreme. The same tendency will be observed again in Chapter 8, when we come to discuss reservations which he expresses about the notion of importance in history. Here it must suffice to say that every time he talks about composing a story or constructing a picture, he undermines his own doctrine.

And he often writes as if he did not himself really believe it. The propriety and utility of pattern-drawing is quite clearly implied, for example, when he declares: 'A long period of history hangs together better than a short; and the loose ends which are left in the plot of any given period are knit up in the fabric of its context' (NAPH 37). He adds: 'History as a whole, if only we could know it as a whole, would certainly reveal itself as infinitely more coherent and systematic, infinitely more pervaded by a plot, than any mere period of history.' He goes on, very properly, to observe that discovering the plot or pattern of the past is not, as some might think, 'philosophy of history'; it is 'simply history'. Clearly, the sense in which it is simply history is not that of presenting an undifferentiated welter of interconnected fact, but that of revealing an individual, and perhaps even unique, pattern in the subject-matter. The historian's task is certainly to discover what happened in history as a whole; but this may require the abstraction of a pattern (at least in the sense of a configuration) from that whole.

7

THE IDEALITY OF HISTORY

§ 1. *Historical Scepticism*

In the last chapter, I examined Collingwood's account of a structural imagination at work in historical inquiry, an account which seeks to do justice to both its a priori and empirical aspects, and which draws attention to certain synthesizing or whole-istic dimensions of historical thinking which go well beyond the idea of understanding as re-enactment. I want to go on now to ask how far he holds that the investigations of historians, so conceived, are capable of attaining objective truth about the past: whether, on his view, historians can reasonably claim, in the words of von Ranke, to recover the past 'as it actually was', or whether their conclusions must be considered subjective, or relativist, or, in some other damaging sense, non-objective. Collingwood's concern about this issue goes back to his earliest writings, although the reasons he gives for questioning the Rankean formula change as time goes by. In *Speculum Mentis*, a philosophical analysis of the historical enterprise is said to show that its aims and methods involve incoherencies which threaten its own breakdown. In the essays of the 1920s, this theme is carried further, Collingwood calling for a limitation of history's pretensions with a view to heading off the threat of scepticism.[1] Many commentators—Walsh is an example—have seen the refutation of scepticism as a major goal of Collingwood's philosophy of history (*IPH* 71), and more than a few have thought it a failure in that regard. Thus Carr maintains that Collingwood's position implies 'total scepticism'; D. M. Mackinnon characterizes its 'underlying

---

[1] The issue here is, of course, scepticism about history, not about philosophy. Collingwood has also been said to be sceptical about philosophy, notably in *EM*, but there is little trace of such a view in *IH*, or in most of his philosophical writings on history.

bias' as 'subjectivist'; Marwick views it as 'justifying historical relativism'.[2]

It is a curiosity of the critical literature on Collingwood that his doctrine of re-enactment has been seen both as an attempt by him to dissolve sceptical worries, and as one of the elements of his theory of history which most immediately generates such worries. Mandelbaum is typical of those who see the requirement that historians re-enact past thoughts as something which must 'inevitably lead to scepticism'.[3] Those who view it this way, however, have generally grounded their position on difficulties believed to arise for Collingwood on the false assumption that he is a Cartesian dualist, who assigns historians the impossible task of gaining knowledge of private mental contents (see Chapter 2, § 3). Others, like Goldstein and Fain, have regarded the re-enactment doctrine as Collingwood's 'answer' to scepticism.[4] But although it may indeed offer an answer to the ill-founded scepticism just instanced, it can hardly be regarded as, in itself, an answer to scepticism in any broader sense. For, considered strictly, it is simply a theory of what would count as understanding an action if we could get it; and such a theory no more entails objectivism than it does indeterminism (see Chapter 3, § 5). A claim actually to have achieved re-enactive understanding of a past thought, since it would include a claim to have got it right, would, of course, entail a repudiation of scepticism in the sense of claiming to know at least something about the past; and Collingwood makes such claims. But although this may be significant for the question whether he was himself an historical objectivist (and I shall argue that it is), it scarcely makes the re-enactment theory of understanding itself an 'answer' to scepticism.

For the way Collingwood himself conceived the threat of scepticism, we must look well beyond his re-enactment doctrine, although remembering always to ask how his response to it jibes with his re-enactive view of understanding. In his writings on history, four considerations are repeatedly stressed as likely to engender scepticism. One is the essential incompleteness, and

[2] *WIH* 21; D. M. MacKinnon, Review of *IH*, in *Journal of Theological Studies*, 48 (1947), 252; Marwick, *Nature of History*, 80.
[3] Mandelbaum, Review of *IH*, 187.
[4] Goldstein, 'Collingwood's Theory', 3–4; Fain, *BPH* 144. Fain adds that, as an answer, it 'misses the mark'.

thus openness to doubt, of any account of the past constructed by an historian, and, further, the incompleteness of any evidence which could be cited for any detail of it. A second is what Collingwood, especially in some of his writings of the late 1920s, calls 'the ideality of history': the fact that what the historian studies no longer exists (or exists only 'in idea'), raising the question of the reasonableness of claiming that a given account 'corresponds' to what originally happened. A third centres upon reasons for saying that historical inquiries must always be conducted from a certain point of view, the latter allegedly distancing the inquirer from his object. A fourth derives from the fact that history is constantly rewritten, it being a commonplace that each generation must write its own history in its own way, and from its own standpoint. What Collingwood has to say about the first two of these sources of concern is one of the reasons why he is sometimes called an idealist rather than a realist in his view of history. What he has to say about the second two is one of the reasons why he has been called an historical relativist or perspectivist. I shall consider the first two issues in the present chapter, and the second two in Chapter 8.

Before proceeding, there are two points on which a brief comment should perhaps be made, both relating to Collingwood's use of key philosophical terms. The first is that, although, as the four reasons cited for embracing scepticism will have suggested, Collingwood conceives the problem of historical objectivity in ways which will be familiar enough to most of his readers, he often distinguishes between what he calls 'subjective' and 'objective' in history in ways which are related only distantly to the problems just indicated. When he asks, for example, whether a re-thought thought or re-enacted experience is subjective or objective, and answers that it must be both, he is not simply contradicting himself, as he would be if he were using these terms in more familiar senses (*IH* 218). All he means is that the historian's re-thought thought must actually be thought by him, and thus be a critical intellectual experience of his own, as well as being something which refers beyond itself to a public world (*IH* 190). So employed, the distinction has no connection with that between thinking truly and thinking falsely, or thinking descriptively and thinking evaluatively, to take just two other contrasts which 'subjective' and 'objective' are sometimes used to mark. In context, however, little confusion need result from what some may regard as a rather peculiar usage. The same could be said of the fact that, when Collingwood calls historical inquiry objective, what he often means is simply that its results make a claim upon all who will consider the evidence—rather than being simply the personal impressions or opinions of particular inquirers. As he rather picturesquely puts it, the historian builds an intellectual habitation not just for himself, but for all historians—and, he might have added, for all who think historically (*IH* 155).

The second point concerns Collingwood's use of the term 'realism' when contrasting his own view of historical knowledge and inquiry with that of some of his philosophical opponents. The most important meaning he gives it is an epistemological one: the claim that historians can gain knowledge of the past 'as it actually was' (L26 394)—although the latter notion, too, is sometimes rather a slippery one in Collingwood's hands, as will appear. An associated, but not identical, epistemological meaning is the claim that knowledge is always achieved 'by acquaintance', always a matter of a knower directly 'apprehending' an object, the paradigm for this being knowledge of physical objects in sense perception (L26 483). A linked meaning is the contention that, in order to be known, a thing must exist, from which it follows that if the historical past is known, it must still (in some sense) exist. From this derives what might be called 'silly realism', the ontological claim that the past studied by historians consists of events which, happily, are still going on 'somewhere'—in some ethereal world where (as Collingwood puts it) 'Galileo's weight is still falling', and 'the smoke of Nero's Rome still fills the intelligible air' (LHK 101). It is puzzling that Collingwood should have thought it necessary to ridicule such a view, which it is difficult to believe any historian or philosopher of history ever held. One of the dangers of his doing so is that undeserved odium may descend upon historical realism in some less silly, and even genuinely challenging, sense.

By historical realism, Collingwood also means, at various points, some other and not obviously equivalent things. Sometimes he conceives it as a view of historical inquiry as passive, this being at odds with his own view of it as a questioning and critically re-enactive activity (*A* 26). Sometimes he sees it as an acceptance of an intuitionist view of what is involved in historical discovery (A 30). At other times it becomes for him a claim that what historians want to know can be completely and finally known, this imposing upon them an unattainable goal (LHK 100). At still other times, it is the strange contention that what happened in the past is not altered by becoming known—or, to put it more strongly, that neither its nature nor its existence depend upon its being investigated by the historian (L28 448). Where the historical task is specifically envisaged as being the re-enactment of thoughts, Collingwood sometimes represents realism as the view that the only proper concern of historians is with what the thoughts were, leaving aside the question whether they were valid or invalid, true or false: i.e. it becomes what he elsewhere calls treating the past as a 'spectacle' (A 59). And sometimes realism means no more than a willingness to distinguish at all between historical fact and the historian's knowledge of it—a position which he denigrates as 'naïve realism' (IH 142, 181).

Clearly, a philosopher might be said to be a realist in some of these senses and not in others. The very multiplicity of meanings, furthermore, which Collingwood never explicitly recognizes, virtually guarantees that some of his pronouncements about the alleged dangers of realism in history will be misleading.[5] In what follows, I shall avoid, when I can, referring to what he wants to attack as 'realism', calling attention rather to more specific theses which, from time to time, he uses this term to indicate. I shall hardly be able to avoid using it altogether, however, if only because of its use by Collingwood in statements which I shall want to cite.

§ 2. The Problem of Incompleteness

Let us look first, then, at the problem allegedly raised for claims to attain objective knowledge in history by the fact that historical accounts are always in one way or another incomplete.[6] Collingwood often brackets this problem with the one he sees

---

[5] In view of such cavalier use of key terms, it is hardly surprising that, as van der Dussen notes (HS 119–29), Collingwood has had ascribed to him almost all the possible positions on historical objectivity.

[6] In Ch. 2, § 2, the problem discussed was whether re-enactive explanations, specifically, are necessarily incomplete. Here it is whether completeness can be attained in historical accounts generally.

deriving from the fact that the ostensible object of historical study is now past and gone, non-existent, only 'ideal'. In the lectures of 1926, he denies that historical inquiry achieves genuine knowledge of its object because we cannot know 'past fact as such and in its entirety' (L26 409). In the lectures of 1928, he says that 'history is an illusion if it means knowledge of the past in its actuality and completeness' (L28 484). But although there may be connections between the two issues which Collingwood thus runs together, the two are not the same, and they require separate treatment. In this section, I shall look mainly at what can be said to follow from conceding that an historical account will necessarily offer an incomplete treatment of its subject, this raising again some of the issues noted in considering Collingwood's view of universal history, but from a different point of view. In succeeding sections, I shall look at the more complicated problem raised by the fact that the past is only ideal.

Collingwood's concern about the necessary incompleteness of historical accounts goes back at least to *Speculum Mentis*, where it appears in conjunction with his conception of history as a study of what is factual and individual (*SM* 231). Besides being stressed in the lectures of 1926 and 1928, it is present also in some of the published essays of the 1920s, especially 'The Limits of Historical Knowledge'. It is not entirely absent from the later works, however, sometimes manifesting itself in remarks made even after (as I shall argue) Collingwood had shown how its challenge could be met. Thus, in *The Idea of History*, we are reminded that nothing is 'a possible object of historical knowledge' taken 'in its entirety' (*IH* 327). In the *Autobiography*, Whitehead is praised for undermining a 'realistic' view of knowledge by making clear the 'interdependence' of things, this suggesting that, for Collingwood, the idea of having complete knowledge of anything is still a problematic idea (*A* 45). In a manuscript of 1938–9, we are told that historians should not even 'try to be complete', such a goal being banished from historical studies even as an 'idea of Reason' (NHV 14). And in the plan which Collingwood sketched for his projected 'Principles of History', he still contrasts knowledge to be gained through re-enactment with vain attempts at knowing a 'Dead Past and Completeness' (NHV 21).

The argument from incompleteness comes in two main forms. Both are present in *Speculum Mentis*, and the second is given special prominence in 'The Limits of Historical Knowledge'. It is pointed out, on the one hand, that, although it may ordinarily be assumed that the goal of historical inquiry is to get to know, or ultimately to get to know, all that happened in the past, it would generally be allowed that this goal can never be reached, there being no possibility of any historical account exhausting its topic.[7] What actually happened was a 'sum total of events'; but every historian is necessarily a specialist (LHK 100). It follows from this, Collingwood maintains, that no historical account can represent the past as it actually was. In other words, the totality that it was cannot be known as what it was: a totality. What is grasped is, at best, an 'abstraction' from it (NTM E-111). In pressing this point, Collingwood sometimes caricatures the 'realist' view which he claims to be attacking. To say that historians should recover the past as it actually was, he declares, means that 'every historian as such ought to know the whole past', which implies that he has as great an obligation to discover 'what Julius Caesar had for breakfast on the day he overcame the Nervii' as to discover 'whether he proposed to become king of Rome' (LHK 100–1; NAPH 53). To say the least, he here ignores what might be said, and what he says himself elsewhere (see Chapter 8), about the way judgments of importance function in history.

But Collingwood sees a difficulty not only in the supposed claims of historians to know the past in all its parts or aspects, but also in their more likely claims to know any of them. For what actually happened, he insists, was an interconnected network of occurrences, not a mere sum of discrete happenings; and no part or aspect of this network can be 'truly ascertained' except in its relationship to everything else (L26 419; L28 452).[8] It follows that no historical work can 'express the complete truth about any single fact' (NAPH 43). We can thus neither know the past as a whole, nor know wholly any of its parts or aspects. To this Collingwood adds the supplementary consideration, not always clearly distinguished from the first two, that the evidence considered for or against even the most minute of factual claims in history is never complete: it never exhausts what might have been

---

[7] Completeness is even more obviously an impossible a goal if, as in *SM*, history's subject-matter is seen as reaching into the future—a notion which Collingwood later repudiated.

[8] Sometimes Collingwood brings the two versions of the argument together by maintaining, that, since whatever the historian is working on at a given time is, for him, the whole of history, the problems of knowing wholes and knowing parts come to the same thing (L28 459).

taken into account (L26 392). A problematic incompleteness thus characterizes not only what the historian says happened, but also his reasons for saying it. It is the first kind of incompleteness which Collingwood has in mind when he questions whether historians will ever know what something like the battle of Hastings really was, and the second when he wonders how fully particular accounts of the battle can be justified (NAPH 42, 49). What he says in this connection clearly owes something to his quite explicit rejection at this point of 'the theory of external relations', the view that the nature of a thing need not depend in an essential way on its relations to other things (L26 419). Collingwood concedes that this theory may have an acceptable application in a subject like mathematics, but maintains that it is 'untrue of relations in history'.

The ostensible solution which he offers to the problem of incompleteness, as described, anticipates what he says later in more detail about the role of question and answer in historical inquiry. The historian's task, he contends, is not to recover the past 'in its actuality and completeness' but to find 'the answer which the evidence in his possession gives to the question he is asking' (L28 487). As Collingwood puts it much later, historians should aim not at completeness, but at 'relevance'—relevance to the question posed (NHV 14–15). This he represents as, at the same time, a renunciation of all thought of gaining knowledge of the past as it actually was.

But this is surely a very unsatisfactory response to the problem as stated, and in all three of its dimensions. First, although it may be true that historical findings should be responses to questions asked, the question an historian asks (see Chapter 6, § 4) may itself call for the delineation of a whole—the career of Alexander, for example, or the state of Celtic art during the Roman occupation. Such wholes are not, of course, history as a whole; but the task of describing them raises, if on a different scale, precisely the same questions about how an infinite whole of fact can be characterized as the ones which set Collingwood's argument in motion in the first place. For small-scale wholes, too, have infinite aspects. It is true that, when Collingwood has the present problem in mind, he generally represents historians as dealing with much more specific questions than these—questions like what Caesar intended in invading Britain for a second time in 44 BC. But he cannot plausibly limit historians to answering questions of that kind; nor does he accept such a limitation in his own historical work.

It needs to be stressed, secondly, that, if, as Collingwood maintains, there is something problematic about the idea of historians coming to know isolated facts, the problem remains even if they are seen as responding to very specific questions. An historian who points to Harold's defeat at Hastings in answering the question when Norman power began in England, for example, can still be asked by some Collingwoodian 'anti-realist' (as Collingwood himself asks at one juncture): 'But what exactly *was* Harold's defeat at Hastings? What exactly did it involve?' (NAPH 43). The supposed problem is that, in order adequately to grasp the nature of something, one must grasp the nature of its relations to everything else. But at no level of detail would such a need be neutralized by the fact that a reputable historical inquiry proceeds by question and answer. The problem remains equally untouched by the more general concession that historians normally deal with something less than the entire history of the world.

It is even more obvious, thirdly, that Collingwood offers no adequate response here to the allegation that an historian's evidence is always incomplete. For this will be quite as true on the assumption that what the historian claims to know, he knows in answer to a question. Collingwood himself sometimes gives the impression of trying to blunt such an objection by hinting that, in any actual inquiry, what is called evidence can never plausibly be said to be incomplete. For 'nothing is evidence', he tells us, 'unless it affords an answer to a question which somebody asks'; and 'nothing is a genuine question unless it is asked in the belief that evidence for its answer will be forthcoming' (L28 487). The suggestion seems to be, in other words, that historical conclusions cannot be asserted on incomplete evidence because it is only to the extent that some document, artefact, or relic provides an answer to a question raised that it gains the status of evidence. Presumably Collingwood does not really want to say that the evidence used by historians is always, by definition, complete. Yet one can see traces of such an idea even in his apparently innocuous declaration that 'historical thinking means nothing else than interpreting all the available evidence with the maximum degree of critical skill' (LHK 99). For the notion of unavailable evidence has been emptied of any meaning.

But Collingwood also offers another, and better, solution to the problem of incompleteness as he states it. This derives from his ultimate acceptance of the theory of external relations—although, characteristically, he gives little indication of having seen this as an important volte-face on his part. In a manuscript of 1935, he describes the idea that 'unless we know everything, we know nothing' as a mistake of idealist philosophers (RAH 20). But even earlier he had, in effect, broken with the idea that nothing can be known about a given thing in abstraction from its total context. By claiming, in his 1928 lectures (and again in more detail in *The Idea of History*) that it would make sense, at least, for an historian to claim to re-think the very same thought as an original agent did, despite a difference of context, he gives the lie direct to the notion that anything torn from its context is thereby epistemologically mutilated (L28 446; *IH* 298).[9] It should be added that, in taking this further position—which Donagan describes as 'adopted' from the realists (*LPC* 225)—Collingwood has no intention of denying the importance of referring historical events to their contexts. He simply no longer represents understanding by reference to context as an all-or-nothing affair; it is now regarded as a matter of degree. The new doctrine leaves him free to claim that historians can know both something about history as a whole and something about its parts, aspects or incidents—to claim for them, in other words, the possibility of piecemeal knowledge.[10]

Collingwood presumably changed his position because he could not otherwise make sense of historical inquiry as he found it and practised it.[11] In his later works, he is increasingly driven by the question *how* history is possible, not *whether* it is, its reality

[9] Collingwood still denies that a past thought can be re-enacted 'as it actually happened' (*IH* 303), meaning 'in its immediacy'; but, on his later account of re-enactive understanding, this would be irrelevant to the historian's concerns.

[10] If the argument from incompleteness were sound, knowledge of the present 'as it actually is' would be equally precluded, since this, too, is something which we cannot know either as a whole, or wholly in any of its parts. This would deprive Collingwood of his most likely contrast when he represents knowledge claims about the past as especially problematic. He seems on the verge of making this point himself in L28 484.

[11] If Collingwood had been discussing the problem of completeness which historians actually have, rather than the artificial problem of (let us call it) absolute completeness, he could usefully have considered issues like the relativity of description to a chosen scale, as he does himself *qua* historian when he calls his survey of Romano-British civilization 'as complete as the narrow limits of this essay permit' (*RB* 143; also *RBES* 247).

being regarded as beyond question. Yet there remain in them residues and recurrences of the earlier position, often associated with the doctrine that history is knowledge of fact or of individuality, which the idea of history as re-enactment never leads Collingwood to renounce. In his lecture to the British Academy, he says that, as presently conceived, history is a study 'whose field is the human past in its entirety' (*IH* 209); yet, in his university lectures of the same year, he denies that an historian can even take a period 'as a whole' (*IH* 329). In 'The Historical Imagination', he asserts it to be 'in principle' the aim of the historian 'to use the entire perceptible here-and-now as evidence for the entire past' (*IH* 247); but adds, prudently, that this is 'impossible in practice'. In its earlier parts, too, *The Idea of History*, preaches awareness of the way 'one new fact added to a mass of old ones' may involve 'the complete transformation of the old' (*IH* 147), and expresses agreement with Oakeshott that 'a mere fact divorced from other facts [is] a monstrosity' (*IH* 157).

Nor is Collingwood's considered position, as I represent it here, entirely absent from earlier works which may seem to leave little room for it. For example, even after denying that anyone can now know 'what exactly it was that happened' at the battle of Hastings, Collingwood adds that the battle will remain something 'partly known and partly unknown' (NAPH 42–3). In a manuscript of 1935, he allows that historians may gain *increasing* knowledge of their objects (RAH 20). Such admissions quite undermine any idea that, because of what the argument from incompleteness shows, the historian can never know 'what actually happened' in the past. This isn't to deny the very real problems which are raised for practice by claims to have partial and increasing knowledge; for, as Collingwood warns, the addition of one new detail *may* require a whole new way of representing something. What he comes to reject is the view that it must.

§ 3. *The Problem of the Non-existent Past*

We turn to the problem raised by the fact that what the historian seeks is knowledge of something which is past and gone, something which is therefore, as Collingwood expresses it for the first time in a paper of 1926, not 'real' but only 'ideal'—quite as unreal, for example, as the future (SPAT 147). He comes back to this consideration again and again as something which no theory of history must ever forget. 'The past is simply non-existent', he writes in an essay of 1928; 'every historian feels this in his dealings with it' (LHK 101). 'The events of history do not "pass in review" before the historian' he declares in *The Idea of History*; 'they have finished happening before he begins thinking about them'—'gone beyond recall' (*IH* 97, 133). In a manuscript of 1931, he calls it 'the paradox of history' that the historian's supposed object, 'because it no longer exists, is not "there" to be known— not "given", not "here", not "anywhere"—completely faded and vanished into the gulf of nothingness which is past time' (L31 2). In these and many similar passages, Collingwood makes it evident how seriously he took the problem raised by the pastness of the historian's object.

That problem, it should be noted, differs in an important way from the one supposedly raised by the incompleteness of what historians claim to discover. For, with regard to the latter, there is an immediate plausibility in trying to scale the problem down by arguing that the historian may still obtain partial, if not complete, knowledge of the past, or knowledge of it which is to some degree probable, if less than certain. There is no room for such notions of more or less, or of degrees of probability, where the problem is the non-existence of the past. For if the latter makes the historian's ostensible object entirely inaccessible to him, or, indeed, deprives him of an object altogether, the consequence would seem to be that he cannot justifiably claim to have any knowledge of the past at all. Collingwood's response to this difficulty has often been thought to be along the following lines. Deprived of what would ordinarily be said to be his object of study, the historian must be seen as dealing with something which *does* exist and which *is* accessible. And the idea of historical thinking as a re-enactment of the past has frequently been thought to show where Collingwood thinks such an object is to be found. To put it at its simplest, the true object of historical inquiry must be conceived not as a non-existent past, but as an existent thinking-of-the-past. Thus Marwick ascribes to Collingwood the view that 'since the past itself has no existence . . . history has reality only in the mind of the historian'; Joseph Levine sees him as holding that history is 'not a description of objective events' but something that takes place 'in the historian's mind'; and J. E. Sullivan concludes that, for him, historical facts are 'the products of the thinking of historians and do not exist apart from that thinking'.[12]

Since Collingwood does make pronouncements which offer some excuse for such an interpretation, it is hardly surprising that his account of historical knowledge has sometimes been hailed by so-called 'constructionists' among contemporary philosophers of history as a clear anticipation of their own views. A notable example is Goldstein, who, besides working through a constructionist position on his own account in an unusually careful and sustained way, has argued persuasively for a constructionist interpretation of Collingwood's theory of history.[13] According to constructionists, what we call facts about the past are not found by historians, they are made; they are not data, they are conclusions. They are not, of course, made capriciously; they are made in accordance with evidence, and apply certain rules. But 'the past that the historian evokes', declares Goldstein, 'is not a real past as it was when it was present, but rather a construction of his own.' Claiming to speak also for Collingwood, he continues: 'the historian does not look for evidence in order to explain the event, as if the event is clearly before him'; rather 'he calls it forth for the purpose of explaining his evidence.' The only historical event which 'figures in the work of the historian', Goldstein avers, is the latter's own 'hypothetical construct'.[14] There is no need, in this connection, he holds, to get involved, as Collingwood did, in difficult metaphysical questions about the sense, if any, in which the past may now properly be said to 'exist'. Collingwood's main point, in denying its existence, was to emphasize its inaccessibility to historical inquiry. For even if a 'real past' does exist, the historian still cannot know which construction placed upon the evidence most nearly describes it. The barrier between object and inquirer is absolute. The 'real' past is therefore irrelevant to historical inquiry. It has, and can have, no role to play in it, and there is no intelligible sense in which historians' conclusions can be said to be 'about' it.

[12] Marwick, *Nature of History*, 79–80; 'The Autonomy of History: R. G. Collingwood and Agatha Christie', *Clio*, 7 (1979), 257; *Prophets of the West* (New York, 1970), 160.
[13] Especially in 'Collingwood's Theory of Historical Knowing'.
[14] 'Evidence and Events in History', *Philosophy of Science*, 29 (1962), 177.

In the remaining sections of this chapter I shall question the view that Collingwood's theory of history is, on balance, a constructionist one, so understood.[15] At the same time, I shall concede that he had constructionist moments, particularly in his writings of the middle and late 1920s, when the idea of the past as non-existent seems to have obsessed him to a degree that even the idea of re-enactment never did. His constructionist tendencies, however, recede into the background of his thought on history thereafter, only occasionally gaining fresh, if generally brief, expression. And when such lapses into constructionism occur, they can generally be traced to identifiable philosophical errors, some of which I shall try to pinpoint. I shall argue, too, that many statements of Collingwood's which may appear on the face of it to be constructionist are open to non-constructionist interpretations. And this, it seems to me, is only what one should expect, since none of the other chief elements of Collingwood's theory of history, properly understood, require him to be a constructionist—including what he has to say about re-enactment and about the role of imagination in historical thinking, two of his doctrines on which constructionists often seize. I say this despite the fact that, when Collingwood expands upon the notion of the ideality of the past in his lectures of 1928, after introducing it in the lectures of 1926, he represents it as an idea so fundamental to his whole view of history that most of his other key doctrines can be 'deduced' from it (L28 427).[16] If I hesitate to say that he was, in consequence, or even ought to have been, a philosophical realist with regard to history, it is only because of the confusion about what 'realism' is to mean that characterizes so many of the passages stressed by constructionists when claiming Collingwood as one of their own.

In the section to follow, I shall call attention to some things which Collingwood says which seem to me quite incompatible with ascribing a constructionist position to him. In succeeding sections, I shall examine, first, some further claims of his which may appear more problematic, but which, I think, still need not be interpreted as constructionist, looking then at some others which, on any natural interpretation, do seem to me to imply constructionism. In a final section, I shall ask how Collingwood

[15] Collingwood does not himself use the term 'constructionism'.
[16] Van der Dussen has reminded me that Collingwood denies having deduced them from it himself; yet he does represent them as deducible.

could have thought his constructionist dicta sound, in view of the difficulty of reconciling them with so many other things which he had to say.[17]

§ 4. Anti-constructionism in Collingwood

In spite of the hostility which Collingwood quite early expressed towards what he called realism in philosophy, his view of history in his earliest works is without much question realistic in at least some of his own senses of the word (*HS* 27). In *Speculum Mentis*, for example, the object of historical knowledge is said to be a world of individual fact existing independently of the historian's knowledge of it, something to be known, if at all, by passively apprehending it (*SM* 210–11, 216, 231). This is the main reason why it is represented there as a defective form of knowledge. Much the same view informs early published essays like 'The Nature and Aims of a Philosophy of History'. Collingwood has been seen as liberating himself from such a view of history in the writings of the later 1920s, tentatively at first in 'The Limits of Historical Knowledge', and then completely in the lectures of 1926 and 1928 with the development of the doctrine of the ideality of history, with its emphasis on there being no independently existing world of fact for the historian to apprehend. Van der Dussen has seen this change of doctrine as among the most important occurrences in the development of Collingwood's thought about history (*HS* 6–7, 34–5); and it is hard to quarrel with that judgment.[18] What I would question is whether what Collingwood often derives from the ideality doctrine represents more than a stage which his thought passed through.[19] Wisps and fumes of his original excitement over the methodological benefits

[17] An abbreviated version of §§ 4–7 appeared in *Collingwood Studies*, 1 (1994), 59–75 under the title 'Was Collingwood an Historical Constructionist?' The argument derives originally from a paper presented to the Collingwood Centenary Conference at Trent University in 1989.
[18] Rex Martin, too, finds a 'sea change' in Collingwood's thought at this point (Review of van der Dusson, *HS*, 74). Yet, when Collingwood looks back on his own intellectual development, what stands out for him is his discovery of the re-enactment doctrine, not that of ideality (*A* 107).
[19] Following van der Dussen, one might apply to the 'anti-realist' position of the lectures of 1926 and 1928 Collingwood's own doctrine that no philosophical system is more than 'a temporary resting place for thought' (Introduction to *IH*, rev. edn., p. xliii).

supposedly accruing to historians from the idea of a non-existent past—for example, their not having to worry about 'correspondence'—do remain in some of the later writings. But, although *The Idea of History* and other later writings scarcely rehabilitate the realism of *Speculum Mentis*, they are not, on balance, plausibly interpreted as constructionist.

As has been indicated already, this is eminently true of the Collingwoodian claim that historians re-enact past thought, reinforced by the associated contention that a re-enacted thought must be identical to the thought of the original agent. Collingwood talks repeatedly of the historian re-enacting, reconstructing, re-evoking, re-creating, re-thinking, reviving, and even repeating, the past. Having noted that the events which the historian studies have 'finished happening', he says that the historian must 're-create them inside his own mind, re-enacting for himself so much of the experience of the men who took part in them as he wishes to understand' (*IH* 97). It would be straining language to interpret this as envisaging anything less than the doing of something in the present which has already been done before in the past, something quite distinguishable from the re-doing of it. Collingwood makes free use of the prefix 're' even in the lectures of 1926 and 1928, which stress so much the doctrine of ideality (L26 407; L28 440–1). Furthermore, he insists that the historian's re-enactment be performed *knowingly*. When the historian re-enacts the past, he says, it must be 'in that re-enactment known as past' (*IH* 158, 289); the historian must re-enact the past 'consciously knowing that this is what he is doing' (L28 445). To say that something is known to be the case is to imply that it is the case. These are all, therefore, claims that the object of historical thinking is past happenings, not present constructions.

A non-constructionist interpretation of the re-enactment doctrine is reinforced by Collingwood's argument, in 'History as Re-enactment of Past Experience', that the re-enacted thought of the historian should be, and can be, the very same thought as that of the agent (*IH* 283 ff.).[20] This whole long section, the burden of which is anticipated in the earlier writings despite what they say

---

[20] In § 1, the argument was that Collingwood is not trying to prove in this lecture that historians ever succeed in thinking the same thought as a past agent. The question at this point is whether the phrasing of his argument does not show that he believes they sometimes do.

about ideality (L28 446–8), has no point on a constructionist interpretation. As Collingwood observes in that section, saying that an
historian's supposed re-enactment of the past is simply a subjective state of his own would mean that 'instead of answering the
question how the past is known we should be maintaining
that the past is not known, but only the present' (*IH* 284).
Martin justifiably seizes upon this passage as a clear indication
that Collingwood's considered view was not constructionist;
and Code remarks, although more guardedly, that it shows
Collingwood to have had 'some brief for realism after all'.[21]

There are many other passages in the writings of the 1930s for
which it seems highly implausible to suggest a constructionist
interpretation. A case in point is the opening section of *The Idea of
History*. The object of historical thought, it is there maintained, is
'the past, consisting of particular events in space and time which
are no longer happening' (*IH* 5). What historians find out is 'actions of human beings that have been done in the past' (*IH* 9). It
is no easier to find even prima-facie constructionism in the
Epilegomena. 'Historical knowledge', maintains Collingwood, 'is
of something which can never be a this, because it is never a here
and now' (*IH* 233). The historian's business, in considering
present relics, is 'to discover what the past was which has left
those relics behind it' (*IH* 282). Nielsen has opined that the
ideality doctrine throws new light on what is said in *The Idea of
History*—and she means constructionist light.[22] But it is hard to see
how this could be said of passages like these. Nor is the thesis
plausible with regard to some of Collingwood's more nuanced
pronouncements: for example, that history is neither 'knowledge
of the past and therefore not knowledge of the present', nor
'knowledge of the present and therefore not knowledge of the
past,' but is 'knowledge of the past in the present . . . the present
revival and reliving of past experiences.' (*IH* 175).[23] This is surely

---

[21] Rex Martin, 'Collingwood's Claim', 522; Code, 'Collingwood's Epistemological Individualism', 554.

[22] Nielsen, 'Re-enactment and Reconstruction', 29.

[23] Even in 1930, Collingwood was making statements about the object of historical inquiry which are difficult to interpret as constructionist, e.g. 'History is
knowledge of the past, and the past consists of events that have finished happening' (PH 136). And even earlier, having asserted that the past consists of 'events
which have finished happening', he maintains that 'these events can be historically known' (L28 449).

a straightforward claim that what historians know is the past, together with a reminder of what attaining such knowledge requires in the way of present experience.

Much the same conclusion can be drawn from the account given early in *The Idea of History* of differences between the ways historians and psychologists study what is ostensibly the same sort of object: human thought. Psychologists, Collingwood observes, are professionally committed to studying thought 'subjectively', i.e. as psychological process. By contrast, historians study the thoughts of past agents as possible instances of knowledge, i.e. as thought in relation to its object. Philosophers of history are said to be interested in the thought of historians similarly as instances of knowledge, not as psychological processes, or mere 'experiences'. Collingwood adds: 'The whole psychological analysis of historical thought would be exactly the same if there were no such thing as the past at all, if Julius Caesar were an imaginary character, and if history were not knowledge but pure fancy' (*IH* 2–3). He thus criticizes those who would psychologize historical thinking for conceiving it exactly as constructionists say we should conceive it. Collingwood's own view of the task of historians is that it is 'to apprehend the past as a thing in itself, to say, for example, that so many years ago such-and-such events actually happened'.

What Collingwood has to say about supposed knowledge of the past through memory, and the relationship of memory claims to historical knowledge, may seem more problematic. Both in *The Idea of History* and in the lectures of the 1920s, he stresses that, whereas historical knowledge is inferential, claims to remember the past are immediate; and in the earlier writings, our not having reasons for remembering, or even for trusting memory as such (by contrast with trusting particular memories), leads him to express doubt about whether we can speak of memories as knowledge at all (L26 366–7; L28 435–6). In *The Idea of History*, while allowing that memory (and testimony, which is memory once removed) may 'in some cases' be accepted as knowledge, he observes that it cannot at any rate be considered 'scientific' knowledge (*IH* 257). Collingwood also evinces some uncertainty at times about how memory claims and claims to possess historical knowledge are to be related to each other. In the lectures he says that 'because we remember the past and thus have an immediate awareness of it, we can build up on this foundation the entire structure of critical history, which starts from memory but goes far beyond it' (L26 411). In *The Idea of History*, he calls for the drawing of an absolute distinction between memory and historical reasoning, any notion that history could rest on memory being rejected as an early-modern, pre-critical fallacy (*IH* 234–5). Yet he also describes historical knowledge as 'that special case of memory where the object of present thought is past thought' (*IH* 294).[24] And while denying that history depends on memory, he concedes that the deliverances of memory may be confirmed or disconfirmed by historical findings (*IH* 252). This implies that he still holds the view, stated in the 1928 lectures, that 'history and memory are akin in that their object is the past' (L28 435). It is hard to give a sense to that assertion while conceiving the historical past as a mere construction.

Collingwood's claim that historical thinking involves an exercise of imagination is also sometimes seen as pointing towards an essentially constructionist conception of historical knowledge. Yet the piece of writing in which he has most to say about the role of imagination in history, the inaugural lecture, does not in the least suggest constructionism.[25] Historical thinking, Collingwood there asserts, is an 'imaginative reconstruction of the past' (*IH* 247). But 'the imaginary, simply as such,' he observes, 'is neither unreal nor real' (*IH* 241; LHK 102). Instructive in this connection is the explicit contrast which he draws between the use of imagination by novelists and by historians. Both, he says, present an account of human actions and experiences. But the account of the historian, unlike that of the novelist, is 'meant to be true'. The historian's task is 'to construct a picture of things as they really were and of events as they really happened' (*IH* 246). This echoes the view expressed in an essay of 1924 that 'the object of art is the imaginary individual, whereas the object

[24] Collingwood's more usual view that historical knowledge 'does not depend upon memory' seems an overstatement (*IH* 238, 269); for if, as he maintains, scientific reasoning can be said to presuppose the validity of some historical claims, so, surely, can historical reasoning be said to presuppose the validity of some memory claims.

[25] Goldstein evidently thinks otherwise. Apropos Collingwood's conclusion, on the evidence of an inscription on a tombstone, that an Irish colony once existed at Silchester, he holds that 'the possibility that such a colony existed we owe entirely to the working of the historical imagination' ('Constitution', 263). Our knowledge that it did, perhaps, but not the possibility, surely.

of history is the real individual' (NAPH 45). Collingwood does, certainly, draw attention from time to time to gaps between the aims and the attainments of historians. But he makes it a major point of difference between historians and novelists that what concerns novelists exists only as thoughts in the minds of those whose imaginations are appropriately stirred, while what concerns historians, if they know their business, is events which actually took place.

The critical attitude which Collingwood frequently displays towards constructionist ways of thinking can be seen as clearly as anywhere in the way he takes issue with some other philosophers of history. Especially significant is his lengthy critique of the views of Michael Oakeshott, a theorist who really does hold something like a Goldsteinian constructionist position (*IH* 153–8). According to Oakeshott, the historian, working with available evidence, builds in his own experience a view of an historical past in accordance with that evidence. But if 'what really happened' is only 'what the evidence obliges us to believe', Oakeshott maintains, then 'the facts cf history are present facts'; 'the historical past is the world of ideas which present evidence creates in the present.' The historian himself, of course, takes his object of inquiry to be past. But that, according to Oakeshott, is a philosophical error which he typically makes *qua* historian, one which it is the function of philosophical reflection to correct. Collingwood's response is to put Oakeshott's view in the form of a dilemma, and then to refuse it. According to Oakeshott, he says, the object of historical inquiry is either a fixed and finished past, a 'dead', no longer existing past, which is therefore inaccessible to historical inquiry, or it is the historian's own experience when (as the historian himself sees it) he 'thinks' of past events and conditions on the strength of present evidence. But there is another possibility: that the historical past is not 'dead' at all, but lives on in the present, notably in the historian's re-enactment of it.[26] 'What [the historian] thinks as past' nevertheless 'really is past'. 'The fact that it is also present does not prevent it from being past, any more than when I perceive a distant object, where perceiving means not only sensation but thought, the fact that I perceive it here prevents it from being there' (*IH* 158).

[26] Collingwood's metaphorical notion of the past 'surviving' in the present is considered further in § 5.

The views of Simmel are given similar treatment. Collingwood takes Simmel to maintain that the historian can make his subjective vision of the past objective only 'by projecting it into the past'. His objection is that this would make of history merely 'the illusory projection of our own states of mind upon the blank screen of the unknowable past' (*IH* 175). Again, the possibility of the historian's having knowledge of a real past is affirmed.

The largely anti-constructionist stance which Collingwood adopts in *The Idea of History* can be found also in other writings of the 1930s. In a lecture of 1932, history is described as 'knowledge of past facts, individual or unique events occurring at definite places in a time-series, and not contemporary with the act of thought by which they are known' (L32 8). The philosophical question, Collingwood says, is how such knowledge is possible. To reply that historians cannot in fact claim such knowledge, and must fall back upon claims of a constructionist type, would not be to answer the question, but to refuse one of its presuppositions. In a lecture of 1936, Collingwood similarly declares that history is 'reasoned knowledge of something not immediately given'—of something with 'a perfectly definite location in space and time' (L36 12). This clearly means something not present, but past. In another manuscript of the same year, he writes: 'The objectivity of historical fact is this: that *there was* such a fact. Historical fact has its objectivity precisely in being past. To be past here means . . . that which not only was, but remains historically knowable' (NHH 17). Again, little room is left for constructionist manœuvre. The ideality doctrine does gain fresh expression in the plan for 'The Principles of History', and in some other late manuscript fragments. It takes ingenuity, however, to place a constructionist interpretation upon what is said there.

§ 5. *Ambiguous Anti-constructionism*

I have drawn attention to some passages in both Collingwood's earlier and later writings which can hardly with plausibility be read as constructionist, or even as compatible with constructionism. There are others, however, of which this cannot so easily be said. Some, although open to a non-constructionist interpretation, are at any rate more ambiguous, so that to find them cited on occasion in support of an opposite conclusion is not entirely surprising. I shall look briefly in this section at three Collingwoodian contentions which have sometimes, although I think questionably, been read as indicating at least a leaning towards constructionism. The first is that the past which the historian 'reconstructs' is not the past 'as it really was', but simply an interpretation placed upon present evidence. The second is that the so-called historical past is not truly past, but is something 'living in the present'. The third, which is related to the second, is that the knowledge which the historian attains, rather than being about the past, is actually about what he has before him, namely, what he calls his evidence; or, alternatively, about what he excogitates from that evidence. I shall argue that, although what Collingwood has to say with regard to all three of these contentions is frequently misleading, it need not commit him to historical constructionism.

Something like the first is commonly taken to be expressed in a passage of 'The Limits of Historical Knowledge' which those who ascribe constructionist views to Collingwood often seem to regard as especially significant. Historical inquiry is there compared to a game whose first rule is that one must not say anything, however true, for which one cannot produce evidence. The game is won, Collingwood says, 'not by the player who can reconstitute what really happened, but by the player who can show that his view of what happened is the one which the evidence accessible to all players, when criticised up to the hilt, supports' (LHK 97). Historical thinking, he continues, 'does not mean discovering what really happened if "what really happened" is anything other than "what the evidence indicates"' (LHK 99). It follows that if there ever 'happened an event concerning which no shred of evidence now survives', it would be 'no historian's business to discover it', and 'no gap in any historian's knowledge that he does not know it'.

Clearly there is much here which would have to be accepted by anyone concerned to elaborate a theory of historical knowledge which takes serious account of what historians do. What historians aim to show, and should surely aim to show, is (to use a phrase of Collingwood's resembling one of Oakeshott's) 'a verdict in accordance with the evidence' (L28 458). But how does that bear upon the question whether historical accounts are to be understood as telling us about the past as it really was? We must ask what exactly it is that the evidence requires us to believe—or, as Collingwood also says, what the evidence 'proves' (LHK 98). Surely that certain actions and events really took place at times past. What else could be meant in this context by 'being evidence for'?[27]

This crucial point may be obscured by the way Collingwood places in apparent opposition to each other 'knowing what the evidence indicates' and 'knowing what really happened', as if the first sort of claim committed us to nothing with regard to the second. The conclusion that some have drawn on the authority of the passage cited is that, according to Collingwood (at any rate at this stage of his development), it is simply not the historian's aim (not his 'game') to know the real past.[28] But that is surely to read a conditional statement as if it were unconditional. What the quoted passages actually (and correctly) maintain is that it is not the historian's aim to know what really happened to the extent that this cannot be discovered by interpreting evidence. This follows, uncontroversially, from the fact that he has no other way of knowing what really happened. If the evidence is misleading, as will sometimes be the case, the historian who deals with it conscientiously will, of course, be professionally in the clear, which is doubtless part of Collingwood's point. But that does not change the fact that any such historian will be wrong about the real past, not right about an unreal one.

The false antithesis which is so strongly suggested by the cited passages recurs in some of Collingwood's later writings. There seems to be a trace of it in the Epilegomenon 'Historical Evidence', where, as Nielsen has remarked, what Collingwood demands is not that an historian's reconstruction be 'true', but only that it be 'right'—presumably in relation to the evidence

[27] As Mandelbaum observes, it is built into the notion of being historical evidence that it is evidence for the way the past really was (Review of Goldstein, *Historical Knowing*, 293). A similar observation could be made with regard to Collingwood's claim that the present is analysable into the necessary and the possible, these representing what we ordinarily call the past and the future (L26 405, 412–13). If this makes sense at all with regard to the past, it must surely mean that what we find in the present necessitates our concluding that certain other things really did happen in the past.

[28] See e.g. Goldstein, 'Collingwood's Theory', 15–16; Rubinoff, 'Collingwood's Theory of the Relation between Philosophy and History', 378.

(*IH* 268).[29] But the harsh way in which the antithesis is stated in the earlier work tends to be softened later. In an essay of 1930, Collingwood expresses something like a half-way position, associating the claim that 'the past does not exist and cannot be perceived' with the declaration that 'we come to know the past . . . by interpreting evidence [which is] something that exists in the present' (PH 136). In *The Idea of History*, past events are said to be ascertained 'by a process of inference according to rational principles from data given or rather discovered in the light of these principles', without any suggestion that what results does not constitute knowledge of the real past (*IH* 176). All that remains of the original doctrine is, again, the justifiable insistence that what historians can know of the real past is limited to what they can find evidence for—in which innocuous sense Collingwood can indeed be called a constructionist.[30]

The second doctrine, namely, that the historian studies a past which is not 'dead', but still 'lives in the present'—this being seen as somehow offering an escape from the problem raised by the 'real' past's no longer existing—is also easily stated in ways which are barely intelligible. When Collingwood declares, in 'The Limits of Historical Knowledge', that what is 'alone knowable' is not 'the past simply as past' but the past 'as residually preserved in the present', what he says, although clearly metaphorical, is intelligible enough taken as an implicit reference to the historian's dependence on evidence (LHK 99–100). The same can hardly be said about his maintaining, in his lectures of 1926, that, since the historical past 'is an element in the present', what 'we are actually coming to know', in studying it, is the present (L26 406). Only slightly less problematic is his observing in the same manuscript that, while the past studied by historians 'exists ideally as the past', it 'exists actually as the present' (L26 405). As van der Dussen remarks, Collingwood seems at this stage to be 'wrestling with the problem' (*HS* 141). His penchant for propounding (or at any rate suggesting) false antitheses is visible again in his claim,

---

[29] Nielsen concedes that this accords badly with *IH* 246 ('Re-enactment and Reconstruction', 28).

[30] Nielsen prefers to call him a 'constructivist', as a way of stressing his belief that 'the historian constructs or reconstructs its history and does not discover it ready-made', a view which she considers 'relativist' but not 'sceptical' ('Re-enactment and Reconstruction', 26). That is not constructionism as it is considered above.

in the lectures of 1928, that, since the historian's inquiry is concerned with 'those elements of the past whose traces in the present he can perceive and decipher', it is 'in this sense . . . the study of the present and not of the past at all' (L28 485). The notion of the past as surviving in the present is rendered even more obscure in a manuscript of 1933, where Collingwood insists that this is not just a survival of something 'in its effects', but a survival *'in itself, alongside of* its effects' (NTM D-38). We seem to be awash here in a sea of metaphors. And, given this background, it is natural to expect some esoteric meaning when Collingwood observes, in *The Idea of History*, that historical knowledge is 'knowledge of the past in the present' (*IH* 175).

There are non-problematic ways, however, in which one can understand the Collingwoodian contention that the past is knowable to the extent that it lives in the present. This can sometimes be seen as just a figurative application of his theory of historical understanding as re-enactment. A past thought is said to live again when it is re-thought, the re-thinking bringing the past to life in the sense of making it understandable in a way especially appropriate to a human subject-matter. The idea of the past living in the present clearly implies nothing here about the historian not understanding it as it really was. By extension, Collingwood also sometimes means by the past living in the present the fact that certain ways of thinking and acting which existed at past times continue to exist, whether or not they are re-thought or re-enacted in historical judgment. Here a living past chiefly means one which it is here and now relatively easy to understand because we have the cultural or intellectual equipment to do it. Collingwood instances the continued knowledge of Latin as facilitating the understanding of ancient Roman documents (*A* 97), or the fact that a body of past thought like Greek mathematics is actually incorporated into our own ways of thinking mathematically (*IH* 225). By still a further extension, it might be said that the past lives on in the present whenever evidence for reconstructing it is readily available to us. In this sense, Roman military thought can be said to live on in the remains of Hadrian's Wall for anyone possessing the archaeological expertise to grasp the purposes for which it was built. In none of these senses, however, does the idea of the historian being able to study only a past which is living in the present carry the implication that what is discovered is not something about the past as it really was. All that is implied is that what can be recovered of that past is limited in certain ways.

Collingwood's notion of a past which is recoverable because still 'living' is thus not a single idea, but a cluster of several; and he sometimes obscures important differences between them. The sense in which Greek mathematics remains alive in our own mathematical thinking, for example, is not at all the same as that in which Caesar's thought is brought to life again when the historian of Roman Britain re-thinks it. The first implies a continuity of expression; the second (notwithstanding some mysterious statements made in 'History as Re-enactment of Past Experience') does not. The first can be unconscious in the sense that those said to keep Greek thought alive by re-thinking it may not know that re-thinking it is what they are doing. And in cases like the continued existence of a Celtic artistic tradition during the Roman period, as Collingwood describes it, the agents may not even realize that they are thinking the thought in question at all. Collingwood sometimes downplays such differences between explicit and implicit re-thinkings by stressing that, in both cases, the past lives on as an aspect of contemporary life. This gives him an opportunity to indulge a recurring tendency to exaggerate the social importance of historiography as it is in fact pursued. Even when historians study apparently remote subject-matters like the civilization of the ancient Sumerians, he declares, they are really dealing with contemporary problems. For Assyriology, he says, 'is just as much a real element of the modern world as coal-mining' (L28 468). Here a metaphor has surely been pushed beyond useful limits.

As for Collingwood's third sense of reliving, to say that the past lives on in the present merely because relics and remains of it are extant, whether or not recognized as such, surely confuses anything that could plausibly be called 'reliving' with the mere possibility of it. To which Collingwood might well reply (thereby collapsing the third sense of reliving into the second) that a relic is not a relic until it is recognized as such, i.e. until the thought which it expresses begins to be re-thought.

The third ambiguous doctrine holds not just that the past of concern to historians is, in some sense, 'in' the present, but that it really is the present, or, at any rate, is an aspect or stratum of it.[31] Like some contemporary constructionists—for example, Goldstein—Collingwood sometimes argues that, since what historians interpret is 'a trace or residue of the past', what their conclusions are really about is the present, not the past (L28 482). In other words, what historical inquiry is about is what historians call evidence. There are times when it is said only that 'the present world, as we apprehend it in perception, is the starting-point of history' (L26 420). But often, the present world is represented not only as history's starting-point, but as its true subject-matter. In history, Collingwood maintains in the lectures of 1926, 'we are in reality talking not about the past but about the present' (L26 409). The 'object of historical thought', he says again in the lectures of 1928, 'is always present' (L28 459).

But if historical inquiry is not really about the past, but about something present which is ordinarily called evidence, what is it that the inquiry tells us about it? Collingwood has a ready answer. What is treated as evidence, he says, is clearly a part or aspect of the historian's present world, and what historical inquiry undertakes is 'to explain this present world by tracing its origins' (L26 420). In an essay of 1930 he maintains that the historian 'is concerned with one special aspect of the present—how it came to be what it is' (PH 139). At another point, he declares even more explicitly that 'all history is an attempt to understand the present by reconstructing its determining conditions' (L26 420). He may appear to take this back at times, as when, in a manuscript of 1934, he asserts that 'to know the past is to know not *how* the present came to be what it is, but *what* it is' (HUP 1). But this should presumably be read in connection with the Collingwoodian doctrine that understanding evidence is a way of perceiving it as what it really is—i.e. as a relic or a residue of some earlier thing, action, or state of affairs. And if so, the whole doctrine begins to wear rather thin. For even if it is true that the aim of historians is to perceive (or explain) correctly what they regard as their evidence, the very notion of what such perception (or explanation) consists in implicitly ascribes to the historian know-

---

[31] There are marks of both the second and third doctrines in the following dubious passage: 'The whole of the present consists of traces or residues of the past, for the present is that into which the past has turned, and the past was that which has turned into the present. To speak, therefore, of traces of the past in the present is to speak of the present and nothing but the present' (L28 482–3).

ledge not just of the present, but of the past. And if that knowledge is really to make it clear how a present document or artefact came to be, it will surely need to be knowledge of the way the past really was.

All that is left to decide is whether the historian's task is better described as accounting for present artefacts by reference to past states, or as justifying the assertion of past states by citing present evidence. If Collingwood frequently shows a preference for the first way of putting it, that may be due, to some extent, to his experience in archaeology, where the immediate question may so often take the form: How am I to account for this vase or this paving stone? In history, as he concedes himself when discussing the way the method of question and answer applies in this field, it is more likely to assume the form: What should I look for here and now (e.g. in the archives) which will help me to determine whether Rupert in fact left the battle of Naseby early? It might be noted that, when not engaged in formulating startling aphorisms with a quasi-constructionist flavour, Collingwood often puts the historian's task the more usual way around. 'What the historian thinks about', we found him affirming in Epilegomena to *The Idea of History*, 'is Elizabeth or Marlborough, the Peloponnesian War or the policy of Ferdinand and Isabella'; not something existing here and now, as in sense perception, but 'events which have finished happening and conditions no longer in existence' (*IH* 233, 251).

A briefer comment might be made on the second form sometimes taken, both in Collingwood's writings and in the writings of modern constructionists, by the doctrine that the true object of historical knowledge is something present rather than something past. The claim is sometimes made that, if that object is historical facts, then, since historical facts are constituted by what the historian thinks, the subject-matter of history is really the historian's own 'mental constructions'. This idea may seem to be supported by Collingwood's sometimes saying that what the historian gains in the re-thinking of past thoughts is self-knowledge, knowledge of his own mind.[32] But the response of those who see Collingwood

---

[32] As Collingwood puts it himself, historical knowledge is 'the self-knowledge of the historian's own mind as the present revival and reliving of past experiences' (*IH* 175). At the same time, however, he describes it as knowledge of the past, even if 'knowledge of the past in the present'.

as a non-constructionist would surely be that what he says about history as yielding self-knowledge in no way requires the con- clusion that the subject-matter of history is other than what really happened in the past. It is not a matter of either one thing or the other. Just as Collingwood can most sensibly be read as maintain- ing that knowledge of the real past is attained *through* the inter- pretation of evidence, so he can be read as maintaining that self-knowledge is attained *through* the reconstruction of the past in a person's own mind—at any rate to the extent that the issue is past thought.

§ 6. *Lapses into Constructionism*

I have argued that Collingwood is, on balance, a non-construc- tionist, not only in *The Idea of History* and in other later writings, but also, to a considerable extent, in his earlier ones, both published and unpublished. Especially in the latter, he does sometimes make statements which invite a constructionist inter- pretation; but these can generally be treated as overstatements or as careless formulations of less problematic positions. However, he sometimes makes ostensibly constructionist claims which are more difficult to explain away, and in the present section, I shall draw attention to four of these. I can only point out that they are not characteristic, and go on in § 7 to speculate a little about why he fell into making them.

As noted already, Collingwood sometimes claims that the ob- ject of historical inquiry must be a past which is still living in the present. But he seems, at times, to go further, maintaining that what historians call the past is to be *identified* with what presently exists, or with certain aspects of it. 'The past as living in the present is wholly real', he writes in an essay of 1926, since it is 'just the present itself' (SPAT 149). Again, in the lectures of 1928, inveighing against the suggestion that, in re-enacting past thoughts, the historian attempts to 'copy' something which is now past, he declares that 'the re-enactment of the past in the present *is the past itself* so far as that is knowable to the historian' (L28 450). One might perhaps be encouraged by the final phrase to argue that all Collingwood really means here is that the only part of the past which can be known by the historian is the past

which is re-enactable in the present, a contention the correctness
of which may be questioned, but which makes prima-facie sense,
and echoes what he maintains elsewhere. To argue in this way,
however, would considerably stretch what is actually said. To
somewhat similar effect, Collingwood sometimes contends that
the past which historians can know must be a past which has
'turned into' the present, the implication being, once again,
that what is actually known is present, not past. In the lectures of
1926, he declares that, while the past exists only 'ideally' as past,
it exists 'actually' as present (L26 405), a doctrine apparently
revived in a manuscript of 1936, where the past in historical
inquiry is said to be 'the analysed content of the present'
(NHH 11). There may be hints of the same idea in Collingwood's
attempt, at one point, to enlarge the idea of the specious present,
apparently with a view to making the present a viable field
for historical inquiry by ascribing a temporal span to it, while
at the same time denying that what is studied is literally past
(RAH 36).

There are many passages which apparently contradict the
strange, if not self-contradictory, idea that the past studied by the
historian is actually present. In the lectures of 1926, for example,
although maintaining that 'the past has become the present',
Collingwood unequivocally (and surely with good sense) affirms
that what 'turns into something else is by definition *not* that
something' (L26 415). In *The Idea of History*, he provides the perfect
riposte to the position we are here considering by objecting that
any account of historical knowledge in which 'the object (in this
case the past)' is 'simply incorporated in the subject (in this case
the present, the historian's own thought)', would not be 'answering the question how the past is known', but would rather be
'maintaining that the past is not known, but only the present'
(*IH* 284). We are nevertheless left with the aberrant statements,
and others like them, which can hardly fail to encourage
constructionist interpretations. Collingwood's strategy does
sometimes *seem* to be: if the historian's account cannot be shown
to be true of the real past, find a surrogate past, however odd, of
which it can be shown to be true.

Perhaps it is unfair to constructionists to suggest that anything
as apparently incoherent as the straightforward identification of

the past with the present gets very close to what they want to maintain. Somewhat closer may be another Collingwoodian contention, the idea that historians, through their re-enactive activity, actually bring into existence what their statements are about, namely, a specifically historical past. Sometimes, when Collingwood talks of 'constructing' history out of the sources, he can plausibly be taken as having in mind only historians' accounts of past events, not what those accounts are about (L26 382; *IH* 170). But not always. In 'Some Perplexities about Time', for example, he maintains that 'by recollecting and by thinking historically' we actually 'call the past, as such, into being' (SPAT 149–50). In the 1926 lectures, he declares that 'it is we who create the past in order that we may understand the present' (L26 418). In the lectures of 1928, he affirms that 'because historical fact is ideal, those parts or aspects of it which we are not studying do not exist', the implication apparently being that the parts we happen to be studying do exist, but only because we maintain them in existence by studying them (L28 477). In an essay of 1930, he observes that there are no historical facts until the historian 'puts' them there (PH 138); and in the 1928 lectures, he assigns to the philosopher of history the task of making clear 'how historical fact is always and necessarily constituted', this by 'discovering how historians always and necessarily think' (L28 435). Clearly, a so-called historical past which is not discovered, but is 'called forth', 'created', 'constituted', or 'put there' by the historian is a poor candidate for the status of the past as it actually was.

The same view of the object of historical study as having the ontological status of a construction, whose date is the historian's own present, is strongly suggested by a remark which Collingwood makes at one point about the way disagreements between serious historians should be interpreted (PH 139). He and Mommsen, he observes, offer somewhat different accounts of certain things done by Julius Caesar. Does it follow that at least one of them cannot be telling us the truth about the historical past? Not at all, replies Collingwood; for if both have pursued their inquiries with diligence, exploiting to the full the possibilities of inquiry in their own context, the difference between them will be due to the fact that their inquiries have different objects. Each, using the materials to hand, has constituted his own object;

each has produced his own specifically historical past.[33] Goldstein supports constructionism with a similar analysis of a disagreement between A. J. P. Taylor and certain other historians about the origins of the Second World War. Taylor's conception of the war's origins, Goldstein maintains, 'involves historical facts which have no existence at all in the conceptions of his opponents; each side thinks the evidence calls for the constitution of different historical facts'.[34] Clearly, Collingwood's writings do contain distinct traces of such full-blown Goldsteinian constructionism, even if these are less characteristic of them than constructionists seem to believe, as well as being at odds with other things which he has to say.

A third Collingwoodian doctrine which has sometimes been taken to entail a constructionist view of the historical past, although in a rather more mysterious and convoluted way, is a denial of the principle, ascribed by Collingwood to his realist opponents, that 'what we know is not altered by our knowing it' (L28 449). The attack on this principle appears very early in his writings, and is stressed as late as 1939 (*A* 44). But it is not at all easy to make sense of Collingwood's position here, which Donagan understandably calls 'absurd' (*LPC* 287–8). For it has the appearance, at least, of denying not just a truth, but a truism: that if one knows something at all, one knows it as it is (or was) not as it is not (or was not). Yet Collingwood's contrary principle that knowing does make a difference to what is known, seems literally to imply that, although things past were a certain way before they become objects of historical study, an historian's gaining knowledge of them retrospectively changes their nature, so that what is known is not how they were but what they have been changed into.[35] Saying this does at least assume (as extreme forms of constructionism do not) that there really was a past, in which

---

[33] Collingwood may appear to make the same claim when he dismisses criticism of Hegel's account of history with the observation: 'Hegel was talking not about the past as known to us but about the past as known to him' (L26 418). But in this case he is contrasting two views of the real past, not two different creations of a 'past' by historians.

[34] *Historical Knowing* (Austin, Tex., 1976), 84.

[35] In *IH*, Collingwood ridicules 'the copy theory of knowledge' as implying that knowledge requires our having a mental copy of what is known, this opening an infinite regress. But the criticism which he levels at the 'realist' position seems also to apply here to his own: for how can one know that things can never be known without changing them?

determinate things occurred. But can it intelligibly be maintained that the battle of Hastings or the passage of the first English Reform Bill are somehow made different from the way they were in 1066 and 1832 by becoming known now by historians—except in the trivial sense that they have acquired the added characteristics of being known by them?

In fact, what Collingwood says along these lines in *Speculum Mentis* suggests that the latter may be all we are supposed to derive from his provocative principle. Towards the conclusion of that book, he argues that the true or ultimate object of knowledge, including historical knowledge, is 'the knowing mind', a doctrine which reappears in *The Idea of History* in Collingwood's insistence that historical knowledge is at the same time self-knowledge. And on Collingwood's theory of mind as a complex of activities, it may make sense to say that a mind is *ipso facto* changed by knowledge of itself, since each increment of self-knowledge changes the complex. But, as already noted, the position generally maintained by Collingwood is not that historical knowledge is self-knowledge of mind *rather than* knowledge of events, but (more plausibly) self-knowledge of mind *through* knowledge of events. And even if Collingwood's strange principle applies intelligibly to an historian's knowledge of his own mind, it would not follow that it applies intelligibly also to his claims to have knowledge of past events. With regard to something like the battle of Hastings, it is, of course, true—assuming the correctness of the Collingwoodian view of historical events as at least partly constituted by agents' thoughts—that what William and Harold knew of the battle, as they made their contributions to it, 'made a difference' to what it eventually became (NHH 20–1). But the issue is not whether agents' thoughts change or help to constitute the historical object; it is whether historians' thoughts do.

Attempts to make sense of Collingwood's contention that historical events do not remain unchanged in being known may well convert it into a special form of the claim that historians create (not just partially, but entirely) their objects of knowledge. Since, at best, what historians come to know is an event as they have changed it, and since *ex hypothesi* what this event was like unchanged cannot be known, what is known is *as good as* created by them. A related sort of contention is a denial that the historian's true object of knowledge has any *independent* existence, any existence apart from that entailed by its being an object of knowledge. Historical thinking, observes Collingwood in an early 'realistic' essay, 'assumes that there is a world of fact independent of the knowing mind, a world which is only revealed and in no sense constituted by the historian's thought' (NAPH 44, 46)—a view which had already been implicitly challenged in *Speculum Mentis*. In 'The Limits of Historical Knowledge', it is flatly denied that 'the realistic account of knowledge as apprehension of an independently existing object' applies to history (LHK 101). However, from the standpoint of the question whether Collingwood in fact expresses constructionist views, it makes little difference whether his position is that historical events cannot be known until we change them in getting to know them, or that, until we get to know them, they do not exist at all. Both positions imply that historical events are not discovered, but are constituted or constructed.

Still a fourth doctrine which often involves Collingwood in making statements which it is difficult not to consider constructionist is his claim at various points that only the actual can be known—a view of the nature of knowledge which he frequently ascribes to his 'realist' opponents, but also asserts himself. By 'actual', he means 'now existing', from which it follows that it is self-contradictory to claim knowledge of an actual occurrence which took place at some earlier time.[36] From this the conclusion is derived that we cannot know the past as it actually was, and the stage is set for the claim that what historians know is something else, something present, and thus actual. Collingwood argues in this way repeatedly in the writings of the 1920s, and even thereafter, although less frequently. In his paper on time, he declares that 'what we know must . . . really exist', it following that 'we cannot really know either the past or the future' (SPAT 146–7). In the 1926 lectures, he denies that either memory or history can give us knowledge of the past 'as such', since what is known must have 'real existence', and 'the present alone is actual' (L26 364–5). In the same manuscript he observes that the only knowable object 'properly speaking' is the present, since the past consists entirely of 'unrealities' (L26 404). One may try to read

---

[36] In the lectures of 1928, Collingwood argues, curiously, that this may be true only of events, not of things, which, he maintains, may exist at different times (L28 440, 443).

something into the qualification 'properly speaking', since Collingwood is here virtually reversing what would ordinarily be said to be real or actual; but he offers little guidance in this connection. In the lectures of 1928, he says again that from the doctrine of the ideality (non-actuality) of the past we must draw the conclusion that 'the object of historical thought is always present' (L28 459).

It is a relief to turn from such puzzling assertions to find it clearly implied in *The Idea of History* that it is perfectly conceivable that something should be known which is not simultaneous with the act of knowing it. The objects of historical knowledge, Collingwood says roundly, are 'events which have finished happening, and conditions no longer in existence. Only when they are no longer perceptible do they become objects for historical thought' (*IH* 233). Again, he insists that all theories which conceive historical knowledge as 'a transaction or relation between a subject and an object both actually existing . . . make history impossible' (*IH* 233). Yet the offending principle lingers on residually in his remark, in a manuscript of 1939, that since 'past thought is known by re-enacting it in the present', it is 'not something that has finished happening'—this presumably making it, in his view, a more satisfactory candidate for knowledge (NHV 12). The assumption remains that only the actual, the presently existing or presently occurring, is knowable. One can only protest that such a view makes nonsense of the idea of historical knowledge.

§ 7. *Acquaintance and Actuality*

I have conceded that many of Collingwood's pronouncements at least invite constructionist interpretations, but denied that constructionism was his considered view, or that adherence to it was required to accommodate other key notions of his philosophy of history, such as understanding through re-enactment, or the need for imagination in historical reconstruction. In fact, it is not required even by the ideality doctrine taken in a straightforward sense, i.e. as a denial that past events are still occurring or past actions still being performed, since the latter entails only that whatever knowledge we have of such things must be indirect, obtained, perhaps through evidence. What I want to do finally is to look at what seem to me two important reasons for the constructionist tendencies which can nevertheless be discerned in Collingwood's writings. One is the attraction which the notion of knowledge by acquaintance clearly had for him, despite the uncompromising way in which he attacked it when he felt justified in ascribing it to others. The other is the conceptual unclarity which characterizes his talk of the 'real' and the 'actual', and especially his use of the expression 'the past as it actually was'.

In *The Idea of History*, Collingwood declares that all theories of knowledge based upon acquaintance with an object actually existing 'make history impossible' (*IH* 233). Again, in a manuscript of 1936, he insists: 'History is not acquaintance at all. The *this* is present only in the data (evidence) of historical knowledge not in historical knowledge itself (its object)' (NHH 16). In his campaign against scissors-and-paste history, which goes back to the essays of the 1920s, he rejects the idea that history might be based upon acquaintance with its object even at second hand, which he calls dependence upon mere 'testimony'. Yet much of what he has to say about the object of historical thought having to be 'real' or 'actual', in his own special sense of these terms, often seems inspired by precisely the theory of knowledge which he warns against. As Nowell-Smith has remarked, Collingwood cannot be declared entirely innocent of some of the fallacies which he attacked, including the view that 'the highest form of knowledge was acquaintance'.[37] Why, for example, does he make such heavy weather of the fact that the ostensible object of historical knowledge is past and gone? Surely because it leaves us with nothing to point to, nothing to observe, nothing presented, nothing to be inspected. The paradigm of knowledge implicitly at work here, despite Collingwood's protestations to the contrary, is that of the perception of physical objects. Collingwood constantly, and properly, focuses attention on evidence as the immediate object of the historian's concern, this being something with which he is, of course, directly acquainted. But in doing so, he too often obscures the fact that the ultimate object of historical concern, what the evidence is taken to be

---

[37] Nowell-Smith, 'Are Historical Events Unique?', 146.

evidence for, is beyond acquaintance, and can be known only by an exercise of reason.

Since historical knowledge cannot coherently be represented as acquaintance with the past, two possibilities were open to Collingwood: either to identify some present object of knowledge with which the historian can plausibly be said to be acquainted, or to elaborate a theory of knowledge which renounces the idea that one must always be acquainted with what one claims to know. In his better moments, and in his later work more often than in his earlier, Collingwood takes the second alternative. His whole treatment of argument from evidence in *The Idea of History* is the elaboration of such a theory of knowledge. History, we are told, is reasoned knowledge of what one can never know by acquaintance; it is warranted belief about what we do not perceive, based upon an interpretation of what we do. In the earlier work, too, the second alternative is sometimes taken. Thus, in the lectures of 1926, he says that what a theory of modern 'critical' historiography must never forget is that, whereas the historian's knowledge of the sources is direct, or mediated only by 'linguistic interpretation' on the historian's part, his knowledge of the events reported is always indirect, mediated by 'historical interpretation', i.e. a critical interpretation of the sources (L26 377, 382). The simple distinction between direct and indirect knowledge, both considered viable, immediately removes any apparent need to represent the historian as acquainted with his object, and makes any search for something present to serve as the true object of historical inquiry both unnecessary and inappropriate.

Yet at other points, and especially in the lectures of the late 1920s, Collingwood seems to opt instead for the first alternative, responding to the problem of the impossibility of becoming acquainted with an object which is genuinely past by finding an object with which the historian can be acquainted, whether this is the evidence he directly perceives, or his thought about it. Collingwood's description of the historian's object as something incapsulated, or still living, in the present often gives this impression, as does his presentation of the ideality doctrine not just as a denial that the past now exists, but as an assertion that it does still exist, if only as something ideal. His reference, in the 1928 lectures, to the way in which re-enactment allows historians to 'actualize' what they study points in the same direction, since, for

Collingwood, to be actual is to exist. So does a remark in a manuscript of 1939 that, contrary to a view expressed earlier (PH 136),
a re-enacted past 'is not a past that has finished happening, it is
happening over again'—therefore, presumably, available, after
all, for inspection (NHV 12).

So strong, indeed, is the grip of acquaintance theory on Collingwood's thought that he sometimes falls back on the idea even
while arguing against its applicability to history. In a curious
passage of the lectures of 1926, for example, he maintains that
history of the second degree, or history of historiography, is easier
to get right than history of the first degree because 'it has a kind
of directness or immediacy, by contrast with which history of the
first degree is always indirect and inferential'. The historian, he
continues, 'has placed himself directly before us by writing for us
to read; there is only a difference of degree between our acquaintance with him and our acquaintance with people whom we meet
and with whom we converse; whereas we can never have this
direct acquaintance, in however slight a degree, with Alexander
the Great or William the Conqueror' (L26 382). Collingwood
seems comfortable here with at least a quasi-acquaintance theory
for second-degree history. But, of course, such a compromise
cannot stand.

The point made here about the inappropriateness of acquaintance theory to a Collingwoodian account of historical knowledge
is to be distinguished from the argument advanced in Chapter 2
against interpreting Collingwood's idea of re-enactive historical
understanding in terms of such a theory. It was pointed out there
that we do not 'observe' thoughts at all, even present ones. Ascribing thoughts to someone is always a matter of interpreting
something observed. In fact, ascribing them to past agents is, on
Collingwood's mature theory, doubly an interpretation, and
doubly to be distinguished from knowledge by acquaintance. For
it is, first, an interpretation of an outside as expressing an inside,
and, secondly, an interpretation of something present as a relic of
the past. Historical knowledge cannot be knowledge by acquaintance, both because it is *of thought* and because it is *of the past*.
Collingwood is very consistent in his opposition to the idea that
knowledge of thoughts could ever be acquired by becoming directly acquainted with them. He does not oppose as consistently
the idea that knowledge of the past requires some kind of direct

acquaintance with the ostensible object. Besides the illustrations already given, one might cite the oddity of his reminding us that historians lack second sight, or a capacity for time-travel (*IH* 252; L26 364)—as if either would do them much good, given the way, on his view, a past thought would have to be known. There may be a hint of the acquaintance paradigm also in Collingwood's curious tendency to describe history, because it does not claim direct knowledge of its object, as 'non-empirical' (NHH 16, 63). In view of all this, I may have been too hasty, at times, in criticizing authors like Gardiner for regarding Collingwood as an acquaintance theorist.[38] Such authors, however, seem generally to have derived this view of him from his theory of re-enactive understanding, not from his theory of the ideality of the past.

Reinforcing the difficulties that flow from Collingwood's having insufficiently sloughed off the acquaintance theory of knowledge, are problems arising out of the ways he characteristically uses notions like 'reality' and 'actuality' when writing about the object of historical knowledge. His use of them, indeed, when not puzzlingly ambivalent, often seems close to perverse, giving an impression of something close to linguistic sleight of hand.

In the work of his middle years, especially, Collingwood repeatedly denies that the historian can have knowledge of the past as it really or actually was, because, no longer being real or actual, the past is not 'there' to be known (L28 449).[39] And he quite explicitly represents himself, in this connection, as repudiating the formula of von Ranke, which he seems happy to leave to those he calls realists (L26 393–4). Yet, in contexts where he is not under the spell of the notion of the ideality of the past, he does not hesitate to write as though he accepts that formula himself. In *The Idea of History*, for example, he applauds Bacon for seeing 'that the essential work of history is to recall and record the past in its actual facts as they actually happened' (*IH* 58). In the same work, he chides medieval historians for not realizing that an historian's

[38] For example, in 'R. G. Collingwood and the Acquaintance Theory of Knowledge', 2 ff.

[39] When Collingwood first gave serious consideration to what he came to call the ideality of history, he showed some uncertainty about the principle that only the 'actual' can be known, saying: 'What we know must, I suppose, really exist' (SPAT 146).

'prime duty' is 'to bestow infinite pains on discovering what actually happened' (*IH* 55). Even in passages which may give the impression of challenging the Rankean formula, he often introduces qualifications which considerably mitigate the challenge. In the lectures of 1928, for example, he complains that 'history is certainly an illusion' if, as realists think, its purpose is 'to know the past, to become acquainted with things as they actually happened' (L28 483). But if all that he is denying is that we can ever know *by acquaintance* how things actually happened, plenty of room is left for the possibility of knowing it in some other way.

Similar considerations apply when Collingwood uses expressions like 'the past as such', or 'the past in itself' or 'the real past'. He writes: 'the past as such is unknowable', adding that what is 'alone knowable' is 'the past as residually preserved in the present' (LHK 100). All that is excluded, apparently, is knowledge of the past which is *not* 'residually preserved' (or 'still living') in the present, that being referred to as 'the past as such'. Nothing follows from this about whether, when we come to know a preserved (or living) past, we are coming to know 'what actually happened'. We can understand in a similar way Collingwood's holding it to follow from Croce's theory of history (of which he approves) that 'the subject-matter of history is not the past as such, but the past for which we possess historical evidence' (*IH* 202). Collingwood does, at times, shake off his own technically-defined senses of these terms and talk about the real and the actual in more ordinary ways. When contrasting the writing of universal history with the writing of more limited historical works, for example, he maintains that any monograph, seriously thought out, will be a 'real history of the world' (L26 421). And in two of the passages quoted earlier from *The Idea of History* (*IH* 2–3, 246), he uses 'actually' and 'really', as we all normally do, to refer to what happened in the past, not to what is happening before our eyes.

What matters most, however, is not Collingwood's inconsistency with regard to the use of 'actual', 'real', and related concepts, but the way in which his frequent juxtaposing of ordinary and special senses leads him to talk literal nonsense at times. Van der Dussen correctly attributes to him the view, in 1926, that what 'explains why we cannot know the past as it actually happened' is the fact that 'the past is in no sense whatever actual'.[40] But if, as seems intended, 'as it actually happened' is understood in an ordinary sense, while 'actual' is taken in Collingwood's technical sense, this statement expresses a blatant *non sequitur*. For its meaning then is that the past's no longer existing explains why we cannot know it as it was. And this simply begs the question; all the work is done by an unjustified hint (backed by a mere linguistic resonance) that to say otherwise would somehow be self-contradictory.[41] But if the Collingwoodian point is rather that the past's no longer existing explains why we cannot know it as something which is actually happening now, it is simply a tautology—simply a reminder that what is non-existent cannot be known as existing, and, as such, no threat to von Ranke's formula. The conceptual morass into which we are lured by the way Collingwood conjures with the ideas of reality and actuality could be further indicated as follows. From the assertion, 'the past is not actual', taking 'not actual' in Collingwood's sense of 'not presently existing', the only conclusion that could be drawn which would even seem to be relevant to the Rankean formula is that we cannot know the past *as it actually is*, not *as it actually was*—i.e. as composed of what is here and now occurring. And that, of course, is a thesis which one hardly has to be a constructionist to endorse.

In fact, Collingwood's denial of the 'actuality' of history, as he sets out to use the term, has no bearing whatever on whether we can know the past as it actually was, as one would ordinarily understand that expression. It in no way puts in question, for example, the propriety of saying things like: 'Although Peter thinks the battle of Waterloo was won by Napoleon, it was actually (or in actuality) won by Wellington.' One might even maintain, with Donagan, and against the views of a number of recent constructionist interpreters of his position, that Collingwood's philosophical account of history, whether or not he realized this himself, expresses a correspondence theory of historical truth. It does this, at any rate, if, as Collingwood often implies, that is

[40] Van der Dussen, 'Collingwood's Unpublished Manuscripts', 294.

[41] There are, of course, real historiographical problems about how knowledge, necessarily indirect, is gained of what is now past and gone, some of them considered by Collingwood when discussing evidence and principles of historical interpretation. But such problems cannot sensibly be addressed until the nonsense derived from the idea of the past as non-actual has been identified and dismissed.

equivalent to holding that historical inquiry may reveal the past as it actually was.[42]

Three final remarks may serve to keep that contention in proper perspective. It is not being implied that one should regard the conclusions of historical inquiry as incorrigible—a claim that would not be made with regard to any other kind of empirical knowledge, including that claimed in natural science (taking 'empirical' here in its more usual, not its peculiar Collingwoodian, sense). Nor is it being implied that historians get to know, or even claim to get to know, everything about the past—although, as was indicated earlier in §2, Collingwood himself frequently obscures this issue by running together the questions whether the past can be known in its actuality and in its completeness. It is not being implied either that historical inquiry into what actually happened involves no element of interpretation. Knowledge of what actually happened is not confined, for example, to knowledge of how past events and processes were experienced by those who lived through them—a misinterpretation of the Rankean claim that Nowell-Smith has called 'psychological realism'.[43] In the present book, I am, of course, claiming knowledge of Collingwood's thought about history as it actually was. But my conclusions are not advanced as either incorrigible or exhaustive; nor do I assume that my understanding of Collingwood's position coincides entirely with the way he represented it to himself.

[42] If, as Collingwood sometimes seems to have believed himself, holding a correspondence theory of truth in history implies that historians can become acquainted with a real (i.e. still existing) past, then, of course, Collingwood was not a correspondence theorist. But he was not a coherence theorist either in the sense that he considered the truth of a statement to lie in its relationship to other statements—unless the correspondence theory is spirited back in by saying 'in its relationship to other true statements'.

[43] 'The Constructionist Theory of History', *History and Theory*, 16 (1977), 8. This article offers a highly effective critique of constructionism.

8

THE PERSPECTIVITY OF HISTORY

§ 1. *Historical Relativism*

We have been considering what Collingwood had to say about the non-existence, or at any rate the inaccessibility, of the ostensible object of historical inquiry as a reason for questioning whether it can hope to tell us what really happened in the past. As was noted at the beginning of Chapter 7, however, this ontological consideration is not the only source of scepticism about historical knowledge which shows itself in Collingwood's writings. An equally important one derives from his representing historical inquiry as essentially perspectival in nature, each historian being said to approach the study of the past from his own point of view, historical accounts, in consequence, not only differing at a given time, but having to be constantly revised as the viewpoints of historians change. Questioning the status of historical conclusions for such epistemological rather than ontological reasons is generally referred to as 'historical relativism', the doctrine that what historians assert must always be understood as expressing a judgment relative to the standpoint of the person making it.[1] It is important not to confuse this position with the scepticism which sometimes arises out of the ideality doctrine. One significant difference is that this further possible source of sceptical concern leaves it open that historians might discover at least *something* about the way the past really was, even if they do not get it all quite right because of distortions introduced by their perspectives. The ideality doctrine, by contrast, is easily seen as requiring

[1] See e.g. Nathan Rotenstreich's useful distinction between scepticism based on doubts about the existence of the object and doubts about the reliability of historical thought ('History and Time: A Critical Examination of R. G. Collingwood's Doctrine', *Scripta Hierosolymitana*, 6 (1960), 60).

the conclusion that historians can discover nothing about the real past, since all they have in view is a past which they themselves 'construct'.[2]

Mandelbaum has plausibly maintained that scepticism about the possibility of historical knowledge has far more often been traceable to a view of historical inquiry as incurably relativistic than to concern about its subject-matter being past and gone.[3] This seems true especially of historians theorizing about their own discipline, notably since Beard and Becker raised their consciousness about such matters—although, in presenting their arguments for relativism, both of the latter also touch upon the problem posed by the non-existent past.[4]

That Collingwood was an historical relativist, and to that extent at least an incipient sceptic about the possibility of genuine knowledge of the past, is almost as commonly accepted as that he held a re-enactive view of historical understanding. Among philosophers, Rubinoff has referred to his relativism as 'explicit', Carr as 'sweeping', Walsh as 'thoroughgoing'.[5] Historians like Gershoy, Veyne, and Marwick have also described his view of historical knowledge and inquiry as relativist.[6] Even critics who, like MacKinnon or Gellner, concede that a mere charge of relativism still leaves much to be discussed, describe him as 'flirting' with relativism.[7] By contrast, Fain sees him as having been 'constitutionally unable to accept philosophical relativism as the last word'; and Nielsen has insisted that, if he was a relativist, he was at any rate not a sceptic.[8]

The question whether Collingwood was in fact a relativist, and,

[2] A further important difference between the problems of relativism and of constructionism is that accepting the former (like accepting re-enactment theory) has implications for the way historians should write history, whereas the latter has no such implications.

[3] Mandelbaum, *Anatomy*, 9.

[4] See e.g. Beard, 'That Noble Dream', 323; Becker, 'What Are Historical Facts?', 125.

[5] Rubinoff, Review of *EPH*, 473; David Carr, Review of Martin *HE*, 216; Walsh, 'The Character', 65.

[6] Leo Gershoy, 'Some Problems of a Working Historian', in Sidney Hook (ed.), *Philosophy and History: A Symposium* (New York, 1963), 60; Paul Veyne, *Writing History: Essays on Epistemology* (Middletown, Conn., 1971), 302; Marwick, *Nature of History*, 80.

[7] Mackinnon, Review of *IH*, 252; Ernest Gellner, Review of Krausz (ed.), *Critical Essays*, in *TLS*, 30 March 1973, 339.

[8] Fain, *BPH* 143; Nielsen, 'Re-enactment and Reconstruction', 28.

if so, just how extreme his relativism was, has sometimes been thought to be settled by a much-quoted passage which Knox included in his preface to the original edition of *The Idea of History*. There Collingwood writes: 'St. Augustine looked at Roman history from the point of view of an early Christian; Tillemont, from that of a seventeenth-century Frenchman; Gibbon, from that of an eighteenth-century Englishman; Mommsen, from that of a nineteenth-century German.' He adds: 'There is no point in asking which was the right point of view. Each was the only one possible for the man who adopted it.'[9] Van der Dussen has discovered that this famous passage was not, as Knox's preface might lead one to believe, derived from the lecture notes upon which the bulk of the text of *The Idea of History* was based, but was taken, rather, from a letter written by Collingwood to Knox.[10] This may seem somewhat to undermine its authority as an expression of his considered views on such a controversial point. But Collingwood's writings contain many similar passages. In the lectures of 1928, for example, he remarks that 'historical fact, as known to the historian, is essentially relative to the thought that knows it' (L26 429). In summing up his reflections on history in 1930, he concedes that 'everyone brings his own mind to the study of history, and approaches it from the point of view which is characteristic of himself and his generation' (PH 138–9). In the historical part of *The Idea of History* itself, when discussing the views of Fichte, Collingwood reiterates the substance of the St Augustine passage when he asserts that 'the judgement passed on the achievements of the Middle Ages will necessarily differ according as the historian is a man of the eighteenth, nineteenth, or twentieth century' (*IH* 108). There seems to be little doubt that it was an established principle of Collingwood's philosophy of history that history is necessarily written from a point of view.

In what follows, I shall argue that nothing which Collingwood says about history being relative to a point of view justifies describing him as a sceptic—especially not on his own definition of scepticism as the view that 'no one opinion is preferable to any

---

[9] *IH*, 1st edn., p. xii. E. H. Carr sees this as amounting to 'total scepticism', likening it to Froude's remark that history resembles 'a child's box of letters with which we can spell any word we please' (*WIH* 21). This remark, however, betrays a common error about relativism, which, as will appear, is quite compatible with holding that historians make mistakes (from their own points of view).

[10] Introduction to *IH*, rev. edn., p. xxii.

other' (NAPH 43). But, taking historical relativism to mean that the knowledge claimed by historians is in some important way conditioned by their points of view, I shall accept it that Collingwood was an historical relativist. What needs to be asked is just how he thinks the knowledge claims of historians are perspectivally conditioned, and to what extent.

Pursuing such questions will make necessary a more systematic consideration of the notion of having a perspective or point of view in history than is offered anywhere in Collingwood's own writings. It will be found to raise questions, too, about some related ideas which are employed, or at any rate instantiated, in those writings: for example, how far and in what ways history must be written from the standpoint of the present; the degree to which historical understanding is retrospective as well as re-enactive; and the sense in which judgments of relative importance and value judgments need to be made in historical work.[11] As I did with regard to Collingwood's ideality doctrine, I shall argue that the claim that historical studies are perspectival, as Collingwood understands and accepts the idea, is quite compatible with an acceptance of the Rankean notion that historians may, within limits, discover how the past actually was, although the reasons for rejecting scepticism in the two cases are very different. A further thesis, and one bearing upon the central interest of this book, will be that a recognition of the perspectivity of historical judgment makes necessary still a further expansion of Collingwood's theory of historical understanding. As in the case of understanding through synthesis, this is not something which is explicitly argued for in his writings; but a basis for it can be found in much of what he has to say.

§ 2. *Point of View in History*

It is a commonplace of philosophical writing on history that, in order to understand the past, it must be regarded from a certain point of view, and Collingwood often repeats this commonplace. As early as his essay on Croce, he shows sympathy for the idea that what is seen in history 'must be seen by somebody, from

[11] It is of interest that these issues appear on Collingwood's list of typical philosophical questions about history (L27 347–8).

somebody's point of view' (CPH 11). In 'The Nature and Aims of a Philosophy of History', he depicts historians as viewing the past each 'from his own centre, at an angle of his own' (NAPH 54). In his paper on Spengler, he insists that historical cycles can be discerned only from a 'momentary point of view' (SHC 75). In his summation of his ideas on history in 1930, he declares that attempts to eliminate points of view in historical work are 'always unsuccessful' (PH 138). The extent to which the view of historical thinking as perspectival is also present in *The Idea of History* has sometimes not been noticed because of the interest which most of its readers have had in what it says about historical understanding as re-enactment. The tendency to neglect its perspectivism in fact goes back to Knox, whose index to the first edition contains many entries for 're-enactment', but none at all for 'perspective' or 'point of view', this in spite of the exposure which his own preface had given to the famous passage about how differently different historians have 'looked at' Roman history. Yet perspectivist passages in *The Idea of History* are not difficult to find. Thus Collingwood commends Bury for making what he calls the 'unusual admission' that his *History of Greece* is 'written from his own point of view' (*IH* 147). One of the merits which he somewhat grudgingly ascribes to the 'internal criticism' stressed by nineteenth-century historiographical theory is that it showed 'how the author's point of view affected his statement of the facts' (*IH* 130). One of the things for which he says philosophy of history is indebted to Kant is the idea that knowledge of an object may be 'relative to the knower's own point of view' (*IH* 60).

In his historical writings, too, Collingwood makes considerable use of plainly perspectivist language. He observes, for example, that, while, from the British point of view, the Roman period in Britain may be seen as 'an isolated and somewhat unintelligible episode', from the point of view of an historian of Rome 'it cuts a slightly better figure' (*RB* 1–2). In support of his thesis that Celtic art continued to enjoy a surreptitious existence in Britain during the Roman period, he points out that, whereas, from the Roman point of view, an art work like the Bath Gorgon is 'merely one feature of the shield, and the shield is merely an accessory of the divine figure that holds it', from a Celtic point of view, it is 'the centre of interest', the shield being 'merely its frame' (*RBES* 255). With regard to Caesar's failed invasion of Britain, he says similarly that, while, from Caesar's point of view, it could be seen as a project deferred, from the point of view of the British, it was more naturally seen as a 'reprieve' (*RBES* 54).

But although the idea of seeing things from a perspective has a prominent place in both Collingwood's philosophical and historical writings, he nowhere offers a systematic account of what he understands by that idea. What is generally offered, in lieu of analysis, is a version of the fashionable analogy between perspectival judgments in history and in sense-perception. In 'The Nature and Aims of a Philosophy of History', for example, having insisted that 'each historian sees history from his own centre, at an angle of his own', each, in consequence, seeing problems that others do not see, Collingwood likens this to the way 'a hundred people looking at the same tree all see different aspects of it, each seeing something hidden from the rest', adding that 'they can never detach themselves from the distinct starting-points at which they took up the process of perceiving' (NAPH 54). In other writings, too, he puts his position in quasi-perceptual language, insisting that historians must always envisage the past from the 'place' or 'position' they 'occupy' in the historical process (CPH 11; *IH* 248). The analogy with sense-perception is employed explicitly in a manuscript of 1935, in which Collingwood writes: 'Because we are bodies situated in the world of bodies, our bodily situation is a factor in the way in which other bodies appear to us; because we are historical individuals having our own place in the historical process, the varying endowments which that process has conferred upon us make it inevitable that we should envisage that process each from his own point of view' (RNI 44–5). However, if we seek further elucidation of what he thinks is involved in historical inquiries being conducted from a point of view, we find little more than scattered remarks.

The essentials of what Collingwood means by inquiry from a point of view can nevertheless be derived from remarks which he does make from time to time. It needs to be said, first, that, for him, 'perspective' is a composite idea: it collects quite a heterogeneous set of considerations, all regarded as relevant to the fact that historians often reach quite different conclusions when dealing with the same subject-matter. Mere differences of investigative skill apart, Collingwood sees these conclusions as varying with at least the following factors. First, and perhaps most obviously, they will vary with the evidence available, since historical conclusions are what the evidence requires (L28 487). A relevant example would be the way views of Roman Britain which Collingwood himself advances differ from those offered by pre-decessors who lacked his access to archaeological findings. A second, and closely related, factor will be the problems (ques-tions) which historians are trying to solve—related because, ac-cording to Collingwood, evidence is only evidence in relation to an envisaged problem (*IH* 281). The problem-relativity of histor-ical accounts is exemplified by the contrast which Collingwood draws between what can be said of Roman Britain from the stand-point of someone writing a history of Britain and from the stand-point of someone writing a history of Rome, these being con-ceived as responses to different assemblages of questions.[12] It is exemplified in a different way by his reporting, as an historian of Roman Britain, that from the strictly economic point of view, the towns were a 'luxury', their true function being 'cultural and political' (*RBES* 199).

Collingwood also mentions, as reasons why historians' find-ings may differ, the different principles of inquiry which they bring to their interpretations of evidence (*IH* 248). An historian who rejects what he calls 'the argument from silence'—the prin-ciple that an absence of evidence for something is evidence for its non-occurrence (L26 388)—will almost certainly look rather dif-ferently at some stretches of the past than does one who accepts it. A related perspectival consideration, although Collingwood sel-dom notes it very explicitly, is the differing concepts frequently employed by historians in constructing their accounts: for example, agents' versus observers' concepts; social versus indi-vidual ones; colligatory versus atomistic ones. A factor difficult to separate entirely from concepts is the different theories of the subject-matter which historians also sometimes bring to their work. One cannot expect Marxist and liberal historians, for exam-ple, always to give the same answers to the same questions, using the same evidence. Still another element clearly belonging to what Collingwood, at least sometimes, calls the perspective of an historian is the differing value judgments which their accounts

---

[12] This might also be described as writing from the standpoint of different interests, but the role of interests will be considered again in § 6.

characteristically express (L28 470), and the judgments of relative importance which structure them.[13]

Even the elements noted—the historian's evidence, questions, principles, concepts, theories, values (in § 5, position in time will be added)—do not exhaust what Collingwood from time to time includes in what he calls the point of view of an historian. For example, he sometimes also mentions the prior knowledge, both historical and non-historical, which historians need to bring to their work: knowledge of Greek letters, for instance, where a document is in Greek (RNI 43), and, more generally, knowledge of 'nature and man', of philosophy, even of mathematics (*IH* 248). Indeed, the historian's reconstructive task is said to require 'all the powers of his own mind' (*IH* 215)—to which one might add his presuppositions, including absolute ones.

It is Collingwood's contention that historians not only do commonly conduct their inquiries from points of view, understood as consisting of some or all of the factors mentioned, but that they must do so.[14] It is clear, furthermore, that the sense of 'must' in which he maintains this is not a merely psychological one. To put it in the language of later analytical philosophers of history, it is logical or conceptual. Collingwood's position is that it simply makes no sense to suppose that historical conclusions could be reached otherwise than on the basis of certain evidence, in response to certain questions, framed in terms of certain concepts, applying certain principles of interpretation, and making certain judgments of value and importance. As he puts it himself, without a point of view, an historian 'can see nothing at all' (*IH* 108; CPH 10). If an attempt to eliminate all points of view ever were to succeed, he says, then 'history itself would vanish' (PH 138). Here, at least, the perceptual analogy may have some value, reinforcing, if only analogically, the idea that what is known can *only* be known perspectivally: for the idea of perceiving a physical object from no point of view is equally senseless. Perspectivity in historical accounts is thus not, as Collingwood conceives it, a weakness to be identified, and then eliminated, as far as this can

[13] The question of value judgment in historical reconstruction is somewhat neglected in *IH*, *A*, and the published essays of the 1920s, but is considered extensively in L26 398 ff., and CHBI 8 ff.

[14] Both Collingwood and his commentators often phrase this claim in terms of a single perspectival element, usually either evidence or question (e.g. L28 459; *IH* 180; *EPH*, p. xxi; MacIver, 'The Character', 48–9; Popper, 'A Pluralistic Approach', 193).

be done, but a fact of historiographical life to be lived with, and perhaps even to be embraced. When Collingwood frames the central question of philosophy of history as 'How is history possible?', clearly part of his answer is: 'By taking up a point of view and reconstructing a portion of the past from its vantage point.' In similar vein, he describes differences attributable to historians' points of view as systematic, not arbitrary (PH 139), and the requirement that the past be known from a point of view as an a priori element in historical thinking (L28 437 n. 5).

There are times when he associates the idea of historians having a point of view with factors of which it cannot be said that they *must* function in historical reconstruction—at any rate, not in the sense just indicated. Thus he sometimes refers to the personal feelings, attitudes, and motivations which may 'colour' an historian's work as elements of the point of view to be ascribed to him. Of none of such considerations can it be said that they are necessary to the writing of history in a logical or conceptual sense. They are the names rather of defects to which historical work is prone: faults which should be banished from it wherever possible. To the extent that they are nevertheless seen as necessary, the necessity will have to be understood as psychological or dispositional. Collingwood makes this point explicitly with regard to value judgment in the lectures of 1928 (L28 470 n. 16). Yet, with characteristic overstatement, he asserts, in a paper of 1935, that no great history can be written without the driving force of prejudice, citing examples of great historians whose work allegedly confirms this dictum. What he might more appropriately have said is that great histories have sometimes been written despite the prejudices which they express, their greatness making it worth the trouble of identifying the latter and discounting them. It makes no sense, however, to talk of identifying and discounting (with a view ultimately to eliminating) all principles of interpretation, or concepts, or value judgments from an historian's work.

But if historical conclusions are necessarily relative to historians' points of view, as characterized, and in a logical or conceptual sense, what is to be said about their status as claims to knowledge? More particularly, can they be regarded as capable of telling us how the past really was? As Gellner has remarked, this is a question on which Collingwood 'wobbled'.[15]

---

[15] Gellner, Review of Krausz (ed.), *Critical Essays*, 338.

He warns, at times, of a need to 'make allowances for the distortions' introduced into historical accounts by the author's point of view, as if a point of view by its very nature distorts (*IH* 130). He concedes, in discussing Croce's philosophy, that, because the past must be seen 'by somebody, from somebody's point of view', it will doubtless 'be in part seen falsely' (CPH 11). In *Speculum Mentis*, he declares that 'to confess frankly that our histories are nothing but an expression of personal points of view' would be 'the very cynicism of history', the 'conscious acquiescence' in 'fraud' (*SM* 237). Interpreters of Collingwood who deny that he was a sceptic are left to make what they can of his saying only that a perspectival view of the past may produce a 'partly' false account, or his holding only that fraudulent histories may be produced by 'personal' points or view, this perhaps suggesting only the illegitimate factor of prejudice. There are times, too, when the way Collingwood responds to the problem of the status of perspectival accounts may seem to imply that he holds truth itself, and not just differences about what was in fact true, to be relative to a point of view in history, so that what is true for us now about the past may not have been true for Grote or Hume, and vice versa. There is at least a suggestion of this in his maintaining that an historian's point of view is 'valid only for him and people situated like him' (*IH* 108), or his asserting that 'the truth about an event is relative to the point of view from which one approaches it' (L28 474). However, in his British Academy Lecture, he retreats decisively from such a view. Taking aim at Herbert Spencer, he declares that, if the ways in which people think at one time were 'ways in which people must think then, but in which others, cast at different times in a different mental mould, cannot think at all,' then 'there would be no such thing as truth'—which Collingwood clearly thinks there is (*IH* 225).

The most considered Collingwoodian response to the problem of the perspectivity of historical thought, and one which, although it appears early, seems to underlie much of what he has to say on this problem thereafter, is offered at two levels in 'The Nature and Aims of a Philosophy of History'. It is there maintained, first, that to see something in a way which is peculiar to someone at a certain perspective, whether in sense perception or in history, is not necessarily to perceive it falsely. What people at different standpoints may perceive, although different, may all of it be true (NAPH 54). In *The Idea of History*, Collingwood applies the perceptual analogy in the following way. The fact that I perceive a physical object 'here', he says, does not prevent me from perceiving it as 'there'. In a similar way, the historian, investigating the past, 'thinks of his object as there, or rather then, away from him in time', although still an object of present experience. His object of study could thus be said to be experienced 'both as then and as now' (*IH* 158).

Collingwood goes on to compare what he sees as the typically different approaches taken by historians and philosophers of history to the problem of reconstructing the past. An historian, he says, is an epistemological monad; his aim is simply to elaborate an account of his subject-matter from his own point of view. The philosopher of history, by contrast, is a monadologist; his interest is in exploring the relationship between the various points of view which historians are found to adopt and what they claim to see from them. What the philosopher discerns, Collingwood declares, is 'not merely a perspective but the space of perspectives'. 'The world of fact, which for history is an external presupposition of thought, becomes for philosophy a world of perspectives each having at its centre an historical consciousness; a world of worlds of thought each relative to its thinker' (*NAPH* 56). A major consideration here is that a philosopher can see *why* the accounts of historians not only differ, but ought to differ: the differences are not accidental or idiosyncratic, but systematic. Each account shows how the past necessarily appears from a certain point of view. Thus, although in one sense different perspectival accounts contradict one another, in a more important sense they are supplementary.

This response to the problem raised by the perspectivity of history closely resembles the one given of our knowledge of physical objects by phenomenalists among British philosophers a generation ago. The object, as it was sometimes put, is to be conceived as the sum of its actual and possible appearances. It is also curiously similar to the way some contemporary philosophers of history like Ernest Nagel have dealt with the problem of the perspectivity of historical claims—philosophers whom Collingwood might, in other respects, consider positivist opponents. Nagel finds no difficulty in the idea of ascribing a merely 'relational objectivity' to the differing conclusions of historians, this consisting in the fact that, provided all have been reached by rigorous argument from the various points of view held, one can use a 'transformation formula' to reason from what is said from one of them to what ought to be said from another.[16] While what is legitimately said from one of these perspectives cannot be called 'the' truth about its subject-matter, there is, in fact, no truth about it to discern beyond what is ascertainable by this means. This conclusion follows inexorably from the doctrine that knowledge of the historical past cannot be other than in terms of the elements which jointly constitute a point of view. In the *Autobiography*, Collingwood relates how he used to apply something rather like Nagel's 'transformation formula' in his philosophical discussions with hostile colleagues at Oxford, criticizing their positions (to their annoyance) not from his own point of view, but from theirs (*A* 57). And he sometimes appears to hold that this is an exercise which philosophically sophisticated historians, conscious of working within a 'space of perspectives', would themselves want to engage in from time to time.

Is such a perspectivism a sufficient response by Collingwood to the threat so often thought to be posed by historical relativism in the perspectivist sense? It should be clear that it at any rate leaves no room for the kind of objection which Carr expresses when he argues against Collingwood that, if the facts are 'always refracted through the mind of the recorder', then 'by and large, the historian will get the kind of facts he wants' (*WIH* 16, 18). What he will get are the facts which his point of view requires him to recognize—or, if he adopts the perspectival eclecticism which Collingwood seems close to advocating at times, the facts which are required by all the points of view which he is willing to take seriously. Joseph Levine commends Collingwood for insisting that an historian can 'think objectively and subjectively at the same time'; but it is clear that his perspectivism does not commit him to regarding historical thinking as subjective in Carr's sense.[17]

A more likely charge is that Collingwood's perspectivism saddles the historian with too many, not too few, 'truths' about the past, even if these are no more than truths about the way the

[16] 'Some Issues in the Logic of Historical Analysis', reprinted in Gardiner (ed.), *Theories of History*, 381–2.

[17] 'Objectivity in History: Peter Novick and R. G. Collingwood', *Clio*, 21 (1992), 116.

past necessarily appears from different points of view. Collingwood holds that, despite its unavoidable perspectivity, history 'remains genuine knowledge' (PH 139).[18] But is it knowledge of the way the past actually was? How many ways can the past actually have been, it might be asked. In the case of physical objects, we ordinarily make a distinction between the way things appear from various points of view and the way they really are, natural scientists being expected to derive knowledge of the latter from knowledge of the former. But here the perceptual analogy, as it so often does, raises difficulties. What we mean, literally, by historians having a point of view is such things as their conceiving their objects of inquiry as falling under certain concepts or as expressing certain values. If it were possible ever to conceive them in ways which transcended this limitation, it is hard to see how those objects could any longer be considered past social reality. To use Collingwood's own words again, history would 'vanish'. The very notion of past social reality, in abstraction from what we have been calling elements of historians' points of view, is incoherent. If this appears to be a hard saying, it should not be forgotten that present social reality is equally unknowable except from a point of view in Collingwood's sense.

§ 3. *Relativity to the Present*

Perspectivism is the position that historical reconstruction is necessarily relative to a point of view in something like the sense just adumbrated. However, Collingwood's perspectivism often takes the more specific form of maintaining that what historians offer is accounts of the past from a *present* point of view. As he puts it himself, 'the historian can genuinely see into the past only so far as he stands firmly rooted in the present; that is, his business is not to leap clean out of his own period of history but . . . to see the past as it appears from the standpoint of that age' (*IH* 60). He 'is not God, looking at the world from above and outside. He is a man, and a man of his own time and place. He looks at the past

[18] Collingwood holds that 'a thoroughgoing relativism' would 'reconcile' the 'Ptolemaic' idea that the past really was a certain way with the 'Copernican' idea that it is that way from our point of view (PP 105 n.). Just how this can be, however, he leaves it to his readers to work out.

from the point of view of the present: he looks at other countries and civilizations from the point of view of his own' (*IH* 108). Collingwood does not always distinguish as clearly as he might have done between the presentism which he sees following from the fact that historians necessarily have a point of view, and the presentism, discussed in Chapter 7, § 5, which he thinks follows from the doctrine of ideality.[19] The two are radically different, however, even if both are sometimes thought to warrant scepticism. If the ideality doctrine makes historical conclusions relative to the present, it will be in the sense that, since the past is allegedly unknowable, there is nothing but the present for them to be about. If the perspectivity doctrine makes historical conclusions relative to the present, it will be because, although the past can be known, it can be known only as it appears from a present point of view.[20]

The idea that all histories express a present point of view needs some initial qualification in two ways. It needs to be noted, first, that it is quite possible for historians to construct accounts of the past from a past rather than a present point of view. This is something, furthermore, which most historians would in fact claim to do from time to time, seeking to convey a sense of what it must have been like to live through past periods and circumstances by describing them in terms of the questions, knowledge, concepts, values, and so on, of those living at the time. Nor is this done only occasionally, or just for special effect, since it is required, to some degree, whenever historians set out to explain what past agents did in terms of what they thought. As has been noted already, there are historians who place special stress upon this aspect of historiography; but there can be few who do not engage in it at all. It needs to be said also, however, that this cannot, with plausibility, be considered the whole of the historical task. For it would express a disputable preference for showing how things appeared (to the agents) over showing how (in the

[19] As van der Dussen notes (*HS* 142), Collingwood sometimes appears to regard the ideality doctrine as a support for his perspectivist theory. But if there can be no knowledge of a no-longer-existing past, perspectival knowledge of it is as much ruled out as any other sort.

[20] As Walsh puts Collingwood's position, the past is necessarily viewed 'through spectacles coloured by the present' ('Collingwood's Philosophy of History', 157). E. H. Carr describes it similarly (*WIH* 19). It is still misleading, however, to say that perspectivism *entails* presentism, for reasons that will appear below.

judgment of the historian) they really were. If historians are to determine what really happened, they will need to make judgments not only on their own authority, but also from their own points of view. Nor is it clear, in any case, that even the most agent-oriented historians could entirely escape the need to make such judgments. For example, where the viewpoints of the agents themselves are at odds, a decision may sometimes have to be made from the historian's own standpoint as to whose views matter most.

The second qualification is required because, just as Collingwood sometimes passes too easily from holding that history must be written from a point of view at all to holding that it must be written from the point of view of the present, so he sometimes passes, without the benefit of argument, from holding that a history must express a present point of view to holding that the point of view expressed will be that of the historian's own age, generation, or culture. In *The Idea of History*, having declared that the historian 'can genuinely see into the past only so far as he stands firmly rooted in the present', Collingwood observes that his business is not 'to leap clean out of his own period of history', but 'to see the past as it appears from the standpoint of that age' (*IH* 60). Again, in one of the passages quoted, having insisted that the historian 'looks at the past from the point of view of the present', he adds, as if merely enlarging upon that statement, that he 'looks at other countries and civilizations from the point of view of his own' (*IH* 108). In 'The Philosophy of History', he similarly maintains that the historian's study of the past is undertaken 'from the point of view which is characteristic of himself and his generation' (PH 138). But there is no logical or conceptual reason why the standpoint from which the past is envisaged must be that of the historian's age or generation rather than some idiosyncratic standpoint of his own. Collingwood often refers to the historian as the 'representative' of his age, or the 'son of his time' (*IH* 305). But, by reason of his values, assumptions, or questions, he may be in revolt against his age, and could well be trying to convey to his contemporaries a revolutionary way of looking at the past.[21]

---

[21] This point is obscured when Collingwood says of the historian's questions that they are 'a function of his individuality, and *therefore* of his generation' (L28 486, n. 18, emphasis added).

In the more usual case, the historian will doubtless view the past from a point of view which is held both by himself and by the community for which he writes. But Collingwood's presentism often goes beyond the mere contention that historical accounts will be structured by the perspectival elements which, representative or not, are brought to the reconstructive task by the historian himself. He often represents the elaboration of historical accounts as relative to the present in more specific ways, stressing the extent to which their concern is only with certain parts or aspects of the past: for example, those which explain present relics (L28 485); or which make it clear how present states of affairs came to be (L26 418; LHK 102; PH 139); or which are still 'alive' in present thought and action (*A* 97–8, 114); or which throw light on present problems (L28 469); or even which simply reflect present interests of one kind or another (L26 347; *IH* 179; NHV 12). Such claims are prefigured in Collingwood's declaration that all historical thinking arises 'out of the attempt to perceive more adequately the world that exists here and now for our perception' (NAPH 53) and resonates with the approval he expresses of the view which he ascribes to Vico that history 'is concerned, in the first instance, with the actual structure of the society in which we live' (*IH* 66).[22] I cannot undertake here to examine seriatim this whole collection of quite heterogeneous presentist considerations. But I should like to make four comments on a common thread which runs through them: the claim that historical accounts are a function of present *interests*.

First, the claim that the past, as historians envisage it, is a function of present interests sometimes passes over into the much more dubious contention that the present circumstances which evoked, or generated, or now sustain, those interests are what historical inquiry is really about. This idea is present in Collingwood's remark, in the lectures of 1928, that, since the historian's 'business' is to interpret records, history is 'in this sense . . . the study of the present and not of the past at all' (L28 484); and it appears again in a manuscript of 1934, in which, in connection with an historian's need to perceive a certain docu-

---

[22] Collingwood nevertheless shows some ambivalence with regard to this, on the one hand, defending Hegel's doctrine that history ends in the present (*IH* 120), and, on the other, describing him as 'worse than all his predecessors in that he tried to explain not history in general but only the present' (NHH 6).

ment as 'a charter of King John', Collingwood observes that 'the ultimate aim of history is not to know the past but to understand the present' (HUP 1). Here he is arguing that what counts as a part or aspect of the historical past is relative to the interest which historians have in something regarded as present evidence for it, rather than, as might ordinarily be said, the other way around. The same mode of argument is placed in a larger setting when Collingwood insists that, although Gibbon described what he was writing about as 'the decline and fall of the Roman empire', his real subject was 'the triumph of barbarism and religion' (NHV 12). This is said to be revealed with especial clarity by his account of the way the idea of his great work came to him, as he 'sat musing amidst the ruins of the Capitol, while the barefooted fryars were singing vespers in the temple of Jupiter'.[23] The implied question to which his whole history can be read as an answer is apparently: 'How did those "fryars" come to be there?'.

When Collingwood offers it as a conclusion required by the ideality doctrine that the true object of historical concern is not the past but the present, there is a certain prima-facie plausibility about what he says, even if it must ultimately be rejected. As a conclusion allegedly required by the perspectivist–presentist view, there is no plausibility about it at all. It is one thing to say (whether true or not) that historians are only concerned with past events and conditions to the extent that they are related to present concerns of various kinds, such as wanting to account for a present artefact, or to throw light on certain political, social, or cultural problems of the present. It is quite another to say that such concerns are what historians' accounts are really about. Even if present concerns determine which parts and aspects of the past are to be judged relevant to an historical inquiry, that doesn't make the subject-matter of history the present *rather than* the past. That Collingwood was somewhat uneasy about saying the contrary is suggested by the frequency with which he only says that this is true 'in a sense', or true 'in the first instance' (PH 139; L28 484–5; IH 66). Perhaps we are to take his contention, then, only as a figurative way of asserting that relativity to some present

[23] Review of Teggart, 'Theory of History', in *Journal of Philosophical Studies*, 1 (1926), 256. Collingwood commends Teggart for holding that 'history sets out from a present situation and is at bottom an attempt to understand the situation'.

interest is a general criterion of what is worth investigating historically. If so, however, it is most misleadingly stated.

A second comment is that, even when maintaining only that historical inquiry is relative to, not about, present circumstances and problems, the way Collingwood sometimes tries to reinforce his contention that this is necessarily the case trivializes the notion of present circumstances and problems. On Collingwood's theory of history, every claim about the past will, of course, be relative to the present in the sense of being what some body of present evidence shows. But, as his remarks about Gibbon suggest, he seems to want to claim more than that. He often gives at least the impression of holding that historical inquiry necessarily arises out of, or is a response to, present problems of a political, social, or cultural sort—for example, 'barbarism and religion', the story of which, Collingwood remarks, is not yet over. But although historical inquiry may often in fact be undertaken in response to such problems, on what basis could it possibly be claimed that it must be? Revealing, in this connection, is what Collingwood has to say about an apparent counter-example (noted in Chapter 7): the study of the history of the ancient Sumerians, something surely as remote from what would be called present concerns as anything could be. What one might have expected Collingwood to argue is that modern life has in fact been influenced by ancient Sumeria more than at first appears, so that in studying it (as, for example, in studying seventeenth-century England), we can expect to throw light, if indirectly, on present-day problems. But his reply is not along those lines at all: he simply points out that what the ancient Sumerians thought and did, to the extent that it becomes a matter of historical investigation, is *ipso facto* a present problem, since historians are now studying it (L28 468–9). This is a remarkably meagre dividend to draw from the promising doctrine ascribed to Vico.

What Collingwood surely needed (and would doubtless have refused) is a firmer distinction between present problems of the sort called to mind by the phrase 'the actual structure of the society in which we live'—problems like ethnic tensions in the Balkans or the need to improve mathematical education in the United States—and problems of the present which are simply problems of historiography: problems about the interpretation to place upon evidence which is apparently relevant to a problem about the past which, if also to be called a problem about the present, is not one in the same sense. Thus, to the extent that Collingwood's claim that history is necessarily relative to present problems is interesting, it is false. To the extent that it is true, it is trivial.

A third comment centres upon the way Collingwood sometimes represents the kind of interest which he thinks an historian would have in present problems which transcend merely historiographical ones. In some of his references to the work of historians of whom he clearly approves, he makes a good deal of what might be called their 'hidden agendas'. What an historian of the ancient world like Grote was really doing, he says, was writing 'the history of the liberal party'; what an historian of the nineteenth-century like Mommsen was really doing was writing 'the history of Prussia' (NHV 12). And by this, he doesn't mean only that they were dealing with matters which they judged to be of contemporary interest; he means that they selected the topics and asked the questions they did because of a pre-existing concern about the fate of liberalism or nationalism in their own day. Making a general principle of such cases, Collingwood declares that 'all genuine historians interest themselves in the past just as far as they find in it what they, as practical men, regard as living issues' (NHV 12). It is true that he sometimes expresses reservations about what he calls a 'pragmatic' approach to history (L26 396–7); but at least in cases like these he sees relevance to issues of direct practical concern as properly determining what history should be about. There is even a hint that the interest of historians in these issues need not be, and even should not be, entirely disengaged: that it is quite proper for them, provided they do not fall into mere propaganda, to pursue their inquiries with a view to promoting certain results. Such a conception of the wider goals of historians meshes well with the social role which Collingwood increasingly came to ascribe to historical studies in his later writings: that of providing the kind of knowledge needed to save modern civilization.

There is no need to deny Collingwood either his recommendation that history be, at least sometimes, written in a quasi-pragmatic way, or his claim that it is often so written by good historians. What needs to be questioned is any implication that this follows necessarily from his account of history as a

thoroughly perspectivally presentist genre of inquiry. What
Collingwood is really doing here, in the guise of descriptive
analysis, is entering an independent plea for 'relevant' history. He
is repudiating mere antiquarianism as unacceptable, not as impossible or incoherent. In a way additional to the one which we
noted earlier—his stressing activity and enterprise as what matters most in human life, and therefore in history—he is projecting
his values upon the historiographical enterprise. In fact, even in
what he has to say simply about inquiry in history being relative
to (non-historiographical) problems of the present, he may be
seen as having, in effect, moved from analysis to prescription:
from a priori argument about what is necessarily involved in
historical reconstruction to exposition of the kind of history of
which he is prepared to approve.[24]

Still a fourth comment concerns broader and narrower ways in
which one might understand Collingwood's contention that the
proper concern of historians is with the past which led to their
own present. Considered in one sense, this may not appear to
limit the historian's subject-matter in any controversial way—
indeed, perhaps not at all, if taken in conjunction with
Collingwood's reminder that the whole of the past must at any
particular time be assumed to have led to the whole of what is
then present (*IH* 247; L28 482). Taking his dictum in a narrower,
but still quite natural sense, however, the implied doctrine is
surely too restrictive. For it may be taken to limit the historian's
subject-matter to those parts of the past which can be shown to
have formed the society to which he belongs, or selected aspects
of it. So conceived, the idea of history becomes the idea of
one's own history—the idea of whatever in the past has led to
oneself or to one's own group—an approach which historians
sometimes call 'Whiggish'. And that would certainly be a good
deal less than would ordinarily be considered the proper task of
historians.

To the extent that Collingwood's slogan issues such an invitation to historical parochialism, his claim that history ought to be
concerned only with the past which led to the present should
surely be resisted. However, there is nothing in his theory of

[24] This in spite of his frequently insisting that the task of philosophy of history
is to make clear what is necessarily the case in historical studies, not simply to
describe desirable practices and emphases (L26 335–7; L28 434–5).

historical understanding as re-enactment, and little in what he says about other aspects of historiography, which lends support to such a position. Collingwood sees skilled historians as achieving re-enactive understanding of past cultures which are quite foreign to, and unconnected with, their own—whose thoughts, to use his own term, are not incapsulated in the present until the historian incapsulates them by reconstructing them. If his conception of the proper scope of history implied otherwise, it is hard to see how he could have represented it as one of the great values of historical study that, in pursuing it, we learn to think in new ways. The only sense in which it could legitimately be said that all history is concerned with what led to the present is that it must be about the past which has deposited evidence of itself in the present. But with that we abandon the empirical and normative issues which we have here found Collingwood considering, to revert to a priori analysis of what historical thinking must be like.

§ 4. *The History of History*

From the fact that historical thinking is presentist, in the sense that the elements of historians' perspectives are all subject to change with the passage of time, Collingwood draws the obvious conclusion that history will constantly be rewritten. Each generation of historians, he says, 'must rewrite history in its own way' (*IH* 248), history being, in consequence, 'a growing and changing body of thoughts, decomposed and recomposed by every new generation of historical writers' (L28 456–7). In historical studies, there is therefore no 'finality' (L26 391), the hope of finality being simply an 'illusion' fostered by textbooks (*IH* 8). The only sense in which an historical work could be final is that it could 'state where our knowledge of its subject stands at the present time' (PH 138). Collingwood sometimes couples certainty with finality (NAPH 44; L26 391–2), but he implicitly distinguishes between them. Van der Dussen has seen as incompatible with Collingwood's denial of finality the frequently noted passage of 'Historical Evidence' in which he asserts that an historian's argument may sometimes prove its point 'as conclusively as a demonstration in mathematics'; also his description of historical inference as 'compulsive', rather than 'permissive' (*IH* 262).[25] However, Collingwood may be presumed to mean only that historical conclusions may be certain or compulsive relative to evidence considered at a particular time. There is no question of his excluding the possibility of a need for revision later, whether because of the discovery of new evidence, or the acceptance of new principles of interpretation, or changes in other elements in historians' points of view.

As Collingwood himself points out, lack of finality raises the question whether scepticism about the possibility of attaining genuine knowledge in history is, after all, justified.[26] In the face of this problem, he sometimes toys with the idea that historians attain only 'relative truth' about the past (L26 391). He sometimes argues, too, that, while final truth is unattainable, that does not mean that one historical account cannot be judged preferable to another, or that any accounts must be regarded as 'arbitrary or capricious' (PH 138–9). While no account, he says, can claim to offer more than 'interim' conclusions, historical inquiry can attain 'genuine knowledge'. At still other times, he at least hints at what may be thought to be an obvious rejoinder to any attempt to base scepticism about history upon its lack of finality, namely, that this is not a peculiarity of history, but is a feature of empirically-based knowledge claims generally. By their very nature, such claims are corrigible in the light of further experience, this being as true of the conclusions of natural science as of the findings of historians. And the parallel with natural science can be made more specific. For in at least some of the ways in which Collingwood represents history as a perspectival type of inquiry, science is perspectival too. Its claims are responses to questions posed, for example, and are formulated in accordance with assumptions and principles of inquiry, all of which change over time.[27]

The common tendency to regard history as perspectival and

---

[25] *IH*, rev. edn., pp. xli–xlii.

[26] Collingwood tends not to distinguish between more and less threatening aspects of changes in points of view. Relativity to questions, which he stresses most, is hardly threatening at all, since answers to different questions are non-competing. Relativity to value schemes or to principles of inquiry may seem more so.

[27] To warrant being conceived differently from natural science in this connection, history would need to be perspectival in a special way. Two elements of historical perspectivity which seem relevant in this regard are its relativity to the historian's position in time (discussed in § 5) and its relativity to value judgments, especially moral ones.

science as not may owe something to the fact that elements of the perspectives of natural scientists do not change as rapidly as do those of historians, nor do scientists disagree about them as extensively as historians frequently do. It is significant that, in *The Idea of Nature*, in tracing the rise of the idea of nature as conceived by scientists, Collingwood feels quite comfortable with a division into three main periods. By contrast, in *The Idea of History*, in tracing the rise of the idea of history as conceived by historians, he finds it necessary, over much the same period of time, to distinguish many more, as well as to concede that different inquirers (sometimes members of opposed 'schools') often worked from contrasting points of view at a given time, with a correspondingly higher incidence of disagreement. It therefore seems fair to say (even post-Kuhn) that, if perspectivity is a problem, it is a greater problem in history than in science. But it cannot be said to be a problem only there; nor does Collingwood so represent it. In a manuscript of 1935, he declares that 'there is no finality in any knowledge whatever'; and he makes no exception even of philosophy (RAH 20).

It ought perhaps to have been enough for Collingwood to argue that lack of finality does not mean that historians cannot have good reasons for preferring some conclusions to others, and even for claiming certainty for some of them, especially when to this is added the reminder that, if claims to have achieved historical knowledge are put in question merely because they are perspectivally presentist, a much more general scepticism threatens. But he offers a further argument against scepticism, and in some respects a rather odd one, when discussing the nature and importance to be ascribed to the history of historical inquiry itself.[28] The fact that history is constantly rewritten, he maintains, 'is not an argument for historical scepticism'. It is 'only the discovery of a second dimension of historical thought, the history of history: the discovery that the historian himself, together with the here-and-now which forms the total body of evidence available to him, is a part of the process he is studying' (*IH* 248). What Collingwood has to say about 'history of the second degree', as he also calls it, is peculiar in two respects (L26 379). It is peculiar,

[28] By this Collingwood means primarily history of historical findings, not history of the principles according to which historical inquiry is conducted (the theme of *IH*, Parts I–IV), although he might resist a sharp separation of the two.

first, in representing history of the second degree not just as useful, but as indispensable to history of the first degree—as an integral part of historical inquiry as such. It is peculiar, second, in pointing to history of history not, as one might have expected, as still another reason for being sceptical about ordinary historical conclusions, but as affording a reason for rejecting scepticism. Let us look briefly at each of these contentions.

As a way of supporting his claim that history of history belongs necessarily to the historian's task, Collingwood is sometimes prepared, as we have seen him doing in some other cases, to advance a merely empirical argument. Remarking that 'an ounce of practice is worth a ton of theory', he notes that historians do engage in history of history as a matter of course, asking not only first-order questions like: 'Why did the Greeks and the Persians fight a battle at Marathon?', but also, as an aspect of the same inquiry, second-order ones like: 'Why have historians expressed such divergent views about the battle of Marathon?' (L26 408). He also argues that history of history is an indispensable enterprise from a cultural point of view. For 'once historical thinking is recognized as a necessary activity of the human mind . . . it follows that the organization and perpetuation of historical thought is a necessary part of the institutions which go to make up civilized life', history of history being, indeed, 'as necessary to civilized man as the history of war or the history of science'. Collingwood thinks this is even more obviously so 'when history itself is objectified into libraries and schools of historical learning'. One cannot say, therefore, 'that the problems of history are of vital interest while those of the history of history are of merely academic interest' (L26 408–9).

But the main case which Collingwood makes for history of history is not empirical or cultural: it is methodological-cum-logical. All history, he says, 'involves and presupposes the history of history' (L28 462); all history is thus a 'report on the progress made in the study of its subject down to the present' (PH 138). Indeed, he alleges that no problem of the first degree can be settled 'until we have settled the problem of the history of its history' (L26 379).[29] For example: 'I cannot compose my monograph on the Peasants' Revolt until after I have completed my

[29] Here is a new sense in which Collingwood, despite his criticism of Hegel on the point, is prepared to say that all history culminates in the present (L26 409).

bibliography of it and studied the works therein contained.' Because the problem 'has been left on my hands by some previous research on the same subject', unless the previous inquiry is reviewed, 'I shall not clearly see what the problem before me is and how it arose' (L28 463).[30]

If Collingwood's aim here were simply to describe what may be involved in good historical practice—to point out a sometimes useful technique which neophyte historians might be expected to pick up from their seniors—this would be unexceptional. But how can he justifiably hold it to be *necessary* that historians thus study the way their predecessors treated their problems, after having more than once remarked that new generations of historians will, and should, ask new questions (*IH* 248; L28 486 n. 18). For he seems to be maintaining, in effect, that only old questions can be adequately treated. In any case, he appears to undermine his own position when he observes that, since historical problems arise 'out of the attempt to understand the world as it stands irrespectively of the existence of any historians', it follows that 'if all historians were guillotined in a revolution and all their books burnt', these problems 'would ensure a speedy revival of historical studies'—apparently without the good offices of history of history (L26 408). Collingwood's most extravagant claims in this connection are made in the lectures of 1926 and 1928. What is said in *The Idea of History* is more nuanced, previous histories being represented there simply as good 'starting points' for further historical work (*IH* 280). In the *Autobiography*, too, his position is put only normatively in the remark that 'no historical problem should be studied without studying . . . its second-order history' (*A* 132). To which, however, it still needs to be added: 'if it had a second-order history'.

But how is the historian's involvement in history of history, whether this is considered indispensable or only highly advisable, thought by Collingwood to yield a response to scepticism? The benefits which he specifically ascribes to second-order history in this connection are in fact fairly modest. One is that close attention to the way previous historians have treated a problem will make it less likely that past errors will be repeated. Another

---

[30] Atkinson has charged that Collingwood 'fails to allow for the way in which an historian's problems typically arise from the works of his predecessors' (*KEH* 25). Here, at least, he seems to allow for it far too much.

is that such study will help to clarify the nature of the problem being dealt with. Even these benefits are put somewhat in question by an argument which Collingwood himself anticipates and claims to rebut, namely, that if one cannot address an historical problem until its own history has been studied, it will surely be necessary to say the same of the problems of history of history. As Collingwood himself remarks, an historian like Mommsen is 'just as much an historical personage as Julius Caesar' (L26 381), and what he wrote is now a relic to be interpreted like anything else that has come down to us from the past. In consequence, an infinite regress threatens, which would seem to exclude the possibility of any successful historical inquiry at all.

Collingwood's response to this can only be described as lame. All history, he reminds us, 'works backwards from the present'. Thus history of history 'is an easier study than history, in so far as the historians who are there the objects of our study stand closer to ourselves and are more open to our inspection than the persons about whom they write'. 'The psychology of Mommsen', Collingwood continues, 'is easier to grasp than the psychology of Julius Caesar', since 'he was a modern European' (L26 381–2). The same advantage holds, he maintains, with regard to our gaining knowledge of more remote historians by contrast with those about whom they wrote. In addition, second-degree history is not only 'better documented', but also 'has a kind of directness or immediacy, by contrast with which history of the first degree is always indirect and inferential'.[31]

It is hard to see how how the fundamental distinction which Collingwood thus tries to draw between interpreting the works of historians as relics of the past and interpreting relics of other kinds, literary or otherwise, can survive what he says elsewhere about the way historical conclusions must be grounded in a critical study of evidence. Indeed, what he says about documents produced by earlier historians being 'easier' for their successors to interpret than those originating in other ways comes close to accepting the intuitive theory of knowledge which, in his later writings, he repudiated with contumely—or, short of that, at any rate to countenancing the acceptance of mere 'testimony'. At the very least, he attributes too much to the idea of there being an

---

[31] As noted in Ch. 7, Collingwood even speaks in this connection of becoming 'acquainted' with past historians.

'affinity' between historians working at different times which he thinks missing from the relations between historians and agents of other kinds. Happily, the problem which leads him into such complications, the threat of an infinite regress, is not a genuine one. It arises only if one begins by accepting the exaggerated value which he ascribes to what is really no more than a sometimes useful methodological procedure.

§ 5. *Presentism and Retrospectivity*

We have been considering Collingwood's doctrine that what historians offer is always a view of the past from a present vantage-point. This makes history an essentially retrospective sort of inquiry. It also makes it a highly corrigible one, changes in the perspectives which historians bring to their work ensuring that it will constantly be rewritten from ever-new 'present' standpoints.

A minor qualification of this doctrine might be noted with regard to re-enactive explanation. To the extent that historians' points of view are taken to include, say, the evidence available to them and the principles of inquiry they regarded as appropriate, then, clearly, changes in their perspectives may require 'second thoughts', and sometimes quite radical ones, about why certain actions were performed. Revisionist studies of Stalin's policy of mass terror might be a case in point.[32] Changes in historians' conceptual systems or schemes of values, however, will generally have more limited implications, since what re-enactive understanding requires is mainly reference to the concepts and values of the agent. The question why Caesar crossed the Rubicon, for example, ought not to be answered differently by conservative and liberal historians, to the extent that both claim to be re-enacting the agent's thoughts. Where explanations are not re-enactive, or are not primarily so, changes in elements of historians' points of view will clearly, at times, require changes in the explanation. If declining agricultural productivity in Rome is judged by a modern historian to owe something to changing climatic conditions, this may be a conclusion which neither those who suffered the decline, nor most of the historians who came

---

[32] On this, see Skagestad, *Making Sense*, 99 ff.

after them, could have reached because they lacked the appropriate theoretical resources. Even re-enactive explanations may sometimes be revisable from the standpoint of knowledge or expertise not possessed by the original agents, as when unconscious motives or beliefs are attributed which it may have been beyond the intellectual horizons of the original agents to discern.

Changes in historians' perspectives will also sometimes require changes in how the past is characterized, and sometimes in ways going quite beyond the conceptions of the original agents. Collingwood himself makes a revisionary judgment of this kind when he says of Kant that, although, in his critical philosophy, he considered himself to be discovering metaphysical truths about the world a priori, what he was really doing was reconstructing and exhibiting the absolute presuppositions of the science of his time (*EM* 243–4). This is a judgment which could not have been made before the formulation of the Collingwoodian theory of metaphysics as presuppositional history. Collingwood contends similarly that the writings of those who, in the eighteenth century, undertook to write universal history, and, in his judgment, did it badly, should be understood less as 'summaries of work done' than as 'forecasts, and in the main fairly accurate forecasts, of the line which historical inquiry was to follow in the next few generations' (L28 454). Walsh has objected that what Collingwood says about Kant is not a truly historical claim; for what it tells us is what he thinks Kant *ought* to have said, such a judgment being critical in a sense which is irrelevant to knowing what the past was really like—quite different, for example, from the way in which re-enactive explanations need to be internally critical.[33] But Collingwood could surely argue—and does implicitly argue— that we cannot equate the way the past was with the way Kant or any original agent thought it was. What he is claiming for historians is the right, from their more privileged, hindsighted, vantage-point, to have 'the last word' about what it was that happened (at any rate, for the time being).

But historians commonly make judgments about past actions and happenings which are retrospective in a stronger sense than is illustrated by such cases. They often do this, for example, when they try to show the significance or importance of what occurred;

---

[33] Walsh, 'Collingwood and Metaphysical Neutralism', 137.

for this characteristically involves taking into account what came later.

Not all judgments of significance or importance, it must be allowed, are retrospective in this sense. An example of one which is not is Collingwood's declaration that, to understand the significance of an edict of the Theodosian Code, one needs, as Fain has argued (*BPH* 271), to grasp not just the meaning of the words, but also the purposes which the emperor had in promulgating it (*IH* 283). Another, although not employing the word 'significance', is Collingwood's describing Caesar's crossing of the Rubicon as 'a defiance of Republican law' (*IH* 231).[34] In the first of these cases, grasping significance is virtually equated with achieving re-enactive understanding of why an act was performed. In the second, it goes beyond that, pointing to ideas which, although they could be said to have been expressed by the action performed, were not among the agent's reasons for acting as he did. However, the significance which Caesar's action had as an illegal act, is still a significance which it had *at the time*. What historians' judgments of significance more commonly affirm is a significance which actions or events, by virtue of their consequences, have accumulated *through time*. When the task is to explain re-enactively, or even nomologically, why something happened or was done, references to subsequent events are, of course, absolutely excluded. It is precisely upon such references, however, that historians' judgments of significance normally turn. The most tentative of them are made with regard to the immediate success or failure of actions or enterprises, calling something a victory or a defeat, for example, at least beginning to consider the results of what the agents intended. The significance which will be ascribed to something like Henry VIII's dissolution of the monasteries or to Hitler's invasion of the Soviet Union can be expected to reach much further into their futures.

In cases of this sort, the idea that historians undertake their inquiries from a point of view acquires an entirely new dimension. Perspectival elements like systems of concepts or values are, of course, time-bound in the sense that they are held, and brought to bear upon the interpretation of the past, at particular times. But judgments of significance which take account of what happened

[34] See Ch. 2, § 4.

after an event's occurrence bring time into the equation in a further way. If historians are to judge the significance of events by reference to what they led to, their conclusions will be relative not just to the ideas which they bring to their work, but to the actual course of history up to the time of their judgment. Retrospective judgments of significance will change not just with changes in historians, but with changes in the process studied, which continually terminates at a different point. The consideration at issue in such cases could therefore be said to be an 'objective' one in a sense in which none of the other elements of historians' points of view can be said to be. It might be noted that, although changes in retrospective judgments of significance cannot be a basis for changing re-enactive explanations, they can be a basis for changing descriptions, historians sometimes incorporating a retrospectively discerned significance into a redescription of an event. Collingwood furnishes a perhaps only half-serious example of this when, looking back, he describes his erstwhile 'realist' colleagues as 'the propagandists of a coming Fascism' (*A* 167). It need scarcely be added that, for an indeterminist like Collingwood, a significance thus dependent upon subsequent events will be something not only unknown to the agents, but in principle unknowable to them.

The notion that the significance of an event derives to some extent from what happened later, and, in principle, from whatever has happened up to the time of inquiry, gives new point to some of Collingwood's otherwise troubling turns of speech. It gives a literal meaning, for example, to his observation that historians writing at different times have different pasts to write about (PH 139; IH 247; IN 274–5). His justification for saying this in the present context is quite different, of course, from the one which he offers for the same conclusion when considering the doctrine of ideality (Ch. 7, § 6). It is not that, at every moment, historians may construct a new and different 'historical' past, but that, at every moment, they will have an extension of the real past to consider. The perceptual parallel also takes on a greater appropriateness with regard to retrospective judgments of significance, even if it still needs cautious treatment. For the idea of historians being able to 'see' objects of interest only from the 'position' or 'location' or 'place' or 'vantage-point' which they 'occupy' in the historical process acquires something closer to a literal sense than it had when applied to historians' conclusions having to be drawn in accordance with the beliefs and principles held by them at particular times and places.[35] The fact that historians make retrospective judgments of significance also, of course, strengthens the case for saying that history will constantly be rewritten. For although one may plausibly say this on the ground that historians will probably change their relevant beliefs and values, or that their successors will probably have different ones, it is even more plausible to say it on the ground that, since the past which is potentially relevant to their conclusions constantly changes, their judgments of significance will probably change too.

Two cautions might be noted. First, one cannot say a priori that what is relevant to judging the retrospective significance of an earlier event will include later happenings right down to the historian's present. As J. H. Hexter has remarked, the consequences of something like the Treaty of Madrid of 1527 'pretty well finished their unfolding a good while back'.[36] But even if the consequences of some such events have in fact petered out, the historian's own position in time remains the ultimate point of reference for retrospective judgments of their significance. Whether or not the consequences of a given event have run their course is something to be discovered empirically. A second caution is that, as was noted in the case of other perspectival elements, historians may occasionally want to make judgments of significance from past standpoints rather than from their own—judgments relative to past presents rather than to present presents. For making clear the significance or importance which has accrued to certain happenings up to a point in the past which is under study may be an aid to understanding the experience and actions of those living at that time. These, however, are not the kinds of judgments which mainly structure their own accounts of what happened.

[35] Changes of available evidence are analogous to seeing further parts of an object in space, changes of value judgment to looking at it through glasses of a different colour, changes of terminal date to seeing it from one location rather than from another.
[36] *Reappraisals in History* (London, 1961), 12. I assume that what is meant by 'consequence' here is what historians ordinarily mean by it, not just something for which an earlier event was a necessary condition. On this distinction, see Hart and Honoré, *Causation in the Law*, 64 ff. As Collingwood himself observes, all events (from signing Magna Carta to filling a pen) have consequences, but only some make them 'historical', i.e. historically significant (NHH 48).

It is easy to find Collingwood making judgments of significance or importance of the retrospective sort in his own historical work, judgments which apply the idea that the measure of importance in history is found in consequences accrued. For example, when he observes that the trade routes across the Channel between Normandy and Hampshire 'increased in importance during the Bronze Age and the earlier phases of the Iron Age', the reason he gives is that 'they were the main agents in developing the Late Bronze Age and La Tène I civilizations of the Wessex uplands' (RBES 15). Consequential importance seems also to be what he has in mind when he remarks, of Domitian's recall of Agricola from Britain in 84–5, that the emperor thought that 'establishing a satisfactory frontier-line through the forests of Germany' was 'a more important piece of work than the completion of Agricola's conquests in Britain'—adding that 'there is no doubt that he was right' (RB 24). Meshing well with such examples from Collingwood's historical writings is his commendation of Vico for promoting the idea that 'what makes a past period of history worth studying' is 'its relation to the general course of history' (IH 68).

It is therefore something of a surprise to find that, when, as a philosopher, Collingwood comes to discuss the idea of import-ance itself, and the role it can legitimately play in historiography, what he has to say is somewhat elusive. He considers the issue most directly in examining the views of Eduard Meyer (IH 178–80; NHH 46–56). Meyer explicates the idea of importance in history as 'efficacy in producing further events'. The more efficacious an event is in this sense, he maintains, the more important it can be said to be. Collingwood responds to this with two arguments, neither of which is very satisfactory.[37]

He argues, first, that to conceive importance in history in this way is to treat historical events as if they formed causal series—to lapse into a positivistic or naturalistic view of the historical pro-cess (this despite Meyer's own criticism of positivism). Earlier historical events, he insists, never determine later ones (IH 180; NHH 49). But this response ignores the fact that historical events can be said to have consequences where the causal relation is

---

[37] Collingwood rejects Meyer's position despite admitting that there are 'em-pirical arguments' to justify it (NHH 47)—presumably meaning that historians can be found pursuing their inquiries in accordance with it.

rational rather than naturalistic—where the term 'cause' bears the special historical sense which Collingwood insists upon at other points. An event like the French Revolution may be judged historically important because of the way people, throughout the nineteenth century, continued to respond to the ideas it represented, even though they were not determined by them. Collingwood argues, secondly, that to derive the importance of an historical event from its consequences is either circular or opens an infinite regress which eventually deprives the notion of all content (*IH* 179; *NHH* 48). For judging an event to be important because of its consequences surely presupposes the importance of the consequences: an event could hardly be judged important because it led to 'consequences themselves devoid of historical importance'. But the importance of consequences cannot coherently be taken to derive, in turn, from their own consequences *ad infinitum*. The only way to stop the regress, Collingwood allows, is to recognize at least some consequences as being important because of their own nature: important intrinsically, not consequentially.[38] But he explicitly rejects this escape from the problem on the ground that intrinsic importance is an idea of which we can give no account (*NHH* 9).

Yet, although he thus brushes aside the notion of intrinsic importance as unacceptable in theory, he does not deny himself the use of it in practice. In *The Idea of History*, for example, he maintains that the historical importance of the philosophy of Spinoza derives from the fact that we can 'appreciate its philosophical value', and see it as 'a noteworthy achievement of the seventeenth-century mind', rather than from the fact, say, that Novalis or Hegel or others who came after him studied it (*IH* 179). In other words, its importance is to be found in its intrinsic intellectual value, not in its influence, Collingwood observing that it would have been important even if it had remained relatively unknown. In his historical writings, too, the idea of intrinsic importance frequently appears without any hint that it is at all problematic. For example, we are told that Cirencester, originally a tribal capital, became a Roman centre because of 'its size and intrinsic importance', the latter deriving from the fact that the town was 'a rich and splendid one' (*RB* 69). And when Tacitus is taken to task

---

[38] Judgments of intrinsic importance will still, of course, be relative to schemes of values; but the issue here is whether they are relative to consequences.

for 'scornfully' dismissing the ten years after Boudicca's rebellion as 'a time of peace, when Roman arms were gaining no glory in frontier-wars, and Roman governors were disgracing their office by conciliating their subjects', Collingwood's objection is clearly to his conception of what is important in itself, not of what is important because of what it led to (*RBES* 105).

It might be added that Collingwood's historical writings, like those of most historians, also contain judgments of importance which are neither intrinsic nor consequential. Thus Silchester is said to be a site of great importance because 'no town in Britain could have given us fuller and more precise evidence for the character of Romano-British urban life at its best' (*RBES* 189). Here importance is ascribed to something because of what it reveals or represents, not because of its own nature or any consequential fertility which it may have had. And when Collingwood remarks, with respect to certain mutinies put down by Pertinax in 185, that 'the real importance of these outbreaks lies in the fact that they foretold a new civil war', still another sense of importance, commonly asserted by historians, is exemplified (*RBES* 154).[39] In this case, what is said to make an event important is neither what it is, nor what it causes, but what it anticipates or foreshadows—a kind of connection made discernible by the historian's gift of hindsight. But both of these further types of importance, like the consequential variety, presuppose a certain relationship to something else judged to be intrinsically important.

In addition to the two arguments which he aims at Meyer, Collingwood occasionally expresses reservations about the role or meaning of the concept of importance in historical studies in other ways. At one point he seems almost to dismiss it, if not as meaningless, then at any rate as 'indefinable' (L27 356); and at another he declares that what makes a fact historically important 'is a question that cannot be answered' (RNI 56). At still another point, he takes most of the interest out of judgments of importance by claiming that, since everything is 'contributory', everything is equally important. 'There is no real distinction of greater and lesser importance in history', he avers; 'the "crucial" inci-

[39] The sense of 'foretold' is not consequential, but approximates to what historians call 'foreshadowing'. In the same sense, Collingwood represents Celtic art as important partly because of the way it anticipated later English art (*RB* 121).

dents are only those whose crucial character we happen to be able to see' (NAPH 39). This curious contention seems to rest upon confusing what is necessary with what is important. Collingwood also sometimes implies that judgments of importance, although meaningful, are subjective in some questionable sense. To say that something is of historical importance because it influenced other things, which in turn influenced others all the way down to the historian's own present, he maintains, is 'only a muddled way of saying that historical importance means importance for us' (NHV 13).

The latter idea—which at least concedes that occurrences may be more or less important, and may sometimes be of no import-ance at all—takes several forms. The most obvious—that what is important is what is relevant, i.e. instrumental, to our own prac-tical life in the present—is the least characteristic. Another is that the important is simply what happens to interest us—something, for example, which we happen to want presently to re-enact, or which just is, in fact, re-enactable (NHV 13). Still another, and an alternative which commends itself especially to Collingwood be-cause of his stress upon the role of questioning in inquiry, is that the historically important is what answers the questions which historians want to ask (NHH 50). 'The importance of the Megarian Decrees', he says, 'consists not in their having caused the Peloponnesian War, but in their providing the answer (or part of the answer) to [the historian's] question' (NHH 52).[40] In this essentially methodologically-based sense, a judgment of import-ance becomes relative to a problem posed more than to a position occupied in time. This seems to be the sense which Collingwood employs when, after explaining the difference between the agri-cultural systems in Roman Britain based on village and villa, he says that 'the distinction between these two types of settlement is of fundamental importance' (RBES 209). He presumably means importance for understanding the economic system of the province.

There are occasional hints of two other positions taken by Collingwood on this difficult matter. When he remarks that 'the state of the weather at the battle of Trafalgar is important to the naval historian because it was important to Villeneuve and

---

[40] Despite Collingwood's implied either/or, two dimensions of importance seem to be instantiated here at the same time.

Nelson', for example, the implication seems to be that, in history, 'important' means 'important to the agents concerned'. The criterion thus advanced is peculiar, however, in representing historians themselves as making no judgments of importance at all in the sense in which historical agents are conceded to make them. A further, and I think the best, position makes a fleeting appearance when Collingwood equates what is historically important with 'what we think worth studying' (L28 470 n. 16). This at least suggests a recognition that, if 'important' is to have a satisfactory meaning in history, it must have it, at least in part, as a value term. Collingwood's occasionally remarking that the concern of history is with what is 'memorable' in the human past points in the same direction.

As might be expected, the reservations thus expressed by Collingwood about the use of the idea of importance in history extend to the related idea of selection. It might ordinarily be assumed that the task of historians, generally speaking, is to select, and to study further, what they see as important about past actions, events, and states of affairs, putting the rest aside. But Collingwood questions the very intelligibility of the idea that historians select. To say that, in reconstructing the past, they select some facts and not others, he says, implies that a totality of facts is somehow 'given' to them. But there is no given totality of facts—or even of known facts, or of evidence available, or of problems to be solved.[41] There is thus no answer to the question: 'From what does the historian select?' (NHH 52–3; also L26 356). Yet, in the inaugural lecture, Collingwood lists selection as one of the three operations of 'critical' history which make evident the historian's autonomy as an inquirer (IH 236). And in a manuscript of 1936, he states it as obvious that historians 'select from the infinite welter of things that have happened the things that are worth thinking about' (CHBI 12). In his historical writings, he takes it for granted that selection is one aspect of the historian's reconstructive task. In his main work on Romano-British history, for example, he observes: 'The history of Britain in the Roman period is primarily the history of its partial conquest and occupation by Rome' (RBES 5). This presumably means that, in Collingwood's selective judgment, it is not primarily the history

---

[41] Collingwood is nevertheless prepared to say that historians select questions or lines of inquiry to pursue (NHH 55), which seems open to similar objections.

of the decline of Celtic art, or of the first appearance of a considerable urban population on the island. It seems fair to say that the more conventional view of selection in history, which Collingwood expresses in the inaugural lecture, is the better considered one.

§ 6. *Retrospective Historical Understanding*

In Chapter 6, it was argued that the conception of historical understanding which has generally been attributed to Collingwood requires expansion in view of what he has to say about the interest of historians in reconstructing large-scale wholes, this giving it a synthetic or whole-istic dimension as well as a re-enactive one. What we now find him saying about the perspectivity and presentism of historical judgment makes necessary still a further expansion of the original theory. For, besides being re-enactive and synthetic, historical understanding is also often retrospective—and this not only in the sense of projecting back upon the past the concepts, values, assumptions, and so on, of the historian, as well as taking account of those of the agents, but also in the stronger sense of making clear the significance which has accrued to certain actions and events up to the time of the historian's judgment.

The further sense of understanding which thus emerges is one which might well be seen as having a better claim to be considered a specifically historical way of understanding things than either the re-enactive or the synthetic sorts. For the task of historical study is often described as that of putting things 'into historical perspective', where by this is meant, in part, making clear the relation of envisaged past events and conditions to what came after them. What could be more natural than to regard a procedure which ascertains the 'place' occupied by something in an ongoing historical process as a 'distinctively historical' mode of understanding? Retrospective understanding, like synthetic, is not, of course, a matter of seeing *why* things happened as they did, the question 'Why?' not being answerable by reference to subsequent events. It is a form of understanding, again like the synthetic sort, which responds to a question 'What?'—perhaps 'What did it come to in the end?' But we have already abandoned, on

Collingwood's behalf (whether or not he was always clear on the point himself), the idea that all attempts to make an historical subject-matter intelligible must take the form of explanations why.

When historians themselves talk of putting things into historical perspective, or of understanding things historically, what they have in mind is quite often the sort of thing just indicated. However, this is not invariably the case. Robert Ashton, for example, wishing to criticize the Whig–Marxist view of early seventeenth-century English history, which he thinks *too* retrospective, contrasts it with 'the historical' view of it, meaning by this something closer to the way it was viewed by the original agents.[42] The idea of understanding things historically also sometimes means, for historians, seeing past events from more than one perspective: for example, from the perspectives of both the agents and the historian, or even from the differing perspectives of agents who were in conflict. In such cases, the idea of placing things in historical perspective becomes the idea of doing justice to all viewpoints: the idea of being comprehensive, or, at any rate, fair. An example would be Christopher Hill's saying of Cromwell's harsh behaviour in Ireland: 'we must try to get the campaign into historical perspective, and try to see it through the eyes of Cromwell and his contemporaries as well as those of posterity.'[43] Collingwood himself, having signified his approval of the dictum that the historian 'must make every point of view his own' (CPH 16), often takes the trouble, *qua* historian, to make clear at least two contemporary points of view on what he is depicting: that of Caesar as well as of the Britons, for example; of Roman artists as well as of Celtic ones; of Roman historians as well as of their successors. But even where putting the past into historical perspective means appreciating the diversity of the ways in which it can be regarded, a presentist, retrospective way is generally one of them.

Notwithstanding this, Collingwood has sometimes been accused of neglecting the retrospective dimension of historical understanding. According to Walsh, his placing re-enactment at the centre of the historian's task requires the turning of a 'blind eye' to the effects of past actions. It allegedly ignores the fact that

---

[42] *The English Civil War* (London, 1978), 17, 25. Weinryb notes how 'deeply rooted' this idea is among some historians ('Re-enactment in Retrospect', 572).

[43] *God's Englishman* (London, 1972), 113.

historians, who generally know the future of the past they study, want to see what happened 'in relation both to what went before and to what came after'.[44] John Higham has complained similarly that Collingwood's view of history, which he takes to include 'nothing but the re-enactment of past thought', ignores the fact that 'an adequate historical explanation should include a retrospective knowledge of consequences and conditions that the actual participants did not have'.[45] Fain has contrasted Collingwoodian history, which he describes as 'centred almost exclusively on discovering a historical agent's conscious reasons for acting the way he did', with what he calls Hegelian history, which is 'concerned, primarily, with evaluating the historical significance of actions', and which he considers more profound (*BPH* 271). Such criticism is no doubt invited by Collingwood's often referring to re-enactment as if it alone counted as historical thinking, a misleading impression which he does not correct by discussing in any sustained way the idea of retrospective understanding. Yet, even if that idea must therefore be regarded as still another of Mink's 'recessive' ones, it is only fair to say that it is signalled by much of what Collingwood has to say on other matters.

How, then, should someone interested not just in criticizing, but in reconstructing, and perhaps developing, Collingwood's account of history conceive the relationship between the ideas of understanding as retrospective appraisal and as re-enactment? A point to be stressed is that, as was true also of synthetic understanding, the two do not simply represent alternative, and perhaps to some extent opposed, ways of approaching the problem of understanding the past. For retrospective understanding, again like synthetic, commonly presupposes a prior grasp of what it was that various agents did. One cannot judge the significance of an action, or of an historical event which consists at least partly of actions, without knowing what the relevant actions were, both inside and outside; and that entails re-enacting the agents' thoughts.[46] Retrospective understanding is thus not only

[44] 'Colligatory Concepts in History', in Burston and Thompson (eds.), *Studies in the Nature and Teaching of History*, 67.

[45] Higham, *History*, 143–4.

[46] This disposes of a criticism of Collingwood by Marrou that the historian's business is to see the past 'as past', not (as he takes Collingwood to advocate) to try to 'resurrect' it as it once was (*Meaning of History*, 45).

compatible with understanding of the re-enactive kind, but, like synthetic, may incorporate it. If I only say 'may', it is because retrospective understanding can be sought not only of actions done in the past, but of anything that happened. It can thus play a role in natural history, as well as in the study of the human past. If retrospective understanding deserves to be called a 'specifically historical' sort, it is not, therefore, because of any exclusive suitability to the kind of subject-matter which interests those we commonly call historians. Yet the fact that it can also be sought in natural history might be considered as enhancing, not diminishing, its claim to be considered a specifically historical sort of understanding. To put it in Collingwoodian terms, it could be regarded as distinctive to history conceived in its most general sense as a study of the sum total of what has happened, taken in its individuality.

Since, in the case of human history, retrospective understanding can incorporate the re-enactive understanding of actions, one cannot properly say, as some critics of Collingwood like Strauss have said, that it represents, in effect, a lapse into what Collingwood himself rejected as a spectator's approach to the human past.[47] Retrospective understanding does not replace the 'inside' view which Collingwood insisted upon; it gives it its due, even while supplementing it. And even then, the supplementation does not entail adopting a spectator's view in the sense which Collingwood often gave to that term, namely, regarding what happened either as a collection of atomic facts or as instantiations of laws.

The relationship of retrospective understanding to understanding of the synthetic sort is also worth noting explicitly. With regard to our present concerns, the crucial point is this: that, just as re-enactments may enter into synthetic judgment as aspects or elements of it, so may retrospective judgments of significance play a role in synthetic reconstruction. As Leff has observed, it is 'only by standing outside events—in being wise after them— that the historian is enabled to see them whole' (HST 26). And Collingwood himself remarks that, in history, 'something has taken shape . . . which certainly was not present to . . . the mind of any one, when the actions which brought it into existence began'

[47] Strauss, 'On Collingwood's Philosophy of History', 575.

(*IH* 42). When discussing the reconstruction of social wholes, it was noted that what historians often claim to discern is something which went on 'over the heads' of the agents concerned. But what was then envisaged was the common failure of historical agents to discern the social wholes in which they participated as they existed at the time. Since social wholes may also be reconstructed as things coming into existence over time—for example, as developments—it needs now to be recognized that they will often be beyond the consciousness of the agents in a more radical sense—beyond it for metaphysical reasons, not just because of limited perception. The colligation of wholes like the Industrial Revolution or the Romantic movement, for example, requires retrospective judgments of significance at least from the standpoints of the past presents in which these processes are alleged to have ended. However, in regarding those endings *as* endings, historians will also make retrospective judgments from the standpoint of their own present, since they will implicitly claim that nothing happened thereafter which can properly be regarded as continuing them.

When considering the reconstruction of social wholes, some attention was given to Collingwood's view of periodization. It will be clear that the retrospectivity of historical judgment can be of importance for dividing history into periods. This is perhaps most obviously the case with regard to what Collingwood calls a priori periodization, a distinction between ancient, medieval, and modern, for example, taking the historian's own present as a temporal reference point. But the discerning of substantive periods, like the Feudal or Romantic period, also requires retrospective judgment in the sense that the historian must identify endings as well as beginnings, which again implies that, after a certain date, nothing more happened which was relevant to their constitution. Retrospective judgments play an even more prominent role, however, in another fundamental technique of historiography: narrative-construction. Since the place of narrative in history has been a major focus of interest for philosophers of history in recent years, it may be of interest to look briefly at what Collingwood has to say about the kind of understanding which historical narration can achieve.

Collingwood uses the word 'narrative' rather freely in his philosophical writings on history, often talking as if we can

simply take it for granted that historical conclusions assume the
form of narratives. The historian's business, he says in the lectures
of 1926, is 'constructing a narrative'; narrative is the 'finished
product' of historical inquiry; history 'consists of nothing whatever but narrative' (L26 389–91). Like the novelist, he says later in
the inaugural lecture, the historian 'has a story to tell' (*IH* 28–9,
33; RNI 37). And at many other points, it is either said or assumed
that narration is the historian's central object.[48] It is hardly surprising, therefore, that Collingwood has often been considered what
is now sometimes called a 'narrativist' philosopher of history.[49]
Yet he nowhere offers a full-scale analysis of narrative as a genre:
he never sets out to elucidate what has sometimes been referred to
as 'the logic of narration', this despite the long section entitled
'Narrative' which he included in his lectures of 1926, and another
on the same topic in the lectures of 1928 under the title 'Relation',
in which he remarks on the need to elucidate the 'inner structure'
of what historians narrate (L28 478). Although he has no worked-
out theory of narrative, however, his writings contain many elements of such a theory, some of them pointing to just the sorts of
considerations which later 'narrativist' philosophers of history
have thought it especially important to stress.[50]

Collingwood draws no explicit distinction between narrative
and mere chronicle, the point from which explications of the
structural nature of narratives often begin; but the idea is implicit
in his declaration that narrative 'is not an enumeration of distinct
events but a statement of their relations or articulations' (L26
419).[51] A narrative evidently goes beyond chronicle in asserting
serial connectedness. Sometimes, as he does in other contexts,
Collingwood puts the connectedness of narratives too strongly,
saying that their task is to show that 'all the elements hang
together in such a way that each of necessity leads on to or arises
out of the rest' (RNI 39).[52] More plausibly, he asserts that narratives must present an 'orderly sequence of events' (L28 472 ff.), or
display continuity (*IH* 36, 245), this leaving room for the idea that

[48] See e.g. HSD 32; NAPH 48; L26 385; PH 129; *EPM* 208; RNI 9.
[49] See e.g. Hayden White, *Tropics of Discourse* (Baltimore, 1978), 83 ff.
[50] Noted by van der Dussen (*IH*, rev. edn., p. xlvii).
[51] See also L28 476–8; NAPH 36; NTM A-68–9. Collingwood sometimes uses
'chronicle' in the unrelated sense of an account based upon mere testimony (*IH*
202–4).
[52] See also NAPH 36; NTM A-68–9.

they may legitimately display connections of a much looser kind. Collingwood also holds that a narrative must have unity of subject, this anticipating a point stressed by Morton White.[53] There must be, he says, 'one thing that develops' (L28 472, 478). Little is said about the basis on which aspects or elements of a chosen subject may gain entrance into a narrative, other than their having to be integrated with those already there. But in saying of Polybius that, 'like all real historians', he had 'a story of notable and memorable things' to tell (*IH* 33), Collingwood seems not entirely averse to the idea that a role may be played in this connection by the value judgments of the historian. He observes also that, beyond their actual story lines, historical narratives presuppose (sometimes he says contain) background information needed to make the story fully intelligible: for example, descriptions of situations, analyses of characters, diagnoses of motivations (*IH* 245; RNI 37). The ensemble of background information and story line he sometimes refers to as 'the picture' (RNI 37).

But Collingwood has more interesting things to say about the structure of narratives than that they must have a central subject, show events leading to each other, and express value judgments. He also ascribes to them a synthetic, whole-istic dimension. The events recounted in a narrative, he says, must constitute an 'organized coherent whole' (NAPH 36): 'what appears chronologically as a sequence must appear as a simultaneous whole in the historian's thought' (L28 478). He seems here to have in mind more than their forming connected series, but in what respects? Some contemporary philosophers of history have put the whole-istic quality of narratives, at the most general level, as the requirement that what is recounted be shown to have a beginning, middle, and end. Collingwood does not quite say this: indeed, at one point he argues that, in history, there are no beginnings—or, at any rate, only relative ones—and no endings either, short of the present (NHV 10, 12). He nevertheless finds acceptable enough the traditional distinction between ancient, medieval, and modern, which is a more particular version of this pattern, declaring it, indeed, to articulate 'the necessary structure of all historical narrative' (L26 416). And he concedes that historical monographs at

[53] Morton White, *Foundations*, 222 ff.

any rate, like Aristotle's tragedies, must have beginnings, middles, and ends (L28 469–70). What narratives recount is also said to have the whole-istic characteristic of being analysable into phases, steps, stages, and so on—or, as Collingwood also calls them, 'epicycles'. What narratives trace, he says, is developments; and a development 'implies a plurality of phases within the process' (L28 478–9).

From the standpoint of our present concerns, the most interesting thing about Collingwood's embryonic analysis of narrative structure is his recognition that narratives are a vehicle of retrospective historical understanding. The elements of a narrative, he maintains, must be more than just connected; they must be connected in a way which could be described as reciprocal (L28 471). The historian must depict 'the earlier phases as preparing the way for the later, and the later as explaining the true meaning of the earlier' (L28 478). Each phase must be seen as 'the fruit of what has gone before and the seed of what is to come' (L28 478). In other words, narrative intelligibility is established not only by explanatory judgments, but also by judgments of significance, the latter requiring the historian to take up a retrospective standpoint. It is to a considerable extent from such a standpoint that selection into a narrative is made—a point well illustrated by Collingwood's own account of the history of historiography in *The Idea of History*, which, as has often been remarked, is really an attempt to show the steps by which, and the circumstances despite which, his own conception of history as a re-enactment of past experience came into being. Beard has accused him of 'sowing' his own ideas in the earlier part of the book; but given the story of their emergence which he wants to tell, he can hardly avoid looking for their prototypes or their antecedents.[54] The characterizations given by historians also frequently reflect a retrospective standpoint: they describe what happened in ways which relate it to future developments already known to the historian.[55] Relevant examples from Collingwood's histories of Roman Britain are his declaring that, with the recall of Agricola in 84, Rome's 'last chance of completing the conquest of Britain was lost' (*RB* 23), or his describing the barbarian crossing of the Antonine Wall in force about 184 as 'the death-knell of an age', the

[54] Review of *IH*, in *American Historical Review*, 52 (1947), 704.
[55] Danto calls these 'narrative sentences' (*Narration and Knowledge*, ch. 8).

initiative (as Collingwood hastens to inform his readers) passing thereafter from the Romans to their enemies (*RBES* 151).

As an aid to conveying his conception of the nature of understanding through narrative, Collingwood at one point calls upon an analogy from music—and he makes a better use of it than he does of a similar analogy when first explicating the idea of reenactment (L28 441). As some later philosophers of history have also done, he points to 'a certain resemblance between the chronological structure of an historical monograph, and the rhythmical structure of a symphony' (L28 477–8). That structure, he says, serves 'to articulate the symphony as a whole'; for it is 'only when we have the whole before us . . . with its successive parts so interpenetrating one another that each colours the rest and gives them their peculiar significance', that we can really grasp its nature. The hearer must 'overcome' the difference in time 'by being conscious of all the parts at once'. Collingwood maintains that 'the substance of an historical monograph must be simultaneously experienced the same way'. One of the techniques by which historians promote such synthesizing experience is their practice of alternating between re-enactive and retrospective standpoints in what they say about a subject-matter. Particular narrative histories may stress one side or other of this 'Janus face' of history, as Leff calls it (*HST* 24); but it is doubtful that any of them succeeds in entirely eliminating the other.

It is clear that the kind of understanding which a full-fledged narrative achieves, tracing out wholes with parts and aspects which have a temporal spread, can be expected to go well beyond what the original agents could have known. To an even greater extent than the delineation of cross-sectional wholes, therefore, they will direct attention to significances which transcend re-enactive understanding.

§ 7. *Reality and Anachronism*

The idea that historians, especially in the narratives they elaborate, convey, among other things, an understanding of the past which legitimately changes with the passage of time, has sometimes been thought to raise special problems for the status of history as a form of inquiry. By way of conclusion, let me briefly consider two of them, one metaphysical, the other epistemological, or, as some might say, methodological.

The first problem arises if we ask about the relationship between historians' claims to achieve retrospective understanding from present points of view and the Rankean notion that their goal is knowledge of the past as it really was. Collingwood, writing as an historian, describes the breaching of the Antonine Wall as the death-knell of the age of Roman conquest in Britain (*RBES* 151). But could he, with plausibility, represent this as what that event amounted to *at the time that it occurred*? Or is this just what it later became, in consequence of the Romans never regaining the military initiative—something which was far from certain at the time? If one says the latter, the uncomfortable implication seems to be that the past itself is open to retroactive change, not just our understanding of it. Among Collingwood's commentators, Meiland is one of the few who find nothing questionable about such an idea.[56] But if we think it in fact questionable, what attitude are we to adopt towards such widely accepted historical judgments as that the assassination of the Austrian archduke at Sarajevo was the beginning of the First World War or that in the English Revolution of the seventeenth century the foundations of the American constitution were being laid? Must we deny that the past thus characterized in terms of its actual future can be called the real past?

A response implied by much of what Collingwood says in contexts where he is stressing the ideality of the past, and hence its alleged unknowability 'as it really was', is that the problem, as posed, simply doesn't arise. Since retrospective judgments of the sort exemplified structure the past which the historian creates in present thought, they clearly structure the only historical past we can know. And that past does indeed change, although unproblematically, because we ourselves constantly change it. This 'solution', however, can have no interest for anyone who rejects the doctrine of ideality, understood as requiring constructionism. Nor do constructionists usually manifest the courage of their convictions in this connection, few, for example, being prepared to say such things as that the ancient Chinese used to be barbarous (not just regarded as barbarous), whereas they

---

[56] Meiland, *Scepticism*, 173 ff. Donagan describes his arguments for this position as 'ingenious' but 'unconvincing' (Review of Meiland, *Scepticism*, 85).

have now become civilized (not just regarded as civilized). A second response sometimes hinted at by Collingwood is that the problem simply dissolves once we identify the past as it really was with the past as the original agents experienced it and as historians now re-enactively reconstruct it.[57] On this view, what revisionary retrospective judgments tell us is not how the past really was, but only how it appears from later standpoints. The appearances change as standpoints change, but the reality does not. But to claim exclusive truth for the re-enactive dimension of history in this way is surely quite arbitrary. And it conflicts with the ordinary practice of historians, who frequently make judgments like: 'It may have appeared at the time as a continuation of an upward movement, but, as we can now see, it was really the beginning of a decline.'

What better response to the problem could Collingwood offer, then, as a perspectivist and a presentist? Surely that the past, as historians conceive it, can change in one respect and not in another. The respect in which it can change is that it can become significant in further ways with the passage of time—ways which justify its re-characterization, as exemplified by Collingwood's statement about the Antonine Wall. It will thus be *correct* to describe the real past in one way at one time, and in other ways at other times—at any rate, with regard to some of its characteristics. What will change is not just the views of historians, but also what can truly be said of their object. The past cannot change, however, in the sense that what at an earlier time was an agent's reason for performing an action later became something else, or that a victory won at a time of battle later became a defeat (except in the sense that its consequences did not measure up to expectations). If what an historian now says about reasons, or causes, or degrees of immediate success is true, then it must also have been true at the time of occurrence. In other words, to the extent that the retrospective judgments of historians are judgments of significance, they can properly be said to report changes in the past; but to the extent that they only revise earlier re-enactive explanations, or causal diagnoses, or ordinary factual descriptions, in the light of superior present knowledge or improved techniques of inquiry, what they tell us is not how the past has changed, but how

[57] Weinryb notes a tendency to equate 'what actually happened' with 'how the past appeared when it was present' ('Re-enactment in Retrospect', 572).

it always was. For an historical determinist, the situation would be quite different, since what was *going* to happen could be said already to confer significance upon an event at the time of its occurrence. For an indeterminist like Collingwood, however, the most that could be said—and all that historians would normally say—is that, at the time of occurrence, a given event *promised* to be significant—i.e. that one might well have guessed a significance-conferring future for it. But historians who make retrospective judgments of significance do not need to guess. Blessed with hindsight, they know the real (if undetermined) futures of the events they study.

The other problem, the epistemological one, concerns the connection which may hold between retrospectivity in historical judgment and a tendency to represent the past in anachronistic ways. Falling into anachronism is not just error about the past; it is having a distorted conception of it due to assuming it to be more like the present than it really was. Collingwood's theory of history, because of its presentism, has sometimes been accused of inviting such distortion. This might be alleged, for example, to the extent that it is taken to imply that it is proper for historians to regard as important what contemporaries would have considered unimportant, or to use concepts which the original agents would have found unintelligible, or to raise questions which the latter would not, and perhaps could not, have raised because they reflect interests of the historian's own time. All this, critics say, may encourage the elaboration of historical accounts which are unacceptable projections of the present upon the past.[58]

In fact, in his own historical writings, Collingwood displays a sharp eye for judgments which he deems too present-oriented, and he represents anachronism as a besetting sin of historians. Thus, having noted S. R. Gardiner's lament that the Britons displayed so little patriotism during the Roman period, he accuses him, because he writes from 'the distorting point of view of an historian of England', of expecting the Britons 'to show loyalty to something which had not even begun to exist' (*RB* 11). He warns strongly also against the anachronism involved in viewing the Roman regime in Britain as 'imperialist' in the way that the rule of the British was in India or that of the French in Algeria, such

[58] Especially by Leo Strauss, but also by others, e.g. Fischer (*Historians' Fallacies*, 196–9).

analogies being rendered quite misleading, he says, by Roman cosmopolitanism (*RB* 4–6). And he remarks, in the same vein, that historians who approach the relation between villa and village in the Romano-British period 'from the point of view of medieval and modern England', thus viewing it as similar to that of manor and cottage in the Middle Ages, will miss the crucial fact that, while the former belonged to different but overlapping social and economic systems, the latter were two elements of a single system (*RBES* 209). What is identified as anachronism in all these cases is assertion or assumption which the evidence does not support because of false expectations about the past carried over from knowledge of the present. One is reminded here of the notorious invitation to anachronistic judgment which Hume issued to historians who wished to understand the Greeks and Romans. 'Study well the French and English', he told them: 'You cannot be much mistaken in transferring to the former *most* of the observations which you have made with regard to the latter.'[59]

Collingwood offers no systematic discussion of the problem about which he thus warns historians; but the general approach which he would take to it appears in remarks which he sometimes makes about when historians may properly use concepts current in their own day but not current in the past. In his chapter on art in *Roman Britain and the English Settlements,* for example, he offers this reply to critics who would accuse him of actually advocating anachronism. 'There is a certain artificiality', he writes, 'in applying to the ancient world, which knew nothing of any distinction between art and manufacture, that separation of the two which is demanded by modern ways of thinking.' The historian is nevertheless justified when he 'applies the modern conception of art to the ancient world' because, although its inhabitants were 'utterly unconscious of the conception itself', that concept was in fact 'brilliantly exemplified' in their activities. We should therefore feel free to distinguish between 'the technical quality of the Romano-British artisan's work and its artistic quality' when studying its remains (*RBES* 247). Collingwood doubtless falls into overstatement when he adds, in further justification of such a procedure, that 'unless we thought in the conceptual vocabulary of our own times we should not be able to think at all'. In fact, he

[59] Hume, *Treatise of Human Nature*, Sect. 8, Part 1.

has no hesitation himself—nor should he have—about using ancient terms like 'trireme' or *'tribunicia potestas'* when he feels that no modern one will quite do. His own use of modern ones, furthermore, sometimes evokes associations which may risk anachronism, as when he refers to King Arthur's knights as a 'mobile field-army' (*RBES* 321), or to Roman legionaries who settled in Britain as 'time-expired men' (*RBES* 137)—not to mention his talk of capitalistic production and individualistic industry in the ancient world. He nevertheless enunciates the relevant principle for settling disputes about such matters, namely, that to use concepts (he could as well have said theories or assumptions) which evidence shows to be applicable to the subject-matter, even if the agents themselves would not have understood them, is not to be guilty of anachronism.[60]

Collingwood's position on how value judgments or questions may or may not be anachronistic can be extrapolated from this. When he observes, having noted the way the Romans deliberately fostered the growth of towns in Britain, that, since their motives were political and cultural, 'it is hardly relevant to judge the results by economic standards', he is presumably only warning that they must neither be *understood* as economically motivated, nor *judged* as failures to achieve economic goals (*RBES* 199). It does not follow from this that he denies to historians the right to ask questions which the agents themselves would not have asked—and, in fact, he goes on himself to discuss the economic effect of the Roman urban policy, seeing this as an issue of interest to us, if not to the original agents.

A point to be noted in this connection is, of course, that, as Collingwood's logic of presuppositions and theory of inquiry by question and answer both stress, questions have presuppositions. A question which makes an inappropriately presentist presupposition should therefore not be asked. The presupposition that the Romano-British had an economic system, however, cannot be debarred for this reason. In criticism of Collingwood, Strauss has maintained that, because the ancients lacked our interest in economics, to write economic history of classical antiquity is somehow a falsification.[61] He concedes that materials can be found for

---

[60] The question when the historian's own value judgments are appropriate and when the agent's, is more complicated and cannot be probed further here.

[61] Collingwood himself wrote both economic and demographic history.

such a history; the historian can use ancient records 'as a quarry or as ruins' for it. But he thinks this preoccupation too alien to the outlook of the agents to be relevant to understanding their life.[62] Strauss himself weakens this criticism, however, by saying only that answers to the agents' questions must be sought by historians *before they ask questions of their own*; for he seems thereby to concede the legitimacy of their asking their own questions eventually. And what he says about the way the two phases of inquiry should be ordered is, in fact, no more than Collingwood also maintains. On Collingwood's view, one does not know what actions were performed until one knows what thoughts were expressed; but once this is known, there is no reason to refrain from asking further questions, provided they presuppose nothing false about the past. Asking what economic (or demographic) trends or structures obtained in the ancient world does not presuppose (falsely) that the agents concerned were aware of them.

Strauss's charge that Collingwood's theory of understanding invites anachronism has a second aspect. I have noted that Collingwood, as much as Strauss, holds that asking one's own questions about past human actions requires first having understood them re-enactively as responses to the questions of the agents themselves. But Strauss goes on to argue that the idea of re-enactment, as Collingwood presents it, necessarily involves the historian in anachronism because of the insistence that re-enactment be critical. If the historian must criticize the agent's thought in understanding his actions, Strauss contends, he will not really grasp it as the agent did. If he is really to understand the political writings of Plato, for example, he will need to take seriously the idea of searching out 'the truth about the highest things'.[63] When Collingwood represents Plato's *Republic* as an account of the Greek political ideal, therefore, he is already guilty of misunderstanding it; he has conceived it anachronistically from the standpoint of a present theory of philosophy.[64] Plato's aim, Strauss avers, was not to characterize the Greek political ideal, but to discover 'the true model of society with reference to which all

[62] Strauss, 'On Collingwood's Philosophy of History', 580. For further consideration of Strauss's criticism, see Saari, *Re-enactment*, 61; van der Dussen, *HS* 96–7. Also Ch. 3, § 2, above.

[63] Strauss, 'On Collingwood's Philosophy of History', 584. See also Ch. 3, § 2.

[64] And thus takes a 'spectator's' approach to it (unkindest cut of all).

societies of all ages and countries must be judged'.[65] Like some other critics, Strauss is here complaining that Collingwood's theory of historical understanding as re-enactment is, in general, too insensitive to the 'foreignness' of the past.[66] He would doubtless see Collingwood's talk of historians and historical agents having to become, in a sense, 'contemporaries', as giving further credence to this charge.[67]

But Strauss here surely misunderstands the way in which re-enactment as Collingwood conceives it involves criticism. As was noted in Chapters 2 and 4, this is entirely internal to putative explanations, and is quite compatible with the historian's taking seriously in a 'provisional' way (Strauss's own term) an alien notion like 'highest things'. What vitiates Strauss's criticism in the end is his not keeping sufficiently distinct the problems of re-enactive explanation and retrospective description. Describing what Plato was doing as setting forth a Greek ideal is an activity which supervenes upon re-enactment, not an aspect of re-enactment itself. If an historian, in trying to understand Plato's political doctrines, ascribes to him an intention to characterize the Greek political ideal rather than to discern the true model of society, then the result will, of course, be an explanation which is erroneous—and in a way which deserves to be called anachronistic. But that is not at all what Collingwood's theory of understanding requires.

[65] Strauss, 'On Collingwood's Philosophy of History', 575.

[66] See e.g. A. C. Danto, 'The Problem of Other Periods', *Journal of Philosophy*, 63 (1966), 573, and response by Alan Donagan, 'Other Minds and Other Periods', *Journal of Philosophy*, 63 (1966), 578.

[67] What Collingwood envisages is, of course, not the historical agent being made a contemporary of the historian, but the historian making himself, in imagination, a contemporary of the agent—precisely what Strauss says he should do.

EPILOGUE

At various points in this study, I have paused briefly to make a summarizing remark or two; however, it may be useful to append to it a brief sketch of where I think the argument has been. While I have not entirely resisted the temptation to explore some of the back-alleys of Collingwood's thought on history, my focus has been largely upon his idea of re-enactment: on its nature, its limits, and its relation to some other ideas which play, or are thought to play, a legitimate role in historical thinking. My approach has combined elucidation of what he says with criticism, and attempts to develop it, along with a few claims of my own which have been evoked from time to time by views which he advances.

Collingwood's idea of re-enactive understanding was examined first as he expounds it with reference to the most plausible sort of case: the action of an individual agent who sought to attain a certain goal by a certain means. My own interpretation of what he says about such cases, which I called the quasi-normative interpretation, envisaged an historian eliciting from the performance of an action an implied practical argument which represents what was done as the thing to have done, given the agent's point of view. As Collingwood himself does, this was contrasted with understanding past happenings in a nomological, or scientific, way: showing them to have instantiated laws linking them with determining antecedent conditions. The quasi-normative interpretation of re-enactive explanation was itself contrasted with two other ways of interpreting Collingwood's position. One of these I called conceptual-analytic, because it holds that an action is understood when its performance can be seen as logically entailed by the agent's reasons for doing it; the other conceptual-probabilistic, because it adds to much the same analysis the requirement that weak generalizations be shown to hold which would allow some degree of probability to be assigned to what was done. The idea that re-enactive explanation might simply be an incomplete form of scientific explanation was noted and rejected. And the idea that a claim to have offered a re-enactive

explanation assumes historical indeterminism was considered and accepted, although the point is one on which Collingwood's own position is not entirely clear.

Since much of the criticism directed against Collingwood's re-enactment theory has centred less upon its acceptability in cases like the one noted, than upon its allegedly applying only in such cases, I then considered some cases which have often been regarded as more problematic. It was argued that the common complaint that Collingwood's theory has no application to unreflective or irrational actions, or to actions with unconscious motives, has little foundation, but conceded that confused or arbitrary actions, or actions characterized in terms of unintended consequences, lie at least partly beyond its scope. Nor can the success or failure of actions be entirely explained in the re-enactive way, despite Collingwood's sometimes appearing to claim the contrary. The applicability of re-enactment theory to forms of human experience other than action—appetites, emotions, or beliefs, for example—was allowed to be less than straightforward, some 'reconceptualization of the re-enactive process' perhaps being called for in such cases.[1] Special difficulties were also noted for the application of the theory to history of art and metaphysics, at any rate as Collingwood conceives them. By contrast, it was maintained that the idea of historical understanding as re-enactment does not, as is sometimes charged, exclude physical events from history's proper subject-matter, if only because the explanatory conditions referred to in re-enactive explanations are often physical. Nor does it exclude social events and processes, which not only enter into re-enactive explanations in a similar way, but are themselves, to a considerable extent, composed of re-enactable elements.

Clearly, the scope of Collingwood's theory is much broader than many of his critics have allowed. A defender of Collingwood like van der Dussen may still go too far, however, when he maintains that 'no aspect of historical thinking is excluded by the re-enactment theory' (HS 324)—unless by this is meant only that understanding certain kinds of things in history re-enactively,

---

[1] A phrase used by Code ('Collingwood's Epistemological Individualism', 556). This is a loose end which it is to be hoped some student of Collingwood will pick up. A useful source in this connection might be what is said about understanding in the writings on folklore, which the present author has only been able to sample.

notably actions of certain standard kinds, is quite compatible with understanding many other things in further ways.

Some of the further ways come into view when one asks about the relation of the idea of re-enactment to some other key Collingwoodian ideas. Among the most important of these are, first, history's subject-matter being to a considerable extent constituted by social wholes, whose nature is to be grasped by a type of thinking which might be called synthetic; second, historians having to consider their subject-matter from a present point of view, this giving their conclusions a characteristic retrospectivity and hindsightedness; and third, historians being interested in their subject-matter primarily as something individual and concrete. All three of these ideas engender further theories of understanding, none of them being reducible simply to understanding as re-enactment, but all being consistent with it, and sometimes closely integrated with it. A central notion in the first case is that of the relation of part to whole (for example, explaining a particular action as a contribution to a joint enterprise); in the second, that of appreciating a significance which has accrued to something after the event (for example, explaining it as having begun or ended an important development); in the third, that of being understood other than as an instance of a recurring type of thing (for example, explaining an action as an expression of the distinctive ideas of a particular individual). Of these ideas, the most problematic is the third, but chiefly because of some incautious passages in which Collingwood appears to claim that historians may grasp past processes in a way which completely transcends conceptualization. The idea finds defensible and important exemplifications in the notion of re-enactive explanation excluding an action's falling under laws (although bringing it under concepts), and, at another level, in that of tracing out large-scale configurations of actions and events, which need not, as a whole, be brought under concepts.

Two other Collingwoodian ideas which were treated at some length were not presented as themselves generating further theories of understanding. One of these is the idea of an a priori historical imagination, this making historical inquiry a matter of filling out a generalized 'picture' of the historical past which, in conjunction with evidence, functions as a criterion of what may and may not be further asserted. It was argued that, important as this idea is for the full-scale philosophical description of historiography, it has no special connection with Collingwood's theory of re-enactive understanding, although it may help to clarify its status by calling attention to more whole-istic ways in which historians can seek to understand their subject-matter. Another is Collingwood's doctrine of the ideality of the past, which, as merely the claim that past persons and states no longer exist, or that past actions and events are no longer occurring, is hardly a matter for controversy. It was argued, however, that the constructionist implications which Collingwood often draws, or seems to draw, from this idea need to be resisted. In fact, when conceived in a constructionist way, the ideality doctrine has no implications for the kind of understanding which historians should seek. All it implies is that, since what they understand is never the real past, any apparent re-enactment of past thoughts will be no more than apparent.

In considering these and other Collingwoodian ideas, I have often, as promised in Chapter 1, criticized certain aspects of what he had to say about them himself. In some instances, I have thought it important to scotch what seems to me an unacceptable aspect so that more defensible elements of Collingwood's view of history could gain a better hearing. In other cases, where I have thought an idea indefensible as stated, I have tried to reformulate and then develop it, aiming to defend Collingwood by modifying him. I hope that it is clear enough that my overall judgment of his philosophy of history is very positive. I would not quarrel at all with fellow critic Atkinson's description of Collingwood as 'the most considerable philosopher of history in English' (*KEH* 25). He is certainly the philosopher whose thoughts about historical knowledge and inquiry seem to me pre-eminently worth trying to re-think.

If I had to say what I value most in his view of history, apart from the fruitful challenge which it presents, it might be something like this. He clearly has many stimulating theses to advance on many of the major issues of philosophy of history: understanding, evidence, factuality, the role of the a priori, the need for imagination, the nature of fundamental historiographical techniques like narrative and periodization, and so on. But one of the most distinctive features of his work is the way it shows, more than most philosophical writings on history, how a thoroughly humanistic theory of historiography can be elaborated. There are doubtless many reasons for regarding history as belonging to the humanities, however proper it may be, at the same time, to insist, as Collingwood himself does, that its methodology is 'scientific'. One which is commonly urged, and which has not been much considered in this book, is that, in characterizing past forms of life, historians apply, and perhaps necessarily apply, moral, aesthetic, and other standards of value to what people did, thus treating them as responsible human beings (as Collingwood rightly complains social science, conceived positivistically, does not).[2] But equally important as a reason for regarding history as a humanistic study, and one which Collingwood himself acknowledges (*IH* 19), is its requiring, among other things, a critical re-enactment of past thought. The point could perhaps be put in this way: that historical understanding, at any rate as it has traditionally been sought by historians, and as Collingwood largely conceives it, both in his own historical practice and in his philosophical reflection, is humanistic in the sense of requiring of the historian an exercise of practical reason. As Collingwoodians sometimes say, historical thinking is 'vicarious practice'. It takes seriously the standpoint of human agency.

[2] Several sections devoted to this topic ended on the cutting room floor, but will appear in another context.

BIBLIOGRAPHY

Works of Collingwood Cited in the Text

Published Works

Religion and Philosophy (Oxford, 1916).

'The Devil', in B. F. Streeter and others (eds.), *Concerning Prayer: Its Nature, Its Difficulties and Its Value* (London, 1916), reprinted in Rubinoff (ed.), *Faith and Reason*, 212–33.

'Croce's Philosophy of History', *Hibbert Journal*, 19 (1921), 263–98 (*EPH* 3–22).

'Hadrian's Wall: A History of the Problem', *Journal of Roman Studies*, 11 (1921), 37–66.

'Are History and Science Different Kinds of Knowledge', *Mind*, 31 (1922), 433–51 (*EPH* 23–33).

Ruskin's Philosophy (Kendal, 1922), reprinted in Donagan (ed.), *Essays in the Philosophy of Art by R. G. Collingwood*, 5–41.

Speculum Mentis (Oxford, 1924).

'Rome in Britain', *Home-Reading Magazine*, 36 (1924–5), 6–8, 37–9, 71–3.

'The Nature and Aims of a Philosophy of History', *Proceedings of the Aristotelian Society*, 25 (1924–5), 151–74 (*EPH* 34–56).

'Hadrian's Wall', *History*, 10 (1925), 193–202.

Review of F. J. Teggart, *Theory of History*, in *Journal of Philosophical Studies*, 1 (1926), 255–6.

'Some Perplexities about Time: With an Attempted Solution', *Proceedings of the Aristotelian Society*, 26 (1926), 135–50.

'Oswald Spengler and the Theory of Historical Cycles', *Antiquity*, 1 (1927), 311–25 (*EPH* 57–75).

'The Theory of Historical Cycles', *Antiquity*, 1 (1927), 435–46 (*EPH* 76–89).

Faith and Reason (London, 1928), reprinted in Rubinoff (ed.), *Faith and Reason*, 122–47.

'The Limits of Historical Knowledge', *Journal of Philosophical Studies*, 3 (1928), 213–32 (*EPH* 90–103).

Review of R. E. Zachrisson, *Romans, Kelts and Saxons in Ancient Britain*, in *Journal of Roman Studies*, 18 (1928), 117–19.

'Political Action', *Proceedings of the Aristotelian Society*, 29 (1928–9), 153–76, reprinted in Boucher (ed.), *Essays in Political Philosophy*, 92–109.

'A Philosophy of Progress', *Realist*, 1 (1929), 64–77 (*EPH* 104–20).

'Roman Signal-Stations on the Cumberland Coast', *Transactions of the Cumberland and Westmorland Antiquarian and Archaeological Society*, NS 29 (1929), 138–65.

Roman Eskdale (Whitehaven, 1929).

The Philosophy of History (London, 1930) (*EPH* 121–39).

'Hadrian's Wall: 1921–30', *Journal of Roman Studies*, 21 (1931), 36–64.

'The Roman Signal Station', in Arthur Rowntree (ed.), *The History of Scarborough* (London, 1931), 40–50.

Roman Britain, rev. edn. (Oxford, 1932).

An Essay on Philosophical Method (Oxford, 1933).

'Britain', *Cambridge Ancient History*, xi (Cambridge, 1936), 511–25.

Roman Britain and the English Settlements, with J. N. L. Myres (Oxford, 1936).

'Roman Britain', in Tenney Frank (ed.), *An Economic Survey of Ancient Rome*, iii (London and Baltimore, 1937), 1–118.

The Principles of Art (Oxford, 1938).

An Autobiography (London, 1939).

An Essay on Metaphysics (Oxford, 1940; rev. edn. 1995).

The New Leviathan (Oxford, 1942; rev. edn. 1992).

The Idea of Nature (Oxford, 1945).

The Idea of History (Oxford, 1946; rev. edn. 1993).

Essays in the Philosophy of Art by R. G. Collingwood, ed. Alan Donagan (Bloomington, Ind., 1946).

Essays in the Philosophy of History, ed. William Debbins (Austin, Tex., 1965).

Faith and Reason: Essays in the Philosophy of Religion by R. G. Collingwood, ed. Lionel Rubinoff (Chicago, 1968).

Manuscripts

The following manuscripts are located at the Bodleian Library, Oxford.

'An Illustration from Historical Thought', 1920–1. Dep. 16/6.

'The Philosophy of History' (fragment of an introduction), 1926. Dep. 12/3.

'Lectures on the Philosophy of History', 1929. Dep. 12/6.

'The Origin and Growth of the Idea of a Philosophy of History', 1931. Dep. 12/8.

'The Philosophy of History', 1932. Dep. 15/1.

'Outline of a Theory of Primitive Mind', 1933. Dep. 16/8.

Notes towards a Metaphysic', 1933–4. Dep. 18/3–7.

'History as the Understanding of the Present', 1934. Dep. 15/2.

'Inaugural. Rough Notes', 1935. Dep. 13/1.

'Reality as History', 1935. Dep. 12/9.

'Lectures on the Philosophy of History', 1936. Dep. 15/3.
'Can Historians Be Impartial?', 1936. Dep. 12/10.
'Notes on the History of Historiography and Philosophy of History', 1936. Dep. 13/2.
'Magic', 1936–7. Dep. 21/7.
'Notes on Historiography Written on a Voyage to the East Indies', 1938–9. Dep. 13/3.

Secondary Works Cited in the Text

Ashton, Robert, *The English Civil War* (London, 1978).
Atkinson, R. F., *Knowledge and Explanation in History* (Ithaca, NY, 1978).
Bagby, Philip, *Culture and History: Prolegomena to the Comparative Study of Civilizations* (London, 1958).
Beard, Charles, 'That Noble Dream', reprinted in Fritz Stern (ed.), *The Varieties of History* (New York, 1973), 315–28.
—— Review of *The Idea of History*, in *American Historical Review*, 52 (1947), 704–8.
Becker, Carl, 'What are Historical Facts?', reprinted in Hans Meyerhoff (ed.), *The Philosophy of History in Our Time* (New York, 1959), 120–39.
Beloff, Max, Review of *The Idea of History*, in *Time and Tide*, 28 September 1946.
Boucher, David (ed.), *Essays in Political Philosophy: R. G. Collingwood* (Oxford, 1989).
Buchdahl, G., 'Logic and History: An Assessment of R. G. Collingwood's *Idea of History*', *Australasian Journal of Philosophy*, 26 (1948), 94–113.
Burston, W. H., and Thompson, David (eds.), *Studies in the Nature and Teaching of History* (London, 1967).
Carr, David, Review of Martin, *Historical Explanation*, in *Southwestern Journal of Philosophy*, 10 (1979), 212–17.
—— et al. (eds.), *Philosophy of History and Contemporary Historiography* (Ottawa, 1982).
Carr, E. H., *What is History?* (London, 1961).
Cebik, L. B., 'Collingwood: Action, Re-enactment, and Evidence', *Philosophical Forum*, 2 (1970), 68–90.
Coady, C. A. J., 'Collingwood and Historical Testimony', *Philosophy*, 59 (1975), 409–24.
Code, Lorraine, 'Collingwood: A Philosopher of Ambivalence', *History of Philosophy Quarterly*, 3 (1986), 107–21.
—— 'Collingwood's Epistemological Individualism', *Monist*, 72 (1989), 542–67.

Cohen, Jonathan, 'A Survey of Work in the Philosophy of History, 1946–1950', *Philosophical Quarterly*, 2 (1952), 172–86.

Conkin, P. K., and Stromberg, R. N., *The Heritage and Challenge of History* (New York, 1975).

Couse, Gordon, 'Historical Testimony in R. G. Collingwood's Theory and Practice', in Carr *et al.* (eds.), *Philosophy of History and Contemporary Historiography*, 259–70.

Danto, A. C., 'The Problem of Other Periods', *Journal of Philosophy*, 63 (1966), 566–77.

—— *Narration and Knowledge* (New York, 1985).

Debbins, William (ed.), *Essays in the Philosophy of History by R. G. Collingwood* (Austin, Tex., 1965).

Donagan, Alan, 'The Verification of Historical Theses', *Philosophical Quarterly*, 6 (1956), 193–208.

—— 'Explanation in History', reprinted in Gardiner (ed.), *Theories of History*, 428–43.

—— *The Later Philosophy of R. G. Collingwood* (Oxford, 1962).

—— 'The Popper-Hempel Theory Reconsidered', reprinted in Dray (ed.), *Philosophical Analysis and History*, 127–59.

—— 'Other Minds and Other Periods', *Journal of Philosophy*, 63 (1966), 577–9.

—— Review of Meiland, *Scepticism and Historical Knowledge*, in *Philosophical Quarterly*, 17 (1967), 85–6.

—— (ed.), *Essays in the Philosophy of Art by R. G. Collingwood* (Bloomington, Ind., 1964).

Dray, W. H., 'R. G. Collingwood and the Acquaintance Theory of Knowledge', *Revue internationale de philosophie*, 42 (1957), 420–32.

—— 'Historical Understanding as Re-thinking', *University of Toronto Quarterly*, 27 (1958), 200–15.

—— 'R. G. Collingwood on Reflective Thought', *Journal of Philosophy*, 57 (1960), 157–63.

—— 'On Explaining How-Possibly', *Monist*, 52 (1968), 390–407.

—— *Perspectives on History* (London, 1980).

—— *On History and Philosophers of History* (Leiden, 1989).

—— 'Was Collingwood an Historical Constructionist?', *Collingwood Studies*, 1 (1994), 59–75.

—— (ed.), *Philosophical Analysis and History* (New York, 1966).

Elton, G. R., *The Practice of History* (London, 1969).

—— *Political History: Principles and Practice* (London, 1970).

Fain, Haskell, *Between Philosophy and History: The Resurrection of Speculative Philosophy of History within the Analytic Tradition* (Princeton, 1970).

Fischer, D. H., *Historians' Fallacies* (London, 1971).

Frank, Tenney (ed.), *An Economic Survey of Ancient Rome* (6 vols.; Baltimore, 1937).

Gallie, W. B., *Philosophy and the Historical Understanding* (New York, 1957).

Gardiner, Patrick, *The Nature of Historical Explanation* (Oxford, 1952).

—— 'The "Objects" of Historical Knowledge', *Philosophy*, 27 (1952), 211–20.

—— 'Historical Understanding and the Empiricist Tradition', in Bernard Williams and Alan Montefiori (eds.), *British Analytic Philosophy* (London, 1966), 267–84.

—— 'The Concept of Man as Presupposed by the Historical Studies', in G. N. A. Vesey *et al.*, *The Proper Study* (London, 1973), 14–31.

—— (ed.), *Theories of History* (London, 1959).

Gellner, Ernest, Review of Krausz (ed.), *Critical Essays*, in *TLS*, 30 March 1973, 337.

Gershoy, Leo, 'Some Problems of a Working Historian', in Hook (ed.), *Philosophy and History*, 59–75.

Ginsberg, Morris, 'The Character of a Historical Explanation', *Aristotelian Society Supplementary Volume*, 21 (1947), 69–77.

Goldstein, L. J., 'Evidence and Events in History', *Philosophy of Science*, 29 (1962), 175–94.

—— 'Collingwood's Theory of Historical Knowing', *History and Theory*, 9 (1970), 3–36.

—— 'Collingwood on the Constitution of the Historical Past', in Krausz (ed.), *Critical Essays*, 241–67.

—— *Historical Knowing* (Austin, Tex., 1976).

Grant, C. K., 'Collingwood's Theory of Historical Knowledge', *Renaissance and Modern Studies*, 1 (1957), 65–90.

—— Review of Donagan, *The Later Philosophy of R. G. Collingwood*, in *Philosophical Books*, 4 (1963), 3–4.

Hart, H. L. A., and Honoré, A. M., *Causation in the Law* (Oxford, 1959).

Hempel, C. G., 'The Function of General Laws in History', reprinted in Gardiner (ed.), *Theories of History*, 344–56.

—— 'Rational Action', *Proceedings and Addresses of the American Philosophical Association*, 35 (1952), 5–23.

—— *Aspects of Scientific Explanation* (New York, 1965).

Hexter, J. H., *Reappraisals in History* (London, 1961).

Higham, John, with Leonard Krieger and Felix Gilbert, *History* (Englewood Cliffs, NJ, 1965).

Hill, Christopher, *God's Englishman* (London, 1972).

Hook, Sidney (ed.), *Philosophy and History: A Symposium* (New York, 1963).

Joynt, C. B., and Rescher, Nicholas, 'The Problem of Uniqueness in History', *History and Theory*, 1 (1961), 150–62.

Knox, T. M., 'Notes on Collingwood's Philosophical Work', *Proceedings of the British Academy*, 19 (1944), 469–75.

Kracauer, S., *History: The Last Things before the Last* (New York, 1969).

Krausz, Michael, 'The Logic of Absolute Presuppositions', in Krausz (ed.), *Critical Essays*, 222–40.

—— 'Historical Explanation, Re-enactment, and Practical Inference', *Metaphilosophy*, 2 (1980), 143–54.

—— (ed.), *Critical Essays on the Philosophy of R. G. Collingwood* (Oxford, 1972).

Leff, Gordon, *History and Social Theory* (London, 1969).

Levine, Joseph, 'The Autonomy of History: R. G. Collingwood and Agatha Christie', *Clio*, 7 (1979), 253–64.

—— 'Objectivity in History: Peter Novick and R. G. Collingwood', *Clio*, 21 (1992), 109–27.

Llewelyn, J. E., 'Collingwood's Doctrine of Absolute Presuppositions', *Philosophical Quarterly*, 11 (1961), 49–60.

Louch, A. R., *Explanation and Human Action* (Oxford, 1966).

McClelland, Peter, *Causal Explanation and Model Building in History* (Ithaca, NY, 1975).

McCullagh, C. B., 'The Rationality of Emotions and of Emotional Behaviour', *Australasian Journal of Philosophy*, 68 (1990), 44–58.

—— Review of van der Dussen, *History as a Science*, in *Australasian Journal of Philosophy*, 61 (1983), 221–2.

MacIver, A. M., 'The Character of a Historical Explanation', *Aristotelian Society Supplementary Volume*, 21 (1947), 33–50.

Mackinnon, D. M., Review of *The Idea of History*, in *Journal of Theological Studies*, 48 (1947), 249–53.

Mandelbaum, Maurice, *The Problem of Historical Knowledge* (New York, 1967).

—— *The Anatomy of Historical Knowledge* (Baltimore, 1977).

—— Review of *The Idea of History*, in *Journal of Philosophy*, 44 (1947), 184–8.

—— Review of Goldstein, *Historical Knowing*, in *Journal of Modern History*, 49 (1977), 292–4.

Marrou, H.-I., *The Meaning of History*, tr. R. J. Olsen (Baltimore, 1966).

Martin, K. M., 'Caesar and Collingwood as Historians', *Latomus: Revue d'études latines*, 28 (1969), 162–74.

Martin, Michael, 'Situational Logic and Covering Law Explanations in History', *Inquiry*, 11 (1968), 388–99.

Martin, Raymond, *The Past within Us: An Empirical Approach to Philosophy of History* (Princeton, 1989).

Martin, Rex, *Historical Explanation: Re-enactment and Practical Inference* (Ithaca, NY, 1977).

—— 'Collingwood's Doctrine of Absolute Presuppositions and the Possibility of Historical Knowledge', in Leon Pompa and W. H. Dray (eds.), *Substance and Form in History* (Edinburgh, 1981), 89–106.

—— 'Collingwood's Claim that Metaphysics is a Historical Discipline', *Monist*, 72 (1989), 489–525.

—— Review of van der Dussen, *History as a Science*, in *American Historical Review*, 88 (1983), 73–5.

Marwick, Arthur, *The Nature of History* (London, 1970).

Meiland, Jack, *Scepticism and Historical Knowledge* (New York, 1965).

Mink, L. O., *Mind, History, and Dialectic: The Philosophy of R. G. Collingwood* (Bloomington, Ind., 1969).

—— *Historical Understanding* (London, 1987).

Modood, Tariq, 'The Later Collingwood's Alleged Historicism and Relativism', *Journal of the History of Philosophy*, 27 (1989), 101–25.

Munz, Peter, *The Shapes of Time: A New Look at the Philosophy of History* (Middletown, Conn., 1977).

Murphy, A. E., Review of *The Idea of History*, in *Philosophical Review*, 56 (1947), 587–92.

Nagel, Ernest, 'Some Issues in the Logic of Historical Analysis', reprinted in Gardiner (ed.), *Theories of History*, 373–85.

—— 'Determinism in History', reprinted in Dray (ed.), *Philosophical Analysis and History*, 347–82.

Nielsen, Margit H. (now Grove, Margit H.), 'Making Sense of History: Skagestad on Popper and Collingwood', *Inquiry*, 22 (1979), 477–89.

—— 'Re-enactment and Reconstruction in Collingwood's Philosophy of History', *History and Theory*, 20 (1981), 1–31.

Nowell-Smith, P. H., 'Are Historical Events Unique?', *Proceedings of the Aristotelian Society*, 42 (1957), 107–60.

—— 'The Constructionist Theory of History', *History and Theory*, 16 (1977), 1–28.

Oakeshott, Michael, *Experience and Its Modes* (Cambridge, 1933).

Olsen, Mark, 'The Re-thinking of History: Comments on Collingwood's Theory of Historical Understanding', *Register*, 6 (1985), 1–24.

O'Neill, John (ed.), *Modes of Individualism and Collectivism* (London, 1973).

Pompa, Leon, 'The Possibility of Historical Knowledge', *Aristotelian Society Supplementary Volume*, 67 (1993), 1–16.

Popper, K. R., 'A Pluralist Approach to the Philosophy of History', in E. Streisler (ed.), *Roads to Freedom: Essays in Honour of F. A. von Hayek* (London, 1969), 181–200.

Reis, Lincoln, and Kristellar, P. O., 'Some Remarks on the Method of History', *Journal of Philosophy*, 40 (1943), 225–45.

Renier, G. J., *History: Its Purpose and Method* (London, 1950).

Rotenstreich, Nathan, 'From Facts to Thoughts: Collingwood's Views on the Nature of History', *Philosophy*, 35 (1960), 122–37.

—— 'History and Time: A Critical Examination of R. G. Collingwood's Doctrine', *Scripta Hierosolymitana*, 6 (1960), 41–103.

—— *Philosophy, History and Politics* (The Hague, 1976).

Rubinoff, Lionel, 'Collingwood's Theory of the Relation between Philosophy and History: A New Interpretation', *Journal of the History of Philosophy*, 6 (1968), 363–80.

—— *Collingwood and the Reform of Metaphysics: A Study in the Philosophy of Mind* (Toronto, 1970).

—— Review of Debbins (ed.), *Essays*, in *Dialogue*, 5 (1966), 471–5.

—— (ed.), *Faith and Reason: Essays in the Philosophy of Religion by R. G. Collingwood* (Chicago, 1968).

Rynin, David, 'Donagan on Collingwood: Absolute Presuppositions, Truth, and Metaphysics', *Review of Metaphysics*, 18 (1964), 301–33.

Saari, Heikki, *Re-enactment: A Study in R. G. Collingwood's Philosophy of History* (Åbo, Finland, 1984).

Simissen, Herman, 'On Understanding Disaster', *Philosophy of the Social Sciences*, 23 (1993), 352–67.

Skagestad, Peter, *Making Sense of History* (Oslo, 1975).

Stone, Lawrence, *The Causes of the English Revolution 1529–1642* (London, 1972).

Stoutland, Frederick, 'The Logical Connection Argument', in Nicholas Rescher (ed.), *Studies in Theory of Knowledge* (Oxford, 1970), 117–29.

Stover, Robert, *The Nature of Historical Thinking* (Chapel Hill, NC, 1967).

Strauss, Leo, 'On Collingwood's Philosophy of History', *Review of Metaphysics*, 5 (1952), 559–86.

Sullivan, J. E., *Prophets of the West* (New York, 1970).

Taylor, D. S., *R. G. Collingwood: A Bibliography* (New York, 1988).

—— Review of van der Dussen, *History as a Science*, in *History and Theory*, 20 (1981), 175–82.

Thompson, David, 'Colligation and History Teaching', in Burston and Thompson (eds.), *Studies in the Nature and Teaching of History*, 85–106.

Toulmin, S. E., 'Conceptual Change and the Problem of Relativity', in Krausz (ed.), *Critical Essays*, 201–21.

Toynbee, Arnold, *A Study of History*, ix (Oxford, 1954).

Van der Dussen, W. J., 'Collingwood's Unpublished Manuscripts', *History and Theory*, 18 (1979), 287–315.

Van der Dussen, W. J., *History as a Science: The Philosophy of R. G.*

Collingwood (The Hague, 1981).

Veyne, Paul, *Writing History: Essays on Epistemology* (Middletown, Conn., 1971).

Von Wright, G. H., *Explanation and Understanding* (London, 1971).

Walsh, W. H., 'R. G. Collingwood's Philosophy of History', *Philosophy*, 22 (1947), 153–60.

—— 'The Character of a Historical Explanation', *Aristotelian Society Supplementary Volume*, 21 (1947), 51–68.

—— *Introduction to Philosophy of History* (London, 1951).

—— 'Colligatory Concepts in History', in Burston and Thompson (eds.), *Studies in the Nature and Teaching of History*, 65–84.

—— 'Collingwood and Metaphysical Neutralism', in Krausz (ed.), *Critical Essays*, 134–53.

—— 'The Constancy of Human Nature', in H. D. Lewis (ed.), *Contemporary British Philosophers* (4th series; London, 1976), 274–91.

Watkins, J. W. N., 'Ideal Types and Historical Explanation', reprinted in Herbert Feigl and May Brodbeck (eds.), *Readings in the Philosophy of Science* (New York, 1953), 723–43.

—— 'Historical Explanation in the Social Sciences', reprinted in Gardiner (ed.), *Theories of History*, 503–14.

—— 'On Explaining Disaster', *Listener*, 10 January 1963, 69–70.

Wedgwood, Veronica, *The King's War* (London, 1966).

—— Review of *The Idea of History*, in *Observer*, 8 September 1946.

Weinryb, Elazar, 'Re-enactment in Retrospect', *Monist*, 72 (1989), 568–80.

Weiss, Paul, *History: Written and Lived* (Carbondale, Ill., 1962).

Wheeler, R. E. M., Review of *Roman Britain and the English Settlements*, in *Journal of Roman Studies*, 29 (1939), 87–93.

White, D. A., 'Imagination and Description: Collingwood and the Historical Consciousness', *Clio*, 1 (1972), 14–28.

White, H. V., *Tropics of Discourse* (Baltimore, 1978).

White, M. G., *Foundations of Historical Knowledge* (New York, 1965).

Winch, Peter, *The Idea of a Social Science* (London, 1958).

INDEX

abstraction 24, 60, 69, 90, 136 n., 171, 235, 238, 283
distrust of 64, 215, 227, 228
acquaintance 40, 232, 263–8, 270 n., 296 n.
Actium, battle of 214, 222
Acton, J. E. E. D. 217–18
actuality 43, 129, 212, 219 n., 234–9, 246, 250–4, 258–9, 262–70, 286, 288, 309
'as it actually was' 62, 63, 64 n., 229, 231, 232, 274, 283, 316, 317 n.
affinity 59, 297
Agricola 302, 314
Albert Memorial 135, 140
Alexander, Samuel 62, 66
Alexander the Great 24, 144, 266
Alfred, King of Wessex 198
Algeria 318
Alps 158, 163, 164
American Congress 184
American Constitution 316
anachronism 65, 319–22
analogy 23, 77, 83, 85, 97, 121, 138–9, 162, 171, 181, 194, 315
in historical reasoning 101–2, 318–19
Kantian 189, 201
Anglican Church 184
Antonine Wall 314, 316, 317
appetite 123, 126–8, 132, 150, 168, 324
a priori 8, 28, 144 n., 156, 290, 291, 298
idea of history 191, 200–10, 192 n., 229, 325–6
structural concepts 85, 218, 220, 225, 279, 311
arbitrary action 121–2, 127, 148, 198, 216, 279, 292, 317
archaeology 12, 18, 48, 97, 100–1, 169, 212, 218, 253, 256, 277
Archimedes 124, 128, 129, 138
Aristotle 314
Arthur, King of the Britons 192, 320
Ashton, Robert 308
Assyriology 254
Aston Villa 170

Atkinson, R. F. 17, 91, 115 n., 151 n., 179 n., 196 n., 295 n., 326
Augustine, Saint 273
Augustus 56, 180
autonomy 18, 53, 193, 197, 199, 241 n., 306
auxiliary sciences 26, 100–1

Bacon, Francis 1, 90
Bagby, Philip 191, 192
Baldwin, Stanley 160–1, 164
Balkans 288
Bath Gorgon 136, 275
Beard, Charles 10, 272, 314
Becker, Carl 10, 272
Becket, Saint Thomas à 188
Beethoven, Ludwig van 135 n., 139
beliefs 39, 91, 117 n., 119, 196, 265, 298, 301
as causes and effects 154, 157–8
as constitutive of social reality 165, 171–2, 176, 186–7, 215
as elements in re-enactments 50, 73, 76, 81–5, 116, 131–2, 146, 179, 189
as re-enactable 132, 147
Beloff, Max 27
Bergson, Henri 26
biblical criticism 25
biography 170
biology 36, 62, 136, 145, 154, 155
Bollandists 25
Borgias 60
Boucher, David 4, 11 n., 148, 171 n.
Boudicca, Queen of the Iceni 169, 174 n., 205, 304
Bradley, F. H. 1, 26, 143 n., 193–5, 200, 201, 202, 203
Braque, Georges 138
British Constitution 171
British Revolution 72, 316
Bronze Age 302
Brutus 81–2, 93
Buchdahl, G. 192 n.
Bury, J. B. 1, 62, 63, 95, 102, 143 n., 182, 222, 275